Drafting Employment Documents for Expatriates

Second Edition

Drafting Employment Documents for Expatriates

Second Edition

Juliet Carp
Solicitor and English Employment Law Specialist

 LexisNexis®

Published by LexisNexis

LexisNexis
Regus
Terrace Floor
Castlemead
Lower Castle Street
Bristol BS1 3AG

© RELX (UK) Limited, trading as LexisNexis 2018

British Library Cataloguing-in-Publication Data

A catalogue record for this book is available from the British Library.

ISBN 978 1 78473 172 4

Typeset by Letterpart Limited, Caterham on the Hill, Surrey CR3 5XL

Printed and bound by CPI Group (UK) Ltd, Croydon, CR0 4YY

CONTENTS

ABOUT THE AUTHOR

Juliet Carp is an English employment law specialist and partner with London law firm Kingsley Napley LLP.

After graduating from Trinity College, University of Cambridge in 1989 Juliet gained a masters degree in employment law from London University, including international and comparative employment law in her choice of specialist subjects.

Juliet completed her Articles with Simmons & Simmons and qualified as a solicitor to practice in England and Wales in 1993. She subsequently worked at Ernst & Young for 8 years, most recently as a senior manager and employment law specialist within Ernst & Young's Global Employment Solutions Department. Juliet joined City law firm Speechly Bircham LLP in 2002 where she was made partner and continued to focus particularly on international employment law, she then moved to the London office of Dorsey & Whitney (a US firm headquartered in Minneapolis), before joining Kingsley Napley as an employment partner.

Juliet is Deputy Chair of the UK Employment Lawyers Association (ELA), following 4 years as Chair of ELA's International Committee.

Juliet is also the elected Board Member for England & Wales at the European Employment Lawyers Association (EELA) and an active member of the International Labor & Employment Committee of the American Bar Association (ABA).

Having been brought up in the Far East and having spent short periods working for law firms in Hong Kong, Sydney and Abu Dhabi; and as an adviser to both multinational employers and senior expatriates over many years, Juliet has a wealth of practical experience to share.

ACKNOWLEDGMENTS

I would like to take this opportunity to thank the following people who have helped me with this book.

I should first thank Jordan Publishing and LexisNexis, including Kate Hather and Claire Banyard, for their help, but particularly Mary Kenny for her encouragement over the years.

I would also like to thank Struan Mackenzie of Buzzacott LLP (share plans and expatriate tax), Rebecca Bernhard of Dorsey & Whitney (US employment law) and Kingsley Napley LLP's immigration team for taking the time to offer helpful comment on technical aspects, and Alan Julyan without whose support the first edition of this book would never have been written.

Finally, and most importantly, I would like to thank my immediate family, that is my partner John Murphy and our sons Peter, Finbar and Conor for giving up so many evenings, weekends and holidays (and especially Peter for his excellent IT support).

CHAPTER 1

INTRODUCTION

WHAT'S NEW?

1.1   The first edition of this book was written when the UK was firmly in the EU, and we expected to remain there. The UK is currently negotiating with the EU about leaving the Union. 'Brexit' is a reality but we do not currently know how that that will work out.

1.2   This book was written by an English lawyer but with other jurisdictions in mind so, in a sense, Brexit does not change anything. The same core principles should apply to drafting expatriate employment documents and the content of the first edition should still be useful to readers.

1.3   However, things have moved on. Brexit, and recent changes in the US, have made knowledge of global mobility basics essential skills for HR teams. Compliance regimes are much more sophisticated, and in many ways more challenging for both employers and employees. Perhaps more importantly, best practice has moved on, and since the first edition of this book was published in 2009, many people have shared their thoughts and suggestions. I hope this book is not only better than the first, but more accessible to readers from other jurisdictions, particularly those based in the US.

PURPOSE AND SCOPE OF THIS BOOK

1.4   Those who review expatriate employment documents are often surprised to find so many problems, and also that the problems are so varied. There are good reasons for this. Employment documents for 'ordinary' UK employees, at least those who work for larger businesses, are usually the result of careful collaboration between HR specialists who understand what the business wants and employment lawyers who know what is needed technically. The employment law specialist will be able to deal personally with most technical issues that arise, even where they are not strictly 'employment law'. For example, the employment lawyer will be able to advise on payroll, pension, intellectual property or immigration-related clauses to be included in the employment contract. Advice is rarely sought from other specialists. Compromises are often made between technical perfection and style, but where competent advice is sought the end result will usually create few commercial problems. The price will usually be fairly reasonable too. The lawyer should be able to make a fair estimate of the cost of producing the first draft and the HR specialist will understand from experience whether this seems reasonable. As a framework employment contract can usually be adapted by the HR team for a large number of employees, and a good contract reduces the risk for the employer substantially, the time and money spent will almost always be 'worth it'.

1.5   Preparation of expatriate employment documents presents additional challenges and a different approach is usually needed to achieve a good result.

1.6   From a technical perspective, expatriate arrangements will usually be far more complex than those for an ordinary employee and one specialist is unlikely to have all the expertise needed to prepare the documents. For example, specialist advice on tax and social security is usually far more important to those preparing documents for overseas assignments, because the structure of the employment arrangements can make a substantial difference to the sums to be paid. Complex issues may arise from the proposed benefit arrangements, and immigration rules are likely to be critical. The employment law specialist is unlikely to be able to deal with all the issues personally and will need to seek advice from other specialists. An additional layer of complexity is added because each specialist is only likely to be an expert on the laws and practices of his own country, and expatriate employment arrangements always involve more than one country.

1.7   The expatriates themselves are likely to have different expectations from typical home-based employees (referred to as 'local hires' in this book). Often, senior expatriates are paid higher salaries than local hires. Even if this not the case, there is likely to be an expectation that expatriates 'should be' paid more. The expectation may need to be managed if it will not be met. As well as higher remuneration, expatriates typically enjoy more complex benefit arrangements than those that would apply to them at home. Whilst some of these may be 'perks' to make the new role attractive, others will be important for the business too. For example, it may be necessary, in order to attract customers in the local market, for an expatriate representative to be seen to be successful. This could, for example, mean housing suitable for business entertaining or an expensive company car and driver. Other benefits may be offered to reduce the uncertainty or worry that could lead to a potential expatriate declining the proposed new role. Medical cover is almost always offered and employers often offer other benefits to make life easier for the expatriate's family, such as flights home or school fees. Some benefits may be offered to save the employee time (ie to free up his time to work for the business) or reduce risk for the business. For example, the employer may offer assistance with finding accommodation in the host country so that the expatriate is not distracted at the start of the assignment or bear the costs of professional advice on completion of tax returns, where the employer also has an interest in making sure the returns are completed correctly and on time.

1.8   From a style perspective, the worried pre-assignment expatriate will usually want to see the arrangements carefully documented. Expatriates rarely complain that contracts contain too much detail: they usually like to know where they stand (and so do their families). Detailed documents tend to suit the employer too. Overseas assignments are expensive. Misunderstandings over the 'deal' can lead to time-consuming disputes that sour the relationship and distract from the job the expatriate is paid to do. These misunderstandings happen more frequently with expatriate assignments than with ordinary employments. The employer and employee can make different assumptions about what the expatriate is entitled to based on what they feel is 'normal', and there is unlikely to be an existing employee in the same situation to refer to as a benchmark.

1.9   For the assignment manager responsible for making the arrangements work this complexity can be a real challenge. If one specialist is asked to prepare the documents he will inevitably approach the task from a perspective that works from his own experience and could easily fail to address problems another specialist would be able to deal with. On the other hand, if the assignment manager seeks exhaustive advice from every possible specialist, he may become so bogged down in the detail that the documents are not ready when needed, or the cost of the advice outweighs its benefit. It is often hard for assignment managers to assess what is needed at the outset, let alone obtain concrete quotes for the work to be done or compare prices. It can also be quite difficult to change specialists if costs escalate.

1.10   So choices must be made and risks must be accepted, and the background of the person who makes that assessment will inevitably affect the outcome of the project.

1.11   Employment lawyers are best qualified to prepare employment documents. They will be familiar with their own country's employment laws and, with some imagination, can probably identify most of the potential pitfalls in other countries. Most importantly, they should have good drafting skills and will be trained to ask questions. However, tax and social security are often considered to be more significant, commercially, than employment law. Expatriate tax and international social security expertise is typically found in large and medium-sized accountancy firms, and not law firms. Many employment lawyers do not have much experience of the drafting implications that may arise from tax or other specialist advice peculiar to expatriates. This can lead to mistakes, delay and increased expense for the employer.

1.12   Multinationals often employ specialist assignment managers, perhaps from a tax, reward or HR background, who become very experienced in managing day-to-day issues facing expatriates and the particular policies of the business. Most specialist assignment managers would not pretend to be experts at drafting documents. What they are usually good at is getting the job done and, with the experience of daily handling, spotting problems and resolving them.

1.13 When I first started doing this sort of work no books were available on how to draft expatriate employment documents. I had studied for a masters degree in labour law, including a course on international and comparative labour law, but knowledge of international labour standards and European Directives did not help much with the nitty gritty of drafting employment documents for people who move between countries. I found myself relying on tax advisers and assignment managers to explain the usual practices, and soon learned that being good at this sort of work depended not so much on a lot of knowledge but on an approach to problem solving. It is simply not possible for one person to know all the answers. All you can do is keep building on your experience and using that experience to try to identify likely problems, ask the right questions of the right people, and make good decisions on how best to manage risk.

1.14 When I started to write this book I intended to share what I had learned so far. And, of course, the more I wrote, the more I realised I did not know. Every international project presents new challenges and usually something totally unexpected, and it is that, of course, that makes international employment work so interesting. One of the great benefits of having the opportunity to produce a second edition is the opportunity to take account of thoughts and suggestions offered by those who read the first edition.

1.15 If you have to draft some employment documents for an overseas assignment and are looking for an answer to a very particular question you probably will not find it in this book. There is no easy or cheap substitute for checking with up-to-date specialists. But I do hope this book will make the job easier and quicker for those who are less familiar with the issues. This is intended to be a general guide to 'how to do it' rather than to 'all you need to know'. The aim is to highlight the things that those drafting the documents will usually need to think about, with a focus on what needs to be done practically. Checklists, sample documents and clauses are included to provide a starting point for preparing the final tailored documents. They are not intended to be 'precedents' in the traditional lawyers' sense.

1.16 As I am a specialist English employment lawyer and anticipate that this book will be of particular interest to other English employment lawyers I have included some 'hard' English and EC law where I think it is relevant. Lawyers from other countries and specialists from other disciplines will have less need of that detail, so I have tried to keep technical information on English employment law separate to allow those sections to be easily skipped by those who are not interested.

1.17 I hope that this book is written in an accessible way so that those engaged in expatriate projects, whatever their background, will find it useful.

USING THIS BOOK

1.18 Few people read textbooks from start to finish. Most will look at the index to find the answer to an immediate question and leave the rest for later. This book is divided into sections that are intended to make that approach easier. However, those who plan skipping bits should at least read Chapter 4 on the identity of the employer and Chapter 6 on structuring assignments before reading the parts they are particularly interested in. If only one thing is remembered about expatriate assignments, it should be that the identity of the employer is critical to almost everything else.

1.19 It may also be worth referring to the Glossary at Appendix 3. It explains most of the technical terms used in the book, and some that have not been used here but are frequently used by others. This may help to avoid some common misunderstandings arising from language or jurisdictional background and make some of the 'expat jargon' easier to understand.

KEY STEPS TO DRAFTING EXPATRIATE EMPLOYMENT DOCUMENTS

1.20 The following flowchart identifies the key steps to drafting expatriate documents.

Establish business objectives and purpose of documents (see Chapter 2)

↓

Obtain preliminary advice on viability of assignment,
particularly immigration and employer registration requirements
(see Chapter 3 and Appendix 1, A1.5)

↓

Assuming assignment is viable, seek more detailed home and
host country technical advice in key areas, eg corporation tax,
income tax, social security, VAT, immigration, employment law

↓

Decide on identity of employer (see Chapter 4)
and assignment length (see Chapter 5)

↓

Determine assignment structure and identify
documents required (see Chapter 6)

↓

Take detailed instructions on practical things to be covered by
documents and benefits (see Chapters 7 and 8
and Appendix 1)

↓

Prepare first draft documents (see Chapters 7 and 8 and Appendix 2)

↓

Obtain home and host country specialist review

↓

Issue documents to employee and conclude agreements

↓

Prepare any translations needed

↓

Submit to relevant authorities

DISCLAIMER

1.21 Opinions expressed in this book are the author's own. They are not intended to reflect the views of LexisNexis.

1.22 The author is an English employment law specialist and does not purport to be an expert in other areas, such as health and safety, pensions, tax, social security, immigration, data protection, share plans, compensation and benefits or the laws of any other jurisdiction.

1.23 Given the scope of this book, reference to the need to seek specialist advice in all the places where it would be appropriate would be irritating to the reader. The reader should take responsibility for seeking his own specialist advice where appropriate and, in particular, should appreciate that many of the explanations, for example in relation to tax and social security issues, have been simplified in order to achieve the objectives of this book.

1.24 Laws, and English employment, tax and immigration laws in particular, are subject to rapid, and sometimes unexpected, change, for example to reflect changes to public policy and developing case-law. This book is not intended to provide a substitute for up-to-date advice from competent specialists.

1.25 In particular, references to the employment laws and other laws of countries other than England are provided for illustrative purposes only and should not be relied upon. The author takes no responsibility for their accuracy.

1.26 Framework documents are provided to give ideas to competent specialists. They are not intended to be 'precedents' in the traditional lawyers' sense and should be adapted before use.

1.27 The information provided in this book is not intended to be advice and should always be checked by competent specialists before it is used.

1.28 It is the reader's responsibility to check information and suggestions before they rely on them. No liability whatsoever is accepted by the author, the author's firm or LexisNexis for any loss, expense or other liability incurred as a consequence of reliance on the contents of this book or as a consequence of any omission from this book.

1.29 Any dispute arising in respect of this book shall be subject to the laws of England and the exclusive jurisdiction of the English Courts.

CHAPTER 2

BUSINESS OBJECTIVES AND PURPOSE OF DOCUMENTS

2.1   Before starting to draft any employment documents it is, of course, important to understand what the business wants to achieve. This is even more important when drafting expatriate employment documents.

2.2   Instructions to prepare expatriate documents rarely come directly from people who decide that an overseas assignment is needed. It is often difficult to separate the original business objectives from technical advice that has been provided by other specialists and 'good ideas' that have been picked up along the way.

2.3   For example, those preparing the documents might be told that the assignment is to last for three years. More explanation is needed, and the adviser should ask for it. The adviser needs to understand, for example, whether there is a potentially flexible company policy (eg 'We find it takes 3 years for an expat to be really useful to us.') or a specific project or technical need (eg 'We need someone there who can oversee completion of the project on site in the host country and that will take at least 3 years.').

2.4   The person preparing the expatriate documents needs to be able to differentiate between what is essential to achieving the business objectives; what is important; and what is preferred, but not important. Expatriate employment arrangements often entail compromise. If the weight that should be given to different objectives is not fully understood, the best compromise may not be reached, or may be reached only after some unnecessary work for the advisers and expense and frustration for the business.

WHAT WILL THE EMPLOYEE DO?

2.5   The adviser should understand what the business wants the employee to do, practically. This is always important when employment documents are prepared, and most employment contracts will include a job title or job description clarifying the role the employee will be required to undertake. However, this is more important for expatriate assignments (see, eg, 'job title and duties' at **8.38**).

2.6 To draft the documents properly a good understanding of the following is needed:

- the employee's duties (including whether there is a specific project to complete);

- whether assignment timing is critical to achievement of business objectives (eg the employee may need to arrive before the previous manager departs or may need to be available until the end of a specific project);

- whether the employee is to carry out any representative function, eg as director (see **13.40–13.48**);

- the employee's seniority, responsibility for other employees and reporting lines.

WHY AN EXPATRIATE?

2.7 The cost of employing expatriate employees is usually much higher than the cost of employing 'local hires'. Prudent employers will naturally weigh the potential benefits of the assignment against likely costs. A clear understanding of potential benefits is, therefore, important. The following are examples of reasons sometimes given by employers for engaging an expatriate rather than a local hire.

Lack of suitably qualified local staff

2.8 Sometimes the particular skills or experience needed are not available locally. The host country employment market may be tight or the skills required for the role may be highly specialised.

2.9 Care should be taken when making a decision on this basis. The business should not reach a conclusion that an expatriate will be necessary without some evidence that that is factually correct. A good way of establishing whether a suitable recruit might be available in the host country is, of course, to try recruiting locally, eg by advertising the role. The issue should not be whether somebody from a particular country would be appropriate but whether they are the right person for the job. Subject to immigration constraints, the role should normally be open to candidates of any nationality. There may sometimes also be a host country immigration requirement to advertise locally first.

2.10 Careful consideration should also be given to whether it is really necessary to offer an expatriate package (ie additional benefits that are not offered to local staff) to attract a suitable candidate for the role. See **12.21** on 'local plus' remuneration and benefits and Chapter 18 on the potential impact of Brexit.

Development

2.11   Sometimes the business, particularly if it is a large multinational group of companies, will have a policy of sending managers with 'potential' on overseas assignments before they take on more senior roles in the home country. For example, if the host country operation is smaller or developing there may be more scope for the manager to experience the demands of a senior role there. The assignment experience may also help to develop the manager's awareness of the different issues and needs of other parts of the business. Conversely, if the manager is from a smaller operation in his home country it may be thought beneficial for him to have a period of time to develop his skills at another location, for example at the head office.

2.12   This sort of investment is long term. If the business is investing heavily in the development of managers it is likely to be particularly concerned about retention and the repatriation process, and the documents should reflect that. It may also be difficult to meet immigration criteria for development assignments.

Consistency

2.13   Multinationals may rotate managers across the group so that consistency of style and approach can be maintained within the group.

2.14   Some businesses give new recruits experience of the head-office culture before they start work and may insist on a short assignment to head office before the recruit settles down in the country where he is to work.

2.15   It can be difficult to obtain immigration permission if a wish to maintain consistency is the key driver for an assignment.

Sharing expertise

2.16   There may be a need for particular knowledge or expertise within the host country business. It may be appropriate to send a home country specialist to the host country to help transfer knowledge or train host country staff.

2.17   The length of time it may take to achieve this objective may determine the preferred assignment length, and the start and end dates may be critical.

Troubleshooting

2.18   Sometimes there is a particular problem in the host country that needs to be managed carefully under close home company supervision. For example, there might be concerns about financial mismanagement or an interim manager may be needed in place of someone who has left the host country business at short notice.

2.19   There is usually pressure for the assignment to start quickly, which may create challenges, for example because it may be difficult to obtain immigration clearance or relocate an expatriate's family quickly.

To help the employee

2.20   This reason comes up surprisingly often. The employee may want to work in the host country because a spouse or partner is to be assigned there; may want to return to a country he is connected with; or may just be excited by the prospect of a period abroad.

2.21   Particular care should be taken if this is the rationale for the assignment. The employee may not expect a full expatriate package but this would still be an overseas assignment. Just because the employee wants the assignment and is happy to work on an informal basis, perhaps from home and for less money, does not mean that the employer can disregard tax, social security, payroll, immigration, insurance and all the other 'extra' concerns that go with expatriate employment arrangements. If the employer (or the group of companies of which the employer is a part) has no existing operations in the host country (and this is of course more likely to be the case where the employee asks to go) then all the additional considerations that apply to 'start ups' will also apply (see Chapter 13 on new locations).

2.22   The proposal may initially seem like a 'win-win' solution, by which the employer keeps a good employee and the employee keeps his job but, in practice, the assignment may be disproportionately expensive to set up and manage.

More than one reason

2.23   The above objectives have been expressed simplistically and many assignments will have been proposed for more than one reason. For example, an employee may be expected to offer a special contribution to the host company business and managers may also see the assignment as a development opportunity for the employee. If a number of interrelated reasons for the assignment are offered then an understanding of the weight to be given to each would be helpful.

POTENTIAL BENEFITS AND EXPENSE

2.24   Most people involved with expatriate assignments will know they are expensive and will try to weigh costs against benefits. However, both the potential expense and expected commercial benefits are likely to be difficult to quantify upfront. There are commercial organisations offering computer-based tools designed to assist with cost assessment and 'return on investment'.

2.25 Factors that might be taken into consideration by an employer weighing costs and benefits could include:

- additional remuneration costs;
- additional benefit costs (eg the higher cost of international medical cover);
- additional tax and social security–related costs (eg higher social security contributions to be paid by the employer), and opportunities to mitigate;
- management time spent by those setting up and managing the assignment;
- professional expenses for a number of specialists prior to, during and at the end of the assignment;
- additional technology costs, eg to facilitate cross-border payroll management;
- less productive lead-in and wind-down times at the start and end of the assignment;
- costs associated with terminating the assignment or dealing with unexpected departure (eg severance pay, repatriation expenses or early termination penalties in respect of host country accommodation);
- the potentially demotivating effect on host country 'local hires' who see their own career prospects limited, or who are generally annoyed, by the imposition of a 'foreign' manager;
- the likelihood of the anticipated benefits materialising (eg whether a manager will actually stay long enough for the business investing in his development to reap the expected benefits).

PURPOSE OF THE DOCUMENTS

2.26 The adviser must understand the purpose of the documents as well as the purpose of the assignment itself. Without this insight the adviser cannot advise on necessary compromises effectively. For example, the adviser would find it hard to assess whether it is worth incurring professional fees in getting the documents right, or when the documents must be ready, if he does not understand their purpose.

For immigration purposes

2.27 Employers are often required to submit the proposed employment documents to immigration authorities with an application for immigration permission to work, such as a work permit. If the employee cannot start the assignment without a work permit and the employment contract must be submitted well in advance of the assignment start date to achieve this, the employment documents must be ready on time. If the assignment is time critical, failure to put the documentation in place quickly enough may mean that the assignment does not take place at all. More likely, there will be a last minute rush and mistakes will be made.

2.28 If the employment documents are needed for immigration purposes they must, of course, demonstrate compliance with immigration requirements. For example, if there are constraints on the role the employee can undertake or minimum remuneration, the paperwork should reflect them. If immigration permission will be granted for a fixed maximum period the assignment documents should reflect that too.

2.29 If the employment documents are to be presented to officials who work in the host country language only (which is likely) then either the documents must be prepared in the host language or a translation will be needed. In some countries there is a legal requirement for the authentic employment contract to be prepared in the host country language. Translations may need to be certified (see 'apostille' in the Glossary at Appendix 3).

2.30 The fact that the documents must be submitted before a work permit can be granted does not, of course, mean that other issues can be left until later. It is easy, for example, to forget to check the tax and social security position before finalising the employment structure if immigration is the most 'urgent' issue.

2.31 Even if there is no need to produce the employment documents to the immigration authorities before the assignment begins it may be prudent from an immigration perspective to ensure that the documents are in place, so that they can be produced if immigration permission is challenged at a later stage. The employer will be able to respond to any request for production more quickly; the documents are likely to have more weight if they have been in place for some time; and the employment is more likely to have been conducted in an appropriate way, if the issues were considered at the outset.

To reduce the risk of tax or social security challenge

2.32 As with immigration authorities, tax and social security authorities may also require sight of employment documents before the assignment begins. For example, sometimes tax advisers will recommend voluntary submission of the papers to the authorities at an early stage so that they can seek approval ('clearance') of the proposed arrangements from a tax perspective before the assignment begins. In some countries payroll arrangements can only be made once employee registration has taken place and an employment contract may be required for the registration application.

2.33 If any dispute about the correct tax or social security treatment arises at a later stage the authorities are likely to ask for the employment documents. They may, for example, be looking for consistency with submissions regarding the identity of the employer or the likely length of the assignment. The documents are likely to have more weight if they are prepared at the start of the assignment than if they are cobbled together halfway through. Both home and host tax and social security authorities may have an interest in reviewing documents.

2.34　Preparation of the documents at the start can also help ensure that the facts properly support the preferred tax treatment. Once the employment is up and running it will not be possible to change the facts retrospectively and it may be difficult to make some changes going forward. If the documents are prepared early, steps can be taken to ensure that the underlying facts are consistent with the preferred terms from the outset. Documents and the underlying facts should be consistent throughout the assignment. Regular review is important.

For pension purposes

2.35　The employee may wish to participate in particular pension arrangements and the identity of the employee's employer may be critical to his ability to do so. The employment documents may also be considered by a pensions or tax authority that wishes to determine whether the employee is, for example, eligible for any tax relief claimed.

To comply with employment laws

2.36　The following are examples of circumstances in which documents may be required from an employment law perspective:

- In all EU countries, and many others, employers are required to confirm key terms of the employment to the employee in writing (see **8.37** on the Employment Particulars Directive). Normally this information is provided in the form of an employment contract.
- As mentioned above, there may be a requirement for a copy of the employment contract to be supplied to an employment authority either on hiring or subsequently.
- Some employment terms may only be enforceable if they are properly documented, for example, post-termination restrictive covenants or where this is a condition of 'derogation' from a collective agreement.
- A copy of the contract may be required on termination of employment if, for example, approval of termination and/or the severance package offered is required from a court or employment authority.
- If litigation relating to the employment arises at a later stage the employment documents are likely to be considered. As in the event of challenge by immigration, pension, tax or social security authorities, the documents would have more weight if they were put in place before the dispute arose.

To provide comfort to the expatriate

2.37　Expatriates generally like to know where they stand. They will usually appreciate detailed documents so that they can understand the complex terms that apply to them and so that they feel they have some 'comeback' if the promised benefits are not delivered. Families will often be reassured by documents too. Expatriates are likely to give far more weight to employment documents than local hires. (See Chapter 22 on employee perspectives.)

To manage the expectations of the expatriate

2.38 Expatriates often make assumptions about the benefits and other terms that will apply to the assignment and these may not be accurate. Expatriate arrangements vary considerably. The expatriate's expectations may be based on home country practices, another employer's policies, or the terms offered to another employee or on a previous assignment. False expectations can be so firmly rooted that the expatriate does not even think to check with the employer that assumptions are correct.

2.39 Careful documentation of the detail can save assignment managers an enormous amount of time later on, particularly if the managers responsible for the assignee at the time of a query or dispute were not involved at the outset and do not know what was promised orally.

2.40 The following are examples of some common problem areas:

- Tax equalisation arrangements are complex and difficult for non-specialists to understand. The arrangements may never be explained properly or it may be assumed that provision of sample calculations by tax advisers is sufficient to confirm the agreement made. Problems can arise because the examples provided do not cover situations that have not yet arisen. For example, the tax treatment of a severance payment or bonus, or the need to seek reimbursement from the tax authorities may not have been dealt with.

- Employees are often made general promises about the benefits they are to receive, without receiving any confirmation of the detail. Disputes might arise over the precise terms. For example:
  - A promise to pay for children's education may not cover university fees (or additional university fees due because the family is no longer resident in the home country).
  - The employee may be promised suitable accommodation and assume that means a house with a garden for the family dog, as in his home country. He may find that he is instead provided with a flat and his children are unhappy because pets cannot go too.
  - The employment may end at the start of a school year after the employee has paid host country school fees for the year and the employee may expect his employer to put him right.

2.41 Apparently small discrepancies can become significant grievances for an employee, particularly if he has made promises to his spouse or partner and is criticised at home for not securing written confirmation from his employer. Expatriates often have a strong sense that they should not lose out financially because they agree to work abroad.

To manage family expectations

2.42 Successful assignments often depend on happy families. Documents provide an opportunity to make things that family members may be particularly concerned about clear. Given that dissatisfied family members are a common reason for early termination of assignments (and all the additional cost that may entail), the opportunity to make the 'deal' clear up front should not be missed. (See Chapter 22 on employee perspectives.)

To reduce the risk of dispute

2.43 Disputes with expatriates can be expensive and time consuming to resolve. Their packages are often generous, professional advice is generally more expensive to obtain, the expatriate is likely to be expensive to replace and a disgruntled expatriate who cannot be closely supervised can sour relations with other employees and business contacts in the host country.

2.44 As with any contract of employment, particular care should be taken with terms that apply on termination of employment. That is a time when the relationship with the employee is likely to be strained and when the employee may have a strong financial incentive to challenge the employer's interpretation of the documents.

CONCLUSIONS

2.45 With a clear understanding of both the commercial purpose of the assignment, and why the assignment documents are required, those producing the documents will be better placed to ensure that appropriate advice is obtained at the right time and that, where necessary, sensible compromises are made.

CHAPTER 3

IS THE ASSIGNMENT VIABLE?

3.1 Before seeking expensive advice on all the detailed issues that need to be resolved, it is worth quickly checking that the assignment is viable in principle. Key considerations are likely to be restrictions on who may employ people in the host country; whether immigration permission will be available; and personal, employee-related issues.

HOST COUNTRY EMPLOYER RESTRICTIONS

3.2 In some jurisdictions there are restrictions on who can employ people. For example, it may only be possible to employ staff in the host country if:

- the employer is a company registered in the host country, or has a branch or representative office registered there;
- the employer has a significant presence in the host country (eg the employer owns or leases premises in the host country);
- the employer is registered as an employer with an employment, or similar, authority in the host country (not to be confused with the company registration requirements referred to above). The employer registration requirements may be difficult or impossible for the group to satisfy or may take time to complete.

These issues may not be a concern if the proposed assignment is valuable and long term. In that case, the employer may simply work though the host country compliance requirements to ensure they are met. However, this type of requirement could make a short-term assignment impractical. For example, the assignment may become impractical if by the time the requirements are satisfied the employee is no longer needed to do the job or because the cost of compliance is too high to justify assignment of a junior employee. (See also Chapter 13 on potential corporation tax effects of meeting this sort of requirement.)

IMMIGRATION PERMISSION FOR THE EMPLOYEE (AND FAMILY)

3.3 Immigration restrictions are likely to be an important concern when assessing viability. As this is the first detailed reference to immigration, some general comments relating to immigration permission have been included in this chapter for convenience, as well as comments on the issues relating specifically to viability.

3.4   See also **8.8–8.23**, for some suggestions about immigration-related terms to be included in the employment contract and **19.4–19.31** on UK immigration requirements.

Consequences of failing to obtain immigration permission

3.5   In many countries it is a criminal offence to allow an individual to work without the appropriate immigration permission. A work permit or similar immigration permission may be needed. The employee, and dependent family members, may also require separate immigration permission to enter and live in the host country, for example residence permits may also be needed. Different terminology for different types of immigration permission may be used in different countries.

3.6   The employer, its officers and employees and/or the employee and family members might be exposed to fines, or even imprisonment, if the employee and family members enter, live or work in the host country without first obtaining appropriate immigration permission.

3.7   In addition to any legal penalty, if the employer is found to have allowed an employee to work without the appropriate immigration permission, the employer's relationship with the host country immigration authority is likely to be damaged. This may make it more difficult for the employer to obtain immigration permission for future assignments and may lead to more rigorous monitoring of the employer's immigration arrangements generally.

3.8   In some countries an employer must be registered as a 'sponsor' with the immigration authority before its employees can be granted a work permit or other immigration permission. (Sometimes, the host company may act as sponsor even where it is not the employer.) Allowing an employee to work without the appropriate immigration permission could lead to loss of the ability to act as a sponsor for other employees working in the host country. This could have severe consequences for the business. (See the Glossary at Appendix 3 for an explanation of 'sponsor'.)

3.9   Even if there is no criminal or significant financial penalty for the employee, the consequences of failing to obtain the correct immigration permission could be serious and distressing. For example, the employee or family members may be stopped and detained at the airport on trying to enter the host country or be deported from the host country after arrival. An incident of this type may make it difficult or impossible for the employee or family members to re-enter the host country.

3.10 Restrictions on the employee's return would have an impact on the employer too. Even if a suitable employee can be found quickly to replace the employee who is not able to work in the host country, the need to make new arrangements for the substitute would result in delay and additional expense. The business purpose of the assignment is likely to be prejudiced.

Timing

3.11 If an immigration application is not submitted early enough, immigration permission may not be obtained in time for the assignment to begin as planned. This may mean the assignment is delayed or that it cannot take place at all.

Type of immigration permission sought

3.12 Typically, immigration permission is given by way of work permit for the employee and residence permits for the employee and dependent family members. However, in most countries, permission can be granted on a variety of different bases. Sometimes the employee may potentially fall into more than 'category' for immigration purposes, in which case the type of immigration permission to be sought should be considered carefully. Factors that may influence the decision to apply for permission by reference to a particular immigration category may include:

- the employee's personal status, for example, nationality, qualifications and age, and the nationalities, etc of family members;
- the length of time likely to be taken to obtain a particular type of immigration permission (some types of permission are quicker to obtain than others, and whether this is a concern may depend on the business reasons for the assignment);
- the timing of the application (some types of immigration permission may only be available at a particular time of year because the number of permits issued is limited and they quickly run out);
- the length of time the type of immigration permission is available for and whether an extension of time is likely to be granted if needed (the time required would depend on the purpose of the assignment, etc, see Chapter 5);
- the likelihood that permission will be granted (the employer or employee may not be eligible to apply for certain types of immigration permission or the likelihood of success may be less certain);
- the effect of the application on existing applications for immigration permission or any other applications to be put forward by the employer or employee (eg because a limited number are available to the business);
- whether the group wants to allow the employee to work for several employers (eg other group companies) or restrict the employee to just one employer during the assignment (eg to reduce the risk of competition) – work permits are often employer and role-specific;

- the fee for the application for immigration permission; and/or
- associated responsibilities and potential liabilities for the employer.

Pre-visits and temporary immigration permission

3.13 Sometimes the employee will want to visit the host country before the assignment begins, perhaps to check schools or accommodation in advance of relocation. The employer may want the employee to meet other staff in the host country or attend critical business meetings. The employee's partner, and possibly children, may want to go too.

3.14 If immigration permission for the assignment has not yet been granted those trips may technically be illegal. Requirements for immigration should always be checked. Sometimes it is possible for the employee to enter lawfully on the basis of another short-term type of immigration permission, for example, as a business visitor. Care should be taken to ensure that the temporary permission is appropriate for the intended purpose and, if it is, that it is obtained before the visit. For example, if the employee enters on a tourist visa and his suitcase is found to be full of suits, business documents and business cards, the authorities may quite reasonably assume that the employee intends to work and that the declared intention of the visit is false. In practice, such a 'mistake' could, eg, prejudice a pending work permit application and may even mean that the assignment cannot take place at all. The employee could also be prevented from entering the host country in the future. (See also 3.5–3.10 on consequences of failing to obtain immigration permission more generally.)

3.15 Similar care should be taken if family members are to visit the host country in advance of the assignment. If a key family member's conduct leads to rejection of their application for residence permission (i e so that they cannot accompany the employee) the employee may then be unwilling to take up the assignment.

3.16 If the rules for applying for a particular type of immigration permission require the employee to be in a particular place (or not to be in a particular place, such as the host country) then a pre-visit while the application is pending may invalidate the application. Similar considerations could apply to applications for immigration permission for the family.

EEA nationals

3.17 If European Economic Area (EEA) or Swiss nationals (see the Glossary at Appendix 3 for a list of current 'EEA' countries) are to be assigned to a country within the EEA or Switzerland then immigration permission is (currently) unlikely to be a concern. However, there may still be potential pitfalls. For example, there may be a need to register the employee with immigration authorities, or the police, even if there is no formal requirement to obtain a work permit to take up employment.

3.18 It should not be assumed that an employee who is already working in one EEA country will be an EEA citizen and will therefore automatically have a right to work in another EEA country. The employee may be working under immigration restrictions in his 'home' EEA country. The rules for non-EEA nationals can vary substantially between EEA countries and permission obtained in one EEA country is unlikely to be sufficient for another (but see 3.19–3.23 in relation to Schengen visas).

Schengen visas

3.19 Most EU countries, and also Iceland and Norway, are party to a common visa policy (see the Glossary at Appendix 3). The aim of the policy is to abolish internal border controls between countries that are party to it, and enable visitors to travel throughout the participating countries. The countries that participate are usually referred to collectively as the 'Schengen area'. (The area is named after the town where the original agreement was signed.)

3.20 Under the Schengen visa arrangements, a visa for entering any country in the Schengen area automatically allows visitors to freely travel throughout the Schengen area.

3.21 The UK and the Republic of Ireland are not party to the Schengen arrangements relating to border controls and visas, so a 'Schengen visa' cannot be used to visit the UK or Ireland. (Confusingly the UK and Republic of Ireland are party to some other aspects of the Schengen arrangements, for example, security and information aspects.)

3.22 A Schengen visa allows free movement between countries in the Schengen area. It does not give an employee who is issued with a work permit by one country party to the Schengen arrangements an automatic right to work in other Schengen countries, although it might be possible to attend business meetings.

3.23 Specific host country immigration advice should always be sought, even where the employee and family members hold EEA passports or have been granted Schengen visas.

Family

3.24 Immigration permission is often needed for the employee's partner and other family members. It is important to bear in mind that the employee's partner and family may not all have the same nationality or immigration status as the employee. If the assignment is to be long term, immigration permission for the partner and children may be a precondition for the assignment.

3.25 If the employee is not married this may create additional difficulties with obtaining immigration permission for the employee and partner. It may not be possible for unmarried partners to accompany the employee to some locations.

Difficulties may also arise if, for example, children were born before the employee and his partner were married; if there are stepchildren; if the family unit includes dependents other than the employee's partner and children, for example an elderly parent; if the employee is separated from his spouse; or if the employee's legal partner is of the same sex as the employee or of a nationality that is unwelcome in the host country. The first step for the employer is usually to understand exactly who the employee would like to accompany him on the assignment. Each individual will need to be considered separately.

3.26 The employer also needs to understand whether the partner, or any other family member, would wish to work in the host country during the assignment, and whether the partner's ability to work is a precondition for the assignment. It may not be possible for women to obtain permission to work in some countries and in others it may not be possible for an accompanying partner to obtain permission unless they qualify for a work permit in their own right.

EMPLOYEE CONSTRAINTS

3.27 In practice, employees are unlikely to be sent on overseas assignments unless they are willing to go. The arrangements tend to be far too expensive for the employer to risk foisting them on a reluctant employee. The employee himself may have some core needs, and if those needs cannot be met then he may refuse to go. The employee's demands may be closely linked to those of family members, as the assignment will affect them too. It is worth checking with the employee that there are no potential 'blocks' before expensive professional advice is sought. This will, of course, be less of a concern if there is more than one potential candidate.

3.28 Employee-related constraints might, for example, include the following:

- adverse impact on home country immigration status, eg for an employee seeking citizenship;
- close family members must be able to accompany or visit;
- safety;
- a child's exam schedule must not be disrupted or adequate host country schooling must be available;
- an accompanying partner must be able to work too;
- demand for career-related reassurance (what will happen on return home?);
- medical constraints.

Checking for potential personal 'barriers' to assignment can raise complex legal issues including the risk of unlawful discrimination. (See Chapter 12 on equality and Chapter 22 on employee perspectives.)

TAX AND SOCIAL SECURITY CONTRIBUTIONS

3.29 Potential taxes are unlikely to be a technical 'block' but could make an assignment prohibitively expensive. Potential issues would usually be checked with the home company's usual internal or external tax advisers. However, it would be sensible to check the immigration requirements and employee constraints first as it may be difficult to obtain answers to the tax and social security questions cheaply.

CHECKING VIABILITY WITH HOST COUNTRY ADVISERS

3.30 See checklist **A1.5** at Appendix 1 for some suggestions regarding the questions that might be asked of a host country adviser to help determine whether the assignment is viable in principle and whether it is worth investing in further advice. This preliminary advice will usually be sought from an employment lawyer in the host country.

CHAPTER 4

IDENTITY OF EMPLOYER

4.1   The identity of the employer is critical to most expatriate assignments.

For example, the identity of the employer may have a significant impact on:

- the costs of employing the expatriate;
- tax and social security compliance obligations;
- the employment documents needed;
- drafting of a significant number (if not most) employment terms; and
- the viability of the assignment.

4.2   Understanding and getting this right from the beginning saves a huge amount of time, reduces the cost of preparing documents and substantially reduces risk.

4.3   The preferred employer will vary with the countries involved, the purpose of the assignment and the perspective of the adviser. However, there are some common themes and it is worth considering these, and seeking appropriate specialist help, before starting to draft the documents.

WHO CAN EMPLOY?

Legal entity

4.4   For convenience, this book normally refers to companies. However, other legal entities may employ the expatriate, for example, a partnership, limited liability partnership or individual person.

4.5   In the UK, employment by a branch or representative office of a company is not possible because the branch or representative office will not have separate 'legal personality' from the company. However, in some other countries it is common for the branch or representative office to be treated as the employer.

Home or host

4.6   Usually, a company registered in the home or host country will employ the expatriate. Sometimes a company registered in a third country will be the employer.

4.7   Care should be taken with the terms 'home' and 'host'. Generally, the 'host' country is the destination country where the employee will work. The 'home' country will be the place from which the employee is assigned.

Host country restrictions

4.8   Employment by a company that is not registered in the host country, or a company that does not have a significant presence in the host country, may not be permitted in some jurisdictions (see **3.2**).

Service companies

4.9   Sometimes a legal entity will be established with the sole purpose of employing expatriates. See **4.56–4.61** below on 'service' companies.

TIMING OF DECISION ON EMPLOYER IDENTITY

4.10   The identity of the employer is one of the most important things to be determined when expatriate employment arrangements are structured. The employer's identity should be settled as early as possible, and certainly before the employment begins. The employer's identity will affect the way all the employment documents are drafted.

4.11   The correct identity of the employer is, in most countries, a question of fact. Carefully drafted documents are not enough. Before the assignment begins arrangements can be put in place to ensure the facts help confirm that the preferred company is really the employer. Once the assignment has begun the practical arrangements will be in place. It will be impossible to change the facts retrospectively, and it will probably also be difficult to change them going forward. (See **4.71–4.107** on facts supporting the identity of the employer.)

4.12   For example, the employer and employee may have a good working relationship and may be relaxed about putting new employment documents in place. However, as soon as the assignment begins the employee will start to earn a salary under the new arrangements. If a particular company pays the employee and bears the remuneration costs, there may be an inference that it is the employer. That will have consequences for both employer and employee. (See **4.86–4.90** on payroll arrangements.)

IMPACT OF EMPLOYER IDENTITY

4.13 The employer's identity can have a significant impact on the costs of employing expatriates. For example, this may lead to a different tax or social security treatment. Other technical issues, such as immigration restrictions, may limit the options that are available. These can be highly technical and complex issues and usually advice should be sought from a number of specialists before a decision on the identity of the employer for the assignment is made. The following is intended to highlight some of the factors that should be considered when determining the correct employer.

Business reasons

4.14 The employee's role is likely to suggest natural reporting lines within the business.

4.15 If the natural line manager is a representative of the home or host company this may make it more difficult for another company to be treated as the employer. However, it may still be possible to put structures in place to separate management of the employee for employment purposes from the employee's commercial reporting line.

4.16 For example, the preferred option, from a cost perspective, may be to employ the individual through the home company, whilst from a business perspective the natural reporting line may be to a manager within the host company. It may be effective to provide for the employee to report to the host company manager on a day-to-day basis on business affairs, whilst ensuring that key employment-related decisions and practical arrangements remain the responsibility of the home country line manager. The home company could still pay the employee, approve holiday and expense claims, provide benefits, deal with appraisals and disciplinary issues, etc. It would be important to check with both home and host country advisers that the particular factual matrix effectively supports home country employment for relevant purposes (see also 4.71–4.107).

Employment laws

4.17 Host country employment laws may not allow a company registered in the home country to employ people in the host country. If this is the case there will be little choice: the business will need to find an employer that meets host country requirements. Sometimes this must be a company registered in the host country but, in other cases, a branch or representative office registered in the host country will be sufficient. Sometimes it is also possible to employ through a host country agency; another connected company (perhaps a joint venture partner); or a state-sponsored employer.

4.18 The identity of the employer may also affect the application of mandatory home and host country employment laws (see **10.30–10.61** on mandatory laws).

4.19 It is sometimes possible for companies registered overseas to employ people on terms that would not be allowed for employment by local firms. This might, for example, be because the host country is trying to make itself attractive to foreign investment by relaxing the employment laws that apply to overseas investors. (Special arrangements may also apply to employees who will work at particular locations within the host jurisdiction, eg at a military base or within a specially designated commercial zone.)

4.20 In other countries the issues may be more complex but the identity of the employer may still affect legal rights and obligations. For example, the identity of the employer may affect the jurisdiction of home or host country courts or employment tribunals (see **10.62–10.74** on jurisdiction). This can have an impact on resolution of disputes, eg, on termination of employment. See Chapter 16 on ending the assignment.

4.21 If the host company is the employer it may be more difficult to offer expatriate host company employees different pay and benefit arrangements from host company 'local hires', for example, because of race discrimination laws or industrial relations issues. Concerns may sometimes be reduced if the home company remains the employer during the assignment. (See Chapter 12 on equality.)

UK

4.22 The place of registration (nationality) of the employer should not normally make a difference to whether UK employment laws apply to employees who work in the UK. However, the place of registration of the employer will often make a difference to whether UK employment laws apply to employees when they are sent from the UK to work in another country (see **10.56–10.60**).

Immigration

4.23 If a work permit or other immigration permission to work in the host country is required, this will often only be granted in respect of a particular role with a particular employer. This usually means that the identity of the employer must be decided before the application for immigration permission is submitted.

4.24 Sometimes immigration permission will not be granted unless the employer is registered in the host country. The employer may also need to be approved as a 'sponsor' before the immigration application can be considered and it may not be possible for a home country employer who is not registered as a sponsor in the host country to obtain the appropriate approval in time, at a reasonable expense or at all. For example, the employer may need to set up premises in the host country or demonstrate that it is capable of complying with host country laws before it can be registered as a potential sponsor for immigration purposes.

4.25 Sometimes immigration approval is available independently of the employer. For example:

• EEA nationals are generally free to work in other EEA countries without the need for additional immigration approval;

• it may be possible for the employee to apply personally for general permission on the basis of skills or personal status, for example, by using the Australian 'points' system or the US 'green card' system, in which case the identity of the employer may be irrelevant to the application.

4.26 Immigration considerations are usually particularly important, as without immigration permission it may not be possible for the assignment to begin at all.

4.27 Because of the length of time that it may take to process an application for immigration permission, the identity of the employer should usually be settled as early as possible so that the assignment is not prejudiced by any delay.

4.28 See **3.3–3.26**, for a more detailed explanation of the potential impact of immigration restrictions on the viability of the assignment.

Income tax and social security

4.29 Employees are normally required to pay both income tax and social security contributions. Employers are normally required to pay employer's social security contributions and may also be obliged to withhold income tax from employees' remuneration and account for the withheld tax to relevant tax authorities ('withholding obligations').

4.30 Differences in income tax rates between countries can be considerable. For example, personal income tax rates may vary from nil for some locations in the Middle East to over 50% elsewhere. Whilst income tax rates directly affect employees rather than employers, the employer is usually also concerned as there may be a commercial need to adjust remuneration to deliver the desired level of net pay.

4.31 UK employer's social security contributions ('National Insurance contributions' or 'NIC') are currently paid at the rate of 13.8% of qualifying remuneration (uncapped). UK employee's social security contributions are currently paid at 12% of qualifying remuneration up to the 'upper earnings limit' with an additional 2% payable on any excess amount. By contrast, the maximum rates of employee's and employer's social security contributions in France are currently around 25% and 45% respectively. Rates change frequently, and the figures should not be relied on, but the comparison illustrates the potential for significant rate differences and the need to check.

4.32 It is particularly easy for employers and advisers from countries where social security contributions are relatively low to underestimate the potential commercial impact of social security contributions due in other countries.

4.33 The identity of the employer may sometimes make a difference to the amount of income tax that must be paid, eg treaty relief may not be available where there is a host employer. (See, also, **6.58–6.69** on dual contracts and **19.47–19.51** on detached duty relief). The identity of the employer will often make a big difference to the social security contributions that must be paid. The identity of the employer is typically (but not always) a bigger issue for social security than it is for income tax.

4.34 Some countries allow employees to remain in their home country social security schemes for a period of time after they start work in the host country. (Sometimes more significantly for the employer, they may also be permitted to remain out of an expensive host country social security scheme.) The agreements between countries that clarify how the arrangements work may be referred to as international social security agreements ('totalization' agreements in the US). Strict conditions may apply. For example, where the expected duration of the assignment is too long, remaining in the home country scheme may not be allowed even at the outset of the assignment. Future intentions may sometimes be as important as current facts.

4.35 Continued participation in home country social security arrangements may only be possible if the employee remains in the home company's employment during the assignment.

4.36 Social security considerations often have an impact on the preferred entity for employing the expatriate during the assignment, particularly where the host country is an EU country. But see **4.71–4.107** below on facts and **4.114** on tax evasion.

US

4.37 In practice, it is common for assignees from the US to remain employed by their pre-assignment US employer during an assignment to Europe and for the assignee to remain outside the host country social security scheme. There may be a variety of reasons for this.

UK

4.38 UK social security contributions are lower than those that apply in some other European countries. It is worth checking potential social security costs where an employee is assigned from the UK to another European country, as additional costs may be surprisingly high. (See **20.14–20.21**.)

Corporation tax

Corporation tax deduction

4.39 Typically, when an employer prepares accounts it is able to deduct remuneration costs (and some costs relating to termination of employment) from profits before the company's corporation tax liability is calculated. The employer may not be able to do this is if, eg, the employee's work does not benefit the employer's business. If employment costs cannot be offset against profits for corporation tax purposes in the relevant jurisdiction(s) this could increase the real cost of employing the expatriate.

4.40 As tax rules vary from country to country, advice should be sought from appropriate specialists to see whether the identity of the employer will have an impact on the availability of corporation tax deduction, before the assignment begins.

4.41 This may affect preferences regarding the identity of the employer. Usually though, the expatriate can be employed by a home employer without too much impact on corporation tax by ensuring that costs are recharged between the home and host companies appropriately and that recharging arrangements are properly documented. (See **6.26–6.31** and **8.73–8.83**, Appendix 1 checklist **A1.10** and Appendix 2 framework document **A2.6** in relation to inter-company expatriate supply agreements.)

Permanent establishment

4.42 A group of companies may structure business in a way that ensures that corporation tax is chargeable only in appropriate countries. They may, naturally, wish to keep profits subject to corporation tax to a minimum in countries where corporation tax rates are relatively high. There will, also naturally, be legal constraints on their freedom to do this.

4.43 When a group starts doing business in a new host country, or where the business activities in the host country change (both of which can coincide with the start of an expatriate assignment) there is a risk that a new or greater corporation tax liability will be created in the host country.

4.44 As always with global mobility, the rules specific to relevant jurisdictions should be checked but, typically, corporation tax liabilities do not arise in a host country where the group undertakes promotional, marketing or similar activities, provided that commercial transactions are not actually made in the host country. If there is a risk that a 'permanent establishment' might be created by employees' host country activities, then a new subsidiary is often registered in the host country to 'ring fence' the host country activities, and keep the home country activities out of scope for host country corporation tax purposes.

4.45 These issues can be relevant to the structuring of expatriate employment arrangements. For example, it may be important to the group that the expatriate does not have connections or reporting lines to the home company or that the expatriate is clearly not employed by the home company. (See also **13.8–13.15**.)

4.46 It is important that those preparing expatriate employment documents keep in mind that an individual assignment is typically less important to a multinational than wider commercial, tax and group structuring implications. Also, that structuring assignments simply to avoid tax (or advising others to do so) may amount to tax evasion, see **4.114**. Employers, and advisers, should keep in mind, too, that facts often evolve over time. It is important to keep documents under review to ensure that they continue to be appropriate going forward.

4.47 Specialist advice on the impact of employer identity should be sought from internal or external corporate tax advisers as appropriate. It should not be assumed that expatriate tax or international social security specialists will raise relevant corporation tax (or sales tax) issues. Engagement terms with third party advisers relating to tax should make responsibility for different types of tax advice clear.

Transfer pricing

4.48 If the employee's services are supplied by one group company to another, fees should be paid. The rate at which those fees are paid may have an impact on the corporation tax to be paid in each jurisdiction. These 'transfer pricing' issues are more likely to arise if a home country employer, ie the home company, supplies the expatriate's services to a host company in the same group of companies. (See the Glossary at Appendix 3 and **13.16–13.18** for more on 'transfer pricing'.) Specialist advice regarding appropriate 'transfer pricing' rates is generally available from international firms of accountants.

Sales tax (VAT)

4.49 If the home company employs and pays the expatriate but he performs services for the host company, the host company should pay for those services. The fee paid by the host company to the home company may be subject to sales tax (known as 'value added tax' or 'VAT' in the UK).

4.50 This may not be an issue for the host company if it can recover the sales tax paid on fees by offsetting it against the sales tax paid by customers on goods or services produced by the host company. However, intra-group fees may sometimes be a significant cost. For example, this may be because no sales tax is charged on services provided by the host company to third parties. This may be a particular concern, eg, for international charities and other not-for-profit organisations and for some organisations in the financial services sector.

4.51 When structuring expatriate assignments it is important to understand:

- whether sales tax is due on fees paid between group companies;
- if sales tax is due, which company should pay it and at what rate;
- whether the fees to be paid for services, on which sales taxes will be due, are at an appropriate level; and
- whether sales tax is a real cost for the business or whether it can be recovered.

4.52 A large fee is unlikely to be paid by the host company to the home company if the host company employs the expatriate directly for the duration of the assignment. This is because the host company rather than the home company will be paying the employee's remuneration costs. Sales tax is usually only a significant issue if the home company remains the employer during the assignment and the fee reflects remuneration costs.

4.53 Sales tax arrangements should be confirmed in the inter-company expatriate supply agreement. (See **6.26–6.31**, **8.73–8.83**, Appendix 1 checklist **A1.10** and Appendix 2 framework document **A2.6**.)

Intellectual property

4.54 The role may involve creation of intellectual property. The starting point in most countries is that the employer owns intellectual property created by its employee in the course of his employment. The group may want that intellectual property to belong to a particular group company, for example, the company that will use the intellectual property. Where intellectual property may be important it is usually best to deal with these issues at the outset so that the intellectual property can belong to the right company from the start. It may be convenient for the preferred intellectual property owner to be the employer so that the correct company automatically owns the intellectual property. However, generally, the same effect can be achieved without the necessity for that company to be the employer by inserting appropriate terms to confirm the owner of the intellectual property in the employment documents. Reassignment of intellectual property rights at a later stage is usually less attractive, for example because transfer of intellectual property, once it has been created and has a value, may create tax liabilities.

4.55 For many expatriate assignments intellectual property rights are not particularly important because the expatriate is not expected to create any valuable intellectual property. Even where intellectual property is important, it is unlikely to be the most important consideration when settling on the identity of the employer.

Service companies

4.56 Employees are frequently employed by companies that do not do much more than provide the services of employees to other group companies. This can be the case even where the employment has no international element. In an expatriate context, particularly where a multinational's expatriate population is large, expatriates are sometimes employed through one group company. This may, eg, make administration more convenient or assist with delivery of employment benefits.

4.57 These entities supplying expatriates, or their services, to other group companies are sometimes referred to as 'service companies', 'employee leasing companies' or 'global employment companies'.

4.58 Service company arrangements can sometimes offer tax and social security savings too.

4.59 There is often concern about whether these entities genuinely employ the individuals whose services they supply. The identity of the employer will usually be a question of fact. Good documents can help but they will not be conclusive. Factors considered to determine the 'real' employer tend to be very similar in most countries (see **4.71–4.107**). Whilst employment by a service company may be desirable, and achievable, facts that cannot be changed may prevent this from being effective in every case.

4.60 Advisers should take particular care to challenge arrangements where the alleged 'global employer' is located in a low tax offshore jurisdiction where the group does not have any other significant commercial activity and where there are few, or even no, 'local hires'. It might, eg, be argued that the relevant entity is simply acting as agent for the employer.

4.61 Some jurisdictions do not allow employees to be engaged by service companies. They may prohibit or restrict the supply of employees through what are sometimes called 'employee leasing' arrangements. Employees might need to be employed by the entity to which the employees are actually providing services.

Benefits

Pension

4.62 The employee may wish to remain in his current home employer pension arrangements, eg, because that is where he plans to retire. This may not be possible if the identity of the employer changes from the home company to the host company.

4.63 For example, the employee might be participating in a generous final salary/defined benefit pension plan. The plan may only allow employees of the home company to participate. If the employee becomes employed by the host company he may be forced to leave the plan at the start of the assignment. If the plan is 'closed' to new members, he may not even be able to rejoin on his return home.

4.64 Participation in home country benefit plans may only be possible if, for example:

- there is an initial period of employment in the home country;
- the expatriate remains employed by a home country employer during the assignment; or
- if there is a 'residual employment relationship' with the home company during the assignment, eg, with the home company promising employment in the home country at the end of the assignment and some other benefits. (In some countries, steps may be needed under the pension plan rules to make this work.)

4.65 Eligibility for continued participation in a pension plan may be determined by the rules of the relevant pension plan and there may be some scope for amendment. However, the benefit of pension arrangements for employees is usually that contributions, investments accumulating in the pension fund and/or payments of pension at a later stage enjoy tax relief. If this tax relief is not available, for example because the employee is not paying home country income tax and cannot obtain host country income tax relief or is not employed by a company registered in the home country, then changing the pension plan rules, even if this is technically possible, may not help resolve the issue. (See **20.66** on continued participation in a UK pension plan.)

4.66 See the Glossary at Appendix 3 on US '401K' retirement plans.

Incentive arrangements

4.67 The employee may wish to continue to participate in particular incentive arrangements. If the employer changes from the home to the host company this may not be possible. This might be the case, for example, if the plan is only open to home company employees or employees paying home country tax. The employee might be excluded from a group plan if the host company is a joint venture company in which the home company owns, say, a 49% stake.

4.68 If the employee ceases to participate this may affect not only future entitlements but also vesting, loss or tax treatment of rights that have already been 'earned'. It may be expensive for the employer to compensate the employee for the lost benefits, particularly any lost tax relief. (See also **15.9–15.15**, **19.106–19.111** and **20.24–20.25** on share plans.)

Medical and other insurance-based cover

4.69 A large employer will usually be able to negotiate employers' liability, private health insurance cover and other insurance-based benefits, such as dental cover, at preferential rates. The policy may restrict the potential scope of the cover, for example, to employees of the home company. If the employee moves abroad and is employed by the host company, rather than the home company, then the host company should provide the agreed benefits. However, the host company may be unable to secure equivalent cover at the same rates. This is normally primarily a matter for resolution through commercial negotiation but there may be more scope, for example, for scaling down the employees' expectations, if this is tackled at the outset. If there is any delay in resolving issues relating to cover the employer may need to accept the risk directly if an insurable event (eg treatment in relation to an accident) occurs before the appropriate insurance is in place.

4.70 Although the identity of the employer may have an impact on the availability and cost of insurance-related benefits, availability and cost will rarely have an impact on the preferred identity of the employer. Note that the change of employer is unlikely to be the only change required to policy terms, eg there may be a need to change a private medical policy from domestic cover to, most likely, more expensive international cover.

FACTS SUPPORTING THE IDENTITY OF THE EMPLOYER

4.71 Given that the identity of the employer in most countries will be a question of fact, care should be taken to ensure that the underlying facts really do support the assumed employer's identity. Identifying the employer correctly is a key concern for assignment managers and professional advisers to consider for all international assignments, and a task that is usually most appropriately undertaken by specialist employment lawyers.

Correspondence and drafts

4.72 It is easy to assume that informal correspondence with the employee before the employment documents are signed or the assignment begins is irrelevant to employment status. (It can be helpful to confirm this expressly in the documents.) However, correspondence between the employee and managers or the HR team is unlikely to attract legal privilege (broadly, protection from disclosure, see the Glossary at Appendix 3 and **15.123–15.128**) and may provide clear evidence of the parties' intentions at the outset of the employment. This could be critical to determining the true identity of the employer. Particular care should be taken with emails because they are often written with less thought than letters or formal documents. Similarly, correspondence after the documents are prepared may provide useful evidence of the facts, both at the time the documents were prepared and as the assignment progresses.

4.73 Ideally, draft employment documents should be prepared through privileged discussion with legal advisers. They should not be sent to the employee until the employer is reasonably comfortable that the documents reflect the preferred arrangements, and certainly not before the preferred identity of the employer has been decided.

4.74 Legal advice privilege may not apply in the same way (or at all) in every country, and may not always allow the parties to resist disclosure to third parties. Documents should therefore always be prepared in a way that takes account of the risk of a need to disclose. If documents are intended to be drafts, subject to discussion, contract etc they should be marked accordingly.

4.75 Because there are so many technical issues associated with preparing expatriate employment documents delays may arise. It is quite common for those responsible for the documents to lose focus whilst they wait for slow advice or permission from authorities, or for momentum to be lost in other ways. This can, unfortunately, mean that an assignment begins, and sometimes ends, before the arrangements are properly documented. The most recent draft documents under discussion with the employees may then be evidence of the employment terms agreed between the parties, or at least of the employer's intentions at that time.

4.76 Even after the employment has begun correspondence can be relevant. Letters from the employer should be written on the employer's headed paper by an appropriate representative of the right employer. Sometimes, great care is given to documenting the assignment arrangements at the outset and then managers (perhaps new managers who were not involved at the outset) forget about the importance of ensuring that the correct entity manages the employee and subsequent correspondence is sloppy. For example, correspondence relating to appraisals, pay reviews, bonus awards, etc should normally be issued by an appropriate representative of the correct employer, and reflect decisions made by the correct employer.

4.77 The employee's own business correspondence, including emails, may also indicate that a particular entity is the employer.

Immigration documents

4.78 Immigration documents will usually specify the employer and often only an employer may make the application for immigration permission.

4.79 All other arrangements should support the identity of the employer specified for immigration purposes. However, applications for immigration permission are often made by different people from those responsible for the employment documents or tax compliance. It is always worth checking to ensure that the application form and other immigration documents specify and support the assumed employer consistently.

Job title, duties and reporting lines

4.80 The employee's job title, job description, and the duties he actually performs may reflect his employment status. Business cards may be important too. Details and documents may be requested by authorities challenging the arrangements. Particular care should be taken with online representations, eg the individual's personal social media accounts may confirm erroneous details of the current role.

4.81 Generally, it will be possible to structure the arrangements so that duties for the host company are consistent with employment by the home company if this is desirable. However, some roles may need to be carried out by a host company employee. For example, the most senior employee for the host company may need to be a host company employee or it may only be possible to grant 'powers' to employees of the host company. (See **13.26–13.29** on 'powers'.)

4.82 The employee should report directly to someone within the employer's business, normally someone more senior than the employee. Ideally, the line manager should be employed by the employer too. (In practice, this does not always happen.) Care should also be taken with arrangements for those that the expatriate may manage in the host country, particularly if they are host company employees and it is intended that the expatriate should be a home country employee.

4.83 The employee may be employed by the home company but actually provide his services to a host company in a different time zone. The employee may, in that case, report on a day-to-day basis to someone in the host country. If this is the case, then the employment documents should, at least, make clear that core employment decisions will be made by an appropriate representative of the home country employer – and that should happen in practice.

Example

4.84 An employee is employed by the home company and assigned to work as IT manager for the host company. The employee may take day-to-day instructions regarding his duties and the host company business from the host company's IT director. However, all key decisions regarding his employment are made by the home company. Feedback for appraisal purposes is sought from the host company, but a home company manager actually appraises him. The home company decides on any pay rise and communicates its decision to the employee. Day-to-day employment issues such as expenses, holidays and sickness are managed by the home company. Only the home company can discipline or dismiss and the home company will hear any grievance raised.

4.85 Sometimes, for example, because managing expatriate assignments is so specialist, a group of companies will have one team employed by one of the group companies dealing with all the expatriate administration, regardless of which company individual expatriates are actually employed by or work for. This can still be consistent with employment by another group company but extra care must be taken to ensure that decisions communicated by the central assignment managers are clearly made by or on behalf of the correct employer and that costs are recharged appropriately.

Pay

4.86 The employer should be responsible for making sure salary is paid to the employee.

4.87 Normally, the employer will pay the employee from the employer's funds and a payslip will be issued in the employer's name confirming the sums paid.

4.88 Sometimes, usually for convenience, the employer will arrange for another entity to make payments to the employee on its behalf. For example, a home company employer might arrange for salary to be paid by a commercial payroll bureau to the employee or the host company to which the employee is assigned may deliver remuneration. The employment contract and payslips should make clear that payment to the employee by a third party is made on behalf of the employer. Remuneration costs should be properly recharged to the employer, and this should be confirmed by the terms of an inter-company expatriate supply agreement, accounts and banking records, as appropriate. (See **6.26–6.31** and **8.73–8.83**, Appendix 1 checklist **A1.10** and Appendix 2 framework document **A2.6** on inter-company expatriate supply agreements.)

4.89 As the employer is responsible for remuneration, letters awarding pay rises, bonus payments, etc should be written on the employer's headed paper. They should be signed on behalf of the employer by an appropriate representative of the employer. It is easy to forget this as pay reviews are often conducted by people who have not been involved in setting up the arrangements at the start. This does not of course mean that a home employer cannot seek feedback from the host company regarding performance etc, but the correct employer should make the relevant decisions.

Tax and social security

4.90 The employer and/or the employee will be obliged to pay tax and social security contributions. There may be requirements to register, obtain identification numbers, complete forms, tax returns, etc confirming the employer's identity. These arrangements should clearly confirm the identity of the correct employer. It is rarely possible to delay paying the employee for any length of time so the identity of the employer must be known before payroll and tax deduction arrangements are established.

Benefits-in-kind (including pension)

4.91 Benefits should be provided by the employer. Many insurance-related benefits specify the identity of the employer. Policies should be checked to ensure they are consistent with employment by the correct employer.

4.92 Where there is a home country employer, pension arrangements will naturally be provided by the employer. Where the host company is the employer, the employee may still wish to remain in the home country plan. The basis on which this happens, if it is possible at all, should be confirmed clearly through the documents to avoid undermining host country employment. For example, this could be confirmed in a residual contract with the home company and/or an inter-company expatriate supply agreement. (See **8.62–8.72**, Appendix 1, checklists **A1.9** and **A1.10** and Appendix 2, framework documents **A2.5** and **A2.6**.) Pensions advice should always be sought, eg because inadvertently including the 'wrong' person in a pension plan can potentially prejudice the plan as well as the individual employee.

Public insurance funds

4.93 In some countries the employer may be required to pay into an insurance or other public fund, separately from social security contributions, which may later be used, for example, to pay benefits following termination of employment.

Absence

4.94 Most countries have mandatory employment laws requiring the employer to make payments to the employee in respect of qualifying periods of absence, for example, in relation to absence due to holiday, sickness or family leave. Those arrangements should be administered by the employer; the employee should report absence to the employer; and any required payments should be made by the employer. (See **15.21–15.28** on managing absence during the assignment.)

Expenses

4.95 Expenses should be approved and reimbursed by the employer and should be subject to the employer's expenses policy. This will usually happen naturally if there is a host country employer. However, if the host company takes some part in the process for a home employer, the host company's role should be made clear through the employment documents. Claim forms etc should be submitted in a way that is consistent with employment status. The home employer might require the host company to provide some indication of whether expenses have been properly incurred but ultimate responsibility for approval and reimbursement to the employee should rest with the employer.

Policies

4.96 Both home and host companies are likely to have employment policies of one sort or another, possibly gathered together in a formal staff handbook. These might include equal opportunities policies, sickness and absence policies, expenses policies, family-related absence policies, redundancy policies, etc.

Host employer

4.97 Where the host company is the employer it will probably be relatively easy to apply the host company policies to the employee during the assignment. The host company will be the employer and the policies will be designed for use in the host country. They should be checked for consistency with the expatriate arrangements.

4.98 Home company policies should not apply as the employee will not be employed by the home company.

Home employer

4.99 If the home company remains the employer during the assignment that will be more difficult. To support the correct employment status the employer's policies should normally apply. For example, grievances should be heard by the home employer. However, the normal home country policies may not be appropriate for use or may need to be varied for the expatriate. For example, home company policies may be incompatible with host country mandatory employment laws or the policies may be designed to comply with home country employment laws or to reflect home country tax arrangements that no longer apply to the employee.

4.100 As a rule of thumb those drafting expatriate documents should make sure that neither host nor home country policies apply to expatriates employed by the home company.

4.101 It is usually most convenient where there is a home country employer to include a general statement in the employment documents making it clear that none of the home company policies designed for home-based employees will apply to the expatriate during the assignment unless the contrary is confirmed in writing.

4.102 Where there is a home country employer, the host company policies should not apply as the host company is not the employer.

4.103 See also Chapter 9 on assignment policies generally.

Power to terminate the arrangements

4.104 Power to discipline or suspend the employee and the power to end the assignment and/or employment should always rest with the employer, and the employment contract should make this clear.

4.105 However, this does not usually prevent the home and host companies from providing in an inter-company expatriate supply agreement (made between themselves and not with the employee) that the assignment can be ended on notice given by one company to the other, or perhaps without notice in certain circumstances. For example, the expatriate supply agreement could allow the host company to give notice to the home company employer that it wishes to terminate the assignment. The home company employer could then decide whether to serve notice of termination of the assignment and/or the employment on the employee under the terms of the employment contract. Thought needs to be given to the length of the notice periods so that this works. (See **16.24–16.34** on notice periods. This is an area where mandatory employment laws may be relevant.)

4.106 See **6.26** for an explanation of what an inter-company expatriate supply agreement is.

The employment documents

4.107 The following are examples of where the employment documents might be used to support the preferred employment status:

- The correct employer should be identified as the employer in all employment documents. The documents should also reflect and confirm the employee's relationships with other relevant companies.

- Reporting lines for key employment issues, for example, approval of holiday, should be clarified. If there are some arrangements that do not support the identity of the correct employer these should be explained.

- The documents should confirm that the employer is responsible for paying remuneration and that the employer actually bears those costs. Any administrative arrangements that may cause confusion should be clarified, for example, where the host company manages the payroll or reimburses expenses on the employer's behalf.

- The employee's participation in the employer's benefit arrangements may be confirmed in the employment documents.

- Only the employer and the employee should be parties to the employment contract and the people signing the contract for the employer should be appropriate representatives of the correct employer. (In some countries only properly authorised representatives can sign an employment contract for the employer: the required formalities should be checked.)

- The documents should make clear the arrangements for termination of the employment, for example arrangements for service of notices by and on the correct employer.

CHALLENGE TO EMPLOYMENT STATUS

4.108 Ordinary employees working in their home country rarely challenge the identity of their employer. Usually the employer's identity will be obvious. Even if it is not clear, whether the employer is one group company or another does not often have commercial significance. This is not the case for expatriate employment arrangements. Both the expatriate himself and a wide variety of public authorities in home and host countries will have interests in the identity of the employer. There may be strong financial incentives to challenge the preferred status identified by those structuring the assignment arrangements.

4.109 The following are examples of situations where there may be an incentive to challenge the assumed employer's identity.

Tax and social security

4.110 Home country tax authorities may have little financial incentive to challenge the identity of a local hire's employer: whether the employer is one group company or another is unlikely to have significant impact on the income tax and social security contributions to be paid. With expatriates the position is different. The identity of the employer can have a significant impact on the amounts of tax and social security contributions to be paid, and also on which country benefits from the payments. Home and host country tax and social security authorities may challenge the assumed employer's status.

Termination of employment

4.111 The identity of the employer may make a difference to the severance pay the employee might expect to receive on termination of employment. For example, the identity of the employer might determine whether mandatory employment laws apply or the home or host company may have a policy providing for generous redundancy payments that applies only to its own employees.

4.112 The employee may therefore have a financial incentive to challenge the assumed identity of the employer. In practice, this does not often happen. For example, a change to the assumed identity of the employer may also have consequences for other matters such as tax and/or social security contributions in respect of remuneration already paid. The employee may lose out too if the identity of the employer turns out to be a different company and he is found to be guilty of historic tax non-compliance. However, the potential for dispute is there, particularly if there are contractual tax equalisation arrangements or mandatory laws that effectively ensure that if a mistake is made the employer must make any necessary extra payments.

CONSEQUENCES OF MAKING THE WRONG ASSUMPTIONS ABOUT THE IDENTITY OF THE EMPLOYER

4.113 If it is assumed that the home company is the employer and the 'real' employer turns out to be the host company, or vice versa, then the consequences can be quite severe, particularly if the employment has continued for some time under the wrong assumption. For example:

- immigration permission may be invalid or curtailed and, practically, the employee may be required to leave the host country within a limited period (see **3.5–3.10** and **4.23–4.28** regarding potential consequences);

- the wrong company may have been registered in the host country as an employer and there may be exposure to penalties;

- this may have an impact on the availability of treaty relief for tax purposes;

- if insufficient income tax and/or social security contributions have been paid, or the tax and social security contributions have been paid to the wrong authorities then the correct payments will probably need to be made and interest and penalties may also be due. 'Mistakes' may trigger further investigation of the company's tax affairs more generally and that may, in turn, lead to other problems being identified and perhaps unexpected penalties being applied. It may be difficult or impossible to recover any of the additional costs from the employee. The issues may also be ongoing. The cost of paying the employee may increase for the future, for example, because higher employer's social security contributions need to be paid or because more tax is due and there is a tax equalisation or tax protection promise;

- additional sales tax or corporation tax may be due from the home or host company;

- if pension arrangements have been set up incorrectly tax relief may be jeopardised;

- insurance policies, for example, health insurance or employers' liability insurance, may not be valid;

- unexpected mandatory employment laws may apply (and the 'real' employer probably will not have complied);

- if the employee has already been dismissed then a finding that another company is, in fact, the employer may mean that carefully planned procedures are ineffective or unfair. The dismissal itself may be void and/or additional compensation may be due;

- intellectual property may belong to the 'wrong' company and transferring it to the correct company may entail additional cost, for example, tax and legal expense;

- the employment status of other employees may be challenged if the 'mistake' triggers an investigation into other similar arrangements operated by the group.

TAX ERRORS AND EVASION

4.114 As highlighted throughout this book, there is close interaction between the structure of an international assignment and underlying facts, and the potential tax and social security treatment of remuneration and other payments. The figures can be significant and there may naturally be a tendency for employers to prefer documents that confirm facts offering a more favourable tax treatment. This is an area where advisers, and employment lawyers and HR specialists in particular, should take care. The documents produced should reflect the facts and it would be unwise to prepare documents without some enquiry into the reality of the arrangements. The following are examples of areas where particular care should be taken:

- the status of an individual as employee or contractor (see **6.2–6.13**);

- the nature of the role and duties of an expatriate in a jurisdiction where no permanent establishment is intended (see **13.3–13.7**);

- the documented amounts to be paid by the host company to a home employer by way of fees for supply of the expatriate and/or his services (see **4.48** on transfer pricing);

- the identity of the employer (see this Chapter 4);

- the intended length of the assignment (see Chapter 5).

See also **20.23** on the UK Criminal Finances Act 2017.

CHAPTER 5

LENGTH OF ASSIGNMENT

5.1 Expatriates may work abroad for long or short periods. For example, they may:

- travel to the host country on one or more short business trips, perhaps to attend meetings with the host company (see Chapter 14);
- undertake a short-term assignment in the host country of, say, a month or two whilst remaining employed by the home company;
- be posted to the host country for, say, two to five years (either the home or host company may employ the expatriate during the assignment, see Chapter 4); or
- go to work in the host country permanently.

5.2 This book is primarily concerned with assignments that are of sufficient length to require proper documentation, and where the employee has an expectation of returning home. These assignments may range in length from, say, one month to five years. The appropriate employment structure and employment documents vary considerably with the proposed assignment length.

BUSINESS NEED

5.3 The appropriate assignment length from a business perspective will be determined by the purpose of the assignment (see Chapter 2). Factors that might be taken into consideration include:

- time required to complete a specific task or project;
- settling in and winding-down time and costs (ie the need for the assignment to be long enough to justify costs and disruption to the business);
- time that might be taken to train local employees to take over on the expatriate's departure, and/or;
- the length of time the employee is prepared to be there for.

TAX AND SOCIAL SECURITY

5.4   Both the expected length of the assignment and the actual length of the assignment may affect the tax and social security treatment of remuneration. (The income tax treatment may be different from the social security treatment.) Tax and social security are usually key considerations because of potential cost implications. Before looking at specific issues relevant to assignment length, it is worth taking a look at tax and social security arrangements more generally so that comments on assignment length can be put into context.

Who is likely to pay income tax?

5.5   Most countries expect employees who work in their country to pay income tax. The income tax due may also depend on the employee's 'tax residency'. For example, an employee may be 'tax resident' in one country and taxable on his worldwide income under that country's rules. He may also work for short periods in another country where he may be taxable in respect of the income earned for those duties only (see **5.14** in relation to potential overlap and double tax treaties.) The employer may have a 'withholding' obligation (ie an obligation to deduct income tax from the employee's pay and pay it over to the tax authorities) and/or the employee may be required to pay over his own income tax directly to the tax authorities.

US income tax

5.6   The US is unusual because US citizens and 'green card' holders are generally taxed on their Worldwide income, regardless of where they are resident or perform duties. This can add an extra layer of complexity and cost when Americans are assigned abroad.

Tax rates

5.7   The rates at which income tax is charged vary enormously from country to country, from nothing at all to over 50% of taxable income. Tax is normally considered the individual employee's responsibility, but where an expatriate assignment is proposed, tax will usually have importance for the employer too. Put simply, if the employee has to pay more tax he will usually expect more pay from his employer. Another approach is for the employer to offer some comfort regarding the tax to be paid, for example, by way of tax protection or tax equalisation policies (see **7.80–7.92**). Either way, the employee's income tax bill is likely to affect the costs of the assignment for the employer.

Day counting

5.8   Many countries, including most EU countries, do not treat an employee as tax resident, and sometimes do not start charging income tax and/or social security contributions at all, until the employee has spent (or is expected to spend) a minimum number of days in the country. If the assignment is short enough, the employee may fall out of the host country income tax net altogether. For example, where the employee travels frequently between countries it is theoretically possible for the employee not to be tax resident in any country.

5.9 The number of days worked in the host country may be critical to whether income tax is due in the host country. Similarly, if the employee travels in the course of his employment the number of days worked in each place may make a difference to whether income tax must be paid in those countries.

5.10 Sometimes the number of days to be spent inside or outside a country will be estimated in advance and the appropriate tax liability will be agreed in advance with the tax authorities on that basis. Day counting may still be important to show that the estimate was accurate or to allow for any adjustments to be made later if this is required.

5.11 Where day counting is important to the tax treatment the employee will need to understand that he must keep proper records. He should also be clear from the outset about how the records should be kept. For example, the expatriate will need to know whether travelling days, whole or half days, or days on which he does not work, should be counted and whether evidence must be kept (detailed itinerary with arrival and departure times, tickets, diary, travel agent's logs, use of mobile apps etc). See also **14.28–14.34** on tracking for business visitors.

5.12 Day counting rules vary between countries so it may be necessary for record-keeping arrangements for a particular assignment to satisfy more than one country's criteria. Rules may also relate to the number of days in tax years that run from different dates (eg the tax year currently runs from April in the UK and from January in the US). Note too that requirements may not align with immigration tracking requirements. It may be helpful to include a general contractual obligation in the employment documents to keep proper records as instructed by the employer from time to time. The contract could also confirm that the employee must give those records to the employer on request (even if the request is made after the employment ends). Some flexibility should be built into the contractual requirements as the rules may change over time. The detail of what the employee must actually do is normally best left to informal communications that can be amended easily. (See also **7.93–7.97** on record keeping, and **19.40–19.42** on UK day counting.)

5.13 NB: It is surprisingly common for expatriates (and their employers) to believe that tax is only due in a jurisdiction if the employee spends a minimum of 180 days of the tax year in that place. This is a myth. The rules are far more complex and should be checked with tax specialists. See also below in relation to tax residence rules.

Double tax treaties

5.14 The same income may potentially be subject to tax in more than one country. However, the potential impact of 'double taxation' on an employee is often reduced through a 'double tax treaty'. A double tax treaty is an agreement, normally between two countries, that determines, for example, which country's tax should be paid if the same income might otherwise be taxed by both countries. Practically, this is achieved either through one country offering tax exemption in respect of all or part of the otherwise taxable income or one country offering 'tax credits' in respect of tax paid to the other country's tax authority. The treaty may also include 'tie breaker' clauses that determine which country the employee will be 'tax resident' in. Day counting (see **5.8–5.13**) and recharging arrangements (see **4.88** and **8.73–8.80**) may be critical to the way that these arrangements operate in practice.

EU

5.15 As a rule of thumb, an employee may be treated as tax resident in an EU country if he spends more than 182 days in the host EU country. (There is currently no uniform EU treaty in this regard and not every EU country applies this rule.) If the employee is tax resident in the host country he will usually be taxed on Worldwide income in the host country. If he is not tax resident he will usually only be taxed in the host country on income earned in the host country. The length of the assignment may be critical to determining the country in which the employee is tax resident. If the employee is only to be taxed in the host country on host country income, the length of the assignment may also be relevant to determination of the proportion of income that should be attributed to work done in the host country.

US

5.16 It is important for non-US advisers to appreciate that US citizens may be subject to Federal, State and local taxes. Advice given by expatriate tax advisers in relation to one US citizen may not be applicable to another. For example, the anticipated duration of the assignment may have an impact on tax relief available on expenses. For different US citizens the threshold assignment length for this purpose may be different.

Short-term 'business visitors'

5.17 Theoretically, tax could be due in the host country where the employee only works for a few days in the tax year. However, most countries do not require the employee to pay tax unless he works a threshold number of days in the country or earns above a certain level of earnings relevant to the days worked in that country. Records of days spent on short-term visits should be kept, as with longer-term assignments. Liability to tax in the host country may also depend on the nature of the duties carried out there. For example, no tax may be due if the employee's activities are only 'incidental' to his other duties. (See **5.8–5.12** on day counting and Chapter 14 on business visitors and international commuters.)

Intentions

5.18 It may be necessary, or helpful, to submit tax forms confirming the employee's intentions regarding the length of his stay in the host country to the relevant tax authorities at the start of the assignment.

5.19 The tax and social security authorities may also look for practical evidence of the employee's intentions, or a change to the employee's intentions, on length of stay. For example, purchase of property or marriage may indicate an intention to remain permanently in the host country and may even be viewed as conclusive evidence of an intention to remain by the host country tax authorities. See **5.29** on overlap with immigration requirements and **8.14** and **A2.4** for examples of terms that could be included in the documents to clarify intentions and reduce related risk.

EU to UK assignment

5.20 Currently, an employee's intentions will have an impact on whether an employee who moves from an EU country to the UK is treated as UK tax resident from the outset of his assignment. See the Glossary at Appendix 3 on UK tax residence. The UK statutory residence definition takes account of a combination of factors including numbers of days in the UK and relevant ties, eg property or family ties.

Social security

5.21 Social security rules are different to income tax rules. For example, an employee will normally only remain in one country's social security scheme at a time. (There are exceptions.) Which scheme that is may depend, to a large extent, on the length of the assignment, or expected length of the assignment. This is expressed simplistically to highlight the importance of assignment length to social security costs. Rules are, in practice, far more complicated and depend on the jurisdictions concerned.

5.22 Home and host country social security authorities may allow the employee to remain in his home country social security scheme provided that the actual and/or expected duration of the assignment is not too long.

EU to EU assignment

5.23 Whilst there is no general EU-wide binding law to eliminate double taxation, there is an EU social security regulation coordinating EU national social security rules. Each EU member state has its own national social security scheme(s) which are subject to, but not replaced by, EU regulations (EC

Regulation 883/2004 on the coordination of social security systems, as amended for the relevant jurisdictions). Under the EU regulations, where the employee is assigned from one EU country (or another participating country) to another, but remains employed by a home country employer, he may normally remain in his EU home country social security scheme for 12 months. That may usually be extended for a further 12 months. Exceptions may apply, eg, if the employee is replacing another assignee. Remaining in the home country scheme may be possible for a longer period in exceptional circumstances. An 'A1' certificate must usually be obtained from the home country social security authority to confirm that the employee remains in the home country social security scheme. The employer may need to present the A1 to the host country social security authority.

UK

5.24 UK employer's social security rates can be substantially lower than the rates that apply in other EU countries. In practice, a UK-based company may remain the employer during assignment from the UK to an EU country and apply for an A1. This is not really an 'option' as the identity of the employer will be driven by facts (see Chapter 4). Specialist advice should always be sought in this regard.

5.25 The potential impact of Brexit on social security agreements made between the UK and other EU member states is currently uncertain. See Chapter 18 on Brexit generally.

Benefits, allowances and expenses

5.26 The duration, or anticipated duration, of the assignment may affect the income tax relief available in respect of expenses and allowances, for example, housing and relocation allowances and expenses. (See **19.47–19.51** on UK detached duty relief.)

IMMIGRATION

5.27 As with tax and social security contributions, immigration authorities may seek evidence both of the expected duration of the assignment and of its actual duration.

5.28 A work permit, or other immigration permission, will usually be granted subject to a maximum period in the host country. Sometimes, the period allowed by the immigration authority initially may be extended subsequently. If so, conditions will usually apply. Immigration permission may not be available at all if the anticipated or actual duration of the assignment is too long.

5.29 Sometimes the immigration authorities will allow a longer period of stay than is really needed for the assignment. Those applying for a work permit, if doing so in isolation, may be tempted to apply for the longest period of cover that can be obtained, on the basis that that will be convenient if the assignment lasts longer than expected. In some jurisdictions that approach could have unfortunate consequences. For example, the work permit application form may indicate that the assignment is likely to last longer than the maximum intended period in the host country allowed by tax and/or social security authorities if the preferred tax/social security treatment is to apply. Work permit applications need to be submitted early. At that stage, tax and social security advice may not yet have been obtained: it is important to seek preliminary advice in relation to all relevant areas early.

EMPLOYMENT

5.30 The actual or anticipated length of the assignment may have an impact on mandatory employment laws. For example, it may be easier to dismiss during an initial period running from the start of the employment. Many countries also allow employers to offer less generous terms or offer less employment protection to employees on fixed-term employment contracts or on fixed-term assignment. There may be limits on the period during which more relaxed rules can apply to fixed-term arrangements.

5.31 In practice, the application of employment laws is rarely the key consideration in determining the appropriate assignment length.

EU

5.32 More favourable employment laws (from the employer's perspective) for short-term or fixed-term assignments are not usually an important consideration for assignments to or from EU countries. See **10.50–10.55** in relation to the EC Posted Workers Directive which, broadly, requires that employees posted from one EU country to another should benefit from the same protection as other host country employees. Also, employees who are employed on fixed-term contracts should, generally, be treated no less favourably than employees engaged on an indefinite basis (see Council Directive 99/70/EC concerning the framework agreement on fixed-term work, the 'Fixed Term Workers Directive').

PENSION

5.33 The actual or anticipated length of the assignment may have an impact on the employee's ability to continue to participate in his preferred pension plan. Tax relief on accumulating funds or on draw down of the pension may also be affected.

SPECIAL FEATURES OF SHORT-TERM ASSIGNMENTS

5.34 Short-term assignments are typically home country employment arrangements. However, this is not always the case. For example, if it is impossible or difficult for the home company to obtain immigration permission for a short-term assignment, there may be a short-term arrangement for the host company to be the employer for the period of the assignment.

5.35 Employment documents should be amended to record special terms that relate to the short-term assignment. Typically, family will not accompany the employee on a short-term assignment and there will be no provision for long-term accommodation.

5.36 The package is likely to include:

- assistance with immigration, tax and social security issues;
- a subsistence allowance and/or reimbursement of some or all of the costs of hotel or other temporary accommodation and meals;
- reimbursement or payment of travel expenses, perhaps including frequent trips home for the employee or for his family to visit him in the host country;
- payment of normal remuneration set in the home currency with some additional remuneration and/or a bonus to encourage the employee to agree to the assignment;
- short-term changes to payment arrangements to reflect any practical difficulties the employee may experience in opening a short-term bank account in the host country; and/or
- additional insurance cover relating to business travel, medical expenses outside the home country etc.

5.37 See also Chapters 7 and 8; checklist **A1.7** at Appendix 1; and the framework short-term home employer assignment letter **A2.3** at Appendix 2, for some suggestions on appropriate terms for a short-term assignment.

EU – Employment Particulars Directive

5.38 EU member states must ensure that employers give each employee a written statement confirming core terms of their employment contract. The full title of the relevant directive is: Directive 91/533/EEC on an employer's obligation to inform employees of the conditions applicable to the contract or employment relationship, referred to in this book as the 'Employment Particulars Directive'. (See the Glossary at Appendix 3 for a list of EU member states and see **8.37** for a description of the Employment Particulars Directive requirements.)

5.39 The Directive includes a specific requirement in relation to expatriates. In addition to the usual information that the employer must provide, if the assignment abroad is for more than a month Article 4 of the Directive makes it clear that the employer must confirm the following in writing to the employee before departure:

'(a) the duration of the employment abroad;
(b) the currency to be used for the payment of remuneration;
(c) where appropriate, the benefits in cash or kind attendant on the employment abroad; and
(d) where appropriate, the conditions governing the employee's repatriation.'

5.40 Different EU member states will have implemented the Directive in different ways. However, if an employee is to be assigned to another country from an EU country for longer than a month then, as a minimum, this information should be confirmed in writing to the employee before the assignment begins. Practically, of course, most sensible employers would choose to confirm this information in writing anyway.

UK

5.41 The Employment Particulars Directive is currently implemented in the UK through the Employment Rights Act 1996. The wording of the original UK legislation pre-dates the Employment Particulars Directive and is slightly different, but the above requirements are broadly the same. It currently seems unlikely that Brexit will lead to change to these UK laws. They are practical, generally helpful for both employer and employee and rarely criticised.

Case study – short-term assignment and identity of the employer

5.42 The following is an example of the way that the assignment length and identity of the employer could interact.

5.43 The home company works closely with a retail business that sells the home company's products in the host country. The retailer asks the home company to provide some experienced employees to train the retailer's staff in the host country. The retailer anticipates that it will need five people for about three months.

5.44 The home company is happy to help and anticipates that the potential assignees will be enthusiastic about the opportunity to spend a few months in a warmer climate. Ideally, the home company would like to put the employees on a plane and send them to the host country without too much fuss.

5.45 The home company's first step is to make some general enquiries of advisers in the host country, to see whether the assignment is viable. The home company discovers that the employees would need immigration permission, and that the employer must apply for permission before the assignment can begin. However, the home company is not able to employ staff to work in the host country unless it first registers with the local employment authority. To register it needs to show that it has a substantial presence in the host country and the host country advisers say that that would involve renting premises. The home company could comply with the host country requirements but that would take time and the expense does not seem worth it.

5.46 The home company would like the staff to remain employees of the home company during the assignment. However, that does not appear to be practical, so it asks the retailer what it can do to help. The retailer offers to employ the five staff for the duration of the assignment. The retailer already has a presence in the host country and is already registered as an employer with the employment and immigration authorities so it can apply for immigration permission easily.

5.47 The home company worries that employees will be uncomfortable about changing employers for a few months. Normally it is not a good idea to confirm two employments for the same job because the potential for dispute, complication etc is too great (eg employment, tax or pension authorities might later decide that the 'wrong' company is the employer or claims may be made against both companies), but here the risk seems worth it.

5.48 The home company makes some further checks, for example, that the proposed arrangement will not create tax, social security or pensions problems and then gives the go ahead for the paperwork to be prepared.

5.49 The following documents are produced:

- applications for immigration permission to be submitted by the host company;
- new short-term contracts of employment to be prepared by the host company and submitted to the host country immigration authority with the application for immigration permission, including, for example, provision for payment of salary and reimbursement of assignment expenses by the host company;
- a short assignment letter for each employee from the home company confirming the changes to the practical arrangements, for example, confirming that salary will not be paid by the home company for the period of the assignment and confirming the arrangements to apply to pension;
- a short agreement between the home company and the host company confirming, for example, that the host company will be responsible for employing and paying the employees during the assignment etc and confirming the fee to be paid by the host company to the home company for their services (the inter-company expatriate supply agreement).

5.50 The home company checks related practical arrangements like employer's liability insurance, medical insurance cover, accommodation, safety arrangements, etc. The home company employer may ask for assurances from the host company that it will do certain things, for example, provide medical insurance cover. Assurances given by the home and host companies to each other are confirmed in the inter-company expatriate supply agreement.

SPECIAL FEATURES OF LONG-TERM ASSIGNMENTS

5.51 Longer-term assignments may be either home or host employer arrangements (see Chapter 6). Typically, the employee will be accompanied by family members and the benefits package will be more comprehensive.

5.52 For example, the package might include:

- assistance with obtaining immigration permission for the employee and family members;
- tax equalisation or protection and/or assistance with preparation of tax returns etc;
- adjustments to pay to reflect the impact of a location change on the employee, for example, a hardship allowance or cost of living allowance;
- longer-term accommodation suitable for the whole family;
- a relocation allowance or reimbursement of relocation expenses at the start and end of the assignment;
- provision of a car or car allowance;
- assistance with education for children;
- assurances regarding repatriation at the end of the assignment; and
- additional insurance cover relating to business travel, medical expenses outside the home country (for the employer and accompanying family members) etc.

5.53 See also Chapters 6, 7 and 8; checklist **A1.8** at Appendix 1; and the framework long-term home employer assignment letter **A2.4** at Appendix 2, for some suggestions regarding appropriate terms for a long-term assignment contract.

CONCLUSIONS AND TRENDS

5.54 The proposed length of the assignment will be driven by the business objectives, but the relevant period may have a significant impact on the viability of the assignment (eg because of the effect on the availability of immigration permission) and the cost of the assignment (eg because of the effect on the ability of the employee to remain within the home country social security scheme). Practically, the decision on assignment length will also have implications for the benefit package likely to be offered to the employee.

5.55 It seems likely that Brexit, and wider political pressure for tightening of immigration controls, will lead to increased use of shorter term assignments and 'business visitor' trips. (See Chapter 14.) This also reflects a longer-term trend towards more shorter-term assignments, international commuter arrangements etc. The broader trend may be influenced by factors such as working partners wishing to keep their jobs; parents wishing to keep children in day schools in their home countries; cheaper and quicker travel; and easier supervision of overseas operations through technology. Employers should be aware that heightened focus on business visitor compliance extends to tax as well as immigration compliance. Informal documents used for trips in years gone by are likely to need updating.

CHAPTER 6

STRUCTURE OF ARRANGEMENTS AND DOCUMENTS NEEDED

TYPES OF ARRANGEMENT

6.1   The following types of arrangement are considered in this chapter:

- Contracts for self-employed individuals ('contracts for services', see **6.2–6.13**).

- Home country employment arrangements (ie where a company registered in the home country is the employer, see **6.14–6.42**).

- Host country employment arrangements (ie where a company registered in the host country is the employer, see **6.43–6.57**).

- Dual employments (ie where one employee has separate employments with two different employers, see **6.58–6.69**).

- Joint employment (ie where two employers employ the same employee to do the same job under the same contract, see **6.70–6.77**).

CONTRACTS FOR SERVICES AND OTHER OPTIONS

6.2   This book is not intended to cover engagement terms for self-employed individuals, but it may be worth looking at this option as an alternative to employment arrangements when considering a new role.

6.3   A contract for services could be a contract with a self-employed individual (sometimes known as a 'contractor' or 'consultant') or with another entity providing that employee's services (sometimes also known as a 'contractor'). The inter-company expatriate supply agreement described below is also, technically, a contract for services. (See the Glossary at Appendix 3 on 'consultants'.)

6.4   Self-employed contractor arrangements often look attractive because they may offer tax advantages for the individual, and sometimes for the company engaging the individual too. For example, typically, social security contributions do not have to be paid by the recipient of services in respect of a self-employed individual.

6.5   The following are examples of terms that might apply to a 'typical' self-employed arrangement:

- the self-employed individual will usually be responsible for his own immigration permission (and if he is not a host country national this may be more difficult to obtain than if he were an employee);

- the company receiving the individual's services is typically under no obligation to operate a payroll arrangement; deduct income tax or employee's social security contributions before paying the individual; or pay employer's social security contributions;

- the income tax and social security treatment may be more favourable for the individual (for example, because social security contributions may be due at a lower rate, the individual may benefit from a cash flow advantage because taxes need to be paid later or more expenses may be deductible);

- the individual will usually be responsible for issuing invoices for his fees, and may be obliged to register for sales tax (VAT) and charge sales tax in respect of fees;

- the individual will not be covered by collective agreements or employment laws that apply to employees only (generally, the individual is likely to receive less legal protection and legal obligations are likely to be less onerous for the company receiving the services. This may include, eg, lower potential termination costs);

- the company receiving the services may not be required to provide a pension or other mandatory employment benefits such as holiday or sick pay and more flexible, for example primarily commission-based, remuneration arrangements may be more acceptable;

- in the EU laws implementing the 'Commercial Agents Directive' (see **6.12** and the Glossary at Appendix 3) may apply if, eg, the employee receives payment through a commission arrangement;

- the individual may not owe such clear, strong or easily enforceable duties to the company receiving the services, for example, in relation to confidential information or competition;

- intellectual property is less likely to belong to the company receiving the services without a formal agreement;

- a self-employed person will usually self-insure, eg, to cover his own negligence, whereas if there is an employment, the employer will usually need to take out more insurance cover to protect itself (eg against actions by third parties where the employer may be vicariously liable for the employee's conduct and/or against claims made by the employee, eg in relation to personal injury sustained at work);

- health and safety obligations may be more extensive in relation to employees, although self-employed contractors are likely to be covered by health and safety laws too.

6.6   Engaging a self-employed contractor may seem an easy option, particularly where the individual is familiar with the host country and the company that will receive the services is not. At first blush, most of the risk and administrative responsibility appears to rest with the individual if he is self-employed, so that an individual's promise to sort everything out and just invoice for his fees may seem attractive. The individual himself may be pleased to enter into the arrangement because self-employment can involve a substantially lighter tax and social security burden.

6.7   For the company receiving the services there are likely to be three principal concerns: controlling the individual; the risk that the individual could be deemed at a later stage to be an employee rather than a genuinely self-employed contractor; and, in the EU, the potential application of onerous 'commercial agency' rules.

6.8   Control is likely to be a particular issue where the company engaging the individual is based in a different country. Without the normal employment structures and reporting lines, close day-to-day management may be more difficult. In addition, far weaker obligations are likely to be imposed automatically on the individual by the general law, and there may be greater restrictions on what can be achieved through the contract. For example, confidential information may be easier to protect and post-termination restrictions may be easier to enforce against an employee than a self-employed individual.

6.9   There may be strong financial incentives for the individual not to challenge self-employed status whilst the engagement continues, and then to claim employment rights on termination. As the 'employer' will probably have terminated the arrangement under the terms of the agreed contract (then assumed to be a contract for services), host country employment laws relating to termination of employment are unlikely to have been complied with. (The 'correct' processes for terminating contractor and employee arrangements are normally very different.) Termination of the 'contractor' arrangement may even be deemed void by the host country authorities.

6.10   If the company engaging the individual is later found to be the individual's employer, the financial exposure of the 'employer' could be substantial. The employer is unlikely to have operated payroll arrangements correctly (and may have no certainty that the individual has even paid over taxes calculated on a self-employed basis). Employee's and employer's social security contributions are unlikely to have been paid in full. As well as back taxes, interest and penalties may also be due, and in some circumstances failure to comply with social security laws may trigger criminal liability. Mandatory remuneration and benefits, perhaps required by a collective agreement, may not have been provided over a substantial period of time. Substantial employment termination costs may not have been anticipated.

6.11   Given the potential financial consequences of treating an individual as self-employed if he is, in reality, an employee, it is always worth considering whether the relationship is in reality an employment relationship from the outset. Host country advice should be sought in that regard (and normally home country advice too). It is important to bear in mind that although tests applied to determine employment status tend to be fairly similar across the World, the weight to be given to different factors and the potential consequences of failing to treat an employee correctly can vary substantially between jurisdictions. The seriousness with which many jurisdictions treat actions that may deprive employees, and their families, of valuable social security rights should not be underestimated. See also **4.114** on tax evasion.

6.12   Directive 86/653/EEC, the 'Commercial Agents Directive', requires EU member states to provide protection for self-employed commercial agents who receive payments linked to sales, ie those paid through commission arrangements. The language and scope of the Directive are not very clear and there is little guiding case law. Moreover, as the directive must be implemented locally by member states, the precise impact of local laws in each member state will also vary. A key concern for the recipient of services is that a commercial agent will be entitled to compensation on termination. The terms on which this compensation must be provided are onerous for the recipient of services and not entirely clear. Engagement of individuals as self-employed commercial agents is not usually an attractive option.

6.13   Notwithstanding the challenges outlined above, engagement of self-employed contractors in overseas locations to undertake initial business development activities is not unusual. Care should be taken to ensure that the individual is treated as self-employed in practice and that, as the business grows and the role develops, the factual context and individual's status remain subject to review. For example, if additional staff are needed as the host country business grows it may not be appropriate to continue to engage people on a self-employed basis. (In practice, prudent employers engaging contractors in the EU will often take care to ensure that the terms of engagement agreed do not trigger the application of laws implementing the Commercial Agents Directive.)

HOME COUNTRY EMPLOYER

6.14   This is where the employee is initially employed in his home country by a company (or other legal entity) registered there (the 'home company'). The employee is sent abroad by the home company and the home company continues to employ the individual throughout the assignment. There is only one employer so there will be only one employment contract, with the home company. The terms of that contract are likely to change at the start of the assignment to reflect changes to the practical arrangements.

6.15   Figure 6.1 illustrates the key relationships between the home company, the host company and the employee, and documents that would typically be needed for home country employment arrangements. Each of these documents will be considered in more detail below and in Chapters 7 and 8 and Appendices 1 (checklists) and 2 (framework documents).

Figure 6.1

Home country employment

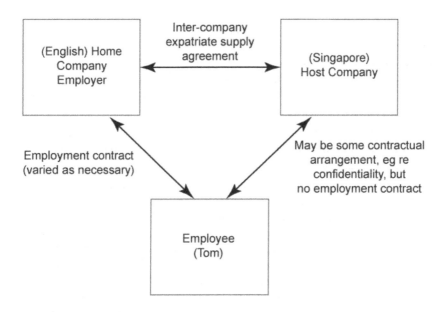

Employment contract with home company – amending, suspending or replacing the existing employment contract

6.16 If the employee is already employed he will also already have an employment contract with the home company.

6.17 Even if there is no written contract, the employee will still have an employment contract. It will just be harder to work out what the current terms are. If there is no existing written employment contract then a new contract document will be needed. (See Chapter 21 on US perspectives.)

6.18 If there is an existing written employment contract, the terms of that contract will need to be changed to reflect the new terms that will apply during the assignment. (See also **8.37** on the requirements of the European Employment Particulars Directive.)

6.19 The current contract documents should be checked before a decision is made as to whether to:

• offer a supplementary assignment letter describing the variations to the existing contract; or
• replace the existing employment documents altogether with new employment documents (either for the duration of the assignment or permanently).

6.20 It is worth bearing in mind that a document that is not perfect, but is still adequate for home country purposes, may not be appropriate for use in the host country. For example:

- host country officials using the document may be unfamiliar with terms that are commonly used in the home country and the consequences of ambiguity under home country law if those laws govern the documents;

- a collection of documents and/or reference to policies and home country collective agreements may be acceptable in the home country but is likely to be confusing to officials in the host country;

- the old employment documents may have been created some time before the assignment and may not reflect current terms (eg because the employee has since been promoted);

- there may be a host country requirement for employment contract terms to be set out in one document (as is likely to be the case in EU countries) and/or to be provided in the host country language or a particular form.

6.21 If there is ambiguity; the documents refer to other documents that are not supplied or legal principles that are not understood; or they do not reflect the terms that currently apply, host country (and home country) officials who need to consider the documents are likely to ask questions. Even if the questions can be easily answered by reference to other documents, dealing with queries is likely to waste time and generate additional expense. For example, immigration permission may be delayed or additional professional advice may be needed.

6.22 If the existing employment contract is unsuitable for use during the assignment (ie if variation through a supplementary assignment letter is unlikely to be sufficient), the employer will need to decide whether the existing employment contract should be suspended for the duration of the assignment or terminated before it begins. If the existing employment contract is satisfactory from a home country perspective; reflects terms that will apply when the employee returns to his old job after the assignment; and is in a form consistent with the contracts of other home country employees, then suspension could be helpful. When the employee returns to the home country, negotiating the terms to apply on his return would probably be more straightforward. Minor variations may still be needed on return (eg to take account of subsequent pay rises or slight changes to the role) but reaching agreement is likely to be easier if there is already a document in place setting out the baseline for negotiations.

6.23 If the existing contract is not well drafted or the employee is unlikely to return to work in the home country anyway, it may be simpler (and easier to explain to officials) if the existing contract is terminated altogether before the assignment begins. The existing contract could be replaced either:

- with a new employment contract and separate assignment letter (technically both documents together would form the employment contract); or, more likely

- with one new employment contract document that covers all the employment terms including those that will apply on termination of the assignment.

Agreement between the employee and host company

6.24 There may also need to be some contract or other written agreement between the host company and the employee, covering, for example, confidentiality, use of host company property, intellectual property, health and safety, etc. This agreement will not be an employment contract as the host company is not the employer.

6.25 Where both home and host companies issue documents it can sometimes be difficult to work out which document is the employment contract and which entity is the employer. If the host company is not the employer then care should be taken to ensure that any agreement between the host company and the employee does not look like an employment contract.

Inter-company expatriate supply agreement

6.26 Finally, to complete the triangle, there will be some sort of agreement between the home and host companies relating to commercial issues, such as the recharging of employment costs or payment of fees for the services provided. This sort of agreement is referred to in this book as an inter-company expatriate supply agreement, though many different terms are used in practice. The agreement is, essentially, a contract for services, ie a contract for the provision of the services of the expatriate by the home company to the host company. Sometimes the agreement will cover provision of more than one expatriate.

6.27 Multinational organisations often fail to document arrangements between the two companies, perhaps assuming that, as they are group companies, dispute is unlikely and a record of the agreement is unnecessary. Agreement between the companies will nevertheless exist, even if only informally. The difficulty, as in any situation where a contract exists but there is no formal document, will be in proving the contract terms if the arrangement is challenged. In practice, even if no dispute between group companies or with the employee arises, a failure to document the inter-company agreement at an early stage can be inconvenient. A variety of public authorities in the home and host countries may be interested in understanding the arrangements. Failure to document the arrangements adequately can have substantial financial consequences.

6.28 For example, tax authorities in the home or host country may expect the host company business to pay the home company employer for the employee's services. If so, they might want to know the precise amounts due, for example, so that they can determine whether a corporation tax deduction should be allowed or whether sales tax should be charged, and if so how much is appropriate.

6.29 It is quite common for different people to be responsible for preparing inter-company agreements from those who prepare the employment documents. From an internal perspective this may seem quite natural, as corporate tax and accounting compliance may be key concerns for inter-company agreements, whilst HR may naturally take the lead in preparing employment documents. Disconnected internal responsibilities, and disconnected external advisers, may account for many of the inconsistencies found between inter-company and employment documentation in practice. See Chapter 17 for practical suggestions for 'joining up' advice provided from different sources.

6.30 An agreement between home and host companies on transfer of personal data may also be required, see **15.73–15.99**, particularly where one of the companies is in the EU. Terms relating to data protection (privacy) compliance may be included in the inter-company expatriate supply agreement. However, they are more often set out in separate documents dedicated to data protection.

6.31 Good paperwork is rarely enough to 'prove' that the home company is really the employer. The underlying facts would need to be consistent and support the preferred structure. Hiring arrangements, reporting lines, pay review communications, bonus and other benefits etc could all be relevant. See **4.71–4.107** on factual arrangements determining employment status.

Case study – home employer

6.32 See figure 6.1, at **6.15**.

6.33 Tom is an IT specialist and has been working with a team in England on development of a new IT system. The new system will be rolled out to group companies in other countries, starting with Singapore. Tom will spend a year in Singapore helping to bed in the new system. After considering all the issues raised in Chapter 4, it has been decided that Tom's English employer will remain his employer during the Singapore assignment. The English home company will supply Tom's services to the Singapore registered host company. The business must decide on the documents that will be needed for the assignment.

6.34 If Tom were a new recruit, his employer should issue him with a new employment contract (as it should with a new local hire). However, Tom is already employed by the English home company so he should already have a written employment contract. Tom's existing employment terms will need to be changed to reflect the new arrangements, for example, his new place of work, role and remuneration package. His English employer explains that, although it is aware that Tom should have been given a written employment contract, in fact, Tom never received one. Even though nothing has been written down, Tom still has an employment contract: it is just harder to work out what the pre-assignment terms are. Tom's English employer decides to issue a brand new employment contract. The new contract will confirm all the terms of Tom's employment, including the special arrangements that will apply during his assignment to Singapore and details of what will happen at the end of the assignment.

6.35 In addition to Tom's relationship with his English home country employer, he will also have a relationship with the Singaporean host company. Unlike Tom's UK employer, the host company always issues employment documents to staff promptly and has an up-to-date employee handbook setting out policies that employees are required to comply with. The Singaporean host company is keen to issue a detailed contract and the policies to Tom as soon as possible, so that he understands what will be expected of him during the assignment. The Singapore company also wants to make sure that Tom is motivated by participation in host company incentive plans designed for the project team and that his employment terms reflect those of his host country peers.

6.36 However, the group needs to ensure that, even though Tom and the Singaporean host company will have a relationship during the assignment, this cannot be confused with an employment relationship. If it is clear that the English home company should be the employer, all the documents should support this. So, as the host company is not his employer, Tom should not be issued with the Singaporean host company's standard employment contract or employee handbook. Nor should the Singapore company issue Tom with other documents designed for its own employees.

6.37 Tom may, nevertheless, enter into some direct agreements with the host company where these are consistent with his employment status. For example, he could enter into agreements dealing with confidential information and intellectual property. The group companies discuss the terms that should apply to Tom during the assignment and it is agreed that the home company employment contract will reflect host country terms relating to shift patterns, public holidays, etc so that host country team relationships are not upset. The English home company puts in place an incentive arrangement to apply to Tom during the assignment. The new cash incentive plan is similar to the plan that the Singapore company has already designed for its own project team, but ensures that the home company is obliged to make the relevant performance assessments (taking account of feedback from Singapore), payments, etc.

6.38 The two group companies then discuss their own relationship. The English home company will agree to supply Tom's services to the Singaporean host company for a fee which is to be set at a level to cover the home company's salary and other direct employment costs with an uplift of 20% to reflect other management costs etc. The companies check with their corporate tax advisers to see if the uplift is appropriate. This arrangement is then documented in a formal 'inter-company expatriate supply agreement'. That agreement also specifies the notice the home and host companies must each give to terminate the assignment arrangement.

6.39 English language documents are acceptable to the home and host companies as well as the employee and there is no host country requirement or practical need for translation(s). It is agreed that as the home company will be the employer; the documents can be prepared in English; and as Singaporean approaches to drafting are reasonably similar, an English employment lawyer familiar with the business will prepare first drafts, taking account of specialist advice received from immigration lawyers and expatriate tax advisers. They will then be submitted to Singapore qualified lawyers for review. Those lawyers will be asked particularly to check for compliance with any applicable mandatory Singaporean employment laws.

Home country employer – no host company

6.40 An employee may be sent by his home employer to work temporarily in the host country for the home employer (ie there may be no separate host company). Figure 6.2 illustrates the relationship between the home company and the employee.

6.41 This is, of course, the ordinary employment relationship that will be familiar to those who prepare employment documents for local hires. The existing employment contract will still need to be varied or replaced, to take account of the new assignment terms. However, there will be no inter-company expatriate supply agreement and no separate agreement with any host company.

6.42 Preparing the employment documents should be relatively easy but corporation tax issues may require more attention. (See **13.12–13.15** on 'permanent establishment' concerns.) Practically, the duties to be performed by the employee and restrictions on freedom to conclude contracts etc in the host country may be important.

Figure 6.2

Home country employment – no host country

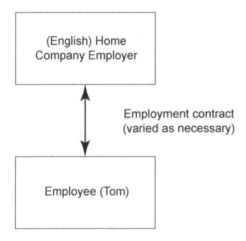

HOST COUNTRY EMPLOYER

6.43 This is where the employee is to be employed by a company (or other legal entity) registered in the host country for the duration of the assignment. The home company employer ceases to be the employer before the assignment begins. There is only one employer so there will be only one employment contract, in this case with the host company.

6.44 Figure 6.3 illustrates the key relationships between the home company, the host company and the employee, and the documents which would typically be used. Each of these documents is considered in more detail below and in Chapters 7 and 8. See also Appendices 1 and 2.

Employment contract with the host company

6.45 There will only be one employment contract with the host company. As there will be no existing employment with the host company, a new employment contract should be drawn up. The contract should reflect host company terms and host country mandatory employment laws, but would also confirm the special expatriate package agreed with the employee.

Figure 6.3

Host country employer

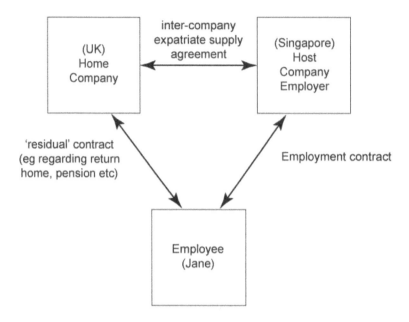

Residual contract between the employee and the home company

6.46 Any existing employment contract with the home company should normally be suspended or terminated during the assignment. However, even though the home company will not be the employer during the assignment, it may be appropriate for the home company and the employee to enter into some direct contractual promises that will apply during the assignment. These may be documented in a 'residual' contract. (This is no term of art and different vocabulary may be used by different organisations for this sort of arrangement.)

6.47 The residual contract may provide, for example, for:

- employment in the home country by the home company at the end of the assignment;
- continued participation in home country pension or other benefit arrangements during the assignment;
- revival of the original home company employment contract on termination of the host company employment.

Note that the existence of a continuing relationship with the home employer may have tax and other implications.

Inter-company expatriate supply agreement

6.48 As with a home country employment arrangement, there should be an inter-company expatriate supply agreement between the home and host companies.

6.49 However, documentation of the relationship between home and host companies is likely to be less critical with a host country arrangement than with a home country arrangement. The host company, as employer, will be bearing remuneration costs and benefiting from the employee's services directly and there are unlikely to be any significant fees paid by the host company to the home company. Sales tax and corporation tax issues may be far less significant as reasons for ensuring that the appropriate inter-company arrangements are properly documented, than would be the case for a home country arrangement. However, it will usually be prudent to document the arrangements anyway, if only to deal with termination of the assignment, make any limited recharging arrangements (or the fact that there are none) clear, and to support the host company's status as employer.

6.50 An agreement between the home and host companies in relation to the transfer of personal data may also be required, see **15.73–15.99**.

Case study – host employer

6.51 Jane currently works in England for her English employer. It is decided that she should be sent to Singapore to work for another group company. After considering all the issues raised in Chapter 4, it has been decided that Jane should be employed by the Singapore-registered company during the assignment. At the end of the assignment, which will be for three years, it is anticipated that Jane will return to her 'old' job in England. In other words, the 'host company' in Singapore will be Jane's employer for the duration of the assignment only. The business is thinking about the documents that will be needed for the assignment.

6.52 As Jane will be employed by the Singaporean host company, she will need a new contract of employment with that company.

6.53 Jane's English employment will end immediately before the employment with the Singapore host company begins. However, she will keep contact with her English home company and they hope she will return. Jane is a member of a generous home company final salary pension plan and would like to retire in England.

6.54 A 'residual' contract with the home company is prepared to record the English company's promise to employ Jane on her return to England at the end of the Singapore assignment, subject to some caveats that will apply if there is no work for her to do.

6.55 Jane has an existing English employment contract. However, it is not well drafted and is out of date, as Jane has been promoted and moved jobs within the company a couple of times since the contract was signed. The notice provisions are inadequate. The home company decides that the existing English employment contract should be terminated. The residual employment agreement will therefore also include some detail about the terms that will apply if Jane is re-employed in England after the end of the assignment.

6.56 The residual contract with the English company will confirm, for example: the notional salary by reference to which Jane's English salary will be set on her return to England (and arrangements for regular review of the notional salary by the home company during the assignment); her seniority; and the terms that will apply if no job is available for her at the time her assignment ends. Care is taken to ensure the termination provisions for the residual contract are compatible with the host company employment arrangements. The residual contract could also document the pension arrangements that will apply to Jane during the assignment but this may not be appropriate. Home country advisers suggest that the Singapore company could 'adhere' to the UK pension scheme. Alternatively, though this may be less tax efficient and could create complications on termination of Jane's employment, the home employer may promise to augment Jane's pension benefits after her assignment ends to take account of the assignment period.

6.57 An inter-company expatriate supply agreement documents the arrangements between the home and host companies. The host company will pay Jane directly under the terms of her employment contract and may also pay a financial contribution to the home company to cover the costs of Jane's pension in respect of the assignment period.

DUAL EMPLOYMENTS

6.58 This is where the employee is employed by two separate employers to do two separate jobs. Typically, each employment will have a different geographical scope. The employers will often be group companies. The arrangement can, theoretically, offer tax advantages, depending on the countries where duties are performed, although in practice these arrangements are open to challenge.

6.59 Figure 6.4 illustrates the key relationships between the two employers and the employee, and the documents that would typically be used for dual employments. (See also **8.57–8.61**.)

Two separate employment contracts

6.60 There are two separate employments, so the employee will have two separate employment contracts, one with each company. These are referred to here as companies 'A' and 'B' rather than 'home' and 'host' companies, as the latter implies that the employee has a closer connection with one of the companies.

Figure 6.4

Dual employments – two employers, two jobs

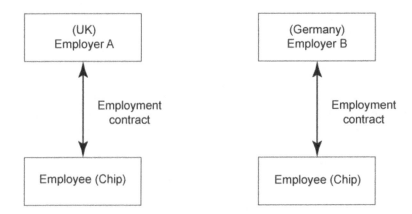

6.61   There is no assignment: the employee is not sent by one company to work for another. No fee is likely to be paid by either company A or company B to the other. Each employer should pay the employee directly. If an inter-company agreement is made between company A and company B, care should be taken to ensure that the agreement is consistent with the dual employment arrangement. Normally, an inter-company agreement will not be appropriate.

6.62   In practice, because dual employments can sometimes offer substantial tax benefits they are likely to be subject to scrutiny by tax authorities, and are frequently challenged. Advisers should be mindful of potential consequences of facilitating tax evasion, both for their clients and for themselves. (See **4.114** on tax evasion.)

6.63   Dual employments should not be confused with 'joint employment', 'split contract' or 'split payroll arrangements'. See the Glossary at Appendix 3, and 6.70–6.77 below on joint employment.

Case study – dual employments

6.64   Chip is an American who is recruited on the open market to work for a multinational group of companies in Europe.

6.65   Chip will have two separate roles. It is anticipated that he will spend roughly three days each week working in London, where he will live with his family. He will be a director of the UK company and will be responsible for a specialist department. A group company registered in Germany is currently working on a project to assess whether similar specialist departments should be established for the group in other European countries. Chip will help the German company with that project. He will spend approximately two days each week working in Europe, travelling between different EU countries, and will share the information he gathers, and his conclusions, with the German company. The establishment of a new specialist department would involve substantial investment and the feasibility project is expected to take a couple of years to complete. Chip's skills would be difficult to find elsewhere and his remuneration package will be substantial.

6.66 As there will be two employers, there will be two separate employment contracts. Each must comply with local requirements and should be consistent with the employment arrangements for the employer's other employees. For example, the UK staff handbook may apply to Chip in relation to his UK duties. German policies should apply in relation to his German arrangements.

6.67 See 8.57–8.61 on facts that would support dual employment status. In practice, establishing two genuinely separate employments is challenging.

UK tax implications – dual employments

6.68 Dual employments were for many years considered a tax efficient way of structuring expatriate assignments involving the UK. The relevant UK tax rules have, however, progressively tightened, and modern technology and expectations of employees make it increasingly difficult to do one job in one place and one in another. It can be difficult to substantiate these arrangements. See the UK tax authority, HMRC, document 'Restrictions on the remittance basis: dual contracts'.

6.69 Detailed analysis of tax and social security issues relating to dual employments is outside the scope of this book, and the author's expertise, but see Chapter 4 and 8.57–8.61 for explanations of some of the issues that should be taken into consideration by those drafting the employment documents if it is decided that the arrangements are appropriate.

JOINT EMPLOYMENT

6.70 Joint employment is where two separate entities employ the same employee to do the same job. Theoretically, this may be possible, for example, where a husband and wife jointly employ a nanny to look after their children. In practice, it is not usually a good idea to try to establish a joint employment arrangement for expatriates, for the reasons described below. Before looking at why joint employment arrangements might cause problems, it is worth having a quick look at why advisers might want to suggest joint employment in the first place. The suggestion is rarely put forward by the business.

6.71 Figure 6.5 illustrates the key relationships between the two employers and the employee, and the documents that would typically be used for joint employment.

Figure 6.5

Joint employment – two employers, one job

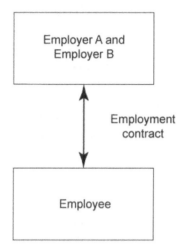

Example – joint employment

6.72 If an employee's services are supplied by one company to another and a fee is paid in return, the fee may be subject to sales tax (VAT). This is usually not a problem as the sales tax due can usually be offset against sales tax received from customers. However, some organisations cannot offset sales tax paid against VAT received from customers, eg, because they do not charge customers sales tax for their services.

6.73 Suppose the employee will not accept the assignment unless he can remain in the home country pension plan, and he cannot participate in that plan unless he is a home company employee. If the host company pays a fee to the home company for the employee's services sales tax will be due. Suppose that, because of the nature of its business, the host company cannot recover the sales tax. The adviser decides to solve the problem by ensuring that the employee is employed by both the host company and the home company at the same time. No fee need be paid which would attract sales tax, the companies just pay part of the remuneration each directly to the employee, and the employee can stay in the home company pension plan. The adviser feels terribly pleased with himself. This is a creative solution that his client will love.

6.74 Unfortunately, things are not quite that simple. Here are some examples of problems the group might face.

- The home country pensions authorities may not accept that joint employment is the correct interpretation of the facts, either at the outset if they are asked for 'clearance' or years later if the arrangement is not drawn to their attention initially. The employee may find that he was not eligible under the pension plan rules to participate in his preferred pension plan after all or that his pension arrangements do not attract the preferential tax treatment he was expecting. The employer may have given assurances to the employee and may be obliged to compensate him for any losses.

- A work permit may be required for the employee to work in the host country and the application may need to be submitted by the employer. The immigration authorities may not accept the joint employment arrangement and may refuse to grant the work permit.

- Tax authorities, who are likely to have a financial incentive to challenge the arrangements, may decide that the home or host company is in reality the sole employer.

- The 'employers' may not be able to comply with host company employment authority or other registration requirements.

- Some decisions would need to be made regarding reporting lines, who would run the appraisal, disciplinary process, etc. Any attempt to make these clear and practical is likely to reinforce an argument that one or other of the companies is in reality the employer.

- After some years the employment may end. An employment court or tribunal may need to make a decision on the identity of the individual's employer. The decision is unlikely to uphold joint employment. As there will have been an assumption that joint employment applied the wrong company representatives are likely to have implemented any dismissal, the correct dismissal procedures are unlikely to have been followed (and the dismissal may even be void) and the 'real' employer may be subject to legal claims, financial penalties, etc. The tax, social security, immigration, etc authorities may take the employment decision as evidence that the arrangements were not, in reality, as presented to them at the outset. All the careful planning may unravel.

6.75 Joint employment arrangements are risky and not usually recommended, and in practice they are rarely deliberately adopted. However, it is quite common for employment documents to be prepared in a way that inadvertently implies that both home and host companies are the employer. Sometimes this comes about because home and host companies issue the documents separately without consulting each other.

6.76 Joint employment should not be confused with a host country employment arrangement where there is a 'residual' contract with the home employer or with dual contracts, or split payroll arrangements (see above and the Glossary at Appendix 3).

6.77 See also Chapter 13 on 'piercing the corporate veil'.

TRI-PARTITE DOCUMENTS

6.78 Sometimes it is thought convenient to enter into tri-partite documents between the home company, the host company and the employee dealing with all the issues relating to the employment (effectively bundling the employment contract, contractual arrangements between the employee and the other company and the inter-company arrangements into one document). This can leave the authorities, and advisers, (in the event of a subsequent dismissal or re-examination of the tax arrangements etc) puzzling over which entity is in fact the employer. The decision on whether the home or host company is the employer may not suit the business. Tri-partite arrangements could also have some unintended consequences, for example:

- the arrangements, particularly the termination arrangements, will be difficult to draft clearly;

- the home and host companies may find that they have effectively guaranteed each other's obligations to the employee;

- any of the parties could become confused about the original intentions, particularly once those who originally drafted them are no longer available to provide an explanation, and could then take action inconsistent with the preferred status without understanding the consequences;

- the preferred employer's identity could be challenged at the outset or years later by the employee or any of the interested home and host country public authorities, see above.

SUMMARY

6.79 The above descriptions are intended to help the adviser ensure that the documents put in place support the preferred structure of the employment arrangements. In particular, it is critical that those documents are consistent with the identity of the preferred employer, and, of course, the facts. Careful thought about the reality of the relationships and the documents required to reflect the facts, upfront, can save a great deal of redrafting and expense later on. The structure should not normally be settled and drafting should not normally begin before specialist immigration and tax advice has been considered and the issues described in Chapter 4 (Identity of the Employer) and Chapter 5 (Length of the Assignment) have been considered in detail. It is also helpful, and more efficient, to review the quality of the existing employment documents before making decisions such as whether to vary, suspend or replace existing documents.

6.80 Chapters 7 and 8 provide some suggestions about the appropriate content of the documents described in this chapter. Appendices 1 and 2 provide checklists and framework documents respectively.

CHAPTER 7

DOCUMENTING EXPATRIATE REWARD

INTRODUCTION

7.1   Both this chapter and Chapter 8 provide information about practical things that should normally be covered by employment documents for an employee on a longer-term assignment (say at least 12 months). This chapter deals with expatriate pay and benefits, whilst Chapter 8 deals with documentation of other matters, such as duties, immigration and the length of the assignment. See **5.36**, checklist **A1.7** at Appendix 1 and framework document **A2.3** at Appendix 2 on practical things that should normally be covered where there is a shorter-term assignment.

7.2   This chapter focuses on some of the special remuneration challenges faced by expatriate employees (and strategies for dealing with them), including:

- differences in 'normal' pay rates between host and home countries (should the employee's pay be 'benchmarked' against home or host rates?);

- the impact of currency and inflation movements on the value of remuneration and the employee's spending power in home and host locations;

- the impact of cost of living and tax and social security differences between home and host locations on the expatriate's net pay;

- the complexity of expatriate benefit arrangements designed to mitigate the impact of relocation on the employee;

- special tax reliefs that may sometimes be available to expatriate employees.

7.3   Pay and benefits should be provided by the employer, so they should normally be promised to the employee through his employment contract. The employment contract could consist of one or more documents. Remuneration could, for example, be confirmed in a separate assignment letter issued by the employer that, together with an 'old' employment contract, forms the complete written employment contract for the assignment. Alternatively, a new employment contract could be prepared especially for the assignment. (See Chapter 6 on the structure of the assignment and the documents needed.)

7.4   More detail about pay and benefits is usually included in a contract for an expatriate than for a local hire. This is partly because expatriates typically receive more valuable and complex remuneration than local hires. It is also because more can go wrong. The expatriate will usually appreciate the comfort this extra detail gives; careful documentation should increase flexibility and reduce the risk of dispute; and more detailed documents can save an enormous amount of (expensive) time if a new company representative, adviser or public authority needs to check the terms that apply.

7.5   This chapter covers:

- Pay (7.6–7.26).
- Allowances and expenses (7.27–7.67).
- Currency and exchange rates (7.68–7.79).
- Tax (7.80–7.98).
- Pension and life assurance (7.99–7.105).
- Share plans (7.106–7.108).
- Benefits-in-kind (7.109–7.142).
- Working time and holiday (7.143–7.154).
- Sickness, health and safety and insurance (7.155–7.163).
- Corporate regulatory constraints (7.164).
- Top tips for documenting expatriate reward (7.165).

PAY

7.6   Pay will be a key concern for both employer and employee and they are unlikely to forget to confirm salary figures in the documents. However, expatriate remuneration packages are usually far more complex than those that apply to local hires. Often the detail is not described in the documents and the parties rely on an assumption that what has worked in practice over a period of time will continue to work in the future. This can cause difficulties, particularly on termination of employment. Expatriates do not always check their pay during the assignment, for example, because they may not properly understand how tax and social security contributions are deducted or the way that tax equalisation works, or maybe just because they are too busy. The employee may well assume during the assignment that the employer will get it right, and if trust breaks down at a later stage the calculations may need to be reopened. It makes sense to be clear about everything that may affect pay from the outset.

7.7   See also **4.86–4.89** on how payment arrangements can support the preferred identity of the employer.

Basic salary

7.8   The most important element of the remuneration package is likely to be basic salary. This may be set by reference to a number of factors. For example, the expatriate will expect a pay rise not a pay cut so his home salary will be a starting point; the group may need to think about comparison with pay for host company local hires in equivalent jobs; and third party 'benchmarking' advice may be sought about the appropriate level of pay for someone performing the particular role in the host country.

Employers should be mindful of the potential application of equality laws when setting pay. (See Chapter 12 on equality.)

7.9 Whatever the mechanism for determining pay, the employment contract should confirm basic salary clearly. That confirmation should include the rate, the currency applicable to that rate and the currency in which salary will be delivered.

Notional salary

7.10 'Notional salary' is a term often used for hypothetical salary used as a reference point for a particular purpose, or for several purposes. Notional salary is not actually paid. Other terms might be used eg 'hypothetical', 'reference' or 'home' salary. As with many other expatriate terms 'notional salary' means different things to different employers and different advisers. If the term is used it should be clearly defined in the documents.

7.11 For example:

- a higher basic salary may be paid for the duration of the assignment and the employer may want to keep the employee informed of the lower salary likely to apply when he returns home, to reduce the risk of disappointment or dispute when he does return;
- notional salary may be used as a reference point for benefit purposes, for example, to determine pension contributions or bonus entitlement;
- notional salary may be important if the expatriate's employment documents confirm net basic salary rather than gross basic salary (normally to give tax comfort), so that there is no specified gross salary to be used as a reference point for other purposes; and
- notional salary may be used as a defined term in tax equalisation or tax protection policies.

7.12 Notional salary will be subject to review, normally (but not always) by the employer and at the same time as basic salary is reviewed. (See 7.20–7.22.)

Bonus

7.13 Remuneration arrangements should support the identity of the assumed employer. (See also Chapter 4 on the identity of the employer.) The employer should give any contractual promise to pay bonus and should bear any bonus costs. Communications about bonus should be made on the employer's headed paper or emails, and should be from a representative of the correct company.

7.14 Although bonus arrangements should be provided by the employer if the home company is the employer, the targets etc to be applied may be adapted to reflect host company goals. (That is, a home country employer should not prevent bonus arrangements taking account of the job the employee actually does in the host country during the assignment.)

7.15 Care should be taken to ensure the arrangements that will apply at the beginning and at the end of the assignment are clear. If the assignment ends part way through the bonus year, targets etc may need to be reset. Particular attention should be given to the way that termination of the employment would affect bonus, as dispute is more likely at that time.

7.16 Currency issues may become significant, for example, if targets are set in a different currency from the currency in which payment is made. (See **7.68–7.79** on currency and exchange rates.)

7.17 Tax arrangements may also need to be clarified. If there is a vague tax equalisation promise there may be doubt about whether the promise applies to bonus as well as salary, and if it does, how it applies to bonus if there is a long period between award and vesting. For example, a bonus might be awarded before the assignment begins and vest during the assignment, or be awarded during the assignment and vest after it ends. (See **7.80–7.92** on tax equalisation.)

7.18 Existing incentive plans may not be appropriate for use in some countries, or may be unlawful. For example, if award of shares is prohibited in the host country it may be better to replace share plan arrangements with a 'phantom' share arrangement, providing cash payments linked to share price. (See also **11.31–11.41** on the potential impact of overseas assignment on post termination restrictions in bonus documents and **15.9–15.15** on share plans generally.)

7.19 See **8.24–8.28** on the effect of mandatory employment laws on bonus, for example, a requirement to make a '13th month' or similar bonus payment.

Pay reviews

7.20 Most employers review pay at least annually. The correct company should review salary, as a decision to increase pay should only be made by the employer. The employer should also make appraisal decisions. If the arrangement is a home employer arrangement, then the host company's views are likely to be sought, but decisions regarding appraisal, pay, etc should be the home employer's.

7.21 The employment contract should record the relevant arrangements, particularly the responsibilities of the employer.

7.22 If the arrangement is a host employer arrangement then the host company should appraise the employee, make decisions regarding salary increase, etc. However, in that case, the home employer may still retain responsibility for reviewing notional salary. Whether the home employer should review notional salary would depend on the purpose of the notional salary, for example, if this is to be used as a reference point for post-assignment salary when the employee returns to the home country then, logically, the home employer should review it.

Payroll arrangements

7.23 The employer should be able to demonstrate that it has paid the employee's remuneration. The employment documents should confirm that the employer is responsible for payment. If another company is to make payments on the employer's behalf, the documents should make the basis on which this is to be done clear. For example, the employee's contract should confirm that payment is made 'on behalf of' the employer; an inter-company expatriate supply agreement should confirm the recharging arrangements between the home and host companies (**8.73**); and both the home and host company accounts should clearly show how the costs have actually been borne. Particular care should be taken where a multinational operates centralised treasury services. There may, eg, be a need to comply with exchange controls.

7.24 Some thought should be given to banking arrangements before the assignment begins, as it may take time for an employee (and employer) to open a bank account in the host country. Practically, the employee may need to ensure that he has funds available, in appropriate currencies, in both home and host countries (see **7.68–7.79** on currency and exchange rates). Where it is not possible for the employee to open a bank account, the employee may still be able to arrange for regular remittance of cash to a local bank for collection.

7.25 The place of payment could also have implications for the tax treatment of payments. It is a common misconception amongst employees that if remuneration is paid in one country it will be taxed in that country and not another. Things are of course much more complex than that and sometimes it can be helpful to anticipate potential misunderstanding and make that clear to the employee in the documents. (See **5.4–5.22** for more general comments on income tax and social security.)

7.26 The employment documents should normally confirm:

- whether payment is made in advance or arrears;
- the rate of accrual;
- payment intervals;
- payment dates;
- place of payment;
- accrual and payment currencies; and

- deductions.

Given that the expatriate is likely to receive a number of different types of payment it can be helpful to include one clause in the employment contract explaining arrangements and provide for those terms to cover all the relevant payments, except as otherwise stated in the agreement. Some or all of this information may be set out in legislation or a collective agreement. (See 8.32–8.35 on duplicating the content of legislation or collective agreements.) The employee should be issued with regular payslips showing payments made and sums deducted. In some countries, eg the UK, provision of a payslip is compulsory.

ALLOWANCES AND EXPENSES

Allowances – general

7.27   Expatriate packages often include allowances.

7.28   There is an important distinction between allowances (usually 'one-off' fixed sums or regular payments at a set rate) and reimbursement of expenses (usually employer payments against receipts for money spent by the employee). The arrangements made will often take account of home and/or host country rules that allow tax relief if reimbursement of expenses or provision of an allowance is made in a particular way or subject to particular conditions.

7.29   The terms used for different types of allowance are not terms of art and tend to take on a particular meaning within businesses that manage a number of overseas assignments, depending on the employer's normal practices. This can result in some inconsistency and uncertainty, perhaps with different managers applying assumed rules in different ways or employees making inappropriate assumptions about what is normal. Whatever the terms applied to the allowances offered, the employer should ensure the documents are clear.

7.30   The documents should normally confirm:

- the rate at which the allowance will accrue;
- whether the allowance will be paid in advance or arrears;
- by whom, when, how, where and in what currency payment will be made (and if the payment currency is different from the currency used to specify the accrual rate, how exchange rates may be determined);
- the arrangements for review, including responsibility for review and whether the allowance can be decreased as well as increased and whether a negative figure is possible.

Expenses – general

7.31 The employment contract should normally describe the methods for seeking approval for and claiming expenses and how expenses will be paid.

7.32 It is worth checking first to see whether any tax concessions may apply so that the arrangements can be structured to take advantage of any tax relief available. For example, tax relief is often available to expatriates in respect of relocation, accommodation and subsistence expenses subject to strict conditions. (See **19.47–19.51** on UK 'detached duty relief'.)

7.33 Expenses are frequently managed in the host country. Expenses are usually incurred in the host country and reimbursement in the host currency and payment to and from host bank accounts may be convenient. However, if the host company is not the employer it will not normally be appropriate for the host company to be contractually responsible to the employee for reimbursing expenses to the employee. If reimbursement is made by the host company on behalf of a home country employer, the documents should clearly confirm this. Ideally, all the administrative arrangements, approvals, etc should be managed by the employer.

7.34 The employment documents should also confirm the arrangements for claiming reimbursement carefully. For local hires a short clause providing for reimbursement of expenses incurred wholly and necessarily in the proper performance of duties, subject to provision of receipts, and with a reference to a more detailed expenses policy, might be sufficient. For expatriates this will not usually be enough. Employees on assignment often incur larger business expenses and are reimbursed in respect of a wide variety of things that might normally be considered 'personal', rather than 'business', expenses. It is unlikely to be appropriate to refer to the employer's normal expenses policy, because that policy is unlikely to have been designed for expatriates.

7.35 Employment documents should confirm:

- the company and nominated representative responsible for approving and reimbursing expenses (usually a proper representative of the employer);
- which expenses will be reimbursed;
- any limits on the amounts that may be claimed and/or time-limits for submitting claims;
- reference to evidence of expenditure and record keeping;
- any float provided (and arrangements for recovery); and
- by whom, when, how, where and in what currency payment will be made (and how exchange rates may be determined).

7.36 Sometimes it will be agreed between a host company receiving the services of an employee and his home country employer that the host company will bear expenses (because, eg, they relate to the host company's business). If this has been decided between the host and home companies, this does not mean that the host company has a contractual obligation to the employee to reimburse his expenses. The employee should claim his expenses from his home country employer in the normal way (with the arrangements documented in the employment contract). The home country employer should, in turn, claim reimbursement from the host company (with the arrangements documented in the inter-company expatriate supply agreement). If the host company does physically reimburse on behalf of the home country employer, the documents (ie the employment contract and inter-company expatriate supply agreement) should confirm the basis on which this is done (ie on behalf of the employer). Management accounts and bank records should also reflect the reality of the arrangements (ie with the costs ultimately borne in the right place).

7.37 Limits on expenses should normally be clearly specified in the documents. Where there is some flexibility the documents may confirm that an appropriate representative of the employer has discretion to make relevant decisions. An employer's freedom to retain discretion to vary pay may be restricted by law.

7.38 Care should be taken with control of the expense arrangements for senior employees, particularly if the expatriate is in the most senior position in the host location or authorises payments for the business. Oversight of employees from another country can be more challenging. See also **15.42–15.46** on bribery.

7.39 Typically, expenses are incurred in the host country in the host currency and are reimbursed in the host currency too. However, currency and exchange rate issues may become important, for example if the employee will travel to other countries in the course of their duties. The documents should confirm any relevant arrangements.

Cost of living allowance (COLA)

7.40 Basic salary for expatriates is often adjusted to take account of relative costs of living in different places. For example, it may be more expensive to live in the US than in South Africa. Beware of assuming that because a country's economy is less developed that the cost of living will be lower. Items that expatriates may consider basic requirements could be surprisingly expensive, for example, if they are not commonly used by local people or heavy import tariffs are applied. Comparative cost of living data is usually purchased from specialist third party providers at the start of, and during, an assignment. It is not normally helpful to the employer to provide for a rigid contractual commitment to one data provider in the documents.

7.41 Cost of living may be taken into consideration before basic salary is set so there is no separate allowance. Alternatively, cost of living may be taken into account by way of a separate cost of living allowance or adjustment (usually referred to as 'COLA'). There are several advantages to specifying COLA and basic salary separately in the employment documents, for example:

- this can help manage expectations at the end of the assignment, by drawing attention to the fact that COLA will be withdrawn or changed if the employee returns home or starts a new assignment;

- it may be easier to adjust COLA upwards or downwards, whereas reducing basic salary is usually difficult, and may be prohibited by law; and

- the employer may set various employee benefits by reference to basic salary only. A separate COLA could, for example, be used to ensure that COLA is not taken into account for pension, bonus and/or tax equalisation purposes. (Alternatively, the employer may use 'notional salary' as a reference point, see 7.10–7.12.)

7.42 COLA is usually paid monthly in arrears with basic salary, but may be reviewed more frequently than basic salary, perhaps twice yearly.

Negative COLA

7.43 Care should be taken when drafting the documents if COLA may be a negative figure (ie if COLA can be applied to reduce, as well as increase, basic salary).

7.44 For example, suppose COLA is a positive figure +€4,000 and salary is €100,000 per year, COLA adjusted salary will be €104,000 per year. If, on the other hand, COLA is a negative figure –€4,000 and salary is €100,000 per year, COLA adjusted salary will be €96,000 per year.

7.45 The language used in the employment documents to describe the way COLA is applied may affect the employee's tax bill (and consequently the employer's costs too, eg, if there is a tax equalisation promise). The key distinction may be between a 'deduction' from salary and a 'reduction' to salary.

7.46 Using the figures above, if COLA of -€4,000 is seen as a 'deduction' from gross basic salary then income tax may be calculated by reference to the 'pre-COLA' gross basic salary of €100,000. If the effect of COLA is to 'reduce' gross basic salary, then tax may be calculated by reference to the 'post-COLA' gross basic salary (ie €96,000). Similar issues may arise if a negative accommodation adjustment is made to take account of rental income from the employee's home country property (see 7.128–7.130).

7.47 If COLA may be reduced or a negative figure it is prudent to check relevant employment laws, particularly in the host country, to ensure that retaining an employer's discretion to adjust pay in this way is lawful. Careful drafting is important and, ideally, should be checked by both employment lawyers and expatriate tax advisers.

Hardship allowance

7.48 Sometimes additional allowances are offered in recognition of the difficulties faced by employees working at a particular location. For example, a 'hardship' allowance might be paid to the employee where social life is limited; family cannot accompany; there are issues with security; or the climate is 'bad'. A hardship allowance is different from COLA. For example, cost of living may be low in a country with a violent history. Employees may, nonetheless, expect to be compensated for the risks they take. Employees from different backgrounds may find different postings difficult. For example, a short posting to Saudi Arabia may not concern a single Muslim man but could be less attractive for a Christian man with a wife and three teenage daughters.

7.49 As with COLA, hardship allowances are usually determined by reference to data purchased from specialist third party providers. The particular employee's allowance may be determined by applying a percentage to his basic salary. It is usually clearer if the employer specifies an actual rate in the contract rather than trying to confirm the formula to be applied or making reference to the source of data. The allowance may then be reviewed and recalculated by the employer at appropriate intervals going forward with less risk of dispute.

7.50 If a percentage figure is confirmed in the contract particular care should be taken in respect of the order in which adjustments are applied. For example, if the hardship allowance is a 5% uplift on basic salary, should the allowance be applied to basic salary before or after COLA is made?

7.51 A hardship allowance is unlikely to be a negative figure.

Disturbance allowance

7.52 Disturbance allowances are often confused with relocation expenses. 'Disturbance allowance' is usually used to describe a small 'one-off' allowance to cover the costs of repurchasing small household goods, such as an iron or kettle, at the outset of the assignment. Receipts may be required, which is less usual where an allowance is paid. As with other allowances, tax advice should be sought before a disturbance allowance is offered.

Subsistence allowance

7.53 A 'subsistence allowance' is usually a regular allowance to cover the costs of hotel expenses, meals, etc. A subsistence allowance is more likely to be offered where the employee is not living in permanent accommodation, eg to short-term assignees in hotels or long-term assignees before they move into permanent host country accommodation. However, subsistence allowances can sometimes be provided throughout a longer-term assignment. Again, tax relief may be available in respect of all or part of the allowance. Daily subsistence allowances are frequently referred to as 'per diems'.

Travel and relocation allowances and expenses

Travel expenses

7.54 The employer may agree to reimburse travel expenses for a variety of reasons, for example, in relation to:

- pre-trips (see **3.13–3.16** and **8.15–8.16** on related immigration issues);
- regular home country visits, for example, for holidays;
- travel between home and host country for children at boarding school (see **7.137–7.139** on education-related benefits);
- relocation and repatriation at the start and end of an assignment (see **7.57–7.64**);
- travel home for medical treatment (**7.156**) or maternity (**12.25–12.34**);
- travel between home and work in the host country;
- travel on business within the host country or abroad.

7.55 The terms offered should be made clear. For example, the following may be clarified:

- whether costs will be reimbursed to the employee or paid directly to the supplier by the employer;
- the qualifying criteria for reimbursement or payment;
- whether limits on costs, number of trips or class of travel etc, will apply or whether this will be discretionary subject to approval;
- the job title of the employer representative from whom the employee should seek approval;
- how termination or reassignment part way through the year may affect entitlement, eg, to home leave flights.

7.56 This is another area where early tax advice may be beneficial. The structure and terms of the arrangements may make a significant difference to the sums to be paid to tax and/or social security authorities in relation to benefits, allowances or reimbursement.

Relocation

7.57 Relocation is an enormous challenge for employees taking up an assignment abroad, particularly if the family will go too. Most employers will offer their employees some help, for example, with shipping their own, and family members', furniture and personal belongings.

7.58 The employer may, for example, offer help with some or all of the following:

- orientation pre-trips, for example, to find schools or accommodation or meet colleagues;
- travel expenses between the home and host country for the employee and family members at the start and end of the assignment;
- lease or sale of the employee's property in his home country (eg by offering a bridging loan or contribution towards estate agents' fees);
- provision of temporary accommodation in the home country, for example, to cover a period after the expatriate's own home is rented but before the assignment begins or whilst the employee is waiting for tenants to vacate his property after the assignment ends;
- obtaining appropriate insurance cover, for example, for a vacant home country property or for possessions in transit;
- transporting belongings, usually by a volume or weight-limited combination of air and sea freight;
- storage of the employee's and/or his family's possessions, for example, if their home country property is let;
- occasionally, transporting pets;
- provision of temporary (eg hotel) accommodation, in the host country while a longer-term home is found;
- services of destination and/or relocation agents to assist, for example, with finding schools or accommodation in the host country.

Limits

7.59 Limits might include limits on volume, weight or cost for the transportation of personal possessions. Usually the expatriate's dependents will be taken into consideration when allowances are set. If it is difficult to predict the appropriate limits at the time the employment documents are prepared, then discretion could be given to a representative of the appropriate home or host company.

7.60 Time-limits for making claims and for reimbursement will probably be important for both employer and employee. Sometimes the employee may be offered an advance on expenses to be incurred or the employer will make payments directly to suppliers to ease cash flow difficulties for the employee.

7.61 Direct payments to suppliers may also help the employer manage the process and/or costs. For example, cost savings may be made if the business for all expatriates is given to one removal company. A better-informed choice of supplier may be made by an experienced mobility team than an individual employee relocating abroad for the first time.

Tax

7.62 Many countries offer some tax relief for relocation costs. The availability of tax relief for the employee is likely to be subject to conditions. For example, expenses may need to be reimbursed by the entity which is the employer at a particular time; there may be restrictions on the items that are covered and/or limits on the total costs that will attract tax relief; the method of payment may be important; or particular documentation may be required. (Note that because the remuneration may be subject to tax in more than one jurisdiction, the rules applicable to both jurisdictions and any applicable double-tax arrangements should be considered.) The employer should take care to ensure that the effect of any tax equalisation promises is clear and that the documents confirm that the appropriate company will approve and bear the costs. The availability of corporation tax deduction should also be considered.

Timing and employer identity

7.63 It is usual for the employer to be responsible for the reimbursement of expenses to his own employee, even if those costs are then reclaimed by the employer from another entity. Particular care with clarity and timing should be taken if the host company will be the employer for the duration of the assignment as there will be a change of employer.

Repatriation at the end of the assignment

7.64 Relocation expenses will also become important at the end of an assignment and the repatriation arrangements to apply on termination should be clear in the employment documents from the outset. The location to which the employee will be repatriated should be made clear, as this will not always be the country from which the employee was assigned, and the selection is likely to have an impact on costs. Sometimes the employee is given a choice. Many employers do not pay repatriation expenses if the employee voluntarily leaves to work for another employer in the host location or does not return home within a fixed period following termination of the assignment. If the relocation package offered to the employee on voluntary termination is to be different a clear definition of 'voluntary termination' (or whatever description the employer chooses to use) including any time-limits should be given. Some jurisdictions may require that the employer meets repatriation expenses. If repatriation expenses will not be met the documents should make that clear. (See also Chapter 22 on 'claw-back'.)

Accommodation and car allowances

7.65 Longer-term expatriate employees are often provided with accommodation and/or cars by their employers. Allowances may, of course, be provided instead. This may allow the employee more freedom in choosing how to spend the money; make managing the expatriate a little easier, because the employer does not need to be so involved with benefit arrangements; and/or help the employer to demonstrate that employees are being treated fairly.

7.66 In practice, provision of accommodation and a car, rather than allowances, will often be appropriate because this makes things easier for the employee at the start of the assignment, allowing him to focus on his job. For example, the employee might otherwise have to be guided through the local process of buying, taxing, licensing, insuring the car, etc. By providing a car the employer may also be able to control the image it projects to customers. (Image may be more important in the host location.) The employee will not have to worry about repairing the car or selling or shipping it at the end of the assignment. The decision to offer a car or a car allowance will often be influenced by tax considerations. (See **7.27–7.30** on delivery of allowances generally, **7.131–7.134** on provision of a car and **7.113–7.130** on provision of accommodation as a benefit-in-kind.)

7.67 Sometimes a fuel allowance or reimbursement of fuel expenses will also be provided.

CURRENCY AND EXCHANGE RATES

7.68 Factors such as movement between home and host currencies, inflation, foreign exchange restrictions, banking practicalities and the timing of delivery may all have an impact on the value of payments to employees working overseas.

Reducing the risk

7.69 Currency is likely to be an issue for most expatriates. There is no 'one size fits all' solution to this. Generally, when currencies move, someone wins and someone loses. If the employer offers more comfort to the employee, the employer will usually have to accept more risk.

7.70 There are a number of tried and tested ways to reduce the impact of currency fluctuation and changes in 'buying power' on employees working abroad. For example:

- cost of living adjustments to remuneration to protect against inflation (see **7.40–7.47** above);

- commercial hedging contracts to protect the employer's costs (see **7.76** below);

- split delivery (ie part of the remuneration paid in one currency and part in another);

- contractual comfort given by the employer to the employee (with or without hedging to give corresponding protection to the employer).

Documents

7.71 The documents should be clear about the currency in which each payment is set, the currency in which each payment will be delivered and the place of payment. If the currency in which remuneration is set is not the same as the currency in which remuneration is delivered, the exchange rate to be applied should be clear.

Currency in which pay is set and delivered

7.72 If the host country currency is unstable it may be important for an employee to have basic salary set in the home currency, particularly if he has substantial financial commitments to meet in the home country. In some cases the currency of a third country may be chosen as a reference point (eg US dollars or Euros), for example, for consistency or because the currency is considered to be steadier or easier to spend. Rarely, remuneration may be pegged to a 'basket' of currencies.

7.73 The employee is likely to use some of his pay in the home country (eg to make pension contributions and mortgage payments) and some in the host country (eg for accommodation, day-to-day living expenses, school fees etc). The place of delivery may, in some cases, have tax implications. Employers often offer employees the opportunity to choose the proportion of pay that will be delivered in home and host countries and currencies. The documents may include limits on the number of times the employee can change the arrangements, or the dates on which they can be changed, for the employer's convenience. For example, the employer may allow all expatriates to revise their preferred arrangements on two set dates each year or if there is a specified currency movement (eg +/- 10% in 3 months) or a life changing event (eg birth of a child).

7.74 If there is a difference between the currency in which payment is set and the currency in which payment is delivered, then the employer will need to use an appropriate currency conversion rate. Sometimes it is possible to clearly reference a third-party source of rates or to provide for review of rates at intervals through the year or annually. Usually the employer will want to ensure that it has some discretion to control or vary the applicable arrangements.

7.75 If the employer does not offer flexibility over the place of payment, the employee may need to make arrangements to transfer money from the home country to the host country or vice versa to meet his obligations. The employer may make a suggestion at the outset as to the appropriate amount to be transferred monthly to the host country (or retained there) to meet living expenses etc. This may be based initially on third party data, though the employee is likely to need to adjust this later on to reflect his own spending pattern. See comments at 7.24–7.25 regarding the availability of host country banking facilities and the effect of place of payment on tax. The employee will need to ensure that his banking arrangements are convenient for expatriate payment arrangements, eg to ensure that making currency transfers etc is not too cumbersome or expensive. The employer may agree to reimburse incidental banking charges.

Hedging

7.76 Where the costs of employing people are incurred in one currency but borne by the employer in another, the employer may be able to 'hedge' these costs commercially in the same way as for other international currency transactions. So, for example, if an employee is sent to the Eurozone with a salary of Euro 200,000 a year, it may be possible for the employer to 'fix' the US dollar value of that salary cost by entering into a commercial hedging contract with a third party.

Trap

7.77 Beware the temptation to increase pay when host currency falls and an employee loses out: the employee may 'win' when the host currency rises again and it may then be hard to reduce salary. In many countries, it is difficult to either retain discretion to vary pay unilaterally or make deductions, even when this is expressly agreed.

Independent financial advice

7.78 Employees can be adversely affected not only by the impact of currency fluctuations on remuneration but by longer term impact on savings, pension etc. Wise (and unregulated) employers generally avoid taking responsibility for employees' personal financial affairs, and most would encourage employees who may have concerns about pension, investments, etc to seek their own independent financial advice. (See Chapter 22 on employee perspectives.)

Equality

7.79 As with other terms, employers should keep an eye to discrimination laws, particularly where 'expatriates' and 'locals' are employed by the same employer in the host country. It is worth asking whether there is a good commercial – and lawful – reason for treating people with different home countries differently? (See Chapter 12 on equality.)

TAX

Tax equalisation and tax protection

7.80 Many expatriates are offered tax equalisation and tax protection arrangements, particularly for long-term assignments. This is because it is accepted that the employee will be most concerned about net pay and that, even if he is provided with third party tax advice, he will want some comfort about the sums he will actually receive.

7.81 The terms 'tax equalisation' and 'tax protection' are not usually used to describe the same thing. A tax equalisation arrangement is usually where the employee is promised that he will be in the same net position after deduction of income tax, as if he had remained an employee subject to the home country's (or another country's) tax regime. Tax protection is where the employee is promised that he will be no worse off than he would have been if he had remained subject to the home country's (or another country's) tax regime. Tax equalisation offers a potential upside for the employer, whereas tax protection does not.

7.82 The documents should clearly explain what has been promised. This is an area where there is often dispute – and where the outcome of a disagreement is often a decision by the employer to pay extra money to the employee to 'put him right' in respect of a misunderstanding.

7.83 The employer will usually have a fairly clear idea of what the intended tax equalisation or protection arrangements are, because the employer will have given the information to tax advisers or in-house payroll specialists to prepare the relevant calculations. However, the employer's intentions are often not clearly communicated to the employee. Typically, the employee will be given some numerical illustrations of the way that a tax calculation might be worked through, based on his remuneration package at the start of his assignment, but little or no attempt may be made to describe the promise clearly in writing. Where circumstances arise that are not dealt with by the illustrations, the correct calculation may be uncertain. For example, uncertainty may be caused by changes in the law, foreign exchange movements or changes to personal circumstances. Employers' preferences for detailed caveats to illustrations and carefully defined written promises in the employment contract documents vary.

7.84 The documents should clearly describe the payments that will be covered by the tax equalisation promise. Normally this would include basic salary. Thought should also be given to whether other payments, such as allowances, bonus and termination-related payments should be covered. The documents could also expressly confirm that certain things will not be covered, for example, share plans, the effects on tax rates of personal wealth, inheritance, etc. Some arrangements will take account of social security contributions and pension, some will not. This sounds simple but in practice it is easy to make mistakes with the drafting. Tax equalisation policies should ideally be drafted by lawyers and checked by expatriate tax specialists.

7.85 For example, if COLA is applied by way of percentage uplift to basic salary and basic salary is tax equalised, should tax equalisation apply to basic salary before or after the COLA is applied? The employment documents should make the employer's intentions clear.

7.86 A simple promise to pay the employee's tax on the relevant payments will usually be inappropriate. There is a risk that the tax may be regarded as pay too, and that tax would then be due on that tax as well.

7.87 The preferred method is usually to first calculate the 'hypothetical tax' (ie an estimate of the home country income tax, and sometimes social security contributions too, that would have been due if the employee had been an 'ordinary' home country employee). The tax equalised pay is then 'grossed up' so that after deduction of the real income tax due and relevant social security contributions, the net payment is the target sum (ie what the net pay would have been after deduction of 'hypothetical tax').

7.88 Care is needed to ensure that drafting reflects reality; that any sample calculations offered by way of explanation are consistent with written terms; and that the priority between illustrations and written terms are clear, in case of conflict.

7.89 Sometimes it is not immediately apparent that the employer is, in fact, offering two types of tax comfort to the same employee. For example, there may be a formal tax equalisation or protection policy that applies to salary etc and the employer may simply 'pay the tax' in relation to other, usually minor, benefits. Care should be taken to ensure that tax advisers and employment lawyers are aware of any additional less formal arrangements and that they are properly documented.

7.90 If tax equalisation or protection is offered and the employee's personal circumstances change this could affect the tax due (ie the employer could end up with a bigger bill). For this reason, the employer may ask the employee not to undertake certain activities and/or to inform the employer if he does so. Tax equalisation could be offered on the basis that certain events or personal circumstances are disregarded or on condition that the employee behaves in a particular way. For example, the employer may insist that the employee does not buy property in the host country; does not spend too long in his home country after the assignment begins; retains records to ensure that tax relief can be claimed efficiently; and/or co-operates in relation to preparation and submission of tax returns (see 7.93–7.97) etc. The employee may also be required to warrant that information he has provided that is relevant to tax is accurate.

7.91 The employee's social security or tax status may also change because of things beyond his control, for example, because the assignment has continued too long for him to remain in his home country social security scheme. Whether this has an impact on costs for the employer or employee will depend on how the tax equalisation promise has been framed.

7.92 As with most benefits, the employer should check mandatory legal requirements before offering tax equalisation or tax protection. In some circumstances these arrangements may not be permitted, or may need to be modified to reflect applicable laws.

Tax returns and record keeping

7.93 Both employer and employee will have an interest in ensuring that tax returns are prepared correctly and filed promptly. Employers often offer expatriates professional help with preparing their tax returns. Typically, the employer nominates a multinational firm of accountants to prepare tax returns for its expatriate workforce.

7.94 The assistance offered by service providers and the employer's expectations for employee co-operation should be prescribed in the employment documents. The advice offered could be cost-limited. More likely, the employer will simply promise to meet the costs of the service and will negotiate with the provider directly on cost. If this is the case, the benefit may be offered subject to limits on the scope of the service provided or other conditions. For example, the employee may be required to provide relevant information and documents within a particular timetable and/or to submit returns on time. The service may not cover the effects of personal wealth, inheritance, sale of property (ie circumstances that may make the tax treatment more complex and the advice more expensive to provide). Assistance is not normally offered at the employer's expense to the expatriate's partner, who may also need to submit tax returns. If the employer wishes to retain some discretion regarding the scope of the assistance to be offered this should be confirmed in the documents.

7.95 Often more than one set of tax returns is required. This is almost always the case for the first and last tax years of the assignment but could apply throughout the assignment. Timing can be awkward if tax years for the home and host countries (and any other relevant country) do not coincide. For example, currently, the US federal tax year runs from 1 January to 31 December whereas the UK tax year runs from 6 April to 5 April each year.

7.96 Where the employee is potentially subject to more than one tax regime, tax advisers are likely to check whether the relevant countries have entered into a double tax treaty or international social security agreement (see **5.14–5.16**).

7.97 Offset of one country's tax against another's, assuming this option is available, may be applied retrospectively. The employer may be obliged to deduct and pay over tax to two different tax authorities in respect of the same income. The employee or employer may then need to apply for reimbursement of overpaid tax from the relevant tax authority. In some cases, this arrangement may apply until a simpler regime is cleared with/approved by the tax authorities. This creates some practical challenges. The documents could help reduce the impact on employer and employee. For example:

- the employer may lend the employee money to cover a temporary cash flow problem, in which case the documents should specify the repayment arrangements, including those that will apply if the employment ends earlier than expected or if the tax authorities refuse to reimburse;

- if the employee is covered by a tax equalisation or protection arrangement, the employer may be out of pocket because of the timing differences. The employer may need the employee's help to recover money from the tax authorities for the benefit of the employer, and repayments made by tax authorities are often delivered directly to employees. The documents could confirm that the employee must assist with any application to the tax authorities for reimbursement; keep the employer informed of progress; and pay over any tax repaid by tax authorities to the employee to the employer promptly;

- the documents could be used to clarify currency issues, eg tax reimbursed may not have the same value when repaid, due to currency shifts;

- the documents could confirm the employee's obligations to keep records (eg to record the number of days spent in different countries, see **5.8–5.13** on the importance of 'day counting') and disclose those records to the employer;

- since tax returns, assistance with reclaiming overpaid tax, etc are likely to be required after the employment ends, the documents should ensure that obligations to co-operate etc clearly continue to apply after the employment ends (this should also be considered if a severance agreement is required. See also Chapter 16 on ending the assignment generally); and

- the employer may reserve a right to make deductions from the employee's pay in the event that required co-operation is not provided.

US employees

7.98 US citizens and holders of US green cards are generally taxable on their Worldwide income. This means, for example, that if a US national is assigned from one EU country to another, US tax treatment would need to be considered as well as the home and host country tax regimes. Federal, state and local taxes may be due.

PENSION AND LIFE ASSURANCE

7.99 Employment documents should confirm the pension arrangement that will apply during the assignment. Normally the details will be confirmed in the employment contract but they may, in some cases, be included in a 'residual contract' (see the Glossary at Appendix 3).

7.100 The contract should normally confirm:

- whether the plan is a money purchase/defined contribution or final salary/defined benefit plan (see the Glossary at Appendix 3);
- the name of plan;
- the rates at which contributions are to be made by employer and by employee (and if they are made by reference to a percentage of pay, the contract should clearly confirm whether this is, eg, basic salary, pre-COLA salary, or notional salary);
- the intervals at which contributions will be paid;
- any flexibility the employer may have to change, replace or withdraw the arrangements;

- a warning that there may be mandatory rules limiting what is possible (eg a cap on contributions set by tax authorities); and
- a warning that continued participation may not be permitted throughout the assignment and confirmation of the arrangements that will apply if participation ceases to be possible under the plan rules or legislation (eg that no alternative benefit would be provided if that is the case);
- whether tax equalisation or tax protection may apply to pension and, if so, how that will work.

The employer may also consider including caveats or warnings relating to the potential impact of relocation on accumulation of funds in the plan or on draw down of pension. US assignees, in particular, should be encouraged to seek independent advice in relation to the impact of relocation on their investments etc, as early as possible and in any event before leaving the US.

7.101 See 10.30–10.61 on mandatory employment laws. Some countries require that the employee and/or employer makes mandatory pension contributions.

7.102 Costs may be recharged through an inter-company expatriate supply agreement.

7.103 Cross-border pensions rules are very complex and are best left to the specialists. Some awareness of the potential application of EU cross-border pension funding rules is helpful and particularly of the potentially very expensive consequences of getting this wrong. Do not allow an employee to remain in a home country pension plan whilst overseas without checking with a pensions specialist first. Given the complexity, sums involved and the potential for problems to only become apparent after a long period of time, pension clauses should always be checked by appropriate pension specialists. In particular, whether the employee is able to stay in the home company plan during the assignment should be checked.

7.104 Life assurance arrangements are often linked to pension. The effect of the assignment on existing life assurance arrangements provided by the employer should be checked too.

7.105 If the employee has taken out his own life assurance cover (eg by way of 'top up' to the cover offered by his employer) then the employee should be encouraged to check that the policy will not be prejudiced by the assignment. As above, the employee should be encouraged to seek independent advice regarding his personal financial circumstances. See also Chapter 22 on employee perspectives.

SHARE PLANS

7.106   Share plans are usually documented separately from core employment contract documents.

7.107   Expatriate employment contract documents may, eg:

- document the fact that the expatriate is not eligible to participate in particular plans;
- clarify the application of tax equalisation or tax protection arrangements;
- warn the employee of the potential impact of relocation on grant, vesting, exercise etc;
- clarify the impact of termination.

7.108   See also **15.9–15.15** on share plans more generally.

BENEFITS-IN-KIND

7.109   Expatriates usually receive a greater range of benefits-in-kind than local hires. There may be a variety of reasons for this, including, for example:

- preconceived ideas held by the employer and/or employee about what an expatriate should expect;
- the employer's wish to provide comfort to the employee (eg the employee may have no realistic idea of what accommodation might cost so confirmation that suitable accommodation will be provided may be reassuring);
- to save the employee time, particularly at the outset of the assignment, so he can focus on his job;
- to save tax or social security contributions (eg if a more beneficial tax treatment is available for a benefit-in-kind than for an allowance or salary);
- to control costs (eg where the employer has greater purchasing power than individual employees because it provides similar benefits, such as medical insurance, to a number of employees);
- to ensure that the employee's status in the host country is not adversely affected by his personal spending patterns (eg by providing a prestigious car or accommodation at a smart address to impress customers);
- to provide the benefit where the employee would not be able to secure it all (eg because a local landlord would be reluctant to let property to a family newly arrived from overseas or because the ordinary waiting list for club membership is too long).

Family

7.110 As many benefits will be provided for the employee's family it can be helpful to define the family members who will receive the relevant benefits. For example, benefits may only be provided by reference to a partner and children under the age of 18 who live with the expatriate.

7.111 As for immigration purposes, the employer should take care to ensure that it understands who the employee regards as his family, their ages and their relationships to him. For example, the employee may have stepchildren, adopted children, children who do not live with him (perhaps because of divorce), children who live with him but are not his natural, step or adopted children (eg his partner's children) and/or elderly dependants. The employee may have a spouse or civil partner or be cohabiting. It may be helpful to understand the partner's role, for example, whether the partner intends to seek new employment in the host country or look after children.

7.112 See also **15.73–15.99** on data protection.

Accommodation

7.113 Rented accommodation is often offered as a benefit to longer-term assignees. Sometimes the employer will buy a property for the use of expatriates, but this is not common.

Suitable accommodation

7.114 The accommodation offered will need to be suitable for the employee's role. For example, if the employee is to have a senior management and/or marketing role he may need to use his home for business entertainment. The impact of the employee's home on his status may be greater in the host country than might be the case at home.

7.115 Any family members that will travel with the employee should be taken into consideration. The employer and/or the relocation agent assisting the employee will need to understand more than just the number of family members. For example, if the employee has school age children he may need to be near a local school, whereas if the children are at boarding school or living with a former partner, considerations will be different. If an elderly or disabled dependant lives with the expatriate then the family may have additional needs. In some locations it may be appropriate to take account of the need to accommodate domestic staff. (See also **15.73–15.99** on data protection issues relevant to the provision of this information to third party and overseas destination service providers.)

7.116 Pets can be important to an expatriate and his family. Even if the employer will not pay for the costs of transport, temporary kennels and/or quarantine, pets may need to be taken into consideration when accommodation is chosen. For example, the family may want a garden and some landlords do not allow pets.

7.117 Of course, the employer does not need to accommodate the employee's every wish but the expatriate and the employer should be clear about the 'deal' from the outset so that the expatriate and family members do not subsequently feel let down and costs do not creep up.

7.118 Security can be an issue and the employer may insist that the employee and his family live in accommodation with satisfactory security. For example, the employer may insist that the employee lives in a gated expatriate 'compound' or a particular part of town.

7.119 The employer may discuss the matter with a specialist relocation agent and set an appropriate budget, and then let the relocation agent help the employee to find appropriate accommodation within the budget.

7.120 The expatriate documents should confirm the promises made.

Cost

7.121 Accommodation is often the most expensive benefit that the employer provides to an expatriate and it is usually worth taking some steps to control costs.

7.122 Tax relief may be available, and this would typically be subject to conditions. The employer should make enquiries before the arrangements are agreed, as the tax regime may play a part in helping the employer to make basic decisions that may be difficult to reverse, such as whether the employer should take out the lease or the employee should take out the lease and whether the employer should pay an allowance or reimburse expenses.

7.123 Sometimes it is cheaper for the employer to provide accommodation on a long lease arrangement. However, if the assignment terminates early this can create difficulties. There may be a substantial penalty to pay if the lease is terminated early. Sometimes it is possible to allocate the vacated property to another expatriate but, in practice, 'matching' available properties with the small pool of employees who may be suitable tenants may be difficult. It may be helpful to note renewal dates, so that the assignment can be reviewed in advance and the risk that a decision to end the assignment will be made shortly after a renewal date is reduced.

7.124 Terms should be clearly documented, particularly if special terms are included to control costs or to apply on termination of employment. This should not only reduce the risk of dispute but should also help anyone who later needs to review the arrangements or provide related advice to understand the current position easily. For example, if the employment documents confirm whether the lease is in the employer's or employee's name that may make things easier for those who later manage termination of the employment on short notice (when it may be difficult to access information from host country employees discretely). It may also be helpful to retain a copy of the lease with the employment documents in the home country, subject to data protection rules.

Payment arrangements

7.125 Documents should make the payment arrangements clear. For example, documents should make the following clear:

- whether the employer or employee will be responsible for payment of any deposit, the amount of the deposit and to whom it should be returned by the landlord;
- whether rent will be paid in advance or in arrears and the intervals at which payments will be made;
- whether rent payments will be made by the employer or the employee (and if the payment is being made by the employer, whether it is being made on behalf of the employer or employee);
- whether the employer will offer any guarantee to the landlord regarding payment of rent by the employee;
- whether the employee must vacate the property at the end of the employment and/or assignment (and any time-limits for doing so);
- whether there are any early termination provisions and whether the employer or employee must meet the cost of penalty payments (this may depend on who is responsible for early termination of the assignment);
- who will pay for any damage to the property;
- whether the employer has a right to make deductions from sums due to the employee from the employer if the employee does not honour his obligations.

7.126 If any terms are confirmed both in the lease documents and the employment documents, care should be taken to ensure that the terms in the employment contract are consistent with the terms of the lease. Care should also be taken if special host country rules apply to the lease of property linked to employment.

Utilities and other accommodation–related bills

7.127 The employee will need basic utilities, for example, gas, electricity and internet, etc. There may also be insurance premiums, connection charges, property taxes, refuse or service charges to pay. It may be difficult for the employee to make the necessary arrangements. The documents should refer to the relevant utilities specifically so that the items covered are clear and make responsibility for payment of expenses, and whether the employer will reimburse the expenses if the employee pays, clear. The arrangements relating to any deposit should also be made clear. There may be liabilities for the employer if the employee leaves the country without paying his bills and this may need to be taken into consideration. For example, the employment documents could provide for offset of outstanding amounts against final pay.

Home country accommodation

7.128   The employer may provide the employee with assistance in relation to his home country property. For example, the employer may help with fees charged by a letting agency. Conditions may be attached to any assistance provided.

7.129   The employee may be required to make reasonable efforts to rent out his home country property and inform the employer of any rent received, and the employer may sometimes make adjustments to pay or benefits to take that into consideration. Third party data, rather than actual rental income, may be used to assess the appropriate adjustment. As with COLA, additional care should be taken if there is to be a negative adjustment to remuneration because the employee rents his home country property. Normally it is better for this to 'reduce' salary than for the adjustment to take effect by way of 'deduction' (see 7.43–7.47 on 'negative COLA'). In practice, adjustments for home country rental income are not common.

7.130   In many cases the arrangements in relation to the employee's home property are left to the employee.

Car

7.131   Expatriates are often provided with a car or a car allowance. Issues arising from the provision of a car are likely to be similar to those that arise with local hires, except that some issues may have more significance. For example, the type of car may be more closely linked to the employee's status and/or be of more concern to managers of similar status in the host country.

7.132   The expatriate may also need to buy or rent an additional car for the use of his family during the day. The employer or its agent may help the expatriate to meet local requirements.

7.133   If it is important for the employee to drive himself to work or for his partner to drive during the day some thought should be given to driving licence arrangements in the host country. The employee and his partner may be able to drive on their home country licences for a while. There may be a requirement to obtain a host country or international licence immediately or after a period of time. If there is likely to be any delay before licences are granted the employee and his partner may wish to apply for the licences before they leave home. In some countries restrictions on the age or sex of drivers may be surprising, so requirements should be checked as early as possible and before arrangements are confirmed in the employment documents.

7.134 A driver may be offered as a benefit or business necessity. For example, a driver could provide additional security, know the area better, be able to ensure that parking difficulties do not affect the employee's work or to support the employee's status. See **7.135** on domestic staff more generally. If the expatriate is likely to want to be able to drive the car himself in the evening, the expatriate may still need a local driving licence, insurance cover, etc even if a driver is supplied for business use.

Domestic staff

7.135 In many host countries domestic staff will be expected. These might include a cook, gardener, cleaner, driver and/or security guard. The employee may be expected to make his own arrangements but sometimes the employer may assist, for example, by facilitating the transfer of domestic staff from an outgoing expatriate to an incoming expatriate, advising on local employment requirements or employing the staff directly. Where the employer helps it will need to ensure that the identity of the employer of the domestic staff is clear; that their employment arrangements (including termination arrangements) are consistent with the arrangements for the assignment; and that it is clear whether the costs of employment will be borne by the employee or employer.

Clubs

7.136 Local practices vary enormously but in some host locations membership of a social club may be appropriate and/or expected. The club may provide access to sports facilities, an opportunity to meet other expatriates and/or to entertain clients. The employer might bear the membership costs and provide assistance with joining arrangements (eg waiting lists or the need for current members to support the employee's application for membership). Given the overall costs of an expatriate assignment a contribution towards the costs of keeping the family happy may be money well spent. The employer's involvement may also give the employer the opportunity to direct the employee towards an appropriate choice of club, for example, a club where the employer's other expatriate employees are members.

Education

7.137 If a long-term assignment is proposed to an expatriate with school age children, the children's education may be critical to whether the expatriate will accept the assignment. Anecdotal evidence and survey data suggest that concern about schooling is one of the most common reasons for refusal to relocate.

7.138 The employer might, for example, provide assistance with locating suitable local schools, provide a financial contribution towards school fees, or help with any deposit required.

7.139   Care should be taken to ensure that the terms on which assistance is provided are clear. For example, the following might be clarified:

- whether nursery care will be provided (this may be a particular issue if the expatriate's partner intends to work and nursery care is free in the home location);
- the age ranges covered;
- whether the promise is being made in relation to named children or whether a change in circumstances may change the scope of the promise (in practice a change leading to increased cost for the employer is unlikely as if new children are born these will rarely reach school age before the assignment is over. However, eg, divorce or remarriage may affect the employee's responsibilities);
- whether the child must live with the expatriate to benefit from the education;
- whether tertiary education is covered;
- whether the employer will pay or reimburse fees;
- whether related items such as uniforms, books, exam fees, music lessons, etc will be covered;
- whether there will be a financial cap on fees, or the choice of school and/or items covered will be prescribed;
- what will happen when school fees increase;
- what would happen if termination of employment took place part way through the school year;
- whether the employer will pay any deposit or offer any guarantee in relation to the payment of fees by the employee;
- what happens if the employee wants or needs his children to change schools;
- if the employee's children are to be educated in the home country whether flights between the home and host countries will be provided/reimbursed for the children and/or a parent (and if so how often and whether this covers half-term breaks and children in tertiary education too).

Language and cultural awareness training

7.140   The employer may provide assistance with language training before and after the assignment begins. The employer may wish to clarify the following:

- when the training will be provided;
- whether approved training will be provided or a contribution to costs;
- which family members, if any, training will be provided for;
- any requirement to reimburse the employer, eg, if a specific standard is not reached or on 'voluntary' termination.

7.141 The employee, and his family, may also be offered cultural awareness training. Typically, this would be provided, at least in part, before the assignment begins. Attendance is likely to be compulsory. See also **12.35** on equality and cultural awareness training.

7.142 Where there is a host country employer, particular attention should be given to whether costs should be borne by employee, host company or home company (eg because of potential tax implications).

WORKING TIME AND HOLIDAY

7.143 Many countries have mandatory employment laws that limit the times at which employees can work (see **8.24–8.38** and **10.30–10.61** regarding mandatory laws).

7.144 For example, the EC Working Time Directive 2003/88/EC (WTD) currently requires EU countries to ensure that employees enjoy a minimum of four weeks' holiday a year; limit working time to an average of 48 hours per week; and ensure that minimum rest breaks are taken. Each EU country will have implemented the WTD in a different way, and some countries may offer greater protection to employees than others.

7.145 Even where there is no legislation on working time (which is unlikely) local practices may dictate the hours that employees normally work whilst in the host country.

7.146 In most, but not all, countries the 'weekend' will include Saturday and Sunday. In some countries work on a Saturday morning may be expected. In Muslim countries Friday may be the most important day of rest and Sunday may be a working day. If a different weekly working pattern will apply, it is worth checking with the employee at an early stage that the change will not cause a problem, for example, because of the employee's religion or the religion of a family member. In some jurisdictions the normal working week does not coincide with the school week.

7.147 Typically, the employee will be expected to take host country public holidays during the assignment, instead of home country public holidays, and to work host country office hours. The number of days that are offered as public holidays can vary considerably between countries. Compare eight public and bank holidays in England to a minimum of 12 in Hong Kong and then consider that the English weekend normally includes Saturday as well as Sunday, whereas in Hong Kong working all or part of Saturday may be normal. In some countries public holidays will be compulsory and in others they will be optional. Within the host country applicable days may also vary between locations.

7.148   The documents should always make clear whether home or host public holidays will apply during the assignment and it is usually prudent to confirm the number of days and which days will be given. If public holidays are not given on critical days for the employee, for example, Christmas for a Christian employee, then it should be possible to confirm that the employee would be allowed to take annual holiday on those days.

7.149   The following website is a helpful (multilingual) source of information about other countries' public holidays, see www.bank-holidays.com (there are a variety of online resources of this type and accuracy has not been checked). In practice, the best sources of reliable information about the days people will expect to take as holiday are usually host company employees or host country advisers.

7.150   The rate at which annual holiday accrues may also change for the assignment, for example to reflect an increased number of public holidays, mandatory host country laws or to achieve parity with the local workforce. Care should be taken with transitional arrangements, for example, in relation to holiday that has accrued before the assignment begins and ends and the treatment of travelling days. Many employers offer extra days at the start and/or end of the assignment to help the employee settle in. Administration is likely to be a more significant concern where there is a change of employer for the duration of the assignment, ie for host employment arrangements.

7.151   Care should also be taken with the administrative arrangements for holiday. The employer should understand whether the employee should be required to take holiday or whether it is permitted for the employee to forfeit holiday or be paid in lieu of holiday that is not taken. Holiday rules may be set out in collective agreement or legislation and, if this is the case, the employer will need to decide whether to duplicate the current rules (see Chapter 17). In some jurisdictions it may be important to clarify the remuneration that will be taken into consideration for the purposes of determining holiday pay.

7.152   Vocabulary can be important too. Some terms related to the calendar can mean different things in different contexts. For example, Good Friday may fall on a different date in Greece than in Spain. Even a 'year' can have different start and end days in different countries.

7.153   Documents should confirm:

- normal hours and days of work;
- any mandatory requirements in relation to overtime/hours of work;
- whether any relevant collective agreement will apply;
- the number of days' annual holiday;
- transitional arrangements at the start and end of assignment if the number of days' annual holiday for the assignment is different from the number of the days that will apply before or after the assignment;

- any special arrangements to accommodate religion etc;
- arrangements for taking holiday (NB approval by employer);
- public holidays that will apply (by reference to the specific location if they vary across the country);
- whether holiday can be carried forward from year to year;
- what will happen to accrued holiday on termination of the assignment and/or employment.

7.154 Take care to check overtime rules with employment law specialists, particularly in the host country. Payment for overtime may be compulsory and ignoring the rules could lead to expensive claims, particularly on termination. If advice is taken early it is often possible to draft remuneration clauses in a way that significantly reduces this risk.

SICKNESS, HEALTH AND SAFETY AND INSURANCE

7.155 See **15.21–15.28** and **15.59–15.67** on sickness and health and safety.

7.156 The employer may consider covering the following in the employment documents:

- an obligation on the employee to ensure that the employee, and relevant family members, receive appropriate vaccinations at the appropriate times before departure and during the assignment;
- a right to recall the employee if the assignment becomes too dangerous (a short notice period for termination of the assignment would probably be sufficient if the employee is on a home company employment arrangement. If there is a host country employer the employer may include a provision allowing the employer to terminate the employment if the assignment becomes too dangerous);
- an express requirement to comply with health and safety policies and any particular security requirements, for example, insurers' requirements or to attend a security briefing arranged through specialist third party providers;
- provision of additional life assurance, death-in-service, accident, travel or 'SOS' emergency cover;
- provision of medical insurance cover (see further below);
- an obligation to submit to medical examination, subject to local laws and/or an obligation on the employee to procure that his family also submits to examination, or perhaps a link between provision of family medical cover and their submission to examination;
- a right to insist that the employee (and/or his family) undergoes appropriate medical treatment or examination in the home country (this may be linked to insurance cover).

Private medical insurance

7.157 Private medical insurance cover is almost always offered to long-term assignees. Even if they qualify for treatment under a free host country arrangement, the treatment available may not be of a quality that the employee and/or employer consider acceptable, or provision may be subject to stringent conditions.

7.158 Sometimes more than one policy applies. For example, the employee may be offered a combination of 'local' cover for minor matters and 'international' cover for others. Care should be taken to ensure that policies are compatible.

7.159 Care should be taken with pre-existing conditions, given the potential for policy change both at the start and end of the assignment.

7.160 Employees assigned from one EU country to another will usually be encouraged (or required) to apply for a European Health Insurance Card (EHIC) (see the Glossary at Appendix 1 for more detail) but medical insurance cover will usually be provided as well. (Note the potential impact of Brexit on EHIC arrangements.)

7.161 It may be helpful to ensure that assignees from the UK are aware of up to date NHS eligibility rules. British assignees may be surprised to learn that they may not be eligible for free treatment during holidays at home. Similarly, if there are restrictions on holiday cover those should be made clear, eg some policies do not cover treatment in the US. It may be more convenient to provide this information separately.

7.162 The documents could specify:

- whether the employer may change the arrangements (eg by substituting a different provider or to reflect change to the insurer's terms);
- which family members will be covered (and any age restrictions);
- the grade of cover provided (if, eg, the provider offers different levels of cover);
- whether maternity is covered (for the expatriate herself or a partner);
- whether holidays and business trips are covered;
- whether the employee is required to contribute to the costs of the cover;
- whether the employee can choose the place of treatment;
- whether the employer can insist the individual travels home for treatment;
- whether provision of cover is subject to any additional conditions (eg family cover could be subject to the co-operation of family members);

7.163 See **15.73–15.99** on data protection and **15.67** on dangerous assignments.

CORPORATE REGULATORY CONSTRAINTS

7.164 In addition to protective employment laws, a wide range of regulatory constraints may apply to remuneration. The detail is beyond the scope of this book. However, it is worth being aware of the following.

- Corporate governance laws and guidelines are most likely to apply to the remuneration of directors of listed companies. There may, eg, be:
  (i) limits on the remuneration that can be awarded;
  (ii) limits on the form in which remuneration can be delivered;
  (iv) reporting obligations;
  (iv) approval requirements.
- A wide range of laws and guidelines apply to senior employees working in the financial services sector, particularly in the EU. These may, for example, restrict the employer's freedom to award bonus or require provision for 'malus' or 'claw-back' arrangements.
- Most companies are governed by company laws and a 'constitution' (eg in the UK the Memorandum & Articles of Association). Any award of remuneration should take account of those requirements. For example, there may be a need for the Board of Directors or a supervisory board or remuneration committee to approve a director's remuneration or contract.
- See **6.12** on commercial agents.

TOP TIPS FOR DOCUMENTING EXPATRIATE REWARD

7.165

- **Why are you documenting the employee's remuneration?** For example, are you aiming to set employee expectations, to persuade the employee to accept the assignment, to reduce the risk of dispute or clarify the arrangements for a public authority? (See Chapter 2 on the purpose of the documents.) Does your document deliver on this?
- **Don't forget the family:** if family 'buy in' is necessary to make the assignment work, make sure the documents clearly confirm the things that will interest them.
- **Get the employer right:** Make sure remuneration clauses support the correct employer's identity. (See Chapter 4.)
- **Consider options for protecting the expatriate's 'buying power':** For example, COLA, tax equalisation, currency-related terms etc. (See **7.68–7.92** above.)
- **Is any tax relief available?** Has your expatriate tax adviser checked that the documented arrangements meet the relevant requirements? Are there any other options?
- **Draft carefully:** getting remuneration clauses wrong can cost a lot of money. Don't, for example, attempt to draft a tax equalisation policy if you do not have the necessary expertise.

- **Think about the future**: consider highlighting downsides to the employee to reduce risk (or consciously accept the risk and set internal expectations accordingly); encourage the employee to seek independent advice; build in caveats and flexibility where appropriate; and try to anticipate potential problems, eg, the impact of early termination on accommodation costs or the birth of another child on education costs. See also Chapter 16 on mitigating termination risk.

- **Can the employee help?** If the employee can do practical things to make things easier for the business or reduce cost or risk, eg, by providing tax advisers with information in good time or keeping receipts, consider providing for this in the document and/or making a benefit conditional on assistance being provided.

- **Be mindful of equality laws:** See Chapter 12.

- **Check local employment laws (and collective agreements) upfront:** Most jurisdictions have legislation protecting employee's pay. Make sure the arrangements are checked locally so that there are no surprises, eg, a requirement to deliver a 13th month payment, a prohibition on share plans or retaining some types of employer 'discretion', or complicated rules relating to deductions from wages and recovery of overpayments from employees.

- **Prioritise:** If you don't have the time or specialist advice needed to get everything absolutely right, make sure you prioritise appropriately. (See Chapter 17 on getting the best from your advisers.)

- **Check the facts and make sure your documents reflect them!**

- **Check the facts again regularly** and make sure the documents are kept under review and updated where appropriate. (See **15.105–15.120** on changing terms.)

CHAPTER 8

PRACTICAL THINGS TO BE COVERED BY DOCUMENTS

INTRODUCTION

8.1   This chapter, and Chapter 7 on pay and benefits, provide some information about practical things that should normally be covered in documents for an expatriate assignment.

8.2   The documents needed might include:

- an employment contract (eg one contract document, or perhaps a base contract and an assignment letter to go with it);
- an agreement between the employee and host company where the home company is the employer (covering, eg, confidentiality);
- a residual contract between the employee and the home company where the host company is the employer (covering, eg, return home); and/or
- an inter-company expatriate supply agreement (covering, eg, recharging arrangements between the home and host companies).

See Chapter 6 for a more detailed explanation of the documents that would normally be needed for the chosen employment structure.

8.3   Many of the practical things to be covered by the employment contract will be the same, or similar, regardless of whether there is a home or host country employer during the assignment. This applies particularly to the pay and benefits arrangements described in Chapter 7.

8.4   This chapter provides information about some of the other terms that are special to expatriates, and that should normally be documented in an employment contract. The terms may need to be adapted to reflect the kind of employment arrangement that has been set up (home, host, dual, etc) but the issues to be covered will be similar.

8.5   Appropriate terms will also depend on the purpose of the particular document being prepared. This chapter includes some explanation of these differences.

8.6   In particular, this chapter covers the following:

- Employment contract/assignment letter (**8.7–8.61**).
- Residual contract (**8.62–8.72**).
- Inter-company expatriate supply agreement (**8.73–8.83**).

It may be helpful when reading this chapter to refer to the checklists at Appendix 1; the framework documents at Appendix 2 and Chapter 9 on assignment policies.

EMPLOYMENT CONTRACT/ASSIGNMENT LETTER

Contractual status

8.7   It usually saves time in the long run to start by thinking about the contractual status of the document being prepared. It may also be helpful to think about the following before starting to draft:

- the business purpose of the assignment and documents generally (see Chapter 2);
- the identity of the employer (see Chapter 4) and the relationships between the employee and the home and host companies (see Chapter 6);
- the length of the assignment (see Chapter 5);
- the nature of the document being prepared (ie what it is for and how it fits with the other documents being prepared; see Chapter 6);
- whether any previous contract(s) or arrangements will be varied, terminated, suspended or retained (see **6.14–6.23**);
- priority between different documents with the same subject matter in case of conflict (eg an existing employment contract that will be retained and a new home country assignment letter being prepared which are, together, to form the new employment contract); and priority between particular clauses and other documents (eg the tax equalisation clause in the contract being prepared and tax equalisation illustrations provided separately); and
- the status of related policies (see Chapter 9 on assignment policies).

See also checklist **A1.6** at Appendix 1 and framework document **A2.4** at Appendix 2.

Immigration

8.8   See **3.3–3.26** for explanations of some of the potential consequences of failing to obtain immigration permission; issues relating to the type of permission sought; accompanying family members etc.

Co-operation

8.9   Sometimes the employer will be responsible for making the application for immigration permission and sometimes the employee will. Occasionally, a host company that is not the employer will be responsible. Whatever the process, all parties will have an interest in ensuring that appropriate advice is obtained and that the applications are submitted properly. It is common for the employer to give the employee an assurance in the employment documents regarding its support and for the employee to agree to provide whatever co-operation and assistance is required (and to procure that accompanying family members co-operate too).

8.10   Co-operation is important not only at the start of the assignment but also during the assignment. Immigration laws can change; there may be a requirement for periodic checking of information or renewal of immigration permission; or there may be a change to the employment arrangements or the employee's status during the assignment that affects immigration permission (see **8.17–8.19** and **15.111**). The employer may wish to include a warranty regarding the accuracy of information provided by the employee in the documents (see **8.46–8.47**).

8.11   The employment documents may also include clauses requiring the employee to co-operate at the end of the assignment with immigration-related requirements, for example, by returning papers that may be required by the authorities, paying bills, and/or leaving the country within the appropriate timeframe. The employer may also consider imposing claw-back arrangements. See Chapter 22 on employee perspectives and claw-back.

8.12   The employer may require that the employee and his family maintain up-to-date passports, with an appropriate length of time before expiry. For some host countries second passports may be helpful (where it is possible to obtain them), eg, to facilitate regional travel where obtaining visas takes time.

Role and job title

8.13   Applications for immigration permission usually include information about the proposed role. (This information is likely to be important for other aspects of assignment planning too. For example, the duties and job title may determine whether particular mandatory employment laws apply, see **8.29–8.31**.) If there are immigration restrictions on the role the employee can take in the host country then the job title and duties specified in the employment contract (and reality) should be consistent with those restrictions. In some situations a more detailed job description may also help support the application for immigration permission.

Length of assignment

8.14 If immigration permission will only be given for a particular period, then the period of the assignment specified in the contract should be consistent with this. (See Chapter 5 for an explanation of some other factors that might be linked to the length of the assignment, in particular, tax and social security treatment of the employee's remuneration.) It is rarely appropriate to simply specify the maximum period the employee is likely to be allowed in the host country by the immigration authorities in the contract. Care should be taken when documenting assignment length. It is worth considering whether a fixed term assignment is intended; or a fixed term subject to earlier termination on notice; or whether the intention is simply to confirm the parties' expectations regarding assignment length. See **8.39–8.41** on the duration of the assignment and Chapter 16 on ending the assignment.

Pre-visits

8.15 Employees and their families will often visit the host country before the assignment begins and before a work permit or other immigration permission is granted. They may, for example, wish to meet colleagues or inspect potential schools or accommodation (see **3.13–3.16** on immigration risks associated with pre-visits).

8.16 In practice, it is unusual to document obligations in relation to pre-visits in the expatriate employment documents. If promises relating to airfares and/or hotel accommodation for an orientation trip will be recorded in the contract, care should be taken to ensure that the rationale for the visit is documented in a way that is consistent with immigration rules and the facts; that the appropriate company reimburses expenses; and that the documents take account of any available tax relief.

Activities that may affect immigration status

8.17 Most employers will anticipate the need for immigration permission before the start of the assignment. Immigration can also have an impact during the assignment.

8.18 Sometimes the employee's activities will affect his immigration status. For example, he may marry, divorce or purchase property in the host country. The employment contract could include restrictions on some of those activities and/or a requirement to report a change that may affect the employee's immigration status. Critical events for immigration purposes may also have tax and social security implications, so it is sometimes easiest to provide for reporting of potentially relevant changes together.

8.19 A change to immigration rules or the employer's actions might also affect immigration status. For example, a change to the employee's role could invalidate immigration permission or lead to a need for further approval.

Employers usually prefer to deal with these issues as they arise rather than give employees up front assurances in the employment documents in relation to potential change. (But see Chapter 18 on Brexit.)

Termination if immigration status changes

8.20   Generally, an employee will only be able to perform a particular job in the host country if he has the appropriate immigration permission. If, for any reason, that immigration permission is not granted as anticipated, or is withdrawn during the assignment, the assignment may need to end. If there is no other suitable job available, then the employment may need to end too.

8.21   It will usually be appropriate to include a term providing that maintenance of immigration permission is a condition of the assignment. The documents could provide for automatic termination of the employment (eg if the employer is the host company) or allow for termination of the employment by a home country employer on notice (or with payment in lieu of notice), if immigration permission is lost. An alternative might be to provide for loss of immigration permission to be treated as a summary dismissal event, entitling the employer to terminate the employment either immediately or on notice.

8.22   It is worth thinking about the impact of these sorts of terms on potential claims.

Whether providing for automatic termination of the employment or including other special terms to apply in the event that immigration status is lost reduces or increases the risk of disputes and claims will very much depend on the jurisdictions involved. For example, if there is a host country employment, the host country employment contract could provide for automatic termination, or summary dismissal, if immigration permission is lost (or the employment may end automatically under host country law, regardless of the terms of the contract). This may lead to the automatic revival of a residual contract with the home company (see **16.43–16.54**), depending on the terms of that contract. The residual contract may need to be terminated separately or the employee may be repatriated to work in the home country or re-assigned elsewhere. Potentially, the employee may make claims under either or both contracts (ie against the home and host companies).

UK

8.23   Whilst options for documenting the consequences of lost immigration status have been considered for years, this issue has recently attracted more interest in the UK because of uncertainty over the consequences of Brexit. Employers of employees who work in the UK should conduct pre-employment immigration checks. It is good practice to include clauses dealing with immigration status in employment documents for all employees who will work in the UK, ie for UK local hires as well as expatriates. Consistent practices generally reduce the risk of race discrimination claims. Options include:

- making offers of employment conditional on production of appropriate documents confirming a right to perform the relevant duties in the UK;

- asking the employee to warrant that information provided to the employer is accurate;

- inclusion of an express obligation to notify the employer of a change of immigration status, or potential change to status;

- making clear that ongoing employment is conditional on a right to do the work in the UK.

There may also be increased pressure from employees who are recruited to the UK for additional contractual comfort on matters such as the costs of immigration advice and the impact of loss of immigration status on repatriation assistance, bonus etc. See Chapter 18 on Brexit and Chapter 22 on employee perspectives.

Mandatory employment laws

8.24 See the Glossary at Appendix 3 for a description of 'mandatory employment laws'. Before the documents are prepared and the assignment begins, a host country employment law specialist should be asked to advise on whether any host country mandatory employment laws (including collective agreements) should be taken into consideration. Practically, it is important to ask about normal practices in the host country, as well as about mandatory requirements. Sometimes other countries' employment laws will be relevant too, for example, home country laws or the laws of a country of which the employee is a national. The host country employment lawyer should also be asked to check the final form documents before they are issued. In some circumstances it may be more efficient to ask the host country lawyer to prepare the first drafts (see **10.22** on governing laws and Chapter 11 on restrictive covenants). The following are examples of mandatory employment laws that may need to be accommodated in the employment documents.

Service dates

8.25 The application of mandatory employment laws in many countries is determined by reference to length of service. Sometimes the period of employment with the particular employer is critical. Sometimes the period of service within a group of companies will be more important. It is usually worth confirming the relevant dates in the documents, even where there is no legal requirement to do so. This reduces the risk of dispute later and will make it easier for a manager or adviser who has not been involved in setting up the assignment to get to grips with the facts quickly if this becomes necessary. The contract should normally confirm:

- the date on which employment with the employer for the assignment began;

- the date on which employment with the group began (an appropriate definition of 'group' would be needed); and
- the date the assignment will begin.

13th month payments

8.26 A host country requirement to provide bonus is surprisingly common. These bonus payments might, for example, be referred to as '13th month payments' or as 'Christmas' or 'New Year' bonus. Additional holiday pay or mandatory profit sharing arrangements may be required.

8.27 Mandatory employment laws may govern the way bonus arrangements are structured, as well as the amounts to be paid. For example, in a particular jurisdiction the employer may be free not to offer bonus but if the employer does choose to provide bonus the way in which the bonus is calculated and paid may be subject to legal rules.

8.28 Checking bonus requirements with a host country adviser in advance could save the employer money and avoid damage to relationships. If the employer knows whether additional payments must be made, or will be expected, and how they will be calculated, bonus could be offered in a compliant way, and the employer could take the additional bonus costs into consideration when setting salary. The employee's attention could be drawn to the total package so that he understands the value of the arrangements from the start. If the employer is not aware of the additional payments before salary is agreed, the additional payments may need to be made at an extra cost. Uncertainty may also arise in relation to the scope of any tax equalisation promise if the arrangements are not clear from the outset.

Effect of job title and duties on mandatory employment laws

8.29 Employment documents invariably provide some confirmation of the work the employee will be required to do. The specified job title and duties may have an impact on which mandatory employment laws apply. Many countries, particularly European countries, provide that different mandatory employment laws apply to different groups of people. For example, more senior (in the English sense) people in a managerial capacity may enjoy more or less protection than less senior workers (eg 'blue collar', clerical or factory workers).

8.30 In some countries, such as the UK, individuals holding the office of director can be employees too. In other countries individuals who hold an office are treated as a separate category and the rules relating to 'ordinary' employees may not apply to them.

8.31 The way the role is described in the documents could have an immediate impact on pay and benefits or on the size of any payments to be made on termination of employment. The role and job title can have other implications too (see, eg, **13.8–13.15** on corporation tax and **8.13** on immigration implications).

Collective agreements

8.32 Many countries, particularly Western European countries, implement mandatory employment laws by means of collective agreements. It is important to understand which collective agreement(s) will apply to the employee during the assignment so that the mandatory laws that apply to the employee are clear. It is usually helpful to refer to the relevant collective agreement(s) expressly in the documents to reduce the risk of dispute with the employee. This could also reduce the risk of someone managing termination at a later stage being unaware of the collective agreement. (See also **8.37** on the requirements of the Employment Particulars Directive.)

8.33 Sometimes, but rarely, it is possible to ensure that some or all of the terms of a collective agreement do not apply by agreement. Not all terms of all collective agreements are 'mandatory', some just provide a 'base line' which the employer and employee can move from by agreement.

8.34 Where a collective agreement sets out detailed employment terms that must apply it can sometimes be unhelpful and/or create additional risk if those terms are recorded in the employment contract as well. For example, the collective agreement may be amended so that it is out of line with the contract and/or the language may be different in translation. Usually it is best to follow local employment lawyers' recommendations on the form of the document, terms for inclusion, language and style.

8.35 Those who are not familiar with the way that collective agreements are used in many European countries may also wish to look at the explanation of 'collective agreements' in the Glossary at Appendix 3.

Sickness and other absence

8.36 Most countries have mandatory laws relating to sickness and other periods of absence from work. The documents could specify relevant arrangements taking those laws into account. For example, if host country laws provide for a long period of full pay during long-term sickness absence, the documents could record that, even if the detail would not normally be spelled out in individual contracts in the host country, see **8.32–8.35** on collective agreements. (See also **7.157–7.163** on private medical insurance, **15.64–15.66** on pre-assignment medicals, **15.21–15.28** on managing sickness absence generally, and the Glossary at Appendix 3 on 'European Health Insurance Cards').

EU – The Employment Particulars Directive

8.37 Directive 91/533/EEC on an employer's obligation to inform employees of the conditions applicable to the contract or employment relationship (the 'Employment Particulars Directive') applies to EU countries. (See the Glossary at Appendix 3 for a list of EU countries.) The Directive requires that employees should be provided with certain information relating to their employments, including, for example, information relating to:

- identities of the parties;
- place of work;
- job title or job description;
- the date the contract or employment began;
- expected duration if it is a temporary contract;
- holiday;
- notice details;
- remuneration and payment arrangements;
- working time;
- applicable collective agreements.

In practice, of course, prudent employers should include the information required by the Directive in the employment contract anyway. Article 4 of the Directive relates specifically to assignees and requires that additional information be provided before departure. (See **5.38–5.40.**) Potential amendments to this directive are currently under consideration.

Job title and duties

8.38 Some care should be taken to ensure that the job title and any job description specified are appropriate, as this can link to a number of other things. For example:

- immigration permission may depend on the employee's role. A description of that role may have been given to the immigration authorities before the assignment began or a copy of the employment contract may be required for the application (see **8.13**);
- the employee's role may have an impact on which mandatory laws apply (see **8.29–8.31**);
- the employee's role may have an impact on the tax and security treatment of the employee's remuneration because, for example, the role may have implications for the identity of the employer (see **4.80–4.85**);
- certain roles will have particular responsibilities that may need to be registered or powers of attorney may need to be granted to ensure the role is effective (see **13.26–13.29**);

- the role may give an indication of who benefits from the employment, which may have corporation tax or sales tax (VAT) implications (see **13.19–13.20** on sales taxes);

- the scope of the employee's duties (eg his authority to conclude contracts) may help determine whether a 'permanent establishment' has been established for corporation tax purposes (see **13.8–13.18** on corporation tax); and

- the documented role may restrict the flexibility of the employer, for example, to insist on a change to duties as the business evolves (**15.105–15.120**).

Duration of assignment

8.39 If the potential need to terminate the employment is not considered at the outset, opportunities to reduce the potential risks may be missed. Employers should always enquire about the mandatory employment laws and procedures for termination of employment likely to apply before an assignment begins. The following are examples of areas where the employment contract might include clauses to reduce the risks on termination of employment.

8.40 It may be easier to dismiss if:

- the individual is engaged on a fixed-term contract;
- the role meets certain criteria so that certain mandatory laws do not apply;
- compensation is fixed up front;
- notice or payment in lieu of notice is expressed in a particular way; or
- a particular redundancy policy is expressly disapplied.

8.41 The employment contract should:

- confirm the date on which the employee was first employed by a group company, the date on which employment with the current employer began and the date on which the assignment is to begin (see **8.25**);
- clarify the expected duration of the assignment (as mentioned earlier, it is worth considering whether a fixed term assignment is intended; or a fixed term subject to earlier termination on notice; or whether the intention is simply to confirm the parties' expectations regarding assignment length);
- include clear coordinated terms to facilitate termination of both the assignment and the employment, ie notice provisions (**16.43–16.59**);
- take account of mandatory laws, for example, in relation to the way notice must be served (**16.60**);
- be consistent with termination arrangements specified in other documents (eg a residual contract or an inter-company expatriate supply agreement);
- confirm repatriation arrangements (see **5.39** and **7.54–7.64**);
- clarify the effect of termination on benefits (eg bonus);

- include appropriate provision for garden leave or post termination restrictive covenants.

See also Chapter 16 on termination of the assignment and/or employment more generally.

Confidentiality, garden leave and post termination restrictions

8.42   See Chapter 11 for further details.

Business expenses

8.43   The arrangements for reimbursement of business expenses should be made clear. (See **4.95** on the need to ensure that the expense arrangements support the identity of the employer, **7.68–7.79** on currency and exchange rates and **7.28** on interaction with tax.)

Intellectual property

8.44   See **15.100–15.104** on intellectual property generally.

Data protection

8.45   The employee should give clear consent to the processing and transfer of employment data for the required purposes, including transfer of data between the home and host companies in the home and host countries. Please refer to **15.73–15.99** for a more detailed explanation of issues relating to international data transfer, particularly transfer of data outside the EU, as the employee's or family members' consents may not be sufficient to satisfy legal requirements. In practice, the employee should normally be provided with a separate document detailing the relevant data protection policy and consent should normally be dealt with voluntarily, separately from the employment contract.

Miscellaneous technical/practical clauses

Warranties

8.46   Many employers ask employees to give warranties in respect of information they have provided that the employer is relying on when offering a new employment. A common example would be a request for the employee to warrant that he is not subject to a contractual obligation to a third party, such as a former employer, that would prevent him from lawfully working for the new employer (ie the employer might seek assurance that a claim from an earlier employer in respect of breach of post termination restrictions is unlikely).

8.47   To ensure that an expatriate assignment runs smoothly, and lawfully, the employer will need the employee to supply information about himself and any family, not only at the start of the assignment but during the assignment too. Important things, such as favourable tax treatment and immigration permission, may depend on the accuracy of the information provided. The employer may ask the employee to warrant that some or all of the information supplied is correct and insist that the employee informs the employer promptly of any relevant changes. For example, the employer may ask the employee to warrant that he has certain qualifications or that he has not previously breached the immigration laws of the host country. The employer may wish to make clear that the employment may be terminated, or some other penalty may apply (eg disciplinary action), in the event of breach of warranty and/or that benefits such as tax equalisation, medical cover or immigration assistance are conditional on the provision of accurate information etc. (Note the potential application of 'penalty' clause rules and restrictions on claw-back of some immigration expenses in the UK.)

Translations

8.48 Some host countries insist that employment contracts, and other documents, are issued in the host country language. In others there may be a requirement to provide a translation of the contract in the host country language to the employee or public authorities. There may be a need for the translation to be certified as accurate in a particular way. (See 'apostille' in the Glossary at Appendix 3.) Although rarely an issue, in practice, with the type of senior expatriate referred to in this book, generally it is important to be able to demonstrate that the employee has received documents in a language that he understands.

8.49 Even where there is no legal requirement to prepare a translation, it will usually be convenient to have a translation ready in case of need.

8.50 The employment documents should confirm which language version is the authentic document and which is the translation prepared for convenience, so that if there is a conflict between the different language versions interested parties will know which version to rely on.

Choice of laws

8.51 Each employment document should include a clear statement confirming the laws that the parties agree will govern the contract. (See **10.3–10.29** on governing laws generally.) It may also be helpful to confirm the law that will govern non-contractual obligations (see Chapter 10).

8.52 It may be convenient to confirm which country's mandatory laws and/or collective agreements will apply too. Sometimes it may be appropriate to expressly confirm that some mandatory laws and/or collective agreements do not apply, for example, if it is possible to exclude the application of mandatory laws through the contract.

8.53 It may be helpful to include a statement confirming the agreed jurisdiction for disputes. Sometimes the parties' choice will be prescribed. (See **10.62–10.74** on jurisdiction.)

8.54 See Chapter 10 generally for explanations of issues relating to applicable laws and Chapter 11 on special considerations relating to post termination restrictive covenants.

Rights of third parties

8.55 Under English law, and some other countries' laws, third parties may have rights in relation to a contract concluded between an employee and his employer. For example, other group companies or family members may have an interest in the terms of the contract. They may have a legal right to be consulted about any change or their consents may be required to amend the agreement.

8.56 Whether it is helpful to include a clause that attempts to limit the rights of third parties will of course depend on the laws applicable to the contract etc. Such a clause should normally be included in employment contracts and severance agreements governed by English law. This is a more important issue for expatriate contracts than for domestic contracts, because of the range of benefits that family members usually enjoy.

Dual employments

8.57 Dual employments arise where the expatriate has two different employments with two separate employers. The expatriate will perform different duties for each employer. Typically, each employment will have a different geographical scope.

8.58 See **6.58–6.69** (including figure 6.4) for an explanation of the key features and structure of dual employment arrangements. Caution should be exercised if the arrangements are intended to reduce tax, see **6.58–6.69** and **4.114** on tax evasion.

8.59 The key things to bear in mind when drafting dual employment contracts are, first, that the two employments should be separate and, secondly, that each is, essentially, a part-time employment.

8.60 The following are examples of the ways that dual employments might differ from single employment arrangements.

- **Separate contracts:** The terms that relate to each employment should be confirmed separately in two separate employment contracts. Ideally, each employment contract should be based on the pro forma documents used for employees of the relevant employer.
- **Job title and duties:** The job title and duties for the particular employment should be clearly documented in each contract (ie these will be different in

each contract). These should be consistent with the actual duties, and the job title specified on business cards, emails and letters. It should be clear from the nature of the duties that they relate to the appropriate employment and that they will benefit the appropriate employer. The jobs must each have commercial reality.

- **Reporting lines:** Reporting lines to a representative of the appropriate employer should be confirmed in each contract.

- **Place of work:** The place(s) where the duties will be carried out should be made clear in each contract. If it is critical that duties are not performed in a particular country under one of the contracts that should be clear from the relevant employment contract.

- **Hours of work:** The clause confirming hours of work should reflect the reality of the two part-time jobs. Time may not be split on the same basis every week so it may be necessary to estimate the period of time spent on each employment.

- **Conflict:** It may be appropriate to include a clause acknowledging the existence of the other contract and dealing with potential conflicts, such as conflicting demands on the employee's time.

- **Holiday:** Annual holiday entitlement should usually be specified on a pro rata basis to reflect the part time nature of each employment. The arrangements for public holidays should be made clear.

- **Sickness:** Separate sick pay arrangements should be provided by each employer. Some thought should be given to how sickness should be reported and there should be no overlap between the responsibilities of the employers for paying sick pay.

- **Salary:** Salaries should reflect the time spent and duties undertaken for each employment. Remuneration does not normally need to be split on a rigid 'time spent' basis. Salaries should reflect the commercial reality of the arrangements.

- **Bonus:** If bonus is offered, separate arrangements should be offered for each employment to reflect the duties performed for that employer.

- **Benefits:** Benefit provision should be organised in an appropriate way, consistent with the apportionment of time between the two employers. If a particular benefit will only be provided by one employer (eg medical insurance cover or pension contributions) then this should be taken into consideration when the overall value of each remuneration package is assessed. Where benefits relate to salary (eg permanent health insurance/long term disability cover), they should normally refer to salary for the relevant employment only. The arrangements for life assurance may be linked to pension arrangements.

- **Place of payment:** If remuneration for an employment must be paid into a bank account in a particular country the arrangements should be confirmed in the relevant contract.

- **Tax:** Dual employments are more likely to be checked. The arrangements relating to the provision of tax advice, assistance with preparation of tax returns and the employee's obligations in that regard should be clarified. Tax equalisation or protection promises may sometimes be combined with dual employments.

- **Costs:** Employment costs for the relevant employment should be borne by each employer and this should be confirmed in the relevant accounts.

- **Administration:** Essential administrative obligations, such as keeping records of duties performed for the relevant employer and 'day counting' arrangements should be specified in each contract or reference should be made to appropriate policy documents or compliance with instructions for each employer. (See **5.8–5.13** on day counting generally and **19.40–19.42** on UK day counting.)

- **Expenses:** Each employer should reimburse expenses separately to the appropriate bank account. Particular care should be taken with the arrangements for reimbursement of expenses relating to travel between the two employments and the provision and use of credit cards.

- **Termination:** Termination provisions in the two contracts should not be linked. For example, one contract should not provide for summary termination in the event that the other employment ends. Each employment should be capable of standing alone and termination of one contract should not lead automatically to termination of the other. Each contract should provide for notices to be served on an appropriate representative of the relevant employer. Separate disciplinary procedures should apply. This could, potentially, mean that where fair and lawful dismissal is possible in respect of one employment that the employee cannot be fairly and lawfully dismissed from the other employment in relation to the same reasons at the same time. The employments should be independent and termination should be independent.

- **Signature:** Each employment contract should be signed by the appropriate employer representative for the relevant employment.

8.61 It is generally critical to the success of dual employments that the documents reflect the reality of the arrangements. See also **6.58–6.79** on why the business might choose to use dual employment arrangements; **4.71–4.107** on some of the facts that are likely to determine the identity of the employer; and **4.113** on the consequences of getting the identity of the employer wrong.

RESIDUAL CONTRACT

8.62 'Residual contract' is not a term of art. Here it is used to describe an agreement between the employee and the home company where the host company will be the employer. (See figure 6.3 and **6.46–6.47**, checklist **A1.9** at Appendix 1 and framework document **A2.5** at Appendix 2.)

The home return promise

8.63 Employees who agree to host employer arrangements are often offered comfort by the home company on the arrangements that will apply at the end of the assignment.

8.64 If the assignment is short term the home company may simply promise the employee that he can return to his old job with the home company when his assignment to the host company ends.

8.65 If the assignment is longer term then there will be more uncertainty. The employer's old home country job is unlikely to be kept open until the end of the assignment and may no longer be appropriate in any case. The home company's ability to offer alternative employment may depend on what is available at the time.

8.66 The residual contract could be used to provide some comfort on the arrangements that would apply if suitable home country employment or a new assignment were not offered. It is rarely appropriate to simply refer to a home country redundancy policy designed for local hires. That could, for example, cause problems with tax or conflict with host country laws. Sometimes it is possible to adapt the home country redundancy policy for ordinary home country employees to create a policy suitable for expatriates or to refer only to particular sections of the policy in the residual contract (eg sections relating to the size of redundancy payments and not tax or procedural sections).

8.67 Care should be taken to ensure that the documents do not inadvertently provide the employee with an opportunity to claim compensation from both the home company and the host company if both the employment and the assignment are terminated. (See **16.43–16.48**.)

8.68 See Chapter 16 generally on termination of the assignment and/or employment.

Benefits

8.69 The residual contract may also provide for continuation of some benefit arrangements (eg potentially pension, see **6.51–6.57** for an example).

Notional salary

8.70 See **7.10–7.11** on the purposes of a reference to notional salary. Essentially this is a hypothetical salary used for reference purposes. Those purposes might include the calculation of pension contributions or to keep the employee informed of the minimum salary that would apply to him at the end of the assignment. If pension and the return home are covered by the residual contract then, logically, confirmation of the initial notional salary and provision for review should be specified in the residual contract too. If notional salary is used for another purpose relating to the employment (eg as a reference point for tax equalisation) it would be more appropriate for the host employer to confirm and review notional salary.

Data protection

8.71 The residual contract may confirm the employee's consent to data processing by the home company and transfer of data outside the home country. Similar issues were considered at **8.45** in relation to the employment contract. (See also **15.73–15.99** on data protection generally.)

Notice and termination

8.72 As with any contract it is important to consider how the residual contract might be terminated if things do not work out. Usually a clause providing for termination of the residual contract by notice, to be given by either the employee or the employer is included. Care should be taken to ensure that the documented notice arrangements are consistent with those confirmed in other documents, for example, the host employment contract and the inter-company expatriate supply agreement.

INTER-COMPANY EXPATRIATE SUPPLY AGREEMENT

8.73 Before starting to draft an inter-company expatriate supply agreement it is worth thinking about the purpose of the agreement (see Chapter 6). The document is likely to be primarily there to confirm the structure of the employment arrangements (ie to support the identity of the employer). The arrangements for recharging employment costs between the two companies are likely to be critical, see further below. (See also checklist **A1.10** at Appendix 1 and framework document **A2.6** at Appendix 2.)

Which expatriates does it cover?

8.74 An inter-company expatriate supply agreement will usually only cover the arrangements between one particular home company and one particular host company.

8.75 The agreement may be prepared for one expatriate assignment.

8.76 Alternatively, the agreement may cover the assignments of several employees between the two companies. The relevant employees could be listed in the agreement and a mechanism for adding or removing particular employees to and from the list could be put in place.

8.77 Whether the agreement covers one or more employees is usually a question of convenience. It is unlikely to be appropriate to include employees employed by both the home and host companies in the same inter-company agreement (as that makes the drafting difficult to get right). Sometimes though a number of employees will be assigned on very similar employment terms and, in that case, one inter-company expatriate supply agreement might conveniently deal with all of them.

Identity of the employer

8.78 The agreement should expressly confirm the identity of the employer during the assignment. The other terms of the contract should support the choice made (see Chapter 4 on the identity of the employer generally).

Responsibilities

8.79 As with any contract for services, an inter-company expatriate supply agreement should specify the obligations of each party clearly. The agreement might include, for example:

- confirmation that the employer will deal with an employer's normal obligations, for example, employers' liability insurance, issue of an employment contract, deduction of appropriate tax and social security contributions, salary review, reimbursement of expenses to the employee, etc;
- an explanation of the respective responsibilities of home and host companies in relation to disciplinary and grievance issues;
- if the host company will assist a home country employer by administering payroll or expense arrangements on the home employer's behalf in the host country, those arrangements should be clarified;
- confirmation of the host company's responsibilities in relation to health and safety;
- responsibility and arrangements for obtaining immigration permission (**8.83**);
- responsibility and arrangements relating to data protection compliance (**8.81**).

Fees

8.80 The inter-company expatriate supply agreement should always document the arrangements relating to fees and disbursements. The agreement should for example clarify:

- the fees to be paid;
- whether the fee is expressed to include or exclude VAT;
- any arrangements for review of the fees;
- the intervals and timing of payment;
- invoicing arrangements;

- payment arrangements;
- currency and exchange rate arrangements;
- arrangements for dealing with disbursements if these are dealt with separately.

Sometimes the fees to be paid will be expressed as a percentage mark up on employment costs.

Intellectual property and data protection

8.81   See **15.100–15.104** on intellectual property. See **15.73–15.99** on data protection. In practice, where data protection laws will apply the data protection arrangements will be detailed and will normally have broader application than just one expatriate assignment. The inter-company expatriate supply agreement is therefore more likely to simply confirm both parties' compliance with the relevant arrangements, leaving the detail to another document.

Termination

8.82   The inter-company expatriate supply agreement should specify the arrangements for termination of the inter-company arrangements. The provision of the services should normally cease on the expiry of notice given by the home or host company to the other. The length of the notice period for the inter-company expatriate supply arrangements should be consistent with the notice required to terminate the assignment and/or employment specified in the employment contract. Immediate termination provisions may also be included to deal with serious breach of contract, loss of immigration permission, etc.

Immigration

8.83 The inter-company expatriate supply agreement could include clauses confirming the home and companies' responsibility for ensuring that the employee and relevant family members maintain the appropriate immigration permissions; a duty to inform the other party of any developments that may have an impact on immigration permission; and confirmation of the consequences of loss of immigration permission on the inter-company contract.

CHAPTER 9

ASSIGNMENT POLICIES

PRO FORMA EMPLOYMENT DOCUMENTS FOR ASSIGNMENT MANAGERS' CONVENIENCE

9.1   It is usually helpful for a business that frequently sends staff abroad to prepare detailed pro forma documents (eg assignment letter, inter-company expatriate supply agreement, etc) for the most common types of assignment for the business. The pro forma documents would set out the typical terms offered by the business. Assignment managers can then use their discretion to amend the documents for the particular assignment, ideally choosing between alternative options set out in the pro forma document (and taking account of advice specific to the assignment).

9.2   Even if the final version of an employment document varies from country to country, a consistent format will help assignment managers explain to advisers what they are looking for. Key terms are less likely to be forgotten (eg details of a benefit arrangement a host country adviser may not be aware of). Considerable time can also be saved by those managing assignments over time if the layout of the documents is consistent. For example, they will be able to find the key clauses quickly and more easily identify non-standard arrangements when they are reviewing documents or considering termination of employment.

9.3   The global mobility team may wish to prepare longer policy documents for their internal use, for example, to describe the 'standard' package being offered so that consistency can be maintained across the business. There will be more scope for explanation and looser language if documents are to be used internally by assignment managers, than if documents are prepared for delivery to employees. However, it is worth noting that even 'internal' guidance can provide evidence for the purpose of legal claims, eg discrimination claims.

EMPLOYMENT POLICIES

9.4   Development of a standard contract or handbook to apply rigidly to all expatriate staff is probably not an achievable goal. The variety of mandatory laws and other issues that need to be considered depending on the countries involved, purpose of the assignment and role would make that difficult, if not impossible. Some areas are particularly problematic because mandatory employment laws or public policy rules are more likely to apply and vary between countries. For example, this is likely to be the case for post termination restrictions (see Chapter 11); family policies and sickness absence (**15.21–15.28**); 'whistleblowing' (**15.47–15.58**); and data protection (**15.73–15. 99**).

9.5   It may be more helpful to document policies on matters that are likely to be less problematic, for example, providing information on benefits that are typically provided to all expatriates. So, for example, if international medical cover is provided to all of an employer's expatriates through one provider then it may be possible to produce a document setting out the applicable terms that can be given to all expatriate employees in the same form.

9.6   Sometimes if the policy has only two or three variations it can be helpful to specify each of the variations in one document, and to confirm to the particular assignee which version applies to him. For example, two policies could be developed on the provision of accommodation: the first to apply where the employer takes out the lease and the second to apply where the employee takes out the lease and expenses relating to accommodation are reimbursed to the expatriate by his employer.

9.7   Care should be taken when preparing the employment contract for a particular employee to ensure that relevant policy documents are clearly referenced and that the contract confirms whether or not the policy, or specific terms of the policy, apply to the employee.

9.8   The status of the policy should be made clear. The policy may, for example, be incorporated in the contract so that both employer and employee are bound by it or may be a document that the employee is required to comply with but not the employer. The employment documents should confirm whether the policy or the particular employment document should take precedence in the event of conflict between them.

9.9   As with policies for local hires, discretion reserved by the employer regarding amendment, withdrawal or replacement of expatriate policies should be made clear in both the policy document itself and the employment documents. This is not always permitted by mandatory laws. (See also **15.107–15.109** on unfair contract terms.)

9.10   Particular care should be taken with language. It is sometimes assumed that the language of policy documents should be more informal and descriptive and that precise language can be saved for the main contract document. However, with expatriate assignments the precise terms of the arrangements may have a substantial impact on potential costs for the employer. Ideally, from a legal perspective, the employer should be careful not to promise too much or give too much unnecessary explanation as that may open the door to challenge by the employee. Some employers of expatriates are happy to make more general/open-ended promises because giving their expatriate workforce comfort takes precedence over managing some legal risks. This is, of course, fine, as long as the employer understands the risks being taken.

Policy change

9.11 Because changes to a policy document relevant to an expatriate contract can have unforeseen consequences, it is also important that the correct version of the policy is referenced.

9.12 For example, a general statement like 'the Company's Redundancy Policy for Expatriates in force from time to time shall apply' could be unhelpful. Unless the employer is exceptionally meticulous it will be difficult for those updating a particular policy document to know whether a change to the policy will affect particular expatriate contracts in an unfortunate way. The work and expense required to check the effect on individual contracts when changes are introduced to the policy may be disproportionate.

9.13 Much of the convenient flexibility of easily amended policy documents for use with local hires is lost when they apply to expatriates.

Case study – local non-contractual equal opportunities policy

9.14 The home employer may have an equal opportunities policy that applies to all local hires. It may include some general statements of principle and some detail about how complaints will be dealt with. It is kept up to date by the HR department who are familiar with home country mandatory laws and review the policy regularly in the light of organisational changes and developments in the law. Employees are informed of any changes by email and the intranet copy is updated centrally. The policy itself is non-contractual but the employees are required to comply with the policy under the terms of their contracts of employment.

9.15 The equal opportunities policy developed for local hires is flexible and relatively easy to administer. A standard policy for expatriates would be far more inflexible, see the example below.

Case study – expatriate accommodation policy

9.16 An employer has a large expatriate population and offers all the expatriates rental accommodation. To reduce administration and to try to be 'fair' to employees performing similar roles, the employer tries to develop a standard expatriate accommodation policy. This includes details of the benefits to be provided by the employer, various conditions and the obligations of the employee.

9.17 An employee, Felix, is sent out on assignment, advice is sought on the suitability of the standard expatriate accommodation policy for him and he is given a copy of the policy. Because some co-operation and commitment is required from Felix, and promises are made by his employer, it seems appropriate to make the policy contractual. To make things easier, Felix's contract makes it clear that his employer has a wide discretion to change the standard policy and any change will apply to him automatically. A year or so later the policy is reviewed and amended by managers who were not involved with setting up Felix's assignment. Some potential consequences may follow:

- it may not be practical to check the effect of any subsequent policy change on each expatriate (including Felix) before it is introduced;

- changes that are necessary to achieve objectives for some expatriates may be detrimental if applied to others;

- there may be doubt as to whether the employer is able to introduce the changes in the host country in that way – for example, there may be a conflict with mandatory employment laws or with the separate terms of the landlord's lease;

- the change of policy may have adverse tax implications;

- there may be a requirement for all the terms of the contract to be provided in the host country language (and even if that is not the case it may be necessary to translate the policy documents into the host language so that host country officials making enquiries can understand what the terms are);

- the informal language of a policy document may result in the employer making promises that it did not mean to make.

Example – effect of maternity policy on expatriate

9.18 Suppose an employee is assigned abroad and has a baby. Both home and host companies may have maternity policies that describe how much maternity leave the employee can take, what she will be paid and relevant procedures. The home country policy may be inappropriate because it contains provisions that conflict with host country mandatory laws, whilst the host country policy may be inappropriate because it does not take account of the employee's expatriate status and reasonable expectations. In practice, unless the employee is particularly concerned about maternity at the outset of her assignment or the group is very keen to maintain and publicise consistent standards between group companies, it may be simplest to ensure that none of the existing maternity policies will apply to the expatriate during the assignment. The employer will then have the flexibility to deal with the appropriate arrangements in the light of home and host country advice if and when pregnancy occurs (see also **12.25–12.34** on maternity and paternity generally).

9.19 If there are few international assignments within the group there will be little point in spending time and energy developing detailed policy documents. Even if there are larger numbers the appropriate arrangements for individual expatriates may be too inconsistent to make preparation of detailed policy documents covering every issue worthwhile. However, where there is a large expatriate population and a number of employees are to be assigned on similar terms, or if the group wishes to move towards more consistency in the treatment of expatriates, then development of some policies in some areas may be helpful.

9.20 The first step is to decide the purpose of the policy documents. If they are intended to be principles to guide those deciding on assignment terms (ie policies for assignment managers) then they will need to be in a different form from policies that will be made available to employees (ie employment policies).

Practical suggestions

9.21 If some policy documents may be helpful for a particular assignment the employer could consider:

- generally making it clear in the employment contract that policies do not apply unless the contrary is confirmed clearly in writing;
- ensuring that only relevant terms of relevant policies are expressly applied;
- ensuring that only active decisions to change policy terms that apply to the particular employee will be effective (eg if mandatory laws permit, the employer could reference a particular version of the policy document and reserve discretion to change terms that apply to the employee as well as the terms of the policy document itself, so that the employee's terms can be changed out of line with the introduction of changes for other employees, ie after the particular employee's contract, mandatory laws etc have been checked);
- ensuring that, in the event of conflict, the express terms of the employment contract override those of any policy document;
- ensuring that the status of the policy document is made clear in the policy document as well as the individual expatriate's contract of employment;
- taking care with policy language so that inappropriate promises are not made.

Practical things that could be covered

9.22 The following are examples of topics that the employer may choose to cover in policy documents where the expatriate population is sufficiently large to justify the work required:

- appraisals;
- benefits eg relocation and repatriation, housing, education, home leave, medical;
- bribery, ethics, conduct, prevention of fraud, modern slavery and whistleblowing;
- business visitors and short-term travel;
- equal opportunities;

- exchange rates;
- health & safety, sources of safety-related information, emergency contact details etc;
- holidays, home leave, sickness absence and family leave;
- immigration support, employee obligations;
- internal contact details and internal jargon;
- IT, social media, intellectual property, confidentiality etc;
- privacy (data protection);
- tax briefings, tax returns and personal obligations;
- personal responsibility reminders and information, eg re a need to seek independent professional advice eg on wills, divorce, death, inheritance, personal wealth;
- practical information regarding the availability of family support, eg contact details of destination services providers etc.

Warnings

9.23 Preparation of good policy documents is not easy and can create substantial risk for a business.

9.24 Employers are strongly recommended to seek appropriate professional advice in respect of both the drafting of the documents and relevant specialist areas, eg equality (see Chapter 12), health & safety, tax and social security etc.

9.25 Policy documents should be kept under review and should be updated promptly. Note that care should be taken with the contractual status of policy documents, to facilitate prompt updating.

CHAPTER 10

WHICH COUNTRY'S LAWS APPLY

GOVERNING LAW

10.1 If an employment dispute involves more than one country it is sometimes difficult to work out which country's laws apply. Suppose a dispute develops between a Greek employee and his Hong Kong registered employer about his job in Singapore. Which country's laws are relevant? What if more than one country's laws apply at the same time? Where and how would the laws be enforced? What are the costs for the business likely to be? Most importantly, can anything be done before the assignment starts to reduce the risks?

10.2 In order to decide what must be done, it is important to have a clear understanding of the differences between three quite technical concepts:

- *Governing law*: This is, broadly, the law used to interpret a document such as the employment contract and is, within limits, something the parties can choose (**10.3–10.29**).

- *Mandatory employment laws*: These are the compulsory employment laws that protect an employee during his employment. They might, for example, include protection against dismissal or discrimination, or provide for minimum pay or holidays. The employer and employee cannot normally choose which mandatory employment laws will apply. They will usually apply automatically and override any conflicting terms in the employment documents (**10.30–10.61**).

- *Jurisdiction*: Most countries' courts and tribunals are subject to rules about which claims they can decide. A court or tribunal has 'jurisdiction' when it is able to hear a claim (**10.62–10.74**).

GOVERNING LAW

Legal position

10.3 The governing laws for a document are, broadly, the laws used to decide what the document means.

10.4 For example, under English law, whilst 'what it says' is usually 'what it means', there are well-developed (and complicated) 'rules of construction' that lawyers use to interpret the document if the meaning is not clear. An example of this is the 'contra preferentem' rule: if the meaning of a term is ambiguous the document may be construed against the party that offered it. Other countries take different approaches to construction, so the document may mean different things depending on which country's rules of interpretation are applied. If the document is clearly drafted then the choice of governing laws will be less important for interpretation.

10.5 In addition, the governing law may determine whether certain terms should be implied into the contract. For example, an employer's 'duty of trust and confidence' and an employee's 'duty of fidelity' may be implied into an employment contract governed by English law. There is no need for the employment contract document to mention these duties expressly, they apply automatically if English governing law applies.

10.6 If an employment is purely domestic, no travel is involved, and both employer and employee are based in the country where the work is done, neither the employer nor the employee is likely to give choice of governing law much thought. It will usually just be assumed, perhaps unconsciously, that the local law will be used to interpret the documents and, of course, it usually will be. In the context of international business and transnational employment arrangements there is need for more thought.

10.7 If the laws governing a document are not clear then the precise meaning of the document will not be clear. Rules have, naturally, developed to help decide which country's laws will govern a particular document. To reduce the risk that different countries' courts might come to different conclusions over laws applicable to the same document, some countries have entered into international agreements on how governing laws should be determined. For example, the Convention on the Law Applicable to Contractual Obligations ('the Rome Convention', as amended by the Luxembourg Convention, Brussels Protocol and Funchal Convention) or, since 2009, the EC Regulations 'Rome I' and 'Rome II' have applied to most European countries, see further below.

10.8 Generally, within reason, parties to a contract are able to choose the governing law for the contract. If the parties have confirmed their choice in writing in the document, their decision will usually be conclusive. If the decision has not been recorded in writing it may still hold if there is sufficient evidence of the choice that they have made. If the choice is not clear, rules must be applied to work out which country's governing laws apply. In the EU the document will typically be governed by the laws of the country where the employee habitually carries out his work.

10.9 Where employment terms are set out in several documents, different laws may sometimes be chosen to govern each document. For example, the laws of the country where the employee works will usually be chosen to apply to the main employment contract document, whilst group bonus arrangements are often set out in a bonus document governed by the laws of the country where the parent company is based (see **11.44–11.45** on why the latter can be unhelpful). Different governing laws may even be chosen for different parts of the same document (eg see Chapter 16 on international severance agreements).

Rome I – overview

10.10 EC Regulation 583/2008 on the law applicable to contractual obligations ('Rome I') came into force from 17 December 2009, replacing the Rome Convention for most EU member states. Rome I does not currently apply to Denmark.

Rome II – overview

10.11 EC Regulation 864/2007 on the law applicable to non-contractual obligations ('Rome II') came into force on 11 January 2009. As with Rome I, Rome II applies to the courts and tribunals of every EU member state except Denmark. However, Rome II did not replace any existing treaty or other arrangements: there was no consensus within the EU regarding the treatment of non-contractual obligations prior to Rome II. As the Regulation applies to non-contractual obligations it is not directly relevant to expatriate employment documents. However, it could, in some circumstances, become relevant to an expatriate employment relationship, for example, if there is an industrial dispute or if one party commits a tort, perhaps a breach of the employer's duty of care towards his employee.

Rome I – text

10.12 Some key provisions of Rome I for expatriates are set out below.

'Preamble

. . .

(34) The rule on individual employment contracts should not prejudice the application of the [Posted Workers Directive].

(35) Employees should not be deprived of the protection afforded to them by provisions which cannot be derogated from by agreement or which can only be derogated from to their benefit.

(36) As regards individual employment contracts, work carried out in another country should be regarded as temporary if the employee is expected to resume working in the country of origin after carrying out his tasks abroad. The conclusion of a new contract of employment with the original employer or an employer belonging to the same group of companies as the original employer should not preclude the employee from being regarded as carrying out his work in another country temporarily.

(37) Considerations of public interest justify giving the courts of the Member States the possibility, in exceptional circumstances, of applying exceptions based

on public policy and overriding mandatory provisions. The concept of 'overriding mandatory provisions' should be distinguished from the expression 'provisions which cannot be derogated from by agreement' and should be construed more restrictively.

. . .

Article 3

Freedom of choice

1. A contract shall be governed by the law chosen by the parties. The choice shall be made expressly or clearly demonstrated by the terms of the contract or the circumstances of the case. By their choice the parties can select the law applicable to the whole or to part only of the contract.

2. [Re: subsequent change of choice of governing law.]

3. Where all other elements relevant to the situation at the time of the choice are located in a country other than the country whose law has been chosen, the choice of the parties shall not prejudice the application of provisions of the law of that other country which cannot be derogated from by agreement.

. . .

Article 8

Individual employment contracts

1. An individual employment contract shall be governed by the law chosen by the parties in accordance with Article 3. Such a choice of law may not, however, have the result of depriving the employee of the protection afforded to him by provisions that cannot be derogated from by agreement under the law that, in the absence of choice, would have been applicable pursuant to paragraphs 2, 3 and 4 of this Article.

2. To the extent that the law applicable to the individual employment contract has not been chosen by the parties, the contract shall be governed by the law of the country in which or, failing that, from which the employee habitually carries out his work in performance of the contract. The country where the work is habitually carried out shall not be deemed to have changed if he is temporarily employed in another country.

3. Where the law applicable cannot be determined pursuant to paragraph 2, the contract shall be governed by the law of the country where the place of business through which the employee was engaged is situated.

4. Where it appears from the circumstances as a whole that the contract is more closely connected with a country other than that indicated in paragraphs 2 or 3, the law of that other country shall apply.

Article 9

Overriding mandatory provisions

1. Overriding mandatory provisions are provisions the respect for which is regarded as crucial by a country for safeguarding its public interests, such as its political, social or economic organisation, to such an extent that they are applicable to any situation falling within their scope, irrespective of the law otherwise applicable to the contract under this Regulation.

2. Nothing in this Regulation shall restrict the application of the overriding mandatory provisions of the law of the forum.

3. Effect may be given to the overriding mandatory provisions of the law of the country where the obligations arising out of the contract have to be or have been performed in so far as those overriding mandatory provisions render the performance of the contract unlawful. In considering whether to give effect to those provisions, regard shall be had to their nature and purpose and to the consequences of their application or non-application.

. . .

Article 21

Public policy of the forum

The application of a provision of the law of any country specified by this Regulation may be refused only if such application is manifestly incompatible with the public policy (*ordre public*) of the forum.'

10.13 The European Court (see the Glossary at Appendix 3) has jurisdiction to give rulings on the applicable governing laws for EU member states under the Rome Regulations. However, we do not yet have extensive case law to guide us on the meaning of the Rome Regulations in an employment context. In the meantime, national courts will make their own decisions on the way that the Rome Regulations should be interpreted. These may not always be consistent and may be overturned later, as EU national courts are obliged to apply European Court decisions.

Practical implications

Choosing convenient governing laws

10.14 Given that employers, and to a lesser extent employees (because of their weaker negotiating position), can within limits choose the governing law(s) that will apply to employment documents, the first step will be to decide upon the most appropriate governing law.

10.15 There is often pressure to ensure that employment documents for group companies are governed by the laws of the country where the group head office is based. This might be because the group wants consistency; because the group likes to litigate at home; or perhaps because in-house counsel based at head office feel more comfortable with familiar rules.

10.16   In practice, the law of the country where the head office is located will not usually be the best choice to govern employment documents for longer term assignments. It is worth thinking about how the documents will be used in practice. Obviously, both employer and employee will want to understand what the documents say as they try to resolve day-to-day queries, such as, 'How much holiday can I take?' or, 'How do the tax equalisation arrangements work?'. However, provided the documents are drafted well, technical legal rules of interpretation and the governing law should not be important for day-to-day conduct of the employment relationship. The governing law is likely to become more important if the employment documents are unclear, particularly if a dispute arises.

10.17   It is generally convenient for the governing laws for the employment contract to be those of the country whose courts or tribunals are likely to hear claims relating to the documents and those of the country whose mandatory laws will apply (usually the same country, see further below).

10.18   In the event of a dispute, legal opinion may need to be sought from lawyers from the country whose governing law applies, so that the employer and employee can understand what the contract promises. If a different country's mandatory laws (see below) apply this will add a layer of complexity, as advice from lawyers from two or more different countries may be required for the parties to understand the full picture. If litigation arises and the court or tribunal with jurisdiction needs to consider a foreign governing law, that may also create inconvenience and additional cost. At the very least 'foreign' legal opinions and translations are likely to be required by the court.

10.19   As a rule of thumb, it will usually be most convenient for the employment documents to be governed by the laws of the country where the employee will work. The most significant mandatory employment laws are likely to be host country employment laws and the host country's courts and tribunals are likely to have jurisdiction to hear those claims. In particular, the payments to be made to an employee on termination of employment will often be decided by host country courts, tribunals or other authorities, and that is the issue that is probably most likely to be the subject of litigation (but see comments in relation to post termination restrictive covenants at **10.44–10.45** and the potential impact of the Posted Workers Directive on intra-EU assignments).

10.20   The decision on governing law should not be made before a host country employment law specialist has been consulted. This is because sometimes the choice of governing law may determine whether host country mandatory laws will apply to the employment, most significantly the laws that deal with termination of employment. It is particularly easy for EU advisers to overlook this as Rome I minimises the effect of governing laws on the application of mandatory laws (see above).

10.21 Decisions about governing law should be made before the employment begins and the documents are prepared, and should be properly recorded in the employment documents.

10.22 The choice of governing law will also affect the way the documents should be drafted, and, practically, who should do the drafting. It may be more cost effective for a lawyer from the country whose governing law will apply to the documents to prepare the first draft of the documents.

Multinational documents

10.23 Some multinationals have documents that are intended to apply to employees who work in more than one country. These might include 'standard' employment contracts, incentive plans and/or assignment policies governed by head office laws.

10.24 The rationale for using the same document in different countries is generally convenience (usually the employer's convenience). This approach can also offer some comfort to an employee who undertakes several assignments, as the employee may be familiar with the employer's 'standard' terms and may have a clearer understanding of whether he is being treated consistently with other employees.

10.25 However, multinationals are unlikely to be able to produce pro forma employment contracts or standard polices that are effective in all the countries in which they operate. This may be partly because employment laws and working practices in different countries are so diverse and partly because multinationals often grow by buying or merging with other businesses, and this inevitably leads to some inherited inconsistency in terms. The goal of a perfectly harmonised employment contract that will work all over the world is an attractive one, but in practice unlikely ever to be achieved (see also Chapter 9).

10.26 A more practical approach is to produce standard framework documents that should be broadly acceptable in most countries and to make the amendments that are necessary to ensure local conformity. One of those appropriate amendments is likely to be a change in the governing law. Governing law clauses should normally be reviewed by both home and host country lawyers, and lawyers from other relevant jurisdictions.

Incentive plans

10.27 Incentive plans deserve a special mention as these are documents that are commonly applied in more than one country and the financial implications of getting things wrong can be substantial. Typically, incentive plans will be governed by head office laws, often the laws of a US state, and may be adapted to reflect local tax or other requirements, perhaps through adoption of a host country 'sub-plan'. From an employment law perspective they can create particular challenges because they often contain post termination restrictions governed by head office laws. (See Chapter 11 for a more detailed explanation of issues relating to post termination restrictions.)

Who should draft documents to be governed by English law?

10.28 The background of the person who drafts the document will be important if the document is to be governed by English law, particularly if post termination restrictive covenants are to be included. This is because of very strict rules used to interpret documents in the UK. Good English is not usually sufficient to ensure that the documents are appropriate. Experience of English legal drafting is important. This can lead to some frustration, particularly for US lawyers, as the natural assumption will be that a document drafted by any competent English-speaking lawyer will work well in the UK. This is not usually the case. US legal drafting styles can create substantial problems in the UK, particularly in relation to post termination restrictions.

10.29 The problem could be addressed either by asking an English lawyer to review and, if appropriate, amend the documents or by providing the relevant information and allowing an English lawyer to prepare drafts for review. The latter approach is usually most cost effective, particularly where there are restrictive covenants.

MANDATORY EMPLOYMENT LAWS

What mandatory employment laws are

10.30 Mandatory employment laws are, broadly, employment laws that must be applied to employees. The parties cannot normally choose which mandatory employment laws will apply. They will usually apply automatically and override any conflicting terms in the employment documents. As a rule of thumb, a country's mandatory employment laws usually apply to employees working in that country, but they may in some circumstances apply to employees working in other countries too. Host country mandatory employment laws are likely to be most significant for an overseas assignment, regardless of whether the employer is the home or host company during the assignment, but all relevant countries' rules should be considered.

10.31 For example, the host country is likely to have mandatory employment laws regulating:

- minimum annual holiday and/or compulsory public holidays;
- hours of work;
- sickness or injury;

- maternity (and sometimes paternity and other family-related) leave and pay;
- notice of termination of employment;
- the ways in which employees can be dismissed and how they should be compensated; and/or
- discrimination, eg on grounds of sex, race, etc.

10.32 Mandatory employment laws might sometimes also include, for example:

- requirements for employer registration;
- regulation of recruitment methods;
- restrictions on part-time, temporary and/or fixed-term employment;
- a requirement that employment contracts must include particular information or be provided in a particular form or language;
- regulations on pay (eg by setting minimum hourly rates or providing for bonus payments);
- arrangements for employee representation and/or consultation;
- requirements to take out insurance or contribute to funds for the benefit of employees (eg to provide for payments in the event of redundancy); and/or
- rules relating to the provision of references.

EU – meaning of 'mandatory laws'

10.33 Mandatory laws are referred to quite specifically in Rome I (see **10.12**), Rome II (see **10.11**) and the Posted Workers Directive (see **10.50–10.55**) and have a particular meaning in those contexts. They acknowledge different types of mandatory law, for example, Art 8(1) of Rome I also refers to 'provisions that cannot be derogated from by agreement' and distinguishes those provisions from 'overriding mandatory provisions' (see para 37 of the preamble to Rome I above). Care should be taken with the phrase 'mandatory laws'. Generally, though (and in this book unless otherwise indicated) the terms 'mandatory laws' and 'mandatory employment laws' are used loosely to cover laws which set minimum employment standards, regardless of the terms of the contract, the governing law, and of whether they are strictly 'mandatory laws' for the purposes of Rome I or the Posted Workers Directive.

Which countries' mandatory employment laws apply

10.34 Various articles of Rome I give priority to mandatory laws.

10.35 Rome I makes clear that the choice of governing law made by the parties will not have the effect of depriving the employee of the protection afforded to him by the 'mandatory rules of the law' which would be applicable in the absence of choice.

10.36 For example, suppose the parties choose English law to govern a contract. If they had not done so French law would have applied to the document under Rome I. The employee will still have the benefit of any French mandatory laws that would have applied if English law had not been chosen. (Of course that is not the same as saying that all French employment laws apply to the employee. That would depend on the way that French law works.)

10.37 It is worth noting that, in this regard, special rules apply to individual employment contracts, intended to counterbalance the unequal positions of employer and employee when they choose the governing law for the contract (ie the fact that in practice this is usually the employer's choice).

10.38 Article 8(1) of Rome I uses slightly different language from the earlier Rome Convention and provides that the choice of law made by the parties may not have the result of depriving the employee of the protection afforded to him by provisions 'that cannot be derogated from by agreement under the law that, in the absence of choice, would have been applicable pursuant to paragraphs 2, 3 and 4'.

10.39 As a rule of thumb, mandatory employment laws (in the loose sense) usually apply to employees working in the relevant country. The precise rules of application will be determined by the laws of each country. More than one country's laws may apply at the same time to the same employee.

10.40 Host country mandatory employment laws are most likely to be relevant to an expatriate assignment. Home country and other countries' mandatory employment laws, for example, those of the employee's country of nationality, may also apply.

10.41 Some countries are party to international treaties, or other agreements between countries, that have an impact on their national employment laws, and this may lead to some consistency between the mandatory laws that apply in those countries. For example, the EU member states must implement the '*acquis communautaire*' (broadly EC laws, see the Glossary at Appendix 3) and so some knowledge of the *acquis* will help employment lawyers predict many of the core mandatory employment laws that are likely to apply in EU countries (see **10.56–10.60** below on when UK mandatory laws apply).

Sources of mandatory employment laws

10.42 In the UK, employment legislation is generally passed by Parliament and subsequently clarified through case law made by Employment Tribunals and Courts. Employment laws generally apply in a consistent way to all UK employees (see **19.63**). There is therefore a natural tendency in the UK to assume that other countries will have similar systems. This is not the case, particularly in Europe where a wide variety of different models apply.

10.43 For example, employment laws may be introduced at national level through legislation and/or by means of national collective bargaining. They could also be introduced by collective bargaining at lower levels, for example through sectoral or industry-level collective agreements. Different mandatory employment laws may apply to employees in different circumstances, for example, to employees with a different status (eg managers and blue collar workers); working in a different industry sector (eg pharmaceuticals and banking) or at a different geographical location within the country.

10.44 Many mandatory laws apply differently to those who are regarded as 'managing', 'senior' or 'top' 'executives' and sometimes the rules will apply in different ways to expatriate employees too (see **10.50–10.55** on the EC Posted Workers Directive).

10.45 It is important to be aware that, in many countries, collective agreements that set mandatory employment laws do not only apply to parties to the collective agreement. The employee is unlikely to need to be a trade union member to benefit and the employee and employer do not necessarily need to agree that the collective agreement will apply to the employment relationship. Neither employee nor employer may take part in the bargaining process and they may not even be aware that the collective agreement exists. The collective agreement may nevertheless apply. Where there is a mechanism for introducing mandatory laws by means of collective agreement, they will still be mandatory and variation by contract is unlikely to be permitted or may only be permitted if the derogation is favourable to the employee or agreed in a particular way. This may be an unfamiliar arrangement for UK employers and lawyers, as collective agreements are not generally used to introduce mandatory laws in the UK, although they may occasionally be used to derogate from laws that would otherwise apply. (See the Glossary at Appendix 3 on 'collective agreements'.)

10.46 Sometimes mandatory rules will not apply if a contrary arrangement is freely agreed. For example, the collective agreement may provide a mandatory starting point for negotiation that may only be varied if particular requirements are met. Often the derogation must be agreed not by the individual employee but through some collective process, for example, through the agreement of employee representatives.

10.47 As there may be overlap, and therefore potential for conflict, between the different legislation, case law, collective agreements and contractual obligations that may apply to an individual employee, it is important to understand the priority that should be applied to the various obligations in the particular countries concerned.

Effect of governing law

10.48 The choice of governing law does not usually affect the application of mandatory employment laws. This is particularly unlikely within EU countries party to Rome I (see **10.10–10.13**).

10.49   In some jurisdictions, particularly outside the EU, choosing a different governing law (eg the home country governing law) for the employment contract may have the consequence that host country mandatory laws do not apply to the employment. Sometimes there is an assumption in the host country that if home country governing laws apply to the contract then home country mandatory laws will apply too, which is of course not usually the case. In that event the employment contract will be critical to determining the rights and obligations of employee and employer.

EU and the Posted Workers Directive

10.50   The EC Posted Workers Directive (Council Directive 96/71/EC or 'PWD') broadly requires member states of the EU to provide employment protection for employees 'posted' from an undertaking in one EU member state to work temporarily in their country (see the Glossary at Appendix 3 for a list of current EU member states). Note the subsequent introduction of the Posted Workers Enforcement Directive 2014/67/EU.

10.51   The Posted Workers Directive applies to home country assignments, where the employment relationship remains with the undertaking in the home country. It does not matter whether the employee is required to perform duties in the host country for his home employer (ie without change to the legal entity) or for another group company, as long as his employment contract remains with the home employer. The Posted Workers Directive also covers employees hired out to work for unconnected companies in the host country, provided they maintain their employment relationships with employers based in the home country.

10.52   Essentially, the host country must ensure that certain mandatory laws, including those provided by collective agreement or arbitration awards 'which have been declared universally applicable', apply to the posted worker. The Directive gives some explanation of what 'declared universally applicable' means.

10.53   The mandatory laws covered by the Posted Workers Directive include:

- maximum work periods and minimum rest periods;
- minimum paid annual holidays;
- minimum rates of pay, including overtime rates (but not supplementary occupational retirement pension schemes);
- the conditions of hiring out of workers, in particular the supply of workers by temporary employment undertakings;
- health, safety and hygiene at work;
- protective measures regarding the terms and conditions of employment of pregnant women or women who have recently given birth, of children and of young people; and

- equality of treatment between men and women and other anti-discrimination provisions.

It is worth noting that this list does not include protection offered in relation to dismissal. Also that some derogation is allowed where the length of the posting does not exceed one month. The Posted Workers Enforcement Directive offers, eg, additional protection to employees of sub-contractors.

10.54 Undertakings established in a non-EU member state must not be given more favourable treatment than undertakings established in an EU member state.

UK and the Posted Workers Directive

10.55 The Posted Workers Directive is not usually a significant issue for employees posted to the UK because of the way that UK mandatory employment laws apply. UK mandatory employment laws, generally, apply to all employees working in the UK anyway and the place of registration of the employer or the fact that the employee is posted is not usually relevant. This was the case before the Posted Workers Directive was adopted so, initially, little was done to implement the Directive and UK employers and lawyers still do not, generally, pay too much attention to it. However, it is important to bear in mind that many other European countries did not apply laws consistently to posted workers before the Directive was introduced. In those countries the Posted Workers Directive has more significance for expatriate assignments. The potential impact of the Posted Workers Directive should always be considered where an assignment is connected to a European jurisdiction.

Application of UK mandatory employment laws

10.56 The position regarding UK mandatory employment laws is fairly straightforward for employees coming to work in the UK from other countries. If they work in the UK, mandatory UK employment laws will almost certainly be deemed to apply and the employment documents should reflect that. If the employee works in England it usually makes sense to make sure the employment documents are drafted in English by an English lawyer and governed by English law (see the Glossary at Appendix 3 for an explanation of differences between England, Great Britain and the UK).

10.57 When an employee is sent abroad from the UK he is likely to lose the protection of most English mandatory employment laws, though there are some exceptions, see further below. The employment could be structured to make the application of English mandatory laws more likely (eg by using a home employer arrangement if the employee is to perform duties abroad for the purposes of the home company). However, other factors (immigration rules, tax, etc) are likely to be far more significant for determining the employment structure so this will rarely be a focus for the parties at the time the contracts are drawn up (see Chapter 6).

10.58 It is important to bear in mind that the fact that UK mandatory employment laws apply will not necessarily mean that the laws of another country, where perhaps employment obligations are more onerous for the employer, will not. Where EU rules do not apply, each country applies its own rules to determine whether mandatory employment laws will apply, and it is possible for the mandatory employment laws of more than one country to apply at the same time.

Serco

10.59 In 2006 the House of Lords decided, in the joined cases of *Serco Ltd v Lawson, Botham v Ministry of Defence and Crofts v Veta* [2006] UKHL 3 that employees can only claim unfair dismissal in Britain if they are 'employed in Great Britain'. Three exceptional situations were described in which employees working in other countries can make claims in Great Britain. These are: (i) 'peripatetic' employees based in Britain (eg airline pilots based in Britain); (ii) employees working in a British enclave abroad (eg on a British army base); and (iii) employees posted abroad for the purposes of a business carried on in Britain. These exceptions are not exhaustive and the House of Lords acknowledged in Serco (as has subsequent case law) that there may be other circumstances in which employees who work abroad have a sufficiently close connection to Great Britain to allow them to make unfair dismissal complaints in Great Britain. The 'posting' exception highlighted above is particularly important for multinationals. However, that situation did not apply to any of the employees who were the subject of the *Serco* cases so, in that respect, the example given was not technically binding on other courts (ie to use UK lawyers' language the decision was obiter dicta on that point). The posting exception has, however, subsequently been applied in other cases.

10.60 Similar principles have been applied to other mandatory laws. However, the case law does not always apply consistently. For example, different mandatory laws are set out in different legislation and some legislation is underpinned by EU laws and some is not. The potential impact of Brexit is also currently unclear.

Post termination restrictive covenants

10.61 See Chapter 11 on confidentiality and post termination restrictions.

JURISDICTION

What jurisdiction is

10.62 Most countries' courts and tribunals are subject to rules that determine the claims they can decide. A court or tribunal has 'jurisdiction' when it is able to hear a claim. More than one country's courts could have jurisdiction, for example, both the home country's and the host country's courts and tribunals may be permitted to hear claims arising from dismissal of an expatriate. Sometimes an employee is also entitled to have his claims heard in a court or tribunal in his country of nationality or domicile.

EU

10.63 Regulation (EU) 1215/2012 (on jurisdiction and the recognition and enforcement of judgments in civil and commercial matters (recast)) ('the Judgments Regulation' or 'Recast Brussels Regulation') can apply to EU countries but does not apply to Denmark (see the Glossary at Appendix 3 for a list of the current EU member states).

10.64 The key provisions of the Judgments Regulation currently read as follows:

'Section 5 – Jurisdiction over individual contracts of employment

Article 20

1. In matters relating to individual contracts of employment, jurisdiction shall be determined by this Section, without prejudice to Article 6, point 5 of Article 7 and in the case of proceedings brought against an employer, point 1 of Article 8.

2. Where an employee enters into an individual contract of employment with an employer who is not domiciled in a Member State but has a branch, agency or other establishment in one of the Member States, the employer shall, in disputes arising out of the operations of the branch, agency or establishment, be deemed to be domiciled in that Member State.

Article 21

1. An employer domiciled in a Member State may be sued:

(a)   in the courts of the Member State in which he is domiciled; or
(b)   in another Member State:
    (i)   in the courts for the place where the employee habitually carries out his work or in the courts for the last place where he did so; or
    (ii)   if the employee does not or did not habitually carry out his work in any one country, in the courts for the place where the business which engaged the employee is or was situated.

2. An employer not domiciled in a Member State may be sued in a court of a Member State in accordance with point (b) of paragraph 1.

Article 22

1. An employer may bring proceedings only in the courts of the Member State in which the employee is domiciled.

2. The provisions of this Schedule shall not affect the right to bring a counter-claim in the court in which, in accordance with this Section, the original claim is pending.

Article 23

The provisions of this Section may be departed from only by an agreement:

1.   which is entered into after the dispute has arisen; or
2.   which allows the employee to bring proceedings in courts other than those indicated in this Section.'

10.65   The Judgments Regulation applies to courts and tribunals of relevant EU member states. (There is a complication because the Judgments Regulation does not apply directly in all EU member states and Denmark has opted out: the conventions that preceded the Judgments Regulation may still apply.) The Judgments Regulation does not apply to the courts of other countries, for example, US courts, and those courts may apply different rules to decide whether they may hear the claim (see further below in relation to disputes over jurisdiction).

10.66   Employees have far more choice than their employers over where they can sue and, in most cases, it will be the employee that takes legal action.

10.67   It is worth noting that if the employer tries to limit the available jurisdictions through a choice of jurisdiction clause in the employment contract, this may not be effective (see Art 23).

10.68   If the employer is not domiciled in a member state then Arts 21–23 do not apply. Assuming there is no relevant jurisdiction clause, then the laws of the relevant country should be used to determine whether the court has jurisdiction.

UK and jurisdiction

10.69   The Judgments Regulation is currently applied directly in the UK, in respect of public and private sector employers and employees, through the European Communities Act 1972. The impact of Brexit is not yet clear.

Claims by employees against employers

10.70   Claims are made more often by employees against their employers, for example, to enforce contractual or mandatory employment rights. Claims might relate, for example, to termination of employment, a failure to pay remuneration or discrimination.

Claims by employers against employees

10.71 In practice, employers rarely sue their employees. However, employers may, for example, take legal action in relation to an employee's breach of a post termination restriction or disclosure or inappropriate use of confidential information; to recover a debt such as a loan, or a sum that must be repaid in a certain event (eg a tax refund that the employee has failed to pay over to his employer); or in relation to intellectual property rights.

10.72 For employers of expatriates the position is complicated because the claim may need to be heard in one country and enforced in another country. For example, the employer is most likely to be concerned about enforcement of post termination restrictions in the host country (because the interests that the business wants to protect are likely to be there). However, at the time of enforcement the expatriate is unlikely to be domiciled in the host country. Even if the employer's claim must be heard in the employee's country of domicile, the decision may still need to be enforced in the host country.

Practical issues

10.73 It is likely to be in the interests of both the employer and the employee to reduce the risk of disputes over jurisdiction. However, unlike disputes over governing laws, there may be little that can be done at the outset of an expatriate assignment to reduce the risk of disputes over jurisdiction at a later date.

10.74 It is worth remembering though that, although a jurisdiction clause may be ineffective if the assignment is between employers domiciled in EU member states to which the Judgments Regulation apply, a jurisdiction clause may be helpful if the assignment is not between two employers domiciled in EU member states. As the issues are complex and will vary depending on which countries are involved this is something in relation to which specialist advice from relevant jurisdictions may be helpful.

ENFORCEMENT

10.75 Council Regulation 805/2004/EC provides for European enforcement orders (EEOS). EEOs allow for the automatic recognition and enforcement of uncontested claims from one EU member state to another, without the need for intermediate proceedings in the member state where the claim is to be enforced before recognition and enforcement. EEOs can now apply throughout the EU, except in Denmark. Employers and employees should also be mindful that, in the context of litigation, it may be necessary to serve proceedings in more than one jurisdiction and that permission to serve documents outside the key jurisdiction may be required to allow the claim to proceed.

UK issues

10.76 Two key UK decisions (*Samengo-Turner and others v J & H Marsh & McLennan (Services) Ltd and others* [2007] EWCA Civ 723 and *Duarte v Black and Decker Corporation and another* [2007] All ER (D) 378 (Nov)) of the Court of Appeal and High Court respectively have highlighted the issues relating to the enforcement of 'foreign' restrictive covenants contained in LTIP arrangements. Developing case law is inevitable, as many highly paid City executives have LTIP arrangements containing covenants governed by US laws.

10.77 These cases give an insight into the way international jurisdiction and enforcement rules apply in the UK, the key conclusions being:

- English public policy rules will be applied to determine whether covenants can be enforced here, regardless of whether a foreign law is chosen to govern the contract (in practice this means that if covenants are governed by another country's laws, the covenants must satisfy that country's requirements, as well as English requirements, if they are to be enforced here);
- an employer must sue an employee in relation to his employment contract in the employee's country of domicile;
- the 'employer' can include group companies.

See **11.33–11.38** for a more detailed explanation of the impact of the *Samengo-Turner* and *Duarte* decisions.

PRACTICAL SUGGESTIONS FOR DRAFTING EXPATRIATE DOCUMENTS – OVERVIEW

10.78 It is helpful for an employer to understand which laws will apply to employment documents from the outset so that it knows where it stands if it has to enforce terms of the contract or if it is sued by the employee. In practice, both the employer and employee are likely to want certainty and, where possible, to avoid litigation, particularly if the claim is likely to be a 'test case'.

10.79 The parties should agree on the governing law that will apply to the employment documents and their choice should be recorded in writing in each employment document. In practice this usually means that the employer will choose the governing law. The expatriate may not be particularly concerned by the choice made and may in any case have little bargaining power in that regard. The important thing is that a choice is made. Most of the complex issues and uncertainty currently arising will be avoided if the choice of governing laws is clearly confirmed in the documents. Making a choice in writing before the assignment begins may significantly reduce legal expense if the governing law becomes relevant later – even if the claim is heard in a country that is not subject to Rome I. If documents have already been issued without a clear choice of law then this can be remedied, with sufficient employee cooperation. In reality employees are rarely interested in these clauses before a dispute develops.

10.80 It is usually, but not always, convenient to choose the host country's laws to govern the employment contract. Claims from the employee are most likely to arise on termination of employment. Host country mandatory employment laws are, in that event, likely to be relevant and claims are likely to be dealt with in host country courts (but if home country or another country's mandatory laws apply this may not be the case.) The most convenient governing law is unlikely to be the law of the country where the group's head office is based if this is neither the home nor the host country.

10.81 For the reasons described above the parties are unlikely to have much choice regarding the mandatory laws that will apply to the employment. The application of mandatory laws will usually not be substantially affected by the choice of governing law but there are exceptions, particularly in non-EU countries. For example, if home country laws are chosen to govern the contract then sometimes the host country's mandatory employment laws will not apply. It is worth checking whether the choice of law will affect the application of home or host country mandatory laws with specialists from the relevant jurisdictions as this could have significant financial consequences, particularly if there is a need to terminate the employment at a later stage.

10.82 Different considerations may apply to post termination restrictive covenants (see **11.44–11.46**). See Chapter 11 on post termination restrictions generally. It is worth remembering that claims in relation to post termination restrictions are likely to be brought by the employer rather than the employee and that this may have an impact on the jurisdiction where the claim will be heard. If appropriate, different governing laws could be chosen to govern the post termination restrictions from the other contract terms.

10.83 The potential impact of Rome II on disputes relating to non-contractual obligations in an employment context is not yet clear but it is worth considering whether a choice of law clause in the employment documents may help.

10.84 Generally, the mandatory laws of the host country will have the greatest impact, although the mandatory laws of other countries should be considered. It is worth trying to understand the potential implications of the application of mandatory laws before the documents are prepared as there may be things that can be done to reduce any adverse impact.

10.85 Issues relating to jurisdiction are more complex and the employer should take advice from relevant jurisdictions as to whether inclusion of jurisdiction clauses in the employment documents may be helpful. However, in many cases the inclusion of a jurisdiction clause will not make much practical difference.

10.86 The applicable laws should be considered before decisions are made about the language for the document (but other practical considerations will also apply) and who is asked to prepare the documents.

CHAPTER 11

COMPETITION AND RESTRICTIVE COVENANTS

PURPOSE OF RESTRICTIVE COVENANTS

11.1 Most senior employees need confidential information to do their jobs properly. Depending on seniority and role, the employee might, for example, have access to confidential information about their employer's financial affairs, customers or intellectual property.

11.2 Confidential information that belongs to the employer will still belong to the employer after it is shared with the employee and, often more importantly, after the employment ends. If the employee uses that information for his own purposes, or for another business, the employer is likely to have a remedy in law. However, employers often find it difficult to prove that their confidential information has been used unlawfully.

11.3 Businesses typically try to restrict their employees' activities after their employments end in order to protect their confidential information. Those restrictions are generally referred to as post termination 'restrictive covenants'. For example, if an employee cannot start work for a competitor for six months after his employment ends, the risk that the competitor will benefit from the former employer's confidential information will be lower.

11.4 In addition to confidential information, the business is likely to have other interests that it wishes to protect during an employment and after it ends. The employer may be concerned that the employee will try to 'poach' customers or staff, for his own benefit or for the purposes of a competitor's business. There may be particular concerns if, eg, the employee has had an opportunity to develop close one-to-one relationships with customers at the employer's expense or has led a team developing cutting edge technology.

11.5 Restrictive covenants are sometimes referred to as 'non-competes', particularly in the US or countries with strong US connections. The phrase is not always helpful as 'non-compete' implies that the aim of the restrictions is to restrict competition, whereas to be enforceable the covenants generally need to restrict activity with the aim of protecting a 'legitimate business interest' such as confidential information, client connections or a stable workforce. If the covenants simply aim to restrict competition, they may not be enforceable at all.

PUBLIC INTEREST

11.6 When viewed from the employee's perspective, post termination restrictions could be considered onerous and unjust. By restricting the employee's activities after his employment ends the former employer may be limiting the employee's ability to secure alternative employment. The freedom to enter into an employment of choice is generally considered to be an important democratic freedom and most countries have developed laws to protect that freedom. In the UK, excessive restriction of an employee's activities after his employment ends may be 'in restraint of trade' and be unenforceable on that basis. Public policy objectives relate to protection of the individual's freedom to do his preferred work as well as free trade.

11.7 There is, of course, potential for conflict between the employer's interests and the former employee's interests, and that conflict has been managed in different ways in different places. These different practical approaches to managing conflicting interests create significant challenges for those drafting restrictive covenants for expatriates. Typically, more than one country's rules will need to be considered and it is often difficult to ensure that restrictions will work effectively in all relevant jurisdictions.

MANDATORY LAWS

11.8 In some jurisdictions obligations are imposed automatically by mandatory collective agreement or legislation. It may, or may not, be possible to vary these through the employment contract documents. In jurisdictions where this is the case, it is common for different obligations to apply to different levels of staff. (See also the Glossary at Appendix 3 on collective agreements.) In the UK confidentiality obligations are implied into employment contracts automatically through the 'common law', but other post-termination restrictions, eg, on taking up employment with a competitor for a period of time, are typically agreed specifically with employees.

Where mandatory laws apply to protect confidential information or offer other protection it is, generally, still helpful to specify obligations in employment contracts, see **11.10–11.12**.

EU TRADE SECRETS DIRECTIVE

11.9 Directive 2016/943 on the protection of undisclosed know-how and business information (trade secrets) against their unlawful acquisition, use and disclosure must be implemented by EU member states by 8 June 2018. A definition of 'trade secret' is set out for this purpose in Article 2 of the Directive. Implementation of the directive will not automatically replace existing requirements that apply in member states but will ensure that a minimum level of protection is applied across the EU. The Trade Secrets Directive expressly recognises the relevance of 'measures taken to protect the trade secret'.

EMPLOYMENT DOCUMENTS

11.10 Typically, employment documents will include both clauses requiring the employee to keep certain information confidential and restrictive covenants restricting activities during and after employment ends. The relevant clauses will usually be included in the employment contract, although sometimes they may be found elsewhere, for example in a 'proprietary interest agreement', staff handbook, policy or incentive document. Confidentiality agreements and post termination restrictive covenants should always be reviewed, and usually need to be amended or replaced, before a new assignment begins.

11.11 In the context of an expatriate assignment, both the home company and the host company are likely to be concerned about post termination restrictions, particularly the latter because this is usually where the relevant business activity, customers etc are. Other group companies may also be concerned, for example the parent company. Where there is a home country employer, clauses may be included both in the home country employment contract and in a direct agreement with the host company (see Chapter 6, figure 6.1). Whether a direct agreement with the host company is needed as well as the clauses in the employment contract will depend on the applicable laws. Some countries also require that covenants should be included in a document that is separate from the employment contract. See also **11.39–11.41** below on the practice of including post termination restrictions in Long Term Incentive Plans (LTIPs).

SCOPE OF RESTRICTIONS

11.12 It may be necessary or appropriate to specify the purposes of restrictions in relevant documents but this is not always the case. It may be unwise to specify the purpose of covenants if the purposes allowed by the relevant law(s) are not clear. Advice should be sought from specialists from the relevant countries. Purposes often accepted as legitimate include protection of confidential information, trade connections and the employer's workforce. As business issues are similar in different jurisdictions it is not surprising that restrictions applied in different countries tend to cover similar ground.

Confidential information

11.13 Generally, there is some legislation or case-law, or a collective agreement, that will help to determine whether particular information is confidential or not. Some types of confidential information may attract protection in a particular jurisdiction, whilst other types may not. For example:

- The employee may be permitted to use information that has become part of his own skill and knowledge. (For example, if the employee is a lawyer he may have used his firm's precedent documents during his employment. Obviously, those valuable precedents will not belong to the employee and he will not be free to take them with him to a new firm. However, the employee's own skill is likely to have developed during his work and he might be free to apply that skill elsewhere to develop 'new' precedents of his own.) Employees' developing skill and knowledge is recognised by the Trade Secrets Directive (see **11.9**).

- The employer is unlikely to be able to protect confidential information that is already in the public domain, even if the initial disclosure of the information was unauthorised. For example, highly sensitive financial information may no longer be sensitive after a company's accounts are published.

- Disclosure may be required by a court or public authority, for example in the context of litigation or a tax enquiry. Generally, the employee will also be permitted to disclose information to his lawyers for the purpose of seeking legal advice.

- Many countries have 'whistleblowing' legislation that either permits the disclosure of confidential information or protects the individual from retaliation where there is a public interest purpose (eg informing health and safety inspectors that secret factory processes are unsafe). See **15.47–15.58**.

- The protection available may depend on how confidential the information is. For example, in the UK an employee can only be restricted in disclosure of highly confidential information and trade secrets after the employment ends. Current case-law and legislation in EU countries clarifying the meaning of 'trade secret' may develop in the light of interpretation of the Trade Secrets Directive.

- The protection available may depend on whether the employee is still an employee. In most countries' employees will owe stronger duties of fidelity etc whilst they remain an employee. See **11.22** and **11.23** on garden leave.

- The confidentiality of information may be time-limited. 'Old' information is far less likely to be confidential. For example, undisclosed information about marketing plans is likely to become less sensitive as time passes.

11.14 It is usually helpful to describe information that the employer (or other relevant companies) regard as confidential in the employment documents, so that the employee is clear about what he must not do, and to reduce the risk of dispute at a later date. The employment documents may also confirm that some information is not covered by the confidentiality restrictions, for example information already in the public domain. The requirements of different countries' laws tend to be more consistent in relation to confidential information than in relation to post termination restrictions so that, provided they are reviewed by appropriate specialists, it is unlikely to be too difficult to produce appropriate clauses. Appropriate confidentiality terms tend to be more consistent between jurisdictions than post termination restrictions.

Customers and clients

11.15 Employers often want to protect their client or customer base. Those drafting employment documents may want to think about the following when deciding on the scope of restrictive covenants designed to protect customers or clients:

- which employer's employees the covenants should apply to (eg the host company's, the home company's or all group companies' employees);
- which of those employees the particular restrictions should apply to (eg the employer's research and development team may have less contact with or influence over valuable customers or clients than the sales team).
- whether restrictions already apply to employees doing similar work (ideally covenants should be consistent);
- which customers should be covered;
- whether prospective customers should be covered;
- how long the restriction should apply for after the employment ends (different periods may apply to different restrictions);
- whether a geographical restriction is appropriate;
- whether it is appropriate to restrict cover to customers who have dealt with the business or the employee personally within a specified period before the employment ends (When do customers renew their business? Do they typically return to the business after periods with no contact? How long are the customer connections really valuable for?);
- whether any period of garden leave should be offset against the period of the restriction;
- whether relationships with those who refer customers to the business should be covered;
- whether the employee should be prohibited from dealing with customers (ie if the customer approaches him) or just from soliciting business from customers (ie from actively seeking business);
- whether the restriction should take account of direct and indirect activities (eg providing information to a new employer which enables the new employer to appoint another member of staff to solicit);
- the potential role of social media, eg LinkedIn or Facebook.

Key staff

11.16   The employer will typically want to prevent senior employees who leave from approaching other members of staff and persuading them to leave or work for a competitor. Those drafting the documents may want to think about the following:

- which companies' employees the restrictions should apply to (eg the host company's, the home company's or all group companies' employees);
- which departing employees the restrictions should apply to (eg a departing receptionist may present no real risk to the business because her influence over key staff may be limited);
- which key employees (and contractors?) does the employer need to protect (eg senior employees, sales staff, developers) and how these can be described accurately;
- whether the restriction should only cover staff who the employee had contact with during his employment or perhaps only those who reported to him within a specified period before termination;
- how long the restriction should apply for after the employment ends (and whether different periods should apply to different staff);
- whether any period of garden leave should be offset against the period of restriction;
- whether the restriction should be limited to solicitation or whether it should cover working with the key staff within a certain period after the employment ends;
- whether the restriction should take account of direct and indirect activities (eg providing information to a new employer which enables the new employer to appoint another member of staff to solicit);
- whether key staff who are still employed should be required to report approaches from current and former employees (this may be prohibited by some countries);
- whether more complex terms relating to team moves should be included.

Suppliers

11.17   The employer may wish to restrict the employee from interfering with relationships with suppliers after the employment ends or from approaching suppliers with a view to persuading them to supply to a competitor as well. Considerations will be broadly similar to those highlighted above.

Working with competitors

11.18   Sometimes the employer will not be satisfied with a restriction on the employee's activities when he goes to work for a competitor. The employer may want to restrict the employee's ability to work with a competitor, or to compete on his own account, at all for a period of time after the employment ends. This type of restriction is likely to be more tightly regulated and may not always be permitted.

11.19 The employer may wish to consider the following:

- which departing employees the restrictions should apply to;
- terms already applied to other employees in similar circumstances (consistency is usually important);
- which companies' competitors the restrictions should apply to (eg the host company, the home company or all group companies);
- who the competitors are (it may be possible to name them or describe them accurately);
- how long the restriction should apply for after the employment ends;
- whether any period of garden leave should be offset against the period of the restriction;
- whether the description of competitors should be fixed or be expressed in a way that will allow for changes to the business over time;
- the practical impact of the restriction on the employee's ability to work after the employment ends.

PAYMENT IN LIEU OF NOTICE

11.20 An employer who breaches the employment contract may not be able to enforce post termination restrictions. An employee may be entitled to a long period of notice of termination of employment and it may be impractical to allow him to remain at work throughout the notice period.

11.21 If he is dismissed without notice or on short notice the employer may breach the contract and lose the benefit of the post termination restrictions. An alternative may be to include a clause in the employment contract allowing the employer to pay in lieu of notice. These clauses may be referred to as 'PILON' clauses for convenience. (See **16.29–16.40** on PILON clauses.)

GARDEN LEAVE

11.22 Instead of, or in addition to, including a PILON clause in the contract, the contract could provide for a period of 'garden leave' at the employer's option. The employee would remain employed during any period of garden leave and be unable to work for a competitor. Remuneration normally continues during the garden leave period (but the potential impact on incentives should be considered). As with PILON arrangements, garden leave is not possible in every country. See also **16.41–16.42** on garden leave.

11.23 If garden leave arrangements are being considered for an expatriate the employer might want to consider the following:

- the effect of a period of garden leave on any immigration permission;
- the effect of the employee's location during garden leave on tax and social security, for example whether the employee should (or can) be required to remain in the host country during the garden leave period;
- whether any specific duties to co-operate should be imposed in respect of the garden leave period (from a commercial perspective and in the light of applicable, particularly host country, laws);
- whether the employer can include clauses allowing the employer to remove the employee from any office at the start of, or during, the garden leave period and how any 'powers' (see **16.11**) should be or can be removed; and
- whether it will be possible to include clauses to facilitate appointment of another employee to the expatriate's post during the garden leave period (this might eg have an impact on the immigration status of the departing expatriate).

ENFORCEMENT

11.24 The methods by which restrictive covenants can, and are, enforced in different countries vary considerably. The principles have been debated for a long time and various legislators, courts and collective bargaining units have come up with different approaches to resolving the issues. The differences between these approaches create some practical challenges for those drafting covenants for expatriates.

11.25 The following methods are quite commonly used to enforce restrictions.

- The employer may be able to obtain an injunction, or other court order, to prohibit the employee from undertaking the restricted activity (eg to stop him from starting a particular job before a certain date). Subsequent breach of the court's order may have severe penalties for the employee, for example criminal sanctions for 'contempt of court'.
- The employee may receive a sum of money or benefit that is forfeited if the restrictions are breached (see **11.31–11.41** on LTIP arrangements).
- The employee may be ordered to pay compensation to the employer based on the employer's losses arising from the employee's breach of the covenants. (Practically those losses will often be difficult to quantify.)
- The employee may be obliged to pay pre-agreed financial compensation, perhaps confirmed in his employment contract or a separate document, in relation to his breach of the covenants.
- A new employer may be subject to an injunction or may be ordered to pay compensation to the former employer in respect of the employee's breach

of the covenants, or more likely the new employer's 'inducement' of that breach. Compensation could be based on the former employer's losses or on the new employer's profits arising from breach of the covenants.

- The Trade Secrets Directive (see **11.9**) provides for remedies relating to 'infringing goods' eg recall from the market.

UK – fixed penalties and injunctions

11.26 Potential difficulty can arise if an employee works in the UK and is subject to covenants drafted to comply with another country's laws, and those laws require that the agreement specifies fixed financial compensation to be paid by the employee for breach of the covenants.

11.27 In the UK restrictive covenants are usually enforced by way of injunction (now called an 'interim order'). This is a quick (if expensive) way for the employer to effectively prevent the employee from doing what he should not be doing. The employer applies to the court for the interim order and, if the order is granted, it will normally apply until the full trial takes place. Damages may be awarded at the full trial. In practice, the availability of the injunction is likely to be more important than the availability of damages because by the time the full trial takes place the critical period during which the business seeks to protect itself may have passed and the effect on the employee may be irreparable. To persuade a court to award an interim order the employer must persuade the judge that the 'balance of convenience' lies in granting the interim order. One of the factors the judge will consider is evidence that a cash remedy will not suffice (ie so that if the interim order is not granted it will not be possible for the court to grant a remedy at full trial that would effectively 'put the employer right'). The employer should be able to show that the damage to the business if the employee is allowed to continue to breach the covenants would be difficult to quantify. If a cash remedy for breach of the covenants is specified in the employment documents then the injunction may not be available at all.

Penalty clauses

11.28 Another problem with the agreed financial compensation approach is that the clause requiring the employee to make the payment or repayment may not be enforceable. For example, in England, a 'penalty' for breach of contract may be unenforceable on public policy grounds unless it can be shown that the specified amount is a genuine pre-estimate of the losses flowing from the breach of contract. If the employer cannot easily show what the real losses are or are likely to be it will be hard for them to be confident that the financial penalty is a genuine pre-estimate of the losses flowing from breach and that the covenant will be enforceable.

Certainty

11.29 Confidence in the likely outcome of litigation is important for the effective protection of the business. This is because litigation to enforce covenants is very expensive. The employer is unlikely to want to incur the potential expense unless it is confident of the outcome. From the perspectives of the employee and his new employer, clearly enforceable covenants will be a far greater deterrent. Deterrence is usually a primary objective for the former employer. Effective deterrence is particularly important in an expatriate context where enforcement can be much more complex and expensive. (See **11.42** for some practical suggestions.)

EMPLOYEE PROTECTION

11.30 As with enforcement mechanisms, practices relating to employee protection vary considerably between countries. Depending on the jurisdiction, 'rules' along the following lines may be applied to protect employees:

- rules allowing the scope of covenants to be cut back if they are too broad (eg reducing the period of application of a covenant if the documents provide for too long a restriction, or limiting the geographical scope of the covenant if the area provided for is too broad);

- rules providing that certain covenants will not be enforceable at all, or that they will not be enforceable at all if they are too broad (giving a strong incentive to the employer to provide for modest covenants in the documents);

- provision for payment to be made to the employee either by way of lump sum consideration for the promises made or, recognising the likely impact of the covenants on the employee's ability to secure future employment and the likelihood of consequent lost future remuneration, at a set rate in respect of the period when the covenants are to apply (eg continued payment of salary or a proportion of salary for six months after the employment ends);

- provision for the employer to pay continued remuneration to the employee even if the employer does not want to enforce the covenant, unless perhaps the employee releases the employer from that obligation (eg on the basis that the employee has a legitimate expectation that he will receive the money);

- provision for compensation to be paid to the employee if the covenant proves to be unenforceable (eg recognising that even an unenforceable covenant may have an impact on the employee, for example because he believes it may be enforceable or he does not want to risk litigation and turns down work he would otherwise have accepted).

It is particularly important to be aware that in some jurisdictions covenants that are too broad may be struck out rather than 'fixed' by the Courts.

APPLICATION OF LAWS

11.31 If they are to be effective, restrictive covenants should be carefully drafted taking account of:

- the governing laws to be applied to the covenants (generally this will be a matter of choice provided the choice is confirmed in writing, see **10.3–10.29**);

- mandatory employment or public policy laws, for example restricting the length of time over which the covenants can apply after termination of employment (see **10.30–10.61**);

- the jurisdiction or jurisdictions where claims may be heard (see **10.62–10.74**); and

- the place or places where the covenants are likely to be enforced (see **10.75**).

Examples

11.32 Two UK cases provide helpful illustrations of the way that restrictive covenants intended to apply internationally might be enforced. (Note that there have subsequently been other decisions in this area in the UK. These cases are referred to only to illustrate the sort of legal challenges that might be made and the complexity of the issues.)

Samengo-Turner

11.33 In *Samengo-Turner and others v J & H Marsh & McLennan (Services) Ltd and others* ([2008] IRLR 237, [2007] EWCA Civ 723) the claimant employees lived and were domiciled in England. They had been employed by an English company, one of a number of companies within a group with a US parent company registered in New York. During their employments the claimants participated in LTIPs. The agreements relating to the LTIP arrangements were with the US parent company. The documents confirmed that New York courts should have exclusive jurisdiction and that New York law should be the governing law (for most of the documents).

11.34 The LTIP arrangements provided for bonus payments to be made over a period of time and also included post termination restrictive covenants. The agreements provided for repayment of some bonus in the event that the covenants were breached. The employees went to work for a competitor and the US parent company started proceedings in New York. The New York courts accepted jurisdiction and the employees then applied in England for a declaration regarding jurisdiction and an anti-suit injunction to restrain enforcement of the New York proceedings in England. They brought their claim in the UK under Council Regulation 44/2001/EC (on jurisdiction and the recognition and enforcement of judgments in civil and commercial matters) (an earlier version of the Judgments Regulation, see **10.62–10.74**). This is an EC Regulation to which the US is not party. Article 20(1) of the old Judgments

Regulation provided that the employer 'may bring proceedings only in the courts of the member state in which the employee is domiciled'.

11.35 In the absence of any useful case-law from the European Court of Justice on the application of the Judgments Regulation, the English Court of Appeal confirmed the following.

- The LTIP arrangements were part of the employees' contracts of employment.
- The employer must sue an employee in relation to his employment contract in the employee's country of domicile.
- The New York claim had been brought by their 'employer' for the purposes of the Judgments Regulation, notwithstanding that it was made by the US parent company not the employer, as it was an employment claim against employees that an employer would be expected to make.
- The anti-suit injunction was granted in relation to the US proceedings. (The group was still free to bring fresh proceedings in England).

Duarte v Black & Decker

11.36 *Duarte v Black & Decker Corporation and another* ([2007] All ER (D) 378 (Nov), [2007] EWHC 2720 (QB)) concerned similar issues. Mr Duarte was employed by Black & Decker and also participated in LTIP arrangements. His LTIP documents confirmed that the laws of the US State of Maryland should govern the LTIP arrangements. Mr Duarte also left his employment to take up employment with a competitor, apparently in breach of two-year restrictive covenants contained in the LTIP arrangements. Mr Duarte applied to the English courts for a declaration that the covenants were void and unenforceable. The High Court considered the application of the Rome Convention to the LTIP arrangements. (The Rome Convention was replaced by Rome I for EU countries except Denmark, see **10.3–10.29**. The Rome Convention applied to the UK but not the US.)

11.37 The English Court of Appeal confirmed the following.

- Mr Duarte's LTIP arrangements formed part of his contract of employment (ie as decided in *Samengo-Turner* above).
- The mandatory rules referred to in Art 6(1) of the Rome Convention were specific provisions, such as those in the Employment Rights Act 1996 whose overriding purpose was to protect employees. Article 6(1) provided no justification for applying English law in preference to Maryland law. Article 6(1) of the Rome Convention reads as follows:

    'Article 6

    Individual employment contracts

1. Notwithstanding the provisions of Article 3, in a contract of employment a choice of law made by the parties shall not have the result of depriving the employee of the protection afforded to him by the mandatory rules of the law which would be applicable under paragraph 2 in the absence of choice.'

- The law governing the enforceability and validity of restrictive covenants in employment contracts was of an altogether different character. It was part of the general law of 'restraint of trade' which in turn was part of the general law of contract. Art 16 of the Rome Convention applied in deciding whether the covenants were enforceable. English laws relating to restrictive covenants are public policy requirements. Article 16 of the Rome Convention reads as follows:

    'Article 16

    "Ordre public"

    The application of a rule of the law of any country specified by this Convention may be refused only if such application is manifestly incompatible with the public policy ("ordre public") of the forum.'

- If the restrictive covenants were valid and enforceable under Maryland law but invalid and unenforceable under English law, injunctive relief would be refused. However, based on the evidence of Maryland lawyers, the Court of Appeal decided that the covenants would not have been enforceable under Maryland law anyway.

11.38 It is worth bearing in mind that the interpretation given to the Rome Convention in the *Samengo-Turner* and *Duarte* cases may not be applied by other EU countries' courts and that the articles relating to mandatory/overriding laws in the current Rome I Regulation are formulated differently from those in the earlier Rome Convention.

COVENANTS AND LTIPS

11.39 For some time there has been a practice within multinationals of developing LTIPs that can be used to reward employees throughout the group. LTIPs are sometimes adapted for use in particular countries, for example by adoption of a sub-plan or by change to communications issued when cash or shares are awarded or share options are granted. The country-specific variations may, for example, allow for minor differences in eligibility criteria (eg to reflect host country discrimination laws) or tax and social security concerns.

11.40 Typically, the plan documents include choice of law clauses providing for the documents to be governed by the laws of the country where the head office is situated, often the laws of a US state. Benefits are usually received by the employees over long periods of time (eg two to three years). LTIPs often provide that benefits under the LTIP will either not be awarded ('malus') or will be forfeited ('claw-back') if post termination restrictive covenants are breached. These arrangements are frequently used and can provide for payment of very valuable benefits, particularly in the financial services sector. (Note that extensive regulation currently applies to some long-term incentives in the financial services sector, including in respect of malus and claw-back arrangements.)

11.41 Although enforcement of those arrangements is likely to be difficult (see above in relation to the *Samengo-Turner* and *Duarte* cases) they continued for some time with little legal challenge. Often an employee seeking a new job would look to the new employer to 'put him right' financially, usually by way of conditional 'sign on' bonus. Neither the employee (who did not then lose out substantially if he lost his LTIP benefits from the old employer) nor the new employer (who was likely to operate similar arrangements itself for its own employees) would have much interest in challenging the status quo. Economic and regulatory developments have since changed the landscape, and LTIP arrangements are often subject to dispute.

PRACTICAL SUGGESTIONS FOR EXPATRIATE CONTRACTS

Focus on where the covenants will be enforced

11.42 Employers of expatriates will often want to be able to enforce restrictions in more than one country. For example, enforcement in both the host country (where relevant customers and staff may be located) and in the home country (where the employer may be obliged to take legal action, particularly if the employee is domiciled in an EU home country) may be desirable. Other countries may be relevant too, for example if the employee's role covers a region and not just one country, if the employee accepts a new role with a competitor in another country or if the competitor's headquarters are located in another country.

Confirm the governing law in writing

11.43 The employer should normally agree the governing law for the covenants with the employee clearly in writing to reduce the risk of unnecessary dispute over which country's governing law applies. This is, eg, important in Europe where there is little European-level case-law relating to the way the Rome I Regulation applies (see **10.3–10.29** for more a detailed explanation regarding choice of governing law).

Choose the governing law carefully

11.44 Given the jurisdiction and enforcement constraints illustrated by the *Samengo-Turner* and *Duarte* cases, the employer should choose the governing law for the covenants carefully. For example, if the covenants are to be enforced against employees domiciled in England it would make sense to ensure that the covenants are governed by the laws of England. The employer will not then be forced to jump the double hurdle of proving that the covenants would be enforceable under English law and the chosen governing law.

11.45 It may sometimes be appropriate to choose different governing laws for the covenants from those chosen from the rest of the employment contract, and this is usually possible.

Comply with as many countries' requirements as possible

11.46 It would be sensible to comply with as many of the mandatory requirements of relevant countries relating to restrictive covenants as is practical. Many compromises can be made that would make the covenants more likely to be enforceable in relevant countries without prejudicing potential enforcement in other countries, for example:

- where there are constraints on the scope of the covenants that might be permitted (eg the period of time during which they are to apply) it may be sensible to choose the narrowest rather than the widest scope;
- where there is a requirement for continuing payment in one country this can generally be accommodated in other countries where there is no such requirement; and
- if a separate document containing the covenants is required by one country then this may be acceptable in other countries even if it is not required.

Be pragmatic about which countries' rules are most important

11.47 Some requirements may be in direct conflict (eg, see **11.26–11.29** on fixed financial compensation). It may not be possible to enforce covenants in all relevant countries. If that is the case the group may need to take a pragmatic view and decide which country is, or countries are, the most important. The employer will need to consider which laws will govern the covenants, where they are likely to be enforced and who they are likely to be enforced against.

Play safe

11.48 Although employees have been engaged on expatriate assignments for a very long time there has been relatively little litigation in the area of international restrictive covenants. With that in mind the employer may wish to 'play safe' in order to benefit from a more likely deterrent effect on the employee and any prospective new employer. New, complicated, forms of covenant should generally be avoided.

Tax

11.49 Tax advice should be sought in relation to the covenants and linked payments so that the potential impact is clear. As with any payment that may be subject to tax the employer should take care to ensure that the scope of tax equalisation or protection promises is made clear in the employment documents. Will tax equalisation apply to payments for post-termination restrictions?

11.50 See **16.29–16.40** in relation to the potential impact of PILON clauses on the tax treatment of severance pay.

11.51 If the proposed arrangements are to include 'claw-back' arrangements under which sums already earned or paid must be repaid by the employee if the covenants are breached, care should be taken to make the extent of the repayment and any tax or social security implications clear. The employee and employer may not be able to recover tax due or already paid in respect of the initial payment. Also, this type of arrangement may not be considered 'fair' or be enforceable in some countries.

UK

11.52 The key issue to remember from a UK perspective is that restrictive covenants are interpreted restrictively. The covenants must go no further than is reasonably necessary to protect the employer's legitimate business interests taking account of both the employer's and the employee's circumstances. Typically, UK covenants apply for shorter periods and are narrower in scope than those that might work in other countries.

11.53 Careful drafting by a UK-qualified lawyer is critical as strict rules of interpretation would be applied to determine whether the covenant is enforceable. Covenants drafted in other English language jurisdictions are often not effective in the UK because of the language used.

The importance of covenants

11.54 The adviser should assess the importance of covenants before starting to draft, and before incurring other specialists' fees for checking and commenting on the draft.

11.55 If the covenants are not particularly important, or the employer takes a pessimistic view of the likelihood of successful enforcement being possible it may be better to specify the governing law, use straightforward 'typical' covenants and not to spend too much time and money on getting the detail perfect.

11.56 If covenants are commercially important they should normally be drafted by an employment law specialist from the country whose governing laws will apply. They should be checked carefully by specialists from every relevant jurisdiction. They should also be reviewed and updated regularly. (Agreement will normally be required to introduce change to contracts.) The law is changing rapidly in this area and 'best practice' is likely to change with it.

OTHER PRACTICAL SUGGESTIONS (OUTSIDE THE CONTRACT)

11.57 There may be other, often easier, ways of protecting the business, either in addition to contractual covenants or instead of them. For example:

- In a country where covenants are not enforceable there may be a strong tradition of protecting confidential information in other ways. Time may be better spent on identifying the relevant information and communicating that carefully to the employee in writing.

- Old fashioned good housekeeping can help, such as: limiting the use of personal equipment for work; ensuring client details are properly entered on office databases; that access to telephones, databases and IT is carefully managed during employment and when employees leave; and that use of social media for business development is managed appropriately.

- Making sure that more than one employee develops key relationships can be invaluable, though this is not always practical.

- Consider the terms of contracts with key clients or suppliers and whether restrictions can be included there.

11.58 As with most aspects of employment law, carrots often work better than sticks. Developing good relationships with people and keeping in touch can make a huge difference to what happens at the end of an employment. Commercial benefits that may flow from an employee's wish to maintain good relationships and desire to be seen as the professional 'good guy' in the local market should never be underestimated. This is particularly the case for expatriates where local relationships are often very close and the pool of potential future employers and clients may be closely connected.

11.59 Taking time to visit host locations regularly and helping individuals out with personal things such as schooling, housing or job hunting may be far more effective than getting the paper work right – and a lot cheaper than cross-border litigation.

CHAPTER 12

EQUALITY

INTRODUCTION

12.1 Treating people 'fairly' can be a challenge for assignment managers. A local hire's family life is usually left at home and it is generally accepted that religion, race, sexuality, family status etc should not be taken into consideration when a promotion is offered or remuneration is determined. By contrast, international selection processes, remuneration and policies are often closely linked to 'protected characteristics'. It can be hard to know what 'fair' is, and to navigate practical and compliance hurdles without reference to these things.

12.2 Few of these equality issues have been litigated thoroughly and, in practice, they tend to be managed largely by applying common sense, rather than through careful analysis of the law. Given this context, it is not possible to remove all risk, but it is possible to reduce risk for the employer and to rationalise some of the inappropriate practices that have become a far too 'normal' part of global mobility, see further below. Employers and advisers who may be tempted to complacency by the relatively few reported cases in this area should bear in mind that employment lawyers have focused on this only relatively recently and that, because of the tendency of expatriate cases to settle, the impact of potential claims (eg on higher confidential settlements) is hard to assess with any accuracy. (See also Chapter 16 on dispute resolution.)

12.3 This chapter looks at:

- Selection for assignment (**12.4–12.8**).
- Host country restrictions (**12.9–12.11**).
- Differential pay practices (**12.12–12.24**).
- Maternity and other family leave (**12.25–12.34**).
- Cultural awareness (**12.35**).
- Special considerations for particular protected characteristics (**12.36**).
- Practical steps to reduce risk (**12.37–12.38**).

SELECTION FOR ASSIGNMENT

12.4 Checking for potential personal blocks or hidden costs to assignment can raise complex legal issues including the risk of unlawful discrimination. A normal 'fair' recruitment or selection process for a role in most jurisdictions does not involve enquiry into family matters, health, sexuality, religion or politics. In most democratic countries it is accepted that candidates for a job should be selected on merit only.

12.5 However, to establish and document an international assignment successfully the employer will need to check some information. For example, if the employee is to be accompanied by family members immigration advice will be required for the family too, to ensure the assignment is feasible. The individual's personal circumstances may also have a substantial impact on the employer's costs, and sometimes may have an impact on viability.

12.6 Those advising on the practicalities will want to have the detail as early as possible so that any blocks can be identified before substantial time and money is spent. Actual or perceived 'problems' may also lead the employer to prefer one candidate over another, and this may in turn lead to potential discrimination claims. Given that substantial remuneration and career benefits can attach to international assignment, these claims could be high value. If there are established practices or policies linked to the discrimination, possibly linking staff with different employers who are subject to a common policy, there may also be increased potential for 'class action' or similar group claims.

12.7 The risk of claims arising on selection may potentially be reduced by making sure that sensitive enquiries are made after the preferred candidate is identified. So, eg, it is common practice in the UK to recruit 'blind' to immigration status and to try to resolve any immigration difficulties that become apparent at a later stage. (It is currently best practice in the UK for an offer of employment to made in writing before immigration checks are carried out.) This will not always be possible when an individual is to relocate internationally because there is often a need for early information when preparing for an assignment if deadlines are to be met. Also, those selected for assignment are often internal candidates whose protected characteristics and related circumstances are already well known.

12.8 It is helpful, too, to resist the temptation to anticipate potential blocks for individuals that may be linked to a protected characteristic without evidence. For example, it would be unwise to assume that a woman would refuse an assignment if offered because her husband would not follow her. It will often be simpler and less discriminatory to offer the assignment, together with related information, and let the individual identify and communicate any blocks to the employer. Fairer self-selection may be facilitated by providing relevant information to all candidates rather than just those assumed to be likely to be affected. For example, if the altitude of a host location may exacerbate certain medical conditions it would be sensible to highlight this to all potential candidates for assignment not just those known to suffer from asthma. Similarly, it may be better to volunteer information that may be relevant without the candidate requesting it. So, eg, if an HIV test is required for entry to the host location that information could be included in the information provided to all candidates at an early stage.

HOST COUNTRY RESTRICTIONS

12.9 The host country may not apply the same equality standards as the home country, and is likely to have a different culture. Sometimes these differences pose insurmountable barriers. For example, if an employer is clear that nationals of a particular country will not gain immigration clearance to allow them to take up a post in the host location, the employer may have no option but to pick another candidate. Note too that apparently similar 'protected characteristics' do not always work in the same way in different locations, eg in the EU age discrimination laws protect all ages, whereas US laws may focus on older employees.

12.10 Some lateral thinking, and close questioning of advisers, may be helpful both to facilitate good decision making and to reduce the risk of unexpected claims. For example, homosexuality may technically be illegal in the host country but may not, in practice, be a barrier to business visitors.

12.11 An employee who does not appear eligible for immigration clearance may also have other options that are not apparent to the employer. For example, an Australian who does not qualify for a work permit may be able to get to the same place by applying for an EU passport because of family history. (See also Chapter 18 on Brexit.)

DIFFERENTIAL PAY PRACTICES

Paying expats more than locals

12.12 Senior expatriates are often paid more than local hires for 'doing the same job'. This raises the risk that race discrimination, or similar laws, may be used to challenge the arrangements. In many countries where race discrimination legislation applies, differential treatment is allowed if there is a legitimate objective reason for the differences that is not connected to race. There does not appear to have been much litigation in this area (yet) but it is still worth thinking about why an expatriate might be offered better treatment, particularly where discrimination legislation may apply. The business rationale might include arguments that:

- a local hire was not available to do the job (perhaps supported by documentary evidence of an earlier advertising campaign);
- comparisons with local hires are not appropriate as the 'extra' remuneration or particular benefits were needed to persuade a candidate with the right skills and experience to take the job (ie the business needed to take account of market forces);

- 'expatriate' benefits were provided to free up the expatriate's time and help him perform his duties effectively (eg provision of a car, services of a relocation agent, etc); and/or

- some of the 'expatriate' benefits, such as a disturbance allowance or reimbursement of relocation expenses compensate for disadvantage caused by the assignment and do not amount to additional remuneration.

Conversely, expatriates may sometimes be paid less than local hires, and this may also potentially trigger claims. This is more likely to be the case with more junior expatriates, eg construction or sesasonal agricultural workers, who are not the focus of this book. See 10.50–10.55 on the Posted Workers Directive which sets some minimum European standards.

12.13 Applicable laws may potentially require comparison between individual benefits rather than the 'whole package'.

12.14 Some legislation relevant to discrimination claims may have extra-territorial effect so that there is the potential for overlap between different countries' laws. For example, see **10.56–10.60** on the application of British discrimination laws to employees posted abroad from Britain.

12.15 In some instances, there may be direct conflict between the requirements of one country's laws and another's, for example between US legislation prohibiting the release of commercial information to employees of certain nationalities and host country anti-discrimination laws.

Variable employer costs

12.16 The costs of employing individual local hires are often fairly similar. Tax rates might be similar and benefit packages are likely to be aligned. It is fairly easy for an employer to ensure local hires are treated consistently with each other and that equivalent sums are spent on them.

12.17 However, international employees are frequently offered benefits to compensate them for 'loss' of their home package or situation. The problem is that the 'we'll put you right' approach will entail varying costs for the employer, depending on personal circumstances, and refusing to do so will have differential impact, see further below.

Family-related benefits

12.18 Employees are often offered benefits linked to family status. This is particularly the case for long-term home employer arrangements, where a typical package might include:

- international medical cover for all the family;
- help with education costs where there are school-age children;

- accommodation reflecting family size;
- a home leave budget reflecting the need for all the family to travel home for holidays;
- higher relocation or repatriation limits reflecting the need to transport more family possessions at the start and end of the assignment.

12.19 A number of 'protected characteristics' may be linked, directly or indirectly, to family status, eg sex, sexuality, marital status, race or age. For example, a 65 year old may be less likely to have dependent children living at home than a 45 year old. Some ethnic or religious groups, and nationalities, may be statistically more likely to have more children or older dependent relatives living with them. Some employers try to manage this by providing family-related benefits in respect of a limited number of children only, eg a maximum of two children. This may also raise a risk of 'indirect' discrimination claims because those from protected groups with more children may be disadvantaged. (In reality, there is no risk-free option because the way equality laws work does not quite fit the way expatriate employment works in practice.)

12.20 A single man who will undertake the same role unaccompanied might 'cost' the employer much less even where a consistent expatriate policy is applied to another candidate. There is potential for the single man to make claims on the basis that he is, in reality, paid less. Similarly, a senior employee with seven children may make claims if he is not offered the job because the costs of providing the 'normal' expatriate package under the employer's policy is too high. In practice, there has been little litigation in this area and it is not yet clear whether an approach to remuneration that is linked to family status can be 'justified' (and even when settled, this is unlikely to be settled consistently across all jurisdictions). Where there is uncertainty, it may be helpful to check that there is at least a clear business rationale for the approach adopted.

Local plus

12.21 'Local plus' is a term used to describe a remuneration and benefits package based on that which would be offered to a 'local hire', but with some expatriate 'extras', eg assistance with tax return preparation. The expatriate 'extras', eg tax return assistance, may be offered on a transitional basis. Employers offering local plus arrangements may be particularly exposed to potential discrimination claims because comparison with local staff may be relatively easy. Often a long-term home employer assignee is employed by a different employer from other staff working in the host location and they may perform very different roles. 'Local plus' staff are far more likely to be employed by the same host employer as the host country local hires and may well be working side by side with people doing exactly the same thing.

12.22 As with family-related packages, it may help in the defence of potential claims if there is a business rationale for the differential treatment. It would also be sensible to focus on benefits that directly relate to the move, eg removal expenses, transitional accommodation, first year's tax returns etc, rather than increased long-term remuneration or benefits, which may be harder to justify.

12.23 Where differential treatment is for a stated reason, eg where increased pay reflects language skills, it would be sensible to check the facts, eg that this reflects a genuine commercial need for language skills, and that the payment is necessary to ensure the need is met, in the particular context. For example, if there is a requirement for a Polish-speaking individual to undertake a particular role and so the business feels it must offer more to encourage a Polish national to relocate, it might be prudent to check both that relocation is necessary to ensure that a Polish-speaking individual is available in the host country and that additional payment is necessary to induce an expatriate to accept the role.

Tax equalisation

12.24 See 7.80–7.92 on tax equalisation more generally. Tax equalisation is a particular concern because many tax equalisation policies provide, essentially, for higher or lower gross and net pay, depending on country of origin. Race laws applicable in many jurisdictions (including eg the EU and US) may potentially apply, though not necessarily in the same way. We do not yet have the benefit of clear case law or other legislation to help assess the risks of discrimination claims based on this sort of differential treatment. The following may help with risk assessment in the interim:

- Arrangements that apply over long periods of time and to larger numbers of highly paid, potentially litigious, people are likely to create greater risk.
- Policy documents are not just 'internal' management tools and may be used in litigation as evidence of the employer's intentions etc. The existence of a policy document may also give a litigant the opportunity to draw 'comparisons' with a wider range of people and may open the door to group action. Where there is a written policy the potential impact of the policy on employees with protected status should be reviewed carefully before it is adopted, or frequently thereafter.
- If tax equalisation or protection is applied it should be applied for a clear commercial reason. For example, tax equalisation by reference to the 'home country' might be justifiable in the short term but may not be appropriate if the employees concerned are career expatriates who have not worked 'back home' for 20 years.
- There will naturally be greater risk if different policies apply to employees who work for the same employer or who work side by side doing the same work.

MATERNITY AND OTHER FAMILY LEAVE

12.25 Maternity and paternity issues tend to be more complex for expatriates than for local hires.

12.26 For example, the following may be concerns:

- Whether medical insurance covers maternity-related treatment in the host country. (This type of cover may be unusual for an ordinary 'local hire' but is common under international medical policies for expatriates.)

- Arrangements for the woman to return to her home country while she is still able to fly before delivery.

- Medical treatment normally provided in the home country for 'free' may not be accessible during the assignment, even if the woman is prepared to travel, because of changes to residency or tax or social security status.

- If the expatriate's partner is to give birth in the home country, the expatriate himself may wish to take a longer than usual period of leave to coincide with birth of the baby.

- Medical facilities in the host country may not be of sufficient quality or there may be capacity problems requiring early 'booking'.

- Efficient application of international health cover and immigration permission (if required) to the baby from birth.

12.27 If the expatriate becomes pregnant, rather than the expatriate's partner, then the employer will need to consider applicable maternity leave and pay laws more carefully. The employer will need to consider whether home and/or host country rules relating to maternity leave and pay will apply. The application of maternity pay rules may not apply in the same way as maternity leave rules. The former are often linked to social security contributions, whereas the latter are often governed by mandatory employment laws. The employer should also enquire about the appropriate source of maternity pay as this may not be paid by the employer. It may be possible to recover all or part of the sums paid out of central funds.

12.28 It is possible for both home and host country requirements to apply at the same time and those requirements may conflict. There may be a risk of sex discrimination claims. (In many countries it is also not possible to dismiss a pregnant woman or a woman who has recently given birth or is breastfeeding.) Sometimes, where there is doubt, or perhaps an expectation that home country maternity pay or leave standards will apply when the arrangements are, in fact, covered by host country mandatory laws, the employer may decide to give the employee the best of both home and host country arrangements. Sometimes an early decision to be generous can be cheaper than trying to resolve all the legal issues. It is worth bearing in mind, though, that whilst the employer may elect to allow additional maternity leave or pay additional maternity pay, the employer's ability to recover any additional maternity pay from central funds is unlikely to be a matter of choice.

12.29 Issues relating to maternity cover can be particularly difficult in an expatriate context where the period of absence is long in relation to the period of the assignment. It may be difficult to put a replacement in place quickly, for example because the replacement would need a work permit and this cannot be obtained quickly or cannot be obtained without the pregnant employee relinquishing their permit.

Example – expatriate working in the UK

12.30 Suppose an employee, Ishil, comes to the UK to work and will have a baby whilst she is here. Her expatriate status will not affect her right to take normal UK statutory maternity leave. If Ishil works in the UK and meets the normal UK qualifying criteria she will have the same maternity leave rights as local hires.

12.31 Ishil may, in addition, have rights to take maternity leave under the laws of another country, for example her home country, or under her contract of employment or a more generous contractual company policy that applies to her. Any maternity leave rights arising under Ishil's contract or under the laws of another country will be in addition to UK rights as it is not possible to 'contract out' or 'derogate' from statutory UK maternity leave rights. The employer needs to comply with each aspect of the UK legislation even if the total 'package' offered under another country's laws or the company policy is better.

12.32 UK statutory maternity pay (SMP) is governed by different legislation. Suppose Ishil does not pay UK social security contributions and so does not qualify for SMP. Her employer may decide to make equivalent payments to Ishil but will not be able to recover those 'voluntary' amounts through the UK social security scheme.

Effect on benefits

12.33 The impact of the birth on the employee's, their partner's, and their child's immigration status should also be checked. For example, if the baby is born in the home country further immigration permission may be required to allow the mother to bring the baby to the host country. Problems may also arise if host country laws do not accommodate illegitimate children.

12.34 An additional family member could potentially lead to increased costs for the employer, depending on how benefit promises have been formulated. For example, an extra child could lead to increases in the costs of:

- providing medical cover;
- education-related expenses (but this is unlikely to be relevant for some time);
- flights (again this is unlikely to be an issue while the child is very young);
- tax equalisation or tax protection if the promise has been given in a way that is linked to additional tax relief allowed to a larger family or which takes account of 'child benefit' offered in the home country;
- dealing with immigration issues;

- assisting with accommodation;
- shipping costs at the end of the assignment.

Marriage and divorce may, of course, also affect benefit costs. (See also Chapter 22 on employee perspectives.)

CULTURAL AWARENESS

12.35 A particularly sensitive area for those concerned about equality is cultural awareness training. (See **15.29–15.32** on what this might entail.) To be useful the training must describe national/ethnic characteristics in generalised and comparative terms. Some descriptions and comparisons may well be considered derogatory by some. Employers may potentially be held responsible for detriment caused to participants and others even where the training is provided by third party providers who have been chosen with care. It would be prudent to discuss and review content in advance and ensure that comments are positioned appropriately. Of greater concern may be 'aptitude' tests that seek to identify characteristics that will enable the individual to adapt effectively to the new environment. Again, careful review of proposals for 'bias' and 'indirectly' discriminatory impact would be appropriate.

SPECIAL CONSIDERATIONS FOR PARTICULAR PROTECTED CHARACTERISTICS

12.36 The following comments are intended only to highlight some issues that arise frequently.

Sex:

- Some countries restrict the freedom of women to do certain things, eg drive a car, or wear certain clothing.
- In practice, women may be less likely to volunteer for, be selected for and/or accept overseas assignments. This may have an impact on career development, eg where there is a heavy focus on international experience for promotion. (Assumptions, without basis, that this would be the case for a particular woman could be just as disadvantageous.)

Sexual orientation and transgender issues:

- There may be additional safety concerns. In some countries illegality may be an issue.
- Same sex marriages may not be recognised.
- Changes to sex may not be recognised.

Marital status:

- Some countries do not recognise unmarried partners, same sex partners or illegitimate children.

Disability:

- The employer may be required to make reasonable adjustments under disability discrimination laws.
- The cost of providing support for a disabled employee or family member may be high. Cost is not a legitimate justification for discrimination in many jurisdictions.
- Appropriate medical or educational facilities may not be available in the host location.

Pregnancy and maternity:

- See **12.25–12.34** and **15.21–15.28.**

Race, ethnic or national origin:

- Access to immigration clearance may be restricted for some nationalities etc.
- Tax equalisation policies are often linked, directly or indirectly, to national origin.

Religion or belief:

- Some countries may restrict entry to individuals with certain religious beliefs or a history of certain, eg political, activities.
- Holiday and weekend arrangements, working time and public holidays may not align with the employee's religious obligations.

Age:

- Note that some laws protect only older employees whilst some protect both younger and older employees who are disadvantaged due to age.

PRACTICAL TIPS FOR REDUCING EQUALITY-RELATED RISK

12.37   Best practice is not fully developed in this area and given the variety of jurisdictions, frequency with which equality laws change and tendency for expatriate claims to settle, may never be. In particular, current case law and guidance related to expatriates is limited. This lack of clarity does not of course mean that practical steps cannot be taken to reduce risk: it just makes it difficult for employers to work out how best to do that.

12.38 The following suggestions may help an employer reduce risk. (NB this list is intended to prompt thought, it is not comprehensive and is not a substitute for proper fact and jurisdiction-specific and up-to-date legal advice.) It should also be borne in mind that many employers seek to reduce disadvantage to employees with protected characteristics voluntarily, with positive outcomes in mind, and not just with a view to reducing risk for the employer.

- Take more care when policies apply to large numbers of people, over significant periods of time or to high value benefits eg pension or tax equalisation arrangements.

- Consider the impact of policies on people with particular protected characteristics eg LGBT+ employees, those with children, women, those with disabilities, older and younger employees etc (see **12.36**).

- Make sure policies, practices and employment documents are reviewed regularly by employment lawyers from appropriate jurisdictions, ie specialists, ideally in the context of privileged legal advice. Ask for professional help when drafting documents.

- Seek feedback from employees and consider the guidance of special interest groups (eg Stonewall in relation to LGBT+ assignees) and governmental or similar organisations.

- When checking policies try to identify potential groups of winners and losers as this will give an indication of where risk lies.

- Take particular care to ensure managers are familiar with the concept of indirect discrimination and try to identify practical examples.

- Ensure that any differential treatment can be justified on genuine objective commercial grounds that are not linked to protected characteristics, and bear in mind that the cost of providing a benefit to a particular individual may not be an adequate defence to failing to provide it.

- Consider the impact of practices, benefits etc on individuals if things go wrong, the assignment is ended earlier etc, as well as the impact on the individual if all is going well. Be particularly vigilant on selection, at bonus time and on termination.

- Ensure that diversity training is adapted to the needs of international assignees and global mobility managers.

- Care should be taken when discretion is exercised as discrimination claims may arise, eg when an employer decides to help one employee out but not another.

- Communicate with individual employees frequently, so that problems are flushed out at an early stage, when they are often easier to resolve.

- Do not underestimate the impact of personality and fair dealing. Happy employees who have had a good working experience are more likely to work constructively with their employers to resolve issues as they arise and are less likely to make complaints (or claims).

CHAPTER 13

NEW LOCATIONS

13.1 When a multinational starts to do business in a country where it has never done business before, making arrangements for employment of the first employee is likely to entail more work than when some employment arrangements are already in place. If the first employee is an expatriate then there will be some additional things to take into account when the expatriate employment documents are prepared.

13.2 This chapter covers:

- Corporate structure (**13.3–13.7**).
- Tax (**13.8–13.20**).
- Administrative requirements (**13.21–13.39**).
- Control and authority (**13.40–13.47**).
- Impact of employee status on employment laws (**13.48**).
- Termination (**13.49–13.51**).
- Conclusions (**13.52**).

CORPORATE STRUCTURE

13.3 Before work starts in the host country the business will need to decide on the legal entity that will operate there. This might, for example, be a new company or partnership set up for the purpose in the host country, or a branch or representative office of an overseas company. The decision is unlikely to be driven by employment law considerations. Tax, particularly corporation tax, is likely to be much more important. Specialist advice should be sought from appropriate experts in the home and host countries, and any other country that may be relevant (such as the country where the product to be sold in the host country is manufactured).

13.4 The group might, for example, decide to set up a new limited liability company in the host country to help 'ring-fence' home country profits from corporation tax in the host country. Alternatively, if there is no need from a tax perspective for any other arrangement, the group might decide to set up a representative office in the host country because less administration is involved.

13.5 Corporation tax considerations are usually the most important considerations for determining the entity through which business will be conducted in the host country.

13.6 An expatriate sent to work in the host country does not necessarily have to be employed by the company responsible for running the business to which he supplies his services (see Chapter 4 on the identity of an employee's employer). However, there are more likely to be constraints on the choice of employer where the expatriate is the first employee to work in the host country. For example, the most senior employee in the host country may need to be employed by the host company. Host country laws may prevent an employee of another group company from undertaking certain roles. On the other hand, if there is only a branch or representative office in the host country, then a host country employment arrangement may not be an option, because there may be no host country legal entity capable of employing the expatriate.

13.7 Practically, the need to set up the right legal entity first may delay the employment of the expatriate or the start of his overseas assignment. If he is to be employed by a new company then that company would need to exist before it can employ the employee. It may, however, sometimes be possible for a new recruit to have an initial period of employment with another group company before the overseas assignment or host company begins to mitigate problems with timing.

TAX

Corporation tax and company residence

13.8 A company is generally obliged to pay corporation tax in the country where the company is 'resident' (and sometimes in other countries too, see further below). How tax residency is determined for companies will vary from country to country.

13.9 The assignment of an expatriate to manage a new host company could, potentially, have an impact on the corporation tax status of the new host company. Issues that may be relevant to the host company's tax residency could, eg, include:

- the seniority of the expatriate;
- his role and responsibilities;
- how, in practice, he manages the host company business;
- where he manages the host company business from (eg if the expatriate manages a region, returns to the home country regularly for meetings or simply travels a lot then the risk of the host company becoming tax resident outside the host country may be higher).

13.10 Corporation tax can, from a financial perspective, be a far more significant consideration than income tax.

13.11 The employment documents can help reduce risk for the employer by confirming facts that support the preferred tax residency status, provided of course that they reflect the reality of the arrangements. Documents must reflect the facts, see **4.114** on tax evasion. It is usually prudent to ask a corporation tax specialist to review the proposed job title, duties, normal place of work, mobility clauses, etc before the employment documents are issued to the employee.

Corporation tax and permanent establishment

13.12 A similar issue can arise where tax authorities try to argue that a company that is not tax resident in their country should, nevertheless, pay corporation tax because the non-resident company has a 'permanent establishment' there.

13.13 'Permanent establishment' will usually be defined in a double tax treaty between the home and host countries and the definition will usually refer to a fixed place of business, where the business is carried on.

13.14 Suppose, for example, that there is a home country employment arrangement and an expatriate is assigned to the host country to help start the home company's business there. The home company is clearly corporation tax resident in the home country. However, the expatriate's role may give the host country's tax authorities scope to argue that the home company has created a 'permanent establishment' in the host country and that host country corporation tax is due on that basis. Whether the host country is successful may depend, amongst other things, on:

- the scope of the employee's authority to conclude contracts for the home company in the host country (eg does he act as intermediary/introducer and refer potential commercial contracts for conclusion by someone else back in the home country or does he actually conclude commercial contracts with customers himself?);
- where the employee works in the host country (eg are there any permanent premises or does the employee work from hotels or customers' premises?).

13.15 As with corporation tax residency the employment documents can help the business to protect itself against arguments that a permanent establishment has been created in the host country, or at least help avoid making things worse. Again, it is usually prudent to ask a corporation tax specialist to review the proposed job title, duties, etc before the employment documents are issued to the employee. In particular, it can be helpful to confirm what the employee does not have authority to do, as well as what he can do. It can also be helpful to distinguish between the employee's authority to conclude commercial contracts related to the home company's core business (eg contracts for the sale of chairs if the home company manufactures and sells chairs) and contracts that relate to day-to-day administration (eg a contract for the purchase of stationery for the office).

Corporation tax and transfer pricing

13.16 When one company pays another for the services of an expatriate the level of the fee may affect the profits of both companies. If those profits are subject to corporation tax in different countries then the level of the fee may have an impact on the corporation tax to be paid in each country. That may give the tax authorities an incentive to challenge the size of the fees paid.

13.17 For example, suppose there is a home country employment arrangement. The host company pays a fee to the home company for the employee's services and the arrangement is properly documented through an inter-company expatriate supply agreement. The size of the fee charged could affect the corporation tax due from the home company in the home country and due from the host company in the host country. Care should be taken to ensure that fees are set appropriately. For example, fees might reflect employment costs (remuneration, employer's social security costs, professional fees, etc) with a small mark up to reflect management time and/or the risks the employer accepts in relation to the employment. The fees should be properly documented in the companies' accounts, as well as through the inter-company expatriate supply agreement.

13.18 Recharging arrangements can, eg, also affect:

- the identity of the employer (see Chapter 4);
- the sales tax (VAT) to be paid (this will be more significant if for some reason sales tax cannot be recovered, see **13.19–13.20**);
- the availability of income tax relief for the expatriate under a double tax treaty where there is a short-term assignment (see **5.13–5.15**); and/or
- the availability of a corporation tax deduction in relation to remuneration costs.

Sales tax (VAT)

13.19 The business may need to register for sales tax (VAT) purposes generally.

13.20 If the home company is an expatriate's employer, the host company will normally pay the home company fees for the expatriate's services. Sales tax may be due in respect of those fees. It may be that the host entity does not charge VAT to its own customers, in which case VAT on fees paid to the home company may not be recoverable by the host company.

ADMINISTRATIVE REQUIREMENTS

13.21 Each country will have its own rules for employers and these will need to be checked locally. The following are some examples of things that may need to be considered before the first employee can be engaged in the host country.

Payroll etc arrangements

13.22 Most countries require employers to register for payroll, income tax and/or social security purposes. Typically, both the employer and individual employees would need to be registered with the relevant host country authorities.

13.23 It is worth remembering that host country payroll obligations may arise from the start of the first employment. This may be the case even if the employee is employed by the home company and the employer plans to continue to pay the employee through the home country payroll into his bank account in the home country. It may still be necessary to set up a host country 'shadow' payroll arrangement to ensure that host country withholding obligations are administered appropriately.

13.24 If the employer has never operated a payroll in the host country before it could consider outsourcing this work to a third-party service provider, depending on whether host country rules allow this. Whatever the requirements, the host country rules should be checked well before the first employee starts work. The employer will need appropriate advice to ensure that the payroll is operated and taxes are deducted and/or paid over to the relevant public authorities correctly.

13.25 The business will also need to ensure that funds are available in good time to make necessary payments in the host country. These would typically include salary payments but could also include other business expenses such as rent, the costs of buying office furniture, etc. Practically, where the expatriate is to be the first employee in the host country he may need to be able to sign cheques etc. To do so he will probably need (an) appropriate bank mandate(s). The host country may also require that the expatriate first be granted formal 'powers of attorney' to confirm his authority, see below. Care should be taken to ensure that appropriate controls are put in place if the expatriate is to have the power to make payments to himself.

'Powers'

13.26 In the UK we tend to be relaxed about documentation of employee authority. This is probably because under our contract law an individual with 'apparent authority' can bind a company even if, in reality, he has not been given the authority to do so.

13.27 This is not the case in many other countries. There may be a requirement in the host country for information about the scope of the employee's authority to be registered or made formally available to the public. The rules relating to the granting and removal of authority can be quite complex and host country advice will almost always be needed to make sure the arrangements comply with local rules. This is sometimes referred to as the granting of 'powers of attorney', or simply as 'powers'.

13.28 When formal arrangements of this type are set up it is important to bear in mind that the expatriate may later be unable, or unwilling, to do what is required by the business. For example, if the expatriate with the 'power' to authorise payment of staff is dismissed then someone else may need to be able to deal with the payroll for the host company quickly. Where possible, more than one person should be given the relevant authority at the outset so that things do not grind to a halt if the expatriate's services are withdrawn at short notice or he is uncooperative. Before any powers are granted the business should seek advice from a host country specialist on any steps it might be able to take to facilitate removal at a later stage.

13.29 If powers are to be granted to an expatriate, the person (or people) authorising grant of powers for the company will usually need to be able to demonstrate his (or their) own authority to act for the company in granting those powers. The documentation needed will vary from country to country but might, eg, include:

- board minutes/a resolution confirming the company's decision to authorise granting of the powers, signed by (an) appropriate company representative(s) (eg a director and/or company secretary);
- documentary evidence that each person who has signed the minutes has been appointed to the relevant position (eg for a UK director this might be done by way of an appropriately certified print out from Companies House records);
- witness of the director's or company secretary's signature by a solicitor or, more likely, a notary public;
- an 'apostille' for the notary public's signature (see the Glossary at Appendix 3 for an explanation of what an apostille is).

See also framework document **A2.8** at Appendix 2.

Employment registration

13.30 The company may need to register with a host country employment authority before it can employ any staff. Registration may be subject to conditions, for example, the business may need to show that it is properly licensed as a business or that it has premises in the host country.

Immigration sponsor registration

13.31 A new start up may find it more difficult to obtain immigration permission for its employees, for example, if there is a requirement for the employer to formally register as a 'sponsor' before work permits can be granted.

13.32 Delays in setting up the legal entity that will make applications for immigration permission are likely to delay the submission of the applications. That, in turn, may delay the start of the assignment. (See **19.4–19.31** on UK sponsorship requirements.)

Insurance

13.33 There may be a requirement to put in place employee liability insurance or similar arrangements to ensure that the business is in a position to meet personal injury claims from employees. Even if there is no legal requirement to do this, the business is likely to want to ensure that appropriate cover against personal injury is in place.

13.34 The host company may also consider taking out key man insurance for its own benefit (ie insurance to cover the situation where an employee critical to the business is unable to perform his duties).

13.35 Some countries also require the employer to contribute to a public fund in relation to potential termination of employment (eg to a fund to provide an 'end of service gratuity'). These contributions may be in addition to social security contributions. Other cover may be required for the employee, eg adequate medical insurance cover.

Data protection (privacy)

13.36 See **15.73–15.99** for an overview of data protection requirements, particularly in Europe.

13.37 Where there is a start-up assignment there will be no data protection arrangements in place in the host country.

13.38 The group will need to think about arrangements to facilitate lawful transfer of personal data from the home country and home company (and perhaps other countries and group companies) to the host country and, if there is to be one, the new host company. (There is also likely to be personal data flow in the other direction.)

13.39 Thought should also be given to compliance with host country laws relating to the processing of data etc. For example, particularly if the host country is a European country, there may be a requirement to register with the local data protection authorities as a data controller. (Note: the European requirements are not consistent in this regard. In some countries notification of the relevant authority may be required before data can be processed.)

CONTROL AND AUTHORITY

13.40   As with any expatriate arrangement, reporting lines should support the preferred employment structure (In particular, certain key decisions in relation to an employee should be made by the employer; see **4.71–4.107**). There are likely to be additional challenges relating to reporting lines if the expatriate is the first employee to work for the host country business.

13.41   Practically, there is unlikely to be anyone else on the ground in the host country to manage the expatriate and/or report any problems or potential problems with his performance. If the employee is employed by the home company, some administrative control can be imposed from overseas, for example, arrangements could be put in place for approval of expenses, holiday, etc and a more senior line manager could visit periodically. If the employee is employed by a new host company and is the most senior employee and a director of that company, then effective supervision is likely to be harder to achieve. The group will need to think about how some control can be exercised. This might be by appointing further directors to the board to represent the parent company's interests (ie so that the expatriate is obliged to report his activities properly and can be outvoted if necessary). The business could also ensure that the employment documents include clauses specifically restricting the employee's authority and activities. Contractual restrictions may not, in practice, prevent an employee from deliberately doing something different but they can help make the employer's expectations clear and may assist if there is later a need to discipline or dismiss the employee.

13.42   The scope of an employee's duties may be particularly important if he is the most senior and/or only employee. As explained above, his duties should reflect the activities that the host entity is able to undertake. If the host entity is a representative office able to perform marketing functions only then the most senior employee on the ground should have a contract that confirms that. There may be a need for express clauses limiting the expatriate's powers to enter into binding contracts on behalf of the employer or other group companies. The clauses may require the expatriate to refer leads to a team based in another country or working for another business where conclusion of contracts might be appropriate. (See **13.8–13.15** on potential corporation tax implications.)

13.43   Regardless of host country requirements or the need to document arrangements with tax consequences effectively, restraints on authority included in the employment documents might need to be quite extensive from a practical point of view. For example, the employment documents could make clear that budgets must be approved; limits could be placed on the expenses that can be incurred without approval; and there may be restrictions on hiring or firing or contact with the media. (Some sample clauses are set out below, see **13.47**).

Care should, however, be taken to ensure that restrictions on the employee's activities in the host country do not inadvertently provide unhelpful evidence of activities carried out in other countries. For example, if the most senior employee in the host country cannot hire or fire without permission then the implication may be that another group company outside the host country must have that authority, which may in turn have positive or negative corporation tax consequences. For example, if the 'wrong' people take decisions that may support arguments that there are, in reality, additional 'off the record' 'shadow directors'.

13.44 Practically, it probably makes sense to include restrictions the company would like to see from a business perspective in the draft employment documents before they are given to corporation tax specialists to check for any potential impact on company residence, permanent establishment, etc. The practical arrangements can then be amended, as may be appropriate, before the employment documents are issued to the employee.

13.45 The business is likely to be more reliant on third party advice to double check information provided by the expatriate, particularly where the expatriate is being recruited to help with set-up because of his local knowledge and experience. There may be potential for conflicts of interest if the expatriate sources the relevant advice for the business alone.

13.46 For example, it would not normally be sensible to rely on the expatriate's own assessment of what he should be paid, on the notice period that should apply to him or in relation to other terms of his own employment contract. Where the employer is the client, advice regarding an expatriate's employment documents should be provided directly to a representative of the employer, and not to the expatriate. This may sound obvious but sometimes where an expatriate is dealing directly with host country lawyers regarding commercial issues the expatriate assumes that he is to take the lead in managing production of his own employment documents. It is not normally sufficient for these to be approved by a representative of the employer only after the expatriate has reviewed the documents, as the employer may lose the benefit of knowledge of the instructions and advice that led to particular decisions being made.

Sample clauses relating to employee control

13.47 These suggestions are intended to provide ideas for drafting and will not be suitable for every senior start up employee.

'The Employee shall:

- not enter into any contract with any customer or potential customer of the Company (or any Group Company) on behalf of the Company (or any Group Company);
- not bind the Company (or any Group Company) to any long term, onerous or unusual commitment without the prior consent of [[*job title*]/the Board];

- provide [[*job title*]/the Board] with such information regarding his duties and the affairs of the Company, and in such form, as [[*job title*]/the Board] may from time to time direct;
- prepare and submit to [[*job title*]/the Board] draft business plans and budgets on a [quarterly] basis, or at such other intervals as [[*job title*]/the Board] may from time to time direct;
- not incur any expense on behalf of the Company that is not anticipated by a budget approved by, or in respect of which specific prior consent has been granted by, [[*job title*]/the Board];
- not engage, employ, instigate formal disciplinary proceedings or dismiss or terminate the engagement of any employee, consultant or contractor on behalf of the Company without the prior consent of [[*job title*]/the Board];
- not authorise, communicate or implement any increase to remuneration or the provision of any additional benefit in respect of any employee of the Company (or any Group Company) without the prior consent of [[*job title*]/the Board];
- not make any communication to the press, television, other media or business analyst regarding the business of the Company (or any Group Company) without the prior consent of [[*job title*]/the Board];
- promptly inform [[*job title*]/the Board] of any matter that may adversely affect the interests of the Company (or any Group Company);
- not seek [or provide] professional advice for or on behalf of the Company without the prior consent of [[*job title*]/the Board], and shall provide copies of any such advice to such person as may be nominated from time to time for the purpose.'

IMPACT OF EMPLOYEE STATUS ON EMPLOYMENT LAWS

13.48 The first expatriate's responsibilities may help determine whether particular employment laws apply to him. For example, if the expatriate is granted powers of attorney giving him, or his employment contract gives him, express authority to hire, fire, bind the company, etc it may be that his employment must be treated as a senior role (managing executive or similar). As a consequence, certain collective agreements or laws may automatically apply or not apply to him, for example, on termination of his employment. This may sometimes be beneficial for the employer, as senior executives may enjoy less employment protection than more junior employees. It is worth noting that the scope of the expatriate's authority may have an impact on the size of any severance payment due later.

In some locations there will be a requirement for the business to appoint a 'General Manager' in the host location, with specific powers and responsibilities.

TERMINATION

13.49 Thinking ahead about the possibility that the employee may decide to leave or need to be removed is particularly important where operations in the host country are new (see Chapter 16 on termination more generally). For example:

- the business may be more dependent on customer and other business connections of a few employees and there may be a higher risk of post termination competition (see Chapter 11 on restrictive covenants);
- the employee may not be supported by an experienced team, and there may be no one in the host country who can easily or quickly step into his shoes;
- it may be difficult to access information before a decision to remove the employee is made known to the employee himself (keeping copies of key documents in the home country is particularly important for an expatriate who is the most senior employee in the host location);
- the skills needed to start a business (eg sales skills, entrepreneurial flair, charisma, etc) may not be those that are needed to move the business on when it is more established (eg financial prudence, orthodox people management skills, etc) and this, in itself, may make potential problems with those leading start-up businesses more likely;
- there may be more opportunity for the employee to damage the business if things do not move quickly than might be the case where an ordinary employee is dismissed.

See Chapter 16 for a description of some of the steps that can be taken at the start of an assignment to reduce these risks.

13.50 As noted above, if the employee holds a directorship or similar office, any steps that may facilitate his removal from office at a later stage should be considered before the appointment is made. In countries where managers need documented powers, for example, to conclude contracts, hire, fire, write cheques, seek professional advice etc for the company, etc there should, wherever possible, be another person or people who will have authority to deal with these things without delay until the expatriate can be replaced.

13.51 Subject to mandatory employment laws, a clause in the employment contract allowing appointment of another person to the same post can be helpful, as can provision for garden leave and post termination restrictions.

CONCLUSIONS

13.52 The following issues apply to all employees but are particularly important for an expatriate who is either the first employee to be employed in the host location or the most senior employee there.

- The business will need to seek commercial and corporation tax advice in relation to the appropriate legal entity to manage the business before employment documents are prepared. The expatriate may be employed by that entity (which may delay the start of the employment) or a different legal entity.

- Care should be taken to ensure that any initial engagement as a self-employed contractor is carefully monitored and that any subsequent transfer to employment status is managed appropriately. (See also **6.2-6.13** on self-employed contractor arrangements.)

- The availability of immigration permission for a particular individual may sometimes be important for the choice of employer.

- More detailed advice is likely to be needed in relation to administrative requirements etc as there will be no established payroll arrangements, employer registrations, etc. It may be possible for the business to outsource some of this work to third party service providers in the host country.

- Particular care should be taken with documentation of the employee's role and responsibilities and any contractual restrictions on his activities. There is more likely to be a need for practical control and the restrictions chosen may have significant corporation tax and employment law implications.

- Special arrangements may need to be made to give the employee legal authority to deal with matters that are intended to be within the scope of his role, for example, to give him authority to hire and fire other staff.

- Care should be taken to ensure that control and business continuity can be maintained if relationships deteriorate or the assignment ends.

CHAPTER 14

BUSINESS VISITORS, INTERNATIONAL COMMUTERS AND VIRTUAL ASSIGNEES

INTRODUCTION

14.1 Cheaper and quicker travel, readily available language skills and better IT have all helped make international business travel easier and more productive. Alongside easier short-term travel there has been some resistance to longer-term relocation, perhaps due to the increasing importance of second incomes, schooling challenges and, more recently, a focus on limiting long-term international migration. The trend to increased short-term business travel seems likely to last and, as volumes increase, we would naturally expect adopting best practice to become more straightforward. The problem for employers is that there is also increasing focus on compliance. Monitoring international business travel is no longer 'optional'. Employers need to track travel, manage staff and engage with enforcement agencies. International business visitor policies must evolve to reflect this increasing complexity and related financial risk.

14.2 This chapter covers:

- What is a business visitor? (**14.3–14.7**).
- Immigration, tax, safety and other compliance (**14.8–14.24**).
- Managing evolution (**14.25–14.27**).
- Monitoring (**14.28–14.34**).
- International business visitor policies (**14.35–14.42**).
- International commuters (**14.43–14.51**).
- Voluntary and virtual assignees (**14.52–14.59**).

WHAT IS A 'BUSINESS VISITOR'?

14.3 A 'business visitor' is, broadly, someone who travels to undertake some kind of business-related activity that is not real 'work'. Typical examples might be travel to attend a conference, or to meet colleagues at an overseas head office when starting a new job. As with much of mobility jargon, though, the term means different things to different people. In particular, it is worth highlighting that 'business visitor' is frequently used as a term of art by immigration and tax authorities. Public authorities do not, however, use the term consistently. Tax and immigration authorities do not mean the same things as each other;

authorities in different jurisdictions mean different things; the definitions used by a particular authority may change; and different definitions may apply to people with different occupations or of different nationalities. This is an area where close scrutiny of current, fact-specific and up to date requirements is essential for compliance.

Short-term assignee v business visitor

14.4 Distinguishing between a short-term assignee and business visitor is not always easy without reference to specific immigration or tax definitions but the following may help those trying to get a 'feel' for the borderline:

- Short-term assignees generally work in a jurisdiction where they do not normally work for a limited period of time, say one to six months.

- Business visitors generally 'visit' on a 'business trip' overseas for a very short time (eg a day or two), and for a purpose that is not normal 'work'. The visitor might be an employee receiving a salary but usually will not be performing core 'work' duties, eg a builder would not build a house on a business trip. (The concrete UK immigration examples at **14.5** below illustrate this.)

- Business visitors often do not have to seek specific advance immigration clearance before they travel or, if they do, the process for seeking clearance may be more straightforward. (See Glossary on US 'ESTA' arrangements.)

- Business visitors will usually stay in hotels. They are not normally provided with a serviced apartment or longer-term accommodation by their employer and will not normally have their own home in the host location.

- Business visitors will not normally be accompanied, or visited, by family members during the trip. (Short-term assignees are not usually accompanied either but sometimes a short-term assignee will take a holiday or weekend break with family in the host country during an assignment.)

- Business visitors do not usually receive extra payments or allowances to induce them to travel. Short-term assignees usually do.

- A short-term assignee should have clear paperwork confirming their assignment terms. This is usually in the form of a short-term assignment letter varying the core employment contract terms for the purpose of the assignment, eg, setting out the accommodation that will be provided, any extra remuneration etc. (See **5.34** on short-term assignees generally, the checklist at **A1.7** and the framework short-term assignment letter at **A2.3**).

- A business visitor does not usually receive tailored paperwork but will often be subject to business visitor, expenses, travel and other employment policies. Policy documents are particularly important because, eg, it is unlikely to be practical to issue an assignment letter for a one-day trip, and also because enforcement agencies may wish to see them, see **14.35**.

UK – standard visitor visa

14.5   UK immigration rules for a 'standard visitor visa' can currently allow, eg:

- coming to the UK for a conference, meeting or training;
- taking part in a specific sports-related event in the UK;
- artists, entertainers or musicians coming to the UK to perform;
- academics doing research in the UK or accompanying students on a study abroad programme;
- doctors or dentists coming to take a clinical attachment or observer post in the UK;
- taking certain examinations in the UK;
- visiting the UK to seek funding to start, take over, join or run a business in the UK.

14.6   The traveller cannot do paid or unpaid 'work'; live in the UK for long periods of time through frequent visits; access public funds; marry or register a civil partnership, or give notice of marriage or civil partnership. These criteria are not complete (please refer to the government website for fuller information about the rules, currently at https://www.gov.uk/guidance/immigration-rules/immigration-rules-appendix-v-visitor-rules). The rules change frequently and the only way the visitor can be sure of meeting the currently applicable criteria is to keep checking.

14.7   For an employment lawyer references to 'paid' and 'work' used in an immigration context can be confusing as, of course, remuneration is typically paid in respect of periods during which the employee is undertaking business visits and 'work' in the sense European employment lawyers use it normally includes business trips made for an employer. It is import to stay alert to the frequency with which common words are used to mean different things in a global mobility context. In practice, the key is to check the specific rules and examples given by the relevant authority.

COMPLIANCE

14.8   The most significant compliance concerns for business visitors are likely to be safety, immigration and tax, see further below.

Immigration

14.9   If an employee tries to enter a country under business visitor rules and is not, in reality, a business visitor the consequences can be severe, eg deportation, fines etc. (See **3.3-3.26** on immigration more generally and consequences of failure to comply.) It is worth highlighting that refused entry and return home may entail a night in prison.

14.10 Visitors should remember that responses to questions; and the content of suitcases, pockets, files, electronic devices and diaries should be consistent with their professed purpose for travel. The traveller should be in a position to answer questions honestly and will feel more confident doing so if he is sure he is compliant. Most frequent travellers will be aware of this. However, they may not all be aware that subtle distinctions between jurisdictions and changes to rules over time can mean that what has been appropriate previously is no longer so. It is important that travellers check the criteria in good time, and that they fully disclose relevant information to advisers. That information might include, for example, previous immigration breaches, other nationalities, criminal records, links to 'undesirable' groups or earlier visits to prohibited destinations. Public authorities are increasingly disclosing information to each other and it is generally unwise for travellers to assume that 'no one will find out'.

Tax

14.11 When addressing tax compliance, it is important to consider different kinds of tax. For example, consideration should be given to corporation tax and social security as well as income tax.

Income tax

14.12 Key considerations here, as with other areas of expatriate compliance, are:

- income tax potentially due in each relevant jurisdiction;
- any relief available (eg double tax treaty relief);
- withholding and reporting obligations; and
- recovery from the employee.

14.13 Withholding obligations do not always mirror tax liabilities. (See Chapter 5.) So, for example, there could be an obligation to withhold and pay over tax in two countries concurrently where relief is available under a double tax treaty. The employee, or employer, may subsequently be able to recover from one of the tax authorities. Normally, the employer will ensure that net pay is not reduced by offering a loan to the employee. Theoretically, it is helpful to make the loan conditional on cooperation from the employee with recovery from the authorities, before the loan is granted. However, business visitors typically travel at short notice and do not normally receive carefully prepared documents dealing with loan arrangements before they set off. Although tax equalisation or protection are rarely promised explicitly the employer will typically make good any additional tax the employee is obliged to pay. Even if motivated to recover from the employee subsequently, the employer will often be unable to enforce against a resistant employee due to inadequate paperwork.

14.14 Care should be taken to stress the importance of compliance to employees and to monitor employee's movements (see **14.28-14.34** on monitoring). A careful employer might also consider including cooperation clauses in standard domestic contracts so that there is less need to deal with loans, tax recovery etc on an ad hoc basis or 'after the event'.

UK

14.15 Business visitors to the UK (and short-term assignees) are theoretically liable to UK income tax withholding (known as PAYE) from their first day in the UK. In practice, most businesses will make applications under Short Term Business Visitor Arrangements agreed with HMRC for exemptions based on treaty relief.

Social security

14.16 See **4.29-4.38** for a general comment on the impact of social security on expatriate employment arrangements. Social security is typically not a 'big issue' for business visitors. Most business visitors will simply remain in their home country social security scheme. It would be unusual for host country social security obligations to be triggered in addition, but this is not impossible. It is prudent to check the social security arrangements applicable to a new host location, particularly to locations outside Europe.

Corporation tax

14.17 As has been highlighted elsewhere, employees who work in another jurisdiction can trigger corporate tax liabilities and transfer pricing issues can arise. Base erosion and profit shifting ('BEPS') is subject to increasing focus from regulators. (See **13.8–13.18** on corporation tax, transfer pricing and permanent establishment issues.)

Employment law

14.18 As a general rule, employment law compliance is straightforward for business visitors. There are rarely any host country employee registration requirements for business visitors and any employment claims etc would normally be made in the home country. The key concern is normally safety, see **14.21** below.

14.19 Laws based on the Posted Workers Directive may potentially apply, eg to require that remuneration meets minimum host country standards. (See Glossary and **10.50–10.55** on the directive.) However, given the short duration and purpose of business visits this rarely has significant practical impact on business visitors.

14.20 Similarly, the Employment Particulars Directive requires that certain information should be provided, see **5.38-5.41**, but only where it is anticipated that the employee will be overseas for a month or longer (see **5.39**). A business visit will rarely last a month.

Health & safety

14.21 The key concerns will normally be to keep employees safe and to ensure that medical services can be accessed.

Practical steps

14.22 The employer will normally retain a 'duty of care' for business visitors. Specific requirements in different jurisdictions may vary but it is a fair bet that most will require the employer to accept some responsibility for the employee's health and safety. Whether or not the employer is legally and financially responsible for the outcome, it is likely that the employer will wish to minimise the risk of harm to employees. Business visitor policies would normally include some guidelines to encourage the employee to think about safety in advance and to act with prudence when abroad. The employee might, for example, be encouraged, or required to:

- check the safety of travel plans and/or destinations with public agencies (eg, information is currently available here for UK travellers: https://www.gov.uk/foreign-travel-advice);
- book through a travel agent and ensure that travel details are noted appropriately;
- check requirements for vaccinations or medications, and related timing;
- ensure that they carry information relating to medical cover etc, eg a travel policy, 'contact' card issued by the employer and/or EHIC card;
- check cultural norms before departure, such as dress expectations or attitudes to public expressions of sexuality;
- arrange connecting travel carefully in advance, eg transport from airport to hotel;
- think about arrival and departure times;
- check insurance arrangements before hiring a car;
- consider whether there are any additional employee-specific safety requirements, eg due to medical condition or sex;
- report any concerns to a nominated person.

14.23 Statistics relating to the experiences of female business travellers are depressing. Because business men and women travel so frequently, there is a temptation to assume that no special care needs to be taken by employers. People do generally know how to book a hotel and get on a plane. That does not mean, for example, that arriving at an US airport late at night and taking a taxi from the rank will always be safe for a lone female business traveller.

Medical cover

14.24 Employers are generally careful to ensure that international medical cover is appropriate for employees and their families undertaking long term international assignments. Similar care is not always taken for ordinary business travellers. Employers should ensure not only that appropriate protection is in place (eg via travel and health policies) but also that employees know how to access the assistance that is available. Most employees will bring details of health cover with them when they take a family holiday. Few seem to think it necessary to print out a copy of their office medical or travel policy before they travel for work. Care should also be taken with the potential for overlapping cover. (See also the Glossary at Appendix 3 on EHICs.) It is also a useful fallback to ensure that emergency contact telephone numbers, provider details etc are clearly visible on policy documents, the company intranet, employer issued mobile telephones etc.

MANAGING EVOLUTION

14.25 A key challenge for those managing business visitor arrangements and short-term assignees is the frequency with which these arrangements evolve.

14.26 An individual may start by making occasional business trips, the trips may get longer, the employee may start to do a different sort of work, may marry a local, buy a holiday home or whatever. The difficulty for the employer is that a wide range of business and personal developments may change the nature of the visits. This is not, of course, all bad as the employee's increasing work in the host country may signal commercial success, but this can make compliance difficult. The changes may mean, eg, that more tax is due or that immigration clearance is no longer valid.

14.27 The key thing for the employer is to ensure that appropriate monitoring arrangements are in place that give the employer the information it needs to prompt focus on compliance. Does an alarm bell ring when the employee spends more than a fixed number of days in the host country and, if so, how does that happen?

MONITORING

14.28 It is, of course, impossible to spot a 'stealthpat', meet compliance requirements or manage the metamorphosis of a business visitor into a short-term assignee without monitoring international travel.

14.29 Monitoring may be constrained by privacy laws, see **15.73–15.99**, but will generally be permissible if consent is properly obtained and proper policies and controls are in place.

Practical monitoring

14.30 At its simplest level, employers should know how many days each member of staff works outside the 'home' jurisdiction.

14.31 'Days' may be counted in many different ways. For example, 'vacation' days or part days may be counted in different ways by different public authorities in different jurisdictions. The business will need to find a way to capture the information that is needed, flexibly and lawfully.

14.32 Some options that may be considered include:

- retaining tickets, receipts etc confirming travel dates;
- monitoring overseas visitors to offices through reception records;
- using timesheets or other self-reporting mechanisms;
- using information collected by corporate travel agents;
- installing apps on mobile devices or purchasing other specialist software.

14.33 In practice, more than one approach may be required to ensure compliance, eg, with both immigration and tax needs. The employer will also need to check local constraints on things like tracking via a mobile phone GPS. Ideally times as well as dates should be recorded. See **5.8-5.13** on 'day counting' and Chapter 15 on ongoing management.

Using employment documents

14.34 Employment documents can be used to secure consent from employees, eg the employee may expressly consent to a particular type of monitoring or agree to report certain events promptly, such as a change to home address. Local privacy rules may limit the employer's freedom, eg data protection consents may not be permissible or effective in some contexts. Generally, though, employers could do more to anticipate the possibility that an employee may travel for work and it would be helpful to include some contract terms to assist the employer. For example, it may be helpful to consider including very direct provisions in the contract of every domestic employee requiring the employee to seek consent from his employer before working outside the home jurisdiction and confirming his agreement to assist with travel, immigration and tax compliance. It is important to ensure that employees are aware of the compliance challenges and the reasons for the employer's requests for assistance.

INTERNATIONAL BUSINESS VISITOR POLICIES

14.35 There are some special challenges relating to business visitors, but before focusing on what needs to be done it may be helpful to take a step back and think about the purposes of a business visitor policy (or policies). These may include, eg:

- making travel easier, more efficient and more productive for the traveller;
- ensuring the traveller is safe;
- helping the business to quantify and manage business development/travel costs;
- reducing compliance-related costs and risks for the business.

14.36 In order to achieve the last two business-focused objectives, the cooperation of employees is needed. The traveller must understand his role in achieving compliance, and why he needs to help (and, more persuasively, why it is in his personal interest help). The traveller is far more likely to cooperate if using the policy assists the traveller, as well as his employer. Needless to say, time-consuming processes that are hard to find and easy to ignore are not helpful. Whereas, putting everything a traveller needs to know in one easily accessible place may be quite useful.

14.37 In common with other areas of expatriate management, business visitor arrangements are multi-disciplinary. However, business visitor compliance is relevant to a much wider group of employees, most of whom will not view a business trip abroad as an 'expatriate' arrangement (after all it is not). They are likely to view international business trips as just that, albeit more expensive trips. Many of the policy directions needed will already be built into ordinary domestic policies and procedures, eg those related to budgeting, expenses, privacy, IT etc. The key difference between domestic and international business travel is that international travel creates additional compliance challenges, particularly the immigration and tax challenges highlighted above. There may well be internal resistance to re-writing existing domestic policies to accommodate international travel and no one 'stakeholder' (eg HR, payroll manager, marketing manager, finance team, data protection officer etc) is likely to be able to keep an international business visitor policy up-to-date.

14.38 One way of pulling together the disparate strands so that they meet travellers' needs without creating too much extra work, is to use an intranet to link from a relatively short international business visitor policy to parts of other domestic policy documents that are relevant to international travellers, such as parts of an expense policy that set out practical arrangements for booking hotels.

14.39 Practically, it can be helpful to explain the reasons for policies to staff. For example, if the decision to require hotel and flight bookings through one travel agent was made to achieve volume discounts, reduce the risk of fraud, or help support travellers who get into trouble, why not say so?

UK business visitor paperwork

14.40 UK business visitors are not normally given formal assignment letters. In the UK we have the useful concept of 'managerial prerogative' which, within limits, allows employers an opportunity to unilaterally issue and update policies with which their employees must comply. It is sensible for business visitor arrangements for UK based employees to be set out in policy documents of this type. The advantage of this approach is that it is flexible. The employer can quickly update the policy as best practice and compliance requirements evolve, without the need for individual employee consents. Also, employers may be less reluctant to make a start if they know the policies can be quickly and easily replaced with something better later.

14.41 If more direct agreement is required (eg consent to release personal data, confirmation that all the information needed to identify immigration concerns has been provided, or an agreement allowing for deductions from remuneration if a company laptop is lost) then this could be achieved by asking employees to sign individual (pro forma) letters or memos that reference broader policy documents. Alternatively, contractual agreement to some things may be included in the employment contract from the start. It is important to understand that this approach may not be sufficient in other jurisdictions.

14.42 It would be prudent to ask relevant advisers, eg the business' regular immigration, tax, privacy and employment law advisers to review the business visitor policy document, and any other linked employment documents, bearing in mind that there may be a later requirement to disclose the arrangements to public authorities or refer to them in the event of dispute.

INTERNATIONAL COMMUTERS

14.43 'International commuters' are essentially people who regularly live and/or work in more than one jurisdiction and travel between the two.

Types of commuter arrangement

14.44 Some of the more common commuter patterns are described below.

Living on the border

14.45 Where there is an 'open' border, people may live on one side of the border and work on the other (sometimes they may work on both sides). This might happen for economic reasons, eg, an employee might choose to work for a higher salary in Switzerland whilst living in 'cheaper' accommodation in Germany. In the UK this occurs commonly along the land border between Northern Ireland and the Republic of Ireland. The job itself may be domestic and very straightforward but the arrangements can still create substantial additional complexity, eg the employer may need to deal with cross-border tax withholding requirements, even for relatively junior employees.

Cross-border roles

14.46 The employee's home and workplace may be based in one jurisdiction but he might be an area manager with responsibility for operations in other jurisdictions or he might be a salesman with a 'territory' that covers than one country. The employee may spend substantial and/or regular periods of time working overseas.

Dual roles or employments

14.47 The employee may have two or more distinct roles, which might be with separate employers (see **6.58–6.69** on 'dual employments') or may simply perform different duties in different places for the same employer (eg an IT worker working on a part-time project basis for two clients whose premises are in different jurisdictions).

Personal commuting

14.48 Employees may commute across borders due to personal circumstances, and in practice many do. For example, an employee might take up a role in one country leaving his partner and children in another. This might happen, eg, if the employee is offered a role abroad and the family are unable to easily relocate due to jobs, schooling or whatever. Personal commuting may be of short duration, eg to the end of a school year, or may continue for a much longer period, eg if an employee agrees to take a role in London on the understanding that family can stay at home in Lille. Even where there is a full-time role abroad the personal commuter will typically spend substantial periods of time working at home. In practice, personal commuters are often also 'virtual assignees', see **14.52** below.

Rotators

14.49 Some businesses engage staff on a formal rota providing for longer periods at home in one jurisdiction and at work in another (eg one month on, one month off). Rotator patterns are often seen in the oil and gas sector. Typically, the working location is a 'hardship' location or the arrangement is on a short-term project basis and unsuitable for accompanying family.

Non-resident directors

14.50 Sometimes the officers of a company are not resident in the same jurisdiction as the company. This is common with multinational groups of companies. For example, a UK subsidiary may have three UK statutory directors who are resident in the UK and one director who is resident in the US. The US director may be employed by the US parent company but travel to the UK for a couple of days each month to attend the UK subsidiary's board meetings. (Special attention should be given to tax compliance for any director visiting the UK to attend board meetings.)

International commuter documents

14.51 International commuters are not business visitors. They typically do 'real' work in more than one country and will not normally meet business visitor requirements for immigration purposes. Additional immigration clearance may be required and there may be a requirement to make payroll (or shadow payroll) arrangements in respect of more than one jurisdiction. By contrast to the ad hoc policy-led business visitor arrangements described above, commuters should normally have very clear personal contractual documents. Commuter arrangements might apply from the outset of an employment arrangement or may develop over time. Either way they are likely to be advantages to documenting the promises made clearly.

See the checklist for gathering information to prepare international commuter documents at **A1.11**.

VOLUNTARY AND VIRTUAL ASSIGNEES

14.52 A 'virtual' employee lives in one location and works for an employer based at another location. A virtual international assignee is similar but the employee works in a different jurisdiction from the employer.

14.53 It is not unusual for businesses in expensive locations to be assisted by workers who are based in another jurisdiction where wages are lower. This might be arranged in an organised way. For example, an insurance company in the UK might be assisted by 'call centre' workers who live and work in India. The insurance company could, theoretically, be running part of its operations in India and employ people to work there. More likely, the insurance company will buy services from a separate legal entity located in India. (See **13.3–13.7** on creating a permanent establishment etc.) Alternatively, the UK operation could directly contract with an individual who works in another jurisdiction.

14.54 A voluntary international assignee or voluntary commuter is essentially someone who chooses their cross-border working arrangements for personal reasons.

Example – 'voluntary' virtual employee

14.55 Jim's wife, Dagmar, is offered a new role in Berlin. Jim has always wanted to live in Berlin, speaks fluent German and naturally wants to go too. However, Jim's UK employer, the Bicycle Company, has no operations in Germany. Jim's employer will be sorry to see him go. Jim offers to continue his current role, designing bicycles, but working 'remotely' from his new home in Berlin using a computer and liaising with colleagues via the internet. Transport is quick and easy between Berlin and London and Jim is happy to fly back to the UK for meetings with colleagues when this is necessary.

14.56 At first blush, home working in Germany seems to be a 'win-win'. The Bicycle Company can retain a good employee, and Jim can live where he wants to. The reality is, of course, that Jim's permanent relocation will have a significant impact on his working arrangements. The Bicycle Company may find itself subject to German withholding tax rules, social security obligations, insurance requirements, privacy laws etc. Jim's work may also trigger a corporate tax liability. All the usual considerations that apply to setting up in a new location would apply to Jim's home office in Berlin. See Chapter 13 on setting up in a new location.

Costs and negotiation

14.57 The key difference between an employee-led 'voluntary' assignment and an employer-led assignment is the negotiating positions of the two parties. With some imagination and will employers and employees can usually find a mutually acceptable working arrangement, as they might with a domestic flexible working request. The employer may, however, wish to consider the following before agreeing:

- the value of the employee to the business (in the above example, can Jim be easily replaced with another London-based employee?);
- how long the arrangements are likely to last (is Dagmar's role in Berlin permanent? Is Jim likely to find a better job in Berlin once he settles there?);
- how the arrangements can be made to work practically (see **14.59** on homeworking);
- the real costs of saying 'yes' taking account of set up costs, ongoing costs and potential termination costs;
- how much the employee wants this (what sort of terms is Jim likely to accept?).

14.58 Typically, a voluntary assignee will not drive a hard bargain or expect potentially expensive 'expatriate' terms such as tax equalisation or help with housing or schooling, but costs can still be substantial. Even finding reliable information from which to prepare a cost model could be expensive. The employer should think hard about whether the voluntary assignee is 'worth it'.

Home working

14.59 Virtual assignees are typically 'home workers'. In addition to the usual international assignment issues, the employer should think about issues normally associated with homeworking in a domestic context. For example:

- Will the employee be able to carry out core duties, eg will there be difficulties with meeting clients, supervising colleagues or attending training?

- How will the quality of the employee's work be monitored and how will the employee be managed? Will it be possible to have those difficult conversations without meeting face-to-face?
- How will working time be measured and controlled and the working environment be checked and monitored from a health and safety perspective?
- How will business security issues be dealt with, eg disposal of confidential paper waste?
- The choice of host location could have an impact on business risk management too. For example, business continuity plans and security can become more important at locations where there is a higher risk of crime or national disaster. There may also be higher risks of governmental interference or unwanted disclosure risks in the host country.
- How will personal data protection principles be complied with?
- Can the employee's home be accessed, practically and lawfully, to deal with these issues?
- Will the employer or employee provide equipment such as desk, chair, computer, printer, paper supplies and pay telephone, wifi or other utility bills?
- Will host country planning restrictions allow the employee to carry out the work at home?
- Will any domestic arrangements impinge on the working environment?
- Are there any business-related regulatory constraints?
- Will employers' liability, professional indemnity cover, software licenses and other insurance arrangements still cover the employee?
- Will a trial period or initial fixed term contract be practical, lawful or appropriate?
- A request to work at home abroad is a 'flexible working request' and all the discrimination issues that can arise when such a request is refused domestically could potentially apply to a request for international flexibility too. This will rarely mean that the proposal must be accepted but process, decisions, communications and documentation should be considered carefully in the light of both home and host country laws. (In the UK the employer may also need to comply with the various pieces of flexible working legislation.)

OVERVIEW

14.60 In practice there are a wide variety of short-term, flexible and innovative working arrangements that cross borders. Often variations on more than one of the types of arrangement described above will apply to the same individuals. To prepare effective documents the employer may benefit from:

- developing good questioning skills and thinking laterally – there is no 'one size fits all' option;
- producing broad policies that will satisfy relevant authorities and guide employees through typical business visitor arrangements;
- keeping policies under review and involving relevant internal and external specialists;
- keeping an eye on costs – particularly evolving costs and costs linked to arrangements that are voluntary rather than business-driven;
- setting up effective and lawful monitoring arrangements so that 'evolution' can be caught early and requests for information by public authorities can be met with confidence;
- ensuring employees understand 'what's in it for them' in supporting compliance.

CHAPTER 15

ONGOING MANAGEMENT

15.1 The issues likely to affect expatriates during an overseas assignment are generally similar to those likely to affect ordinary employees. Dealing with them, however, can be a bit more complicated.

15.2 This chapter covers:

- Pay reviews, bonus and share plans (**15.3–15.20**).
- Absence, including holiday, illness and family leave (**15.21–15.28**).
- Cultural awareness and language training (**15.29–15.32**).
- Poor performance and discipline (**15.33–15.40**).
- Complaints (**15.41**).
- Bribery, codes of conduct and 'whistleblowing' (**15.42–15.58**).
- Health and safety (**15.59–15.67**).
- Death (**15.68–15.71**).
- Divorce (**15.72**).
- Data protection (privacy) (**15.73–15.99**).
- Intellectual property (**15.100–15.104**).
- Changing terms and conditions, including 'localisation' (**15.105–15.120**).
- Continuous employment (**15.121–15.122**).
- Disclosure (**15.123–15.128**).

PAY REVIEWS, BONUS AND SHARE PLANS

15.3 Remuneration arrangements should support the preferred employment structure (see **4.86–4.89**). The employer should be responsible for payment of salary and for appraisals and pay reviews. All communications about bonus or pay reviews should be made on the employer's headed paper, emails, memos, etc. This sounds straightforward but decisions are made by the 'wrong' people and communications are delivered on the 'wrong' headed paper surprisingly often. See Chapter 4 on the identity of the employer for an explanation of why this matters.

Pay reviews

15.4 Pay reviews may be more complex for expatriates, for example, because of a need to reassess various allowances and benefit arrangements in the light of new third-party data, exchange rate changes or changes to tax or social security laws, and the need to consider any impact on notional pay for reference purposes. Changes may take effect more than once a year.

15.5 The possibility that pay reviews may leave the employee worse off should be addressed at the outset. For example, if a Cost of Living Adjustment (COLA) can decrease pay, as well as increase it, the employment documents should make this clear (see **7.40–7.47**).

Bonus

15.6 Incentive arrangements should be provided by the employer, and the employer should make decisions on the size of bonus awards. If the home company is the employer, the targets etc may need to be adapted by the employer to reflect goals that are appropriate for the employee's host country role.

15.7 The issues that arise in relation to bonus and pay reviews should normally be those considered at the outset of the assignment when the documents were prepared (see **7.13–7.19**). These could include, for example:

- the effect of exchange rates;
- interaction with tax equalisation or protection promises;
- transitional arrangements at the start and end of the assignment and/or employment;
- the effect of mandatory laws, for example, restrictions on making share awards or a requirement to make a 13th month or similar bonus payment or to allow the employee to participate in profit-sharing arrangements; and/or
- host country expectations and parity with colleagues.

15.8 If new incentive terms, plans or targets are introduced during the course of the assignment then this may be as anticipated and provided for in the contract or may be a matter within the employer's discretion. In some cases, the proposed change may not have been anticipated by the employment documents and the change may be significant enough to amount to a change to the employment contract. (See **15.105–15.120** below on changes to contract terms generally and **15.107** on unfair contract terms and discretion).

Share plans

15.9 Senior employees, and particularly those engaged in the financial services sector, often participate in incentive arrangements under which they are awarded shares or granted share options.

15.10 The arrangements may offer the employee the opportunity to gain from a low or nil share purchase price, increases in share value and/or to receive tax efficient remuneration. The arrangements are generally put in place to benefit a number of employees, rather than for an individual executive, and specific tax approval may be sought from public authorities in relevant jurisdictions. Because most share plans are long-term arrangements, the timing of the executive's assignment may have a significant effect on the value of the arrangements to him.

15.11 Key timing points from an incentive plan perspective may include the date(s) on which:

- the assignment starts and ends;
- the identity of the employee's employer changes if there is a transfer from home to host country employment;
- the employee's tax status changes (which may, eg, fall at the end of a home or host country tax year or on a date when the employee's intentions change, rather than on the start or end date for the assignment);
- the start of the plan year(s) to which performance targets etc relate (typically the start of the financial year of the business);
- shares or share options are awarded or 'granted' to the employee (typically at the start of the employment and then annually after the end of the plan year to reflect individual, team or company performance during the plan year);
- shares or share options 'vest' or become 'unconditional' (ie when the employee is free to take the benefit, which may, eg, be as long as two or three years after the grant date);
- the employee 'exercises' his share option right(s) to buy shares;
- shares are sold or transferred;
- conditional or unvested shares or share options lapse or are forfeited, for example, because of termination of employment in specified 'bad leaver' circumstances before vesting, or because restrictive covenants are breached;
- any 'claw-back' provisions, providing for repayment or forfeiture, bite.

15.12 The employee's assignment may start or end, or his tax residency may change, before or after any of the critical dates that relate to the share plan. This may have some potentially significant effects on arrangements that relate to his pre-assignment role, as well as on arrangements that relate to the period of his assignment. For example:

- a change to the employee's location, tax status or the identity of his employer may mean that under the plan rules he is no longer able to continue to participate in the plan (and it may not be possible or easy for the employer to arrange for a change to the rules, particularly if it is a group-wide plan);
- continued participation in a share plan or further award of shares or share options may be prohibited under mandatory laws that did not apply before the assignment began, for example, host country laws may prevent the employer from giving the employee shares or share-related benefits;
- the structure of the pre-assignment arrangements may be designed to support goals relevant to the employee's former home country role and not his contribution to the host country business during the assignment;
- a change to the expatriate's tax status may mean that the real value of the arrangements changes; and/or
- a change to the status of a plan participant may have an impact on taxation of the wider plan; and/or
- a lack of clarity in the documents may leave employer and employee uncertain as to what has been promised.

15.13 Commercially, these can be significant issues. For example, suppose the employee expects to receive valuable share-related benefits during his assignment but the value of the shares or share options will be significantly less if he is not tax resident in his home country on the grant, vesting, exercise or disposal date. The employer may be obliged to compensate the employee for the extra tax and/or social security contributions that he has to pay, in order to persuade the employee to accept the assignment. That compensation would be a real cost to the employer and might not reflect the value of the expatriate's role during the assignment.

15.14 If the expatriate might expect to participate in a particular share plan but is unable to, for example because of host country laws prohibiting the award of shares, the employer may set up 'phantom' share arrangements to mirror the benefits that the employee would have received if he had not been assigned abroad. Phantom arrangements, being essentially cash bonus arrangements, are unlikely to attract any beneficial tax treatment. If the employer offers a tax equalisation or protection promise, that would also add to the assignment costs for the employer.

15.15 Those drafting the expatriate documents may wish to consider the following:

- clarifying the impact of the new assignment on existing arrangements and documentation of any agreement that the employee will give up existing pre-assignment rights or be compensated for them;
- clarifying incentive arrangements to apply in respect of the assignment period and checking that any flexibility needed to vary or withdraw the arrangements can be retained;

- ensuring that tax implications are understood and that any corresponding tax protection or tax equalisation promises made in the documents are clear;
- whether any restrictions on the employee's ability to take certain actions (eg exercise option rights at a particular time) should be documented and whether tax protection or equalisation promises should include any conditions; and/or
- whether any linked post-termination restrictions or claw-back arrangements will remain effective.

Regulated incentive arrangements

15.16 Incentives awarded to employees may be covered by national or international regulatory restrictions. For example, those that apply in the financial services sector. The detail is beyond the scope of this book (and changes too often for static comment to be useful) but clearly ongoing management of incentive arrangements should include monitoring and compliance with regulatory developments, and where appropriate change to employment documents.

Example

15.17 Suppose Sunil is employed on a home employer assignment to Country A and participates in a Long-Term Incentive Plan ('LTIP'). The LTIP provides for vesting of shares over a three-year period, subject to conditions. Sunil is employed in Country A subject to the terms of an assignment letter that clearly sets out how tax equalisation promises will apply to his LTIP.

15.18 After a couple of years, Sunil is re-assigned to Country B and is given a new assignment letter with new tax equalisation terms. After re-assignment to Country B further shares vest. Do the tax equalisation terms set out in the first or second assignment letter apply? How do they work in practice? Most likely the answers will depend on the way the letters were drafted.

15.19 The key point is that when employees have existing benefits that will continue into an assignment, or subsequent assignment, it is helpful to think ahead and agree on the way the overlap will be worked through at the time the contract is negotiated. One of the challenges for both employees and employers is, of course, that potential costs and outcomes (ie winners and losers) are unlikely to be very clear at the outset. In this case they may not even be clear during the course of the second assignment, because the tax advice is likely to be quite complicated and expensive to obtain, and rates and rules change quite frequently. Nonetheless, clarity on the principles can help avoid expensive disputes. Some employers may actively choose not to clarify the terms that will apply, preferring to deal with ambiguity on an ad hoc basis.

Specialist advice

15.20 Specialist tax/share plans advice should be sought in relation to the particular plans, employee and home and host countries. (See Chapter 11 on the link between share plans and post termination restrictions and **19.106–19.111** and **20.24–20.25** in relation to assignments to and from the UK.) As with other highly technical and potentially high value areas, it makes sense to ask all relevant specialists to check the drafting of the documents. (See Chapter 17 on holding advisers to account.)

ABSENCE, INCLUDING HOLIDAY, ILLNESS AND FAMILY LEAVE

Holiday

15.21 Annual and public holiday entitlements and procedures should be considered when the employment documents are prepared (see **7.143–7.154**). Issues to be considered are likely to include:

- minimum requirements set by mandatory laws (eg on the number of days' holiday, accrual rates, pay during holidays, carry forward or forfeiture of unused holiday);
- transitional arrangements for the start and end of the assignment and/or employment;
- consistency with host country colleagues;
- which public holidays will apply (usually those applicable to host country colleagues);
- flights for the employee and/or family members for 'home leave';
- flights between the home and host countries for children being educated in the home country;
- approval procedures and consistency with employment status.

Illness

15.22 Sickness and absence policies should, normally, as a minimum, reflect host country mandatory laws. It may help to confirm the arrangements that will apply in the contract of employment, even if the sickness arrangements apply automatically through application of a collective agreement or other laws. The practical impact of doing so should be checked with host country employment lawyers as sometimes documenting obligations that are set out in mandatory collective agreements or employment legislation can be unhelpful. See Chapter 17.

15.23 Like holiday and expenses, illness is something that the employer will almost inevitably need to manage at some stage during the assignment. In addition, the arrangements may be a factor in determining employment status and there may be a legal requirement to specify the arrangements that will apply. It makes sense to deal with these issues in employment documents at the outset.

15.24 If the employee is seriously ill the employer may consider terminating the assignment unilaterally or with the employee's agreement, for example, to allow for better medical treatment in the home country or because the position is critical and the employer cannot arrange for appropriate replacement cover on a temporary basis. It may assist if the employment contract gives the employer rights to terminate the assignment and/or employment where appropriate. Mandatory employment laws, for example, those preserving the employment in the event of sickness or allowing claims based on disability discrimination, should always be checked before the employment terms are finalised and again before any decision to require a temporary or permanent return home, or other action, is taken.

15.25 The possibility that an employee may become ill, or become unable or unwilling to perform his duties, during the assignment should be considered at the outset. This is particularly important if the employee is the only employee in the host country, holds 'powers of attorney' or has some similar authority or appointment that is necessary for the smooth running of the business (see **13.40–13.46**).

15.26 Similar issues may arise if family members become seriously ill, for example if the employee's partner or child needs medical treatment in the home country. That eventuality is unlikely to be dealt with expressly in the employment documents but the employer and employee could agree if and when the circumstances arise that the assignment will end or that an additional period of paid or unpaid leave will be granted to the employee to assist. In some countries mandatory laws may protect employees in the event that they are needed to care for a dependent and this should be checked with advisers. See also **7.155–7.163**.

15.27 See also Chapter 12 on equality generally and on reasonable adjustments to accommodate disability.

Family leave

15.28 See **12.25-12.34** on maternity leave and family policies.

CULTURAL AWARENESS AND LANGUAGE TRAINING

15.29 It is common for employers to offer cultural awareness and/or language training to expatriates both before and during their assignments. What is offered varies considerably, from provision of a booklet to read on the plane and a chat with the outgoing assignee on arrival, to regular sessions with a third party 'destination' service provider for all the family. What will be useful may depend on the employer's resources, the employee's role in the host country, the length of the assignment and the differences between home and host country practices.

15.30 It is clear that this sort of training offers huge potential benefits both for the business directly and for ensuring the employee and his family settle in quickly (which will usually benefit the business indirectly).

15.31 Training might cover, for example:

- essential information about local laws (eg rules on consumption of alcohol, sexual activity, confidentiality etc) to reduce the risk of avoidable unlawful activity;
- driving;
- orientation information (eg on shopping, medical, leisure facilities, etc)
- dress;
- formal and informal greetings;
- managing business meetings (business cards, seating, decision-making practices, appropriate forms of communication, etc);
- accepting and giving social invitations and behaviour at social gatherings (eg when to turn up and what to bring by way of gift);
- avoiding unintentional embarrassment (eg use of a gesture considered normal in the home country and offensive in the host country); or
- local religions and related practices.

15.32 Cultural awareness training should be carried out with care. See Chapter 12 on equality, particularly **12.35**.

POOR PERFORMANCE AND DISCIPLINE

15.33 Technically, the employer should deal with any disciplinary issues. This would normally be the case even where a home country employer does not have first-hand knowledge of problems arising in the host country.

15.34 Where informal approaches (discussion at appraisal, with line managers etc) have failed, the employer may consider instigating a more formal disciplinary process.

15.35 The appropriate process is likely to be governed by host country laws, in particular laws relating to potential dismissal. Advice should always be sought from advisers in relevant jurisdictions before formal disciplinary action is taken. This should always include host country advice but will usually include home country advice too, and may include advice from another jurisdiction (eg a country of which the employee is a national if the employee may be able to make claims there).

15.36 One of the difficulties that employers may face is that most countries have laws designed to protect employees in the event of dismissal for poor performance. Some evidence will usually be required, not only of the poor performance but also of discussions with the employee about his poor performance over a period of time. Line managers are generally reluctant to tackle poor performance early, and this tendency is even more pronounced when line managers are located in a different place. The issue of poor performance is often first raised with the employee when the employer is already contemplating dismissal. (It is not unusual for recent appraisal documents to confirm that performance is satisfactory even where performance is actually considered to be poor.) In practice, even if the employer were to promptly adopt a formal step-by-step process to tackle poor performance, including formal warnings and opportunities to improve, it would run the risk of causing a rapid deterioration in its relationship with the employee. Damage to the employment relationship may not be easy to manage from another country, particularly if the employee is very senior or the only employee in the host country. Whatever the underlying reasons, the end result is often that it is impractical for the employer to satisfy host country requirements relating to termination for poor performance. It may be better not to instigate a formal disciplinary procedure at all.

15.37 This may mean that the employer is obliged to pay a larger termination payment to the employee or, in some cases, that it will not be possible to dismiss the employee for poor performance or to dismiss the employee at the preferred time. (See also Chapter 16 on termination more generally.)

15.38 The employer should consider potential disciplinary (and grievance) issues from the outset so that policies are referenced appropriately. Even where there is a home country employer, the home company's normal disciplinary and grievance policies are unlikely to be appropriate for use in the host country (or may lead to unnecessary and time-consuming complications).

15.39 It may be appropriate to confirm the employer's responsibility for disciplinary matters in the employment documents and to expressly confirm that the employer's home country disciplinary policy will not apply during the assignment. Where there is a home country employment arrangement, the host company could agree to co-operate with the home company through the inter-company expatriate supply agreement.

15.40 It may also be appropriate to draw the employee's attention to behaviour that could cause unexpected problems, offence or embarrassment for the business in the host country, or which is contrary to group policy at an early stage. This might be done informally through cultural awareness training or more formally by inserting terms in the employment documents requiring compliance with minimum standards. Some multinationals adopt formal 'codes of conduct', see further below in relation to financial misconduct, bribes and whistleblowing (**15.42–15.46**).

COMPLAINTS

15.41 It is particularly important that expatriates have a clear channel through which they can raise any complaints. Many of the relationship problems that arise between assignees and their employers could be avoided with good communication. It normally helps to offer an alternative channel that the expatriate can use informally or appeal to formally if he does not feel his line manager is resolving things to his satisfaction.

BRIBERY, CODES OF CONDUCT AND 'WHISTLEBLOWING'

Bribery

15.42 Employers of expatriates will naturally need to be conscious of home and host country legislation relating to bribery and corruption. They should also be aware of the existence of key cross-border legislation, in particular the US Foreign Corrupt Practices Act (FCPA) and Sarbanes-Oxley Act 2002 (SOX) (see **15.53**) and the UK Bribery Act 2010, which can have extra-territorial effect.

15.43 Both the FCPA and SOX give employees an opportunity to win very substantial 'bounties' from the relevant public authorities, by reporting misconduct. Employees who do so also receive protection from employer retaliation for such reporting (See **15.47–15.58** on whistleblowing.) In addition employers will be conscious of the significant damage that corruption allegations can cause to a business and of the potential for vicarious liability for the expatriate's actions to bite at home as well as abroad.

15.44 At a more practical level, it is important to bear in mind that in some locations bribery is endemic and that taking a stand can be dangerous for employees. Anti-bribery policies should be very clear about how expatriates should deal with difficult issues that may arise if they are to be effective. More training is also likely to be required for expatriates than for local employees to ensure that they really understand what is and is not acceptable.

Codes of conduct

15.45 It is generally helpful for the employer to issue expatriates with a formal code of conduct to guide them during their assignments. The policy should be issued by the particular expatriate's employer for the reasons described in Chapter 4 but is likely to be either in the form of a loose group-wide policy or an adaptation of that policy suitable for the host country (which may include more specific instructions). The code of conduct might, for example, address expectations regarding:

- bribes, political links and contributions;

- financial propriety;
- industry-specific regulation;
- disclosure and recording of conflicts of interest;
- insider dealing;
- environmental principles;
- fair trade, anti-slavery and supply-chain issues;
- equality and harassment;
- use of emails and the internet (monitoring may also be covered but this is likely to be subject to host country rules and may not be appropriate for inclusion in a group-wide policy);
- standards of communication; and/or
- issues linked to maintaining brand standards.

15.46 The code of conduct may be linked to other policies, for example to a whistleblowing policy (see below) or equal opportunities policy. Data protection issues would usually be dealt with separately if an EEA country is involved because of the complexity of the legal requirements.

Whistleblowing

15.47 Many countries have legislation protecting employees who 'blow the whistle' in the public interest.

15.48 For example, suppose Jack, a nurse, works at a residential home where vulnerable adults are systematically abused and neglected. Jack complains to his employer but nothing is done. He calls the public authority responsible for health and safety inspections and asks for an inspector to visit the home. The employer is fined and forced to implement improvements. The employer finds out that Jack was responsible for triggering the inspection and dismisses him.

15.49 Many countries offer enhanced employment protection to employees in situations of this type, for example those who may suffer victimisation, harassment or dismissal because of their decision to 'do the right thing'. This may be because of a wish to ensure that those who sacrifice themselves for the common good are protected, or more likely a concern that lack of protection will deter employees from coming forward to help prevent accidents etc from happening.

15.50 Whistleblowing legislation has generally been developed to protect the public interest. Different countries have approached the challenge of balancing the need to protect employees from retaliation against employers' needs to keep their business affairs confidential in different ways.

15.51 Whistleblowing does not always refer to disclosure to public authorities. Often a business will want to encourage staff to raise concerns through appropriate internal channels. For example, an employer in the financial services sector may want to encourage employees concerned about financial impropriety or breach of internal rules to raise their concerns internally to those responsible for compliance. There may be formal legal reporting requirements in relation to some matters, eg money laundering suspicions. As complaints may concern line managers it may be appropriate to put in place a formal grievance or whistleblowing procedure so that employees understand what they are expected to do and what their employer will do to protect them from their peers and managers, if that becomes necessary.

15.52 Whistleblowing laws can create additional challenges where there is an expatriate employment relationship because more than one country's rules may be relevant, and the rules may be inconsistent. It may be impossible to fully comply with both sets of rules at the same time.

US – SOX

15.53 The US Sarbanes-Oxley Act 2002 (known as 'SOX') gives whistleblowers some protection under US law. The Act is primarily aimed at US-based employment arrangements. However, case law indicates that in some circumstances, and provided there is sufficient US connection, there could be extra-territorial effect (see *Carnero v Boston Scientific Corp* 433 F 3D 1, 7 and *O'Mahony v Accenture Ltd* 07 Civ 7916 (SDNY, 5 February 2008)).

15.54 For example, suppose Betty works in the UK for a US employer and makes internal complaints about her US-based line manager's fraud. The employer dismisses Betty for making the complaints. The fraud and the decision to dismiss are both made in the US. Betty may potentially have claims in both the UK, because she has been dismissed for making a 'protected disclosure', and the US, under SOX.

France – hotlines and privacy

15.55 The French 'Commission Nationale de 'Informatique et des Liberte's (known as 'CNIL') is responsible for compliance with French data protection (privacy) laws. There has been much discussion about whether whistleblowing procedures adopted by multinationals to comply with other countries' laws (in particular SOX) are compatible with French (and other continental European) legal requirements. The debate has centred on anonymous whistleblowing and ethics reporting 'hotlines'.

15.56 Some reflection on cultural and historical context may help employers better understand the natural tension between anti-corruption legislation and civil liberties. It is also worth bearing in mind that in many European jurisdictions policy documents in this area will be of interest to works councils and other employee participation and representation bodies. There are often public authority registration requirements.

15.57 There has been dialogue between the US SEC and French CNIL and, over the years, useful practical guidelines regarding implementation of whistleblowing arrangements intended to satisfy both countries' rules have evolved. Most recently, the French 'Sapin II Law' (2016-1691 of 9 December 2016) relaxed French hotline restrictions. For up-to-date practical guidance a good place to start is CNIL's website at www.cnil.fr.

15.58 Those drafting whistleblowing policy documents that will apply to expatriates should take care to ensure they are reviewed by home and host country employment law specialists before they are applied or used. It is worth bearing in mind too that potential financial penalties for breaching data protection laws in the EU are very significant (and, from a risk management perspective, may dwarf concern about the potential costs of failing to comply with employment laws).

HEALTH AND SAFETY

15.59 Employers who send employees abroad will usually retain some responsibility for their employees' health and safety during their assignments, even if the home country employer's ability to protect the employees on a day-to-day basis is limited or the practical working arrangements are host country employment arrangements.

15.60 All the usual health and safety issues and risks relating to employment may arise in an expatriate context, but there are some additional risks and practical steps that should be taken that are particularly relevant to expatriate working arrangements. Some examples are set out below.

Host country working arrangements

15.61 Host country health and safety standards may be different from home country standards.

15.62 A home country employer is unlikely to be relieved from responsibility for the employee's working environment just because the employee is working at another company's premises or in another country. Advice should be sought from appropriate specialists regarding responsibilities under both home and host country rules before the assignment begins and should be revisited at appropriate intervals, particularly if concern arises at a later stage.

15.63 It may be appropriate to include more detailed provisions regarding insurance, practical obligations and indemnities in the inter-company expatriate supply agreement, particularly if the home and host companies are not group companies.

Pre-assignment medical checks and consultations

15.64 It is usually sensible to require the employee, and any accompanying family members, to submit to medical examination before the assignment is confirmed. This could have a number of potential benefits. For example:

- assignments are expensive and the check may help identify potential problems that may affect the employee's ability to obtain immigration clearance, perform his assignment duties or receive appropriate medical treatment, whilst the cost of a change of plan to both the employer and the employee is not too high;
- this may help ensure that any special risks are identified and where possible mitigated, for example, to ensure that the employee and his family are properly inoculated against appropriate diseases or that the potential effects of high altitude, pollution or stronger sun are understood;
- if the employer's medical policy includes exceptions for pre-existing conditions or the employer is offering a guarantee in relation to treatment not covered by insurance the medical may help identify potential costs or significant 'gaps' in cover.

15.65 If disability discrimination laws may apply these should be taken into consideration before any pre-assignment checks are undertaken. It will usually be appropriate to clarify the purpose and scope of the checks and how the data will be used in the employment documents, both to reduce the risk of discrimination claims and to ensure compliance with data protection requirements (see **15.73–15.99**). See also Chapter 12 on equality and reasonable adjustments for disability.

15.66 Some employers will provide for regular medical checks in the home or host country during the assignment. Others may insist that the employee and his family submit to medical checks whilst on 'home leave'.

Dangerous assignments

15.67 Some assignments are more dangerous than others. If the employer suspects that the assignment could be dangerous it might consider the following:

- obtaining further information from appropriate third parties (eg the UK Foreign Office or specialist commercial organisations) before the assignment arrangements are finalised and ensuring that this information is updated at appropriate intervals during the assignment;
- ensuring that the employee is aware of security issues and health risks as early as possible and that he is free to refuse the assignment (this might help in the event of subsequent claims but is unlikely to free the employer from all responsibility for potential consequences);

- ensuring that appropriate insurance cover is in place (eg employer's liability, medical, life, accident, key man and/or disability cover);

- giving an appropriate briefing to the employee, and any accompanying family members, on the relevant risks before the assignment begins, on arrival and at appropriate intervals during the assignment, so that they understand what their employer is doing and what they are required to do to reduce risks;

- ensuring that the employee is met at the airport on arrival by host country employees who understand the local environment;

- providing practical security cover in the host country (a driver, security guards, armoured vehicles, etc);

- requiring that the employee live in secure (or relatively secure) accommodation;

- making it clear from the outset that family members will not be permitted to accompany and/or visit the employee during the assignment;

- ensuring that more frequent breaks are offered to reduce the risk of illness or adopting working patterns that allow holiday to be more easily taken away from the host country;

- although this is unlikely to affect the employer's exposure to claims, the expatriate is likely to expect additional remuneration ('danger money') of some sort to reflect the additional risks he will be taking.

DEATH

15.68 All assignees should be encouraged to think about whether they, or any other relevant person, may die whilst they are on assignment, regardless of whether the assignment itself is particularly dangerous.

15.69 Laws and tax rules that would apply to wealth that the employee (or family members) may inherit may be different because they are living in a different country or have a difference tax residency status during the assignment. Similarly, rules that would apply to the employee's own estate if he dies during the assignment may be different.

15.70 For example, the assignment may have an impact on inheritance as follows:

- an employee (or a member of his family) who inherits during the assignment may find the inheritance subject to a different tax treatment, possibly in more than one country;

- if the employee dies his estate may be taxed in a different way and at higher rates than he might otherwise expect;

- compulsory rules regarding the beneficiaries of the employee's estate may apply, even if the employee has made a will, for example, to ensure that property passes to the employee's eldest son rather than his wife;

- more than one country's laws may apply to the estate;
- documents required to ensure that the employee's estate is dealt with properly may not be easily located by the executors if thought is not given before departure to ease of access during the assignment; and/or
- existing life assurance policies may be affected by the assignment.

Practical suggestions

15.71

- The employer should make the employee aware that the assignment may affect inheritance.
- The employee should be encouraged to ensure that his, and his partner's, wills are reviewed by appropriate independent professionals in the light of the proposed assignment, before the assignment begins, and that the practical arrangements to apply to any children are clear. The employer may sometimes offer to contribute to the costs of obtaining appropriate advice.
- The employee may decide, for example, to take out additional life assurance cover and/or make a new will and may encourage his partner to do so too.
- If the employer provides tax equalisation or tax protection benefits, the scope of the comfort offered should be made clear in the employment documents. Most employers do not take account of the effect of an assignment on personal matters such as inheritance or existing personal wealth and if this is the case the documents should make that clear.
- If the employer pays for tax or other professional advice for the employee, the scope of the advice covered should be made clear in the employment documents and/or the contribution to costs should be capped. The costs of tax planning in relation to personal wealth is not normally covered by the employer and this should also be made clear in the employment documents.

DIVORCE

15.72 See Chapter 22 on employee perspectives, including post-nuptial agreements, divorce, settlements and custody.

DATA PROTECTION

15.73 Many countries have laws designed to protect personal data.

EU

15.74 EC Directive 95/46/EC (the 'Data Protection Directive') currently applies to EU countries and imposes obligations and restrictions in relation to the processing of personal data and transfer of personal data outside the EU. Iceland, Norway and Liechtenstein have also introduced laws based on the Directive. (See the Glossary at Appendix 3 for a list of current EEA countries.) A failure to deal with personal data properly may also amount to a breach of Art 8 of the European Convention on Human Rights (ie the right to private and family life).

15.75 The Data Protection Directive will be replaced by the General Data Protection Regulation ('GDPR') from 25 May 2018. The GDPR will apply directly to employers without the need for national implementing laws or collective agreements. The GDPR applies to processing carried out by organisations operating within the EU. It also applies to organisations outside the EU that offer goods or services to individuals in the EU.

15.76 Further information on the GDPR, from a UK perspective, is available here: https://ico.org.uk/for-organisations/data-protection-reform/overview-of-the-gdpr/. (The ICO is the current UK regulator.)

Transfer of data to another organisation

15.77 Generally, the employer, home or host company, or other entity subject to European data protection rules may transfer personal data where the organisation receiving the personal data has provided adequate safeguards. Individuals' rights must be enforceable and effective legal remedies for individuals must be available following the transfer.

15.78 Under the GDPR, adequate safeguards may be provided for by:

- a legally binding agreement between public authorities or bodies;
- binding corporate rules (agreements governing transfers made between organisations within in a corporate group);
- standard data protection clauses in the form of template transfer clauses adopted by the European Commission;
- standard data protection clauses in the form of template transfer clauses adopted by a supervisory authority and approved by the European Commission;
- compliance with an approved code of conduct approved by a supervisory authority;
- certification under an approved certification mechanism as provided for in the GDPR;
- contractual clauses agreed authorised by the competent supervisory authority; or

- provisions inserted in to administrative arrangements between public authorities or bodies authorised by the competent supervisory authority.

Transfer of data to another country

15.79 In addition to a need to transfer data between organisations, where there is an expatriate employment arrangement there is likely to be a practical need for personal data to be transferred from one country to another. For example, the home and host companies may both need personal information about the employee's family members in order to ensure that arrangements for immigration, housing, schooling, etc are managed appropriately.

15.80 The employer should ensure that the employee, and any relevant family members, have given their clear written consent before personal data is transferred between companies or countries. However, technically, consent will not always be sufficient to satisfy data protection laws and protect the employer where data is transferred abroad.

15.81 The Data Protection Directive prohibits (and GDPR will prohibit) the transfer of personal data to any country outside the EU unless:

- the European Commission is satisfied that the country to which the information will be sent has laws providing adequate protection for personal data; or
- steps are taken by the entity sending the information outside the EU to ensure to the satisfaction of the local data protection authorities that the data will be adequately protected after leaving the EU; or
- some other, limited, exceptions apply.

15.82 The European Commission maintains a list of the countries that it considers have adequate data protection laws. These currently include EU countries, Andorra, Argentina, Faroe Islands, Guernsey, Isle of Man, Israel, Jersey, New Zealand, Switzerland and Uruguay. The European Commission's list of countries with adequate data protection laws does not currently include the US.

15.83 Practically, the home and host companies, or all group companies, may enter into a formal agreement or agreements to deal with the way that data will be managed. The form of the agreement will be important if it is to satisfy the relevant data protection authorities and specialist advice will be needed to ensure that it is prepared properly. Once a compliant agreement is in place, arrangements for transfer of personal data in relation to new assignments should be relatively straightforward.

Example: UK to US assignment

15.84 It is proposed that, after some years working in the UK, Bill should be sent to work for another group company in the US on a home country employment arrangement. The UK home company will remain Bill's employer throughout his assignment. Before the assignment details are confirmed, the US host company asks the UK home company to provide some information about Bill to help the US company decide whether he is suitable for the assignment. Once the arrangements are firmed up the UK home company sends more detailed information about Bill, his wife Joan and their three children to the US host company and to various third parties, such as US-based relocation agents. After the assignment has begun, the UK employer will still be responsible for appraisals, bonus, salary review, etc and will need to deal with any disciplinary issues that may arise. There are regular exchanges of personal data about Bill and his family between the UK and US companies, for example by email, throughout the assignment.

15.85 As mentioned above, the European Commission currently takes the view that US laws do not provide adequate protection for personal data. The group has some options if it wishes to comply with UK data protection legislation in relation to the transfer of information to the US:

- the UK home company and the US host company could enter into a 'transborder data flow agreement', including one of a choice of two sets of 'model clauses' approved by the European Commission;
- all the group companies could enter into 'Binding Corporate Rules' (ie a global code of data protection conduct); or
- the UK Information Commissioner's Office's (ICO) guidance could be followed to ensure adequacy by due diligence and codes of conduct.

15.86 Previously it was thought that the US 'Safe Harbor' programme offered adequate protection, but following the decision of the Court of Justice of the European Union (CJEU) on 6 October 2015 in *Schrems v Data Protection Commissioner (Ireland) (Case C-362/14)* that is no longer the case. The Safe Harbor arrangements have been replaced with the EU-US Privacy Shield. This is a binding legal instrument which may be used for transferring personal data from the EU to the US.

15.87 Each of the options has advantages and disadvantages and specialist advice should be sought on the form of agreement that would work best for the particular assignment, home and host companies, and the group more generally.

Home and host country requirements

15.88 Different data protection laws may apply in different countries so the rules of both home and host countries, and any other relevant country (eg the country where the group's head office is based), should be checked. This is particularly important where there is an assignment between two European countries, as both are likely to have laws in place to comply with the Data Protection Directive (or GDPR). The particular requirements of each country are unlikely to be entirely consistent.

Data protection principles

15.89 The Data Protection Directive provides (and GDPR will provide) for eight 'data protection principles' that are worth bearing in mind. The personal data must be:

(1) processed fairly and lawfully;

(2) processed only for specific, limited purposes and not in any manner inconsistent with those purposes;

(3) adequate, relevant and not excessive in relation to those purposes;

(4) accurate, complete and kept up to date;

(5) kept in personally identifiable form no longer than necessary;

(6) processed in accordance with the rights of the data subject under applicable law;

(7) kept secure; and

(8) only transferred to countries that have 'adequate' data protection laws unless the 'data exporter' takes certain specific steps to ensure that the data is 'adequately protected' (see **15.79–15.88**).

Consent

15.90 The explicit consent of the data subject should usually be obtained before personal data is sent outside the EEA. This is not a specific legal requirement in every European country. Also, as noted above, consent will not always be sufficient for compliance purposes, particularly in an HR context. For example, the data protection authorities in some countries may consider that consent given by an employee to his employer is not freely given. In some countries the consent of the relevant data protection authority must be obtained to send data outside Europe.

15.91 Generally, the 'data controller' should have a clear document setting out its data protection policy and make that available to employees. The data controller is likely to be the home company at the start of the assignment but the host company could also be a data controller, for example, in relation to feedback sent to the home country for appraisal purposes.

15.92 The data protection policy would, for example, explain why certain data is kept; how it should be updated and corrected; what is done with it and why; how long it will be kept; how a 'data subject access request' can be made by an employee who wants copies of the data, etc.

15.93 In addition to the data protection policy, the employer will probably wish to provide the employee with consent forms to be completed by himself and his family so that clear consent is given in relation to the data that is actually collected, processed, sent abroad, etc for assignment purposes. Where the home company frequently sends employees on overseas assignments it will usually be helpful to have pro forma consent forms that can be adapted if necessary for each assignment.

15.94 It is also usually helpful to appoint a Chief Privacy Officer (or similar) to take responsibility for data protection generally. In some countries appointment of someone to take this role is mandatory. Because data protection requirements are complex, generally do not appear urgent and can be quite tedious to deal with, it is important that managers and employees have a clear and easy channel to which they can direct data protection queries. This should help reduce the risk of mistakes, missed deadlines and unnecessary audits, fines and compliance orders.

Sensitive personal data

15.95 Stricter rules often apply to the handling of 'sensitive personal data'. Data that is processed and transferred between countries in the context of an international assignment often includes sensitive personal data. For example:

- details of the national origins of the employee and his family may be required for immigration purposes;
- the employee's religion may be disclosed in the context of discussions about the normal working week;
- the employee's sexual orientation may be relevant where host country laws or practices could cause problems; and
- information about health may be processed and transferred frequently, for example, when insurance arrangements, pre-assignment check-ups, vaccinations, etc are dealt with.

Host company compliance

15.96 As well as considering the issues relating to transfer of data outside the EU, the group will need to think about compliance in the home and host countries where the data is processed. (See **13.36–13.39** in relation to start ups, where there are unlikely to be existing arrangements for handling personal data.)

Audit

15.97 It is worth bearing in mind that some data protection authorities will require regular audit of the data protection arrangements that are in place.

Data subject access requests

15.98 See **15.127** below.

For global mobility advisers

15.99 Responsibility for data protection compliance rarely sits within a mobility team, and is unlikely to be the responsibility of HR either. Data protection compliance usually encompasses client, supplier and other third-party data, as well as employees. This should not be a problem as long as those responsible for data protection are aware of the particular compliance issues that arise in the context of global mobility. It is worth highlighting that:

- consents given in an ordinary domestic employment context are unlikely to be sufficient for compliance, eg relevant consents are unlikely to have been obtained from affected family members or with transfer overseas in mind;

- it is the responsibility of the 'home' or 'host' employer within scope of European data protection rules to take steps to ensure compliance by those to whom they transfer personal data. This means that if a new supplier is engaged, eg a destination services provider, additional compliance steps are likely to be required;

- global mobility invariably involves transfer of personal data between jurisdictions. Where a new jurisdiction is involved, new compliance obligations are likely to arise.

INTELLECTUAL PROPERTY

15.100 Different rules will, of course, apply in different countries. However, normally, when an employee creates intellectual property the intellectual property will belong to the employer automatically, even if the employment contract does not mention intellectual property.

15.101 Where intellectual property is unlikely to be important, the employers of expatriates may not wish to make already complicated employment documents longer by including detailed intellectual property clauses.

15.102 However, where the creation of intellectual property is important it may be helpful to include clauses relating to the ownership of intellectual property and the employee's obligations regarding co-operation in the employment documents.

15.103 If the business wants to make sure that intellectual property will not be owned by the employer at the outset, for example because a subsequent transfer of the intellectual property rights between group companies may have tax implications, then this should be dealt with at the outset.

15.104 If intellectual property becomes important after the assignment begins it may still be possible to enter into documents to improve the companies' legal position.

CHANGING TERMS AND CONDITIONS, INCLUDING 'LOCALISATION'

15.105 Terms and conditions of employment may need to be changed during the assignment. For example, the scope of the role may change or the employer may wish to adjust benefit arrangements to reflect changes to tax legislation or exchange rate fluctuations. Agreement is likely to be required from both employer and employee to effect any significant change not envisaged by the original contract.

Mandatory employment laws

15.106 Mandatory employment laws may have an impact on the process to be followed and may prevent some changes from taking effect at all. For example, it may not be possible to agree on changes to terms set by mandatory collective agreement.

Unfair contract terms and discretion

15.107 Generally, it is helpful for a contract to be drafted in a way that gives flexibility to the employer to introduce change to the employee's current terms, without the need to reach specific agreement with the employee. However, the retention of flexibility by the employer may cause problems in some countries where laws offer protection against 'unfair' employment contract terms. Those laws may, for example, cause problems when terms allowing for flexibility are agreed or when terms in the contract providing for flexibility are relied upon. Examples of the sort of clause that might cause problems include clauses:

- providing for mobility or relocation once the assignment has started;
- allowing the employer to change the employee's duties unilaterally (this may also cause immigration problems);
- restricting the employee's ability to make certain employment claims;
- providing for the recovery of costs, for example, relocation expenses, incurred by the employer if the employment terminates early or the employee leaves to join a competitor;
- allowing for non-payment or claw-back of bonus in some circumstances, for example if the employee leaves to work for a competitor (see Chapter 11);
- allowing the employer to provide benefits on a 'discretionary' basis (ie allowing the employer to withdraw benefits unilaterally);
- providing for fixed financial penalties to be imposed on the employee, for example, in the event of breach of contract by the employee; or
- providing for negative adjustments to pay, for example, reduction in the level of COLA offered (see 7.40–7.47).

15.108 The relevant laws may prohibit particular types of clause or may allow for the contract terms when viewed as a whole to be challenged if they are not sufficiently 'balanced'.

15.109 Practically, problems should be avoided if copies of the draft employment documents are reviewed, and amended where necessary, by employment lawyers from appropriate countries before the agreements are concluded.

Effect on the identity of the employer

15.110 Where agreement is required, change should be discussed and agreed between the employee and the correct employer and the correspondence and amended employment documents should reflect that.

Potential consequences of change

15.111 Change may be restricted and/or have unexpected consequences for the assignment. For example:

- a decision to extend the length of the assignment may have tax, social security, employment law and/or immigration implications, for example it may not be possible to obtain an extension to the work permit or tax and social security expenses could increase substantially;

- a change to the role may need to be cleared with immigration authorities (eg in some cases an existing work permit may be invalidated);

- a change to the role may affect the application of collective agreements and/or mandatory employment laws;

- a change to an employee's family size (through marriage, divorce, birth, etc) might not normally have significant consequences for an employer but if valuable family-related benefits are offered (as is often the case for an expatriate) the employer's costs may sometimes increase either through agreement to meet the expatriate's expectations or because the contract or the employer's policies already provide for a link between benefits and family size;

- a change to terms that is to the detriment of the employee may be prohibited by mandatory laws or a particular process may need to be followed before the change can take effect.

Extension of fixed-term contracts

15.112 Many countries (including EU jurisdictions) have quite strict rules that control the circumstances in which a fixed-term contract can be agreed with an employee. The rules may, for example, limit the type of employee who can enter into a fixed-term employment contract; the period of time for which the fixed-term can apply or the terms offered (eg by comparison with those available to employees employed for an indefinite period). Typically, the attraction of a fixed-term employment contract for the employer will be the ability to terminate the employment without the application of onerous mandatory employment laws.

15.113 Specialist advice should always be sought if a fixed-term contract is to be extended, as further conditions may apply. A typical penalty for failing to meet the relevant requirements might be automatic transition to an indefinite employment arrangement. (See **15.111** on the potential impact on immigration permission or tax and social security arrangements.)

Localisation

15.114 Employees are often assigned to work in the host country on favourable expatriate terms, including perhaps a higher salary and a range of 'expatriate' benefits arrangements that local hires do not enjoy. (See also **12.21–12.23** on 'local plus' arrangements.) For all sorts of reasons, the assignment may last longer than expected. For example, the assignment may be so successful that neither the employee nor the home or host companies want the assignment to end, or the employee's personal circumstances may change, for example, through marriage to a host country national.

15.115 The employer may be happy for the assignment to continue but may feel that, after a period of time, the employee should be treated like a local hire. The employer may also worry about discrimination issues where there is no longer justification for treating the expatriate differently from local hires. The employer may therefore look for a way to move the employee onto 'local terms'. This is often referred to as 'localisation'. Localisation could also include movement from a home to a host country employment arrangement and the severing of ties with the home country.

15.116 Few employees will readily agree to a reduction in their remuneration package or any change to their contract that will leave them worse off, without some advantage being offered as a 'carrot'. In practice, this means that localisation is likely to be easier where the employee wants to stay in the host country and is prepared to make some sacrifices to do so; the home and host companies are happy to accommodate him; and the employee would find it difficult to find alternative employment on expatriate terms or other similar terms with another employer in the host country.

15.117 An additional difficulty is that most countries' mandatory employment laws offer protection to employees who suffer negative changes to their contracts. It may not be possible to vary the contract to the employee's disadvantage even with the employee's agreement to the changes. Dismissing and offering re-employment on less favourable local terms may also trigger employment claims.

15.118 Employers may try to set expectations by time-limiting the provision of expatriate terms and making it clear from the outset of the assignment that the expatriate will be required to move to local terms if the assignment lasts longer than a specified period. In practice, this sort of agreement is unlikely to be watertight because at the start of the assignment the employer is unlikely to be in a position to give the employee a very clear picture of what those local terms might eventually be. However, inclusion of a general statement regarding an intention to localise or specific provisions time-limiting certain expatriate benefits may help to manage expectations. That, in turn, could help with maintaining goodwill through subsequent negotiations. This approach could also reduce the risk of employment claims in relation to forced changes.

15.119 Another problem with making statements about localisation from the outset can be the impact on immigration, social security, etc where a maximum anticipated duration of the assignment may be critical to achievement of the employer's goals. For example, a general statement about localisation after five years' assignment may be inappropriate and harmful if a work permit can only be obtained if the employer expects the assignment to last for a maximum of three years.

EU

15.120 Directives 94/45/EC, 97/74/EC and 2009/38/EC (the European Works Council (EWC) Directives) require multinationals with at least 1,000 employees in the EU and at least 150 in each of two member states to set up an EWC if employees request this. If an EWC exists there should be an 'EWC agreement' that explains the way that the EWC operates, its goals, etc. This will include information and consultation arrangements. An EWC is unlikely to be concerned with an individual expatriate employment assignment, changes to the terms of the assignment or its termination. However, if the proposed changes are part of a bigger project affecting employees in more than one country then it would be worth checking whether there may be any EWC implications.

CONTINUOUS EMPLOYMENT

15.121 Many employment benefits and employment rights depend on length of service.

15.122 Length of service is often referred to as 'seniority' in Europe. This can be a bit confusing for English or US advisers who are more likely to use the term 'seniority' to describe the level or status of the employee's role within the business, for example whether he is a senior or junior manager. (See **19.88–19.90** and **20.40–20.53** for an explanation of the way 'continuous employment' for UK statutory purposes may be affected by an expatriate assignment.)

DISCLOSURE

15.123 When managing any employment issue it can be helpful to consider whether communications attract legal privilege or can be regarded as 'without prejudice' – the key concern being whether the communications might need to be disclosed.

Legal privilege

15.124 Legal privilege has developed in many countries to allow lawyers to give legal advice to their clients without the client needing to be concerned about disclosure to third parties. Legal privilege may, for example, arise because of the nature of the communications made (eg because they provide legal advice) or because of the nature of the relationship between those that are engaged in communications (eg lawyer-client). Exceptions may apply. For example, the lawyer may be required to report certain matters to public authorities (eg if money laundering or tax evasion is suspected). Where the protection is offered to communications with lawyers qualifying criteria may be applied. For example, in-house counsel may not be recognised as independent lawyers for this purpose in some countries.

15.125 It is important to be aware that the relevant rules vary considerably from country to country and allow for that in communications. Practically, the assignment manager is unlikely to want to delve into the detail of whether communications might be subject to disclosure at a later stage. It may make more sense to take care with the accuracy of communications so that if disclosure is required problems are less likely.

Without prejudice

15.126 'Without prejudice' communications are those that are intended to facilitate settlement of a legal dispute. For example, the employer and employee may wish to discuss severance terms freely without the risk that the discussions may somehow be used to undermine their case. Without prejudice communications are generally protected from disclosure unless perhaps the parties waive their rights at a later stage or the communications are relevant to costs. As with legal privilege the concept of 'without prejudice' communications varies considerably from country to country. If the issues are significant it is usually worth establishing the ground rules before dialogue begins.

Data subject access requests

15.127 In countries where European data protection rules apply it may be possible for employees to, easily and very cheaply, require disclosure of documents containing personal data.

Practical suggestions

15.128 Whilst technical requirements relating to disclosure can be very important in the context of disputes or investigations, they are far too complicated for ordinary people (and lawyers) to navigate perfectly. Managing day-to-day expatriate issues requires communication, and because of time zone and location differences, communication by email is often most efficient. It is probably more effective to focus on a few simple principles to reduce the risk than to focus on the technicalities every day. After all, when things are going well concealment really should not be a top priority and slowing communication to snail pace to allow for constant checking carries its own risks. Here are some practical suggestions that may help:

- Never destroy documents that may be important to a future dispute or investigation.

- Don't copy people in on emails unnecessarily or use 'reply all' without thinking, particularly where other people are in a different jurisdiction.

- Think carefully about how you share 'sensitive personal data' and make sure all staff are aware of data processing principles. Don't keep sensitive personal data in a place where it is easy to share accidentally.

- Don't mix the content of emails unnecessarily. For example, don't mix managerial discussion with privileged advice.

- Let lawyers give their own advice – don't repeat it informally in emails internally or send it to third parties. If others need to see it, ask the lawyer to send it to them.

- Think about whether it is appropriate to communicate the reasons for decisions (sometimes it will be, sometimes not).

- Don't copy employees in on professional advice to justify your actions or tell employees you are seeking professional advice.

ONGOING MANAGEMENT – OVERVIEW

15.129 It is impossible to prepare good employment documents without giving thought to ongoing management issues. Many of those issues will be easier to manage if they are anticipated when documents are prepared. The above are examples of areas where advice is often sought during an assignment. There will be many more and it is important to keep abreast of developments so that documents can be adapted as best practice develops. Expatriate employment terms are frequently replaced as employees are relocated and repatriated so there are often easy opportunities to update paperwork to reflect issues as they are identified. Employers may find it helpful to join networks of global mobility professionals as well as reading global mobility newsletters and other materials as they become available. It is important to keep an eye on developments in other disciplines that may interact with the managers and advisers core skills, eg reward, tax, immigration, privilege, health & safety, employment law etc. Most importantly, documents should be kept under review.

CHAPTER 16

ENDING THE ASSIGNMENT

AT THE START

16.1 Parties to a contract should always think about what might happen if things go wrong. It is the lawyers' job to help clients focus on the 'what ifs' and, particularly, to anticipate the end. The aim is to identify things that can be done now to make things easier later. Employment contracts are no different.

16.2 For an ordinary local hire there are various issues relating to termination of employment to consider before the employment begins, such as:

- the notice period and arrangements for serving notice;

- how termination might affect benefits such as bonus;

- whether the employer should have a contractual right to pay in lieu of notice;

- whether additional termination payments should be promised, for example, contractual redundancy pay or 'change of control' payments if certain conditions are satisfied;

- whether a 'garden leave' clause should be included, allowing the employer to keep the employee in employment during all or part of his notice period but not let him work;

- whether any post termination restrictive covenants may be appropriate, for example, preventing the employee from soliciting business from customers after his employment ends;

- how the employee would be removed from any office or appointment, for example, as director, and/or how any 'powers' would be withdrawn; and

- the likely cost of ending the employment and how long this is likely to take.

These issues should be considered for expatriates as for other employees. However, there are some additional considerations that are peculiar to expatriates, and the financial consequences of failing to think about these issues at an early stage may be far more severe if the employee is on assignment abroad.

REASSIGNMENT

16.3 If the business wishes to reassign the expatriate to another country or group company then the issues relating to termination of the assignment will be different to those that would apply if employment with the group were also to end.

16.4 The employment documents should be structured in a way that facilitates termination of the current assignment, for example, by making it clear that the employer, but not the employee, has a right to terminate the assignment by serving notice, without terminating the employment. The bigger issue on reassignment is likely to be the need to reach agreement on the terms of the new assignment. If the employee is happy with the new assignment and the terms offered to him, then the old arrangements can usually be terminated or amended easily by agreement. If the employee is unhappy with the new assignment arrangements then, naturally, agreement will be harder to reach.

16.5 If the overseas assignment is short-term, the employee's home country arrangements can usually be suspended for the period of the assignment and easily revived on his return. In that case, the employment documents for the assignment can be clear about the arrangements that will apply when the assignment ends and there should be little problem with transition to the agreed new terms.

16.6 However, many expatriates who have been away for a longer period are unable to return to their former job in the home country. The job may no longer be there or may have been given to another employee. Often the expatriate moves on in his career so that the old role is no longer appropriate anyway. If the employee is a 'career expatriate', enjoying a series of international assignments in different host countries, the next job may depend on the vacancies that are available when the current assignment ends.

16.7 Some parameters may be set through the employment documents for the initial assignment. For example, notional salary and/or notional grading can help the business to manage the employee's expectations about his likely remuneration and status for the next role. If the employee is likely to be returning to an 'ordinary' home country employment, then it can be helpful to ensure that the employment documents for the initial assignment make clear which benefits are 'expatriate' benefits that will be withdrawn at the end of the assignment.

16.8 The reality, though, is that expatriate assignments are expensive and many businesses are reluctant to encourage an employee to take up a new role if he is not committed to it. The employer may prefer to offer the option of a redundancy package if the employee considers the proposed new role to be unsuitable. This may be preferable to the additional disruption and expense of the employee returning home or starting a new assignment and then leaving shortly afterwards, or performing badly in the role.

16.9 Even if the employee is enthusiastic about the new assignment and the proposed new package there will still be some issues to resolve. For example, it might be necessary or helpful to deal with the following.

Termination of the current employment or terms

16.10 If the employee is employed under a host employer arrangement, the employment with the host employer should be terminated effectively at the end of the assignment. If the current assignment is a home country employment arrangement and the new employment is to be with the home company too there will be no need to terminate the employment, but the current assignment terms will need to be terminated. In most cases this can be done simply by confirming in writing that the old employment has ended and/or the old terms have been replaced by mutual agreement. In other situations it may be necessary to use a more formal severance agreement to ensure that loose ends are tidied up. There will often be some administrative obligations to notify relevant host country authorities of the termination.

Removal from appointments etc

16.11 Many senior expatriates hold appointments, for example, as director, or other formal powers that are linked to a particular assignment. The business will need to follow the proper formalities to ensure the expatriate's effective removal from appointments, and the withdrawal of any related powers. This may also involve the appointment of another person or people to take the expatriate's place. For example, if the expatriate is the only employee in the host country with authority to authorise payroll arrangements, it would usually be appropriate to grant that authority to another employee to reduce the risk of administrative difficulties. In some cases it will not be possible to effectively remove the expatriate from an appointment until a replacement is appointed.

Transition from one tax and social security regime to another

16.12 If the employee is to take up a new assignment, the employer will need to seek tax and social security advice regarding the new assignment in the ordinary way. The employer should also be concerned about the effect of the changes on tax and social security arrangements for the current assignment. The timing of the expatriate's departure and the new and old host countries may make a difference to the outcome. Reassignment is unlikely to take place conveniently at the end of the tax year for the countries relevant to both the old and new assignments, so there are likely to be additional requirements in relation to overlapping tax returns etc. There may also be a need to limit the amount of time that the employee spends in his home country between assignments. The effect of tax equalisation or protection promises may need to be considered. The employer may also wish to seek advice regarding tax treatment of the relocation package.

Relocation

16.13 Relocation or repatriation expenses should be dealt with. Even where the employer's obligations are confirmed in the existing employment documents this will still need some care as it may, for example, be more appropriate to deal with expenses and allowances in a different way now the new host country is known or because tax laws have changed. Often the employer's policies will have evolved since the original arrangements were agreed and the employee may be asked to agree that the new policies will apply.

16.14 Practical arrangements will need to be made regarding the payment of outstanding host country bills, school fees, etc. Early termination penalties may be due and there may be a need to recover deposits.

16.15 The most significant issue is likely to be termination or transfer of the lease on the employee's accommodation in the host country. This is because accommodation tends to make up such a large part of assignment costs. Diarising renewal dates may help.

Immigration

16.16 There may be a requirement to notify the immigration authorities and/or return immigration papers. Immigration issues may also affect the timing of the transition. For example, the expatriate may have to wait for immigration permission for his next assignment or there may be a need for the expatriate to stay in post until immigration permission can be obtained for his replacement in the host country. Immigration permission cannot usually be passed from one employee to another where a substitute is appointed to the same role, without the involvement of governmental officials. Timing issues may be managed through an interim period of different work or holiday, perhaps in the home country, or the outgoing expatriate may remain in post to settle in his replacement. Care should be taken to ensure that return to the home country for a short period does not create unnecessary tax liabilities (see also **16.82–16.83**).

Holiday

16.17 If the employer is to change when the employee starts his new assignment then the usual holiday arrangements on termination of employment would normally apply. Typically, holiday entitlement for the year is calculated on a pro rata basis and the employee is asked to take any outstanding holiday or is paid in lieu of accrued holiday that has not been taken. Care should be taken to ensure that the practical arrangements satisfy mandatory employment laws.

16.18 If the employer does not change there may still be some transitional arrangements to deal with. For example, there will be an impact on holiday arrangements if the number of days' annual holiday allowed will change with the assignment, or if there is a need for the employee to take, or not take, holiday before the new assignment begins to help manage timing issues.

Bonus

16.19 The expatriate's bonus arrangements are likely to change with the assignment, because his employer changes or because targets will need to reflect his new role.

16.20 The new arrangements should be set out in the new assignment documents. The employee's entitlement under the old arrangements would need to be determined and any tax equalisation issues resolved. (See also **15.7**.)

Timing

16.21 The timing of the assignment change can be a challenge. A wide variety of factors might be taken into consideration, for example:

- expiry of the outgoing expatriate's immigration permission or the need for him to wait for immigration clearance for the new assignment (see **16.16**);
- the need to allow for a period of overlap so the outgoing expatriate can help settle in his replacement;
- delays affecting the arrival of the replacement expatriate (eg due to the requirements of the replacement's current role, the need for the replacement to obtain immigration clearance before his new assignment begins etc);
- issues relating to the objectives of the new assignment (ie when the expatriate will be needed to start his new role);
- a need to minimise disruption to the natural business cycle;
- cost and benefit issues (eg it may be cheaper for the company to terminate a lease at particular times or it may be helpful for the expatriate to leave the role before timing affects his immigration status);
- the expatriate's personal situation (eg children's school terms or exams, constraints relating to his partner's employment, etc); and
- tax and social security (eg because early return to the home country could create unnecessary tax liabilities).

Documents

16.22 If any of these arrangements are to be recorded in the employment documents thought will need to be given as to whether these issues should be dealt with in the new employment documents or in a separate agreement with the 'old' employer. For example, if the employee will move from a home to a host employment arrangement (ie if he will change employers) it will generally not be appropriate to deal with issues relating to termination of the old home employment in the new host country employment contract. The entity that is responsible for bearing expenses or allowances may also have an impact on the tax treatment for the relevant expenses or allowances.

TERMINATION OF EMPLOYMENT

16.23 If the employee will not be offered another role, either with the same employer or another group company, both the assignment and the employment will need to end and more care should be taken with the termination process and severance terms.

Notice to terminate employment

Length of notice period

16.24 The employment documents should set out the length of the notice period that must be given by the employer and the employee to each other to end the employment. In some countries the period to be given by the employer may need to be the same, or at least as long as, the period to be given by the employee but they may be different.

16.25 Most countries have laws, or collective agreements, setting minimum, and in some cases maximum, notice periods. These may apply by way of default if nothing else is agreed, may override the terms of any contract or may apply unless derogation is agreed in a particular way, for example with employee representatives or in writing. In some countries different rules may apply through different means, for example, by way of national legislation or case law; regional law; national or sectoral collective bargaining agreement; local collective bargaining agreement and/or the contract of employment. It is important to understand the priority in which the relevant requirements should be applied if they conflict, as this varies.

16.26 In some countries where the notice period is set by mandatory rules there may, technically, be no need to specify the relevant notice period in the employment contract and it may be the normal host country practice not to do so. However, it usually makes sense to specify the relevant period for expatriates, or at least make clear reference to the relevant sources of the mandatory rules in the employment documents.

16.27 Additional up-to-date copies of the employment documents should be kept at an accessible location outside the host country, subject to data protection rules and subject to any relevant data protection policy. If it is proposed that a senior expatriate should be dismissed, it may be difficult to find the relevant employment documents and source appropriate host country advice quickly and discretely. For example, enquiries may alert staff in the host country to the potential dismissal. Sourcing information from the host country can be particularly difficult if the expatriate to be dismissed is the most senior employee in the host country.

16.28 If the documents are clear, and include all the relevant information, there is likely to be less work, expense and delay at the end of the employment; mistakes are less likely to be made; and there is less likely to be dispute with the employee over key facts, such as whether a particular collective agreement applies. Even when the paperwork has been prepared and retained meticulously, up-to-date advice should be sought, particularly from a host country employment lawyer to ensure that relevant laws have not changed.

Payment in lieu of notice

16.29 The employer may wish to consider inserting a payment in lieu of notice (PILON) clause in the employment contract. This may allow the employer to end the employment without giving the appropriate notice and by making an agreed payment. The effect may be to avoid breach of the employment contract by the employer if the employer ends the employment without first allowing the employee to work out his notice period. This could be beneficial in some countries, as breach of the contract by the employer may mean loss of the benefit of other terms of the contract for the employer, for example, loss of the ability to enforce post termination restrictions (see Chapter 11).

16.30 In other countries inclusion of a PILON clause could be important because otherwise it would not be possible to dismiss quickly (ie without allowing the employee to work out his notice period in full).

16.31 An additional practical advantage of including a PILON clause is that there is less room for the parties to fall out over calculation of appropriate termination payments.

16.32 There may be tax and social security implications too. For example, the decision may affect deductions to be made in respect of termination payments or the employee's ability to claim social security benefits for a period of time.

16.33 In some places, for example Hong Kong, the employee may also end the contract by making a PILON.

16.34 The rules, advantages and disadvantages of including clauses of this type vary considerably between countries. Mandatory rules prescribing the way in which the PILON should be calculated vary too, for example, whether benefits such as bonus should be taken into consideration or only fixed pay.

UK

16.35 In the UK a PILON clause will usually be included in the employment contract for a senior employee so that the employment can be terminated on short or no notice without breaching the contract. If the employer breaches the contract it is unlikely to be able to enforce post termination restrictions.

16.36 A downside of this approach is that any PILON made under the contract will be taxable whereas termination payments may otherwise, and subject to strict qualifying criteria, qualify for tax relief. Tax relief for an ordinary UK-based employee is currently available only on up to £30,000 of aggregate qualifying termination payments (including the value of benefits). Commercially, for senior employees, the loss of potential tax and social security relief on the PILON will usually be more than outweighed by the benefit to the employer of the protection offered by the PILON in respect of the post termination restrictions.

16.37 For expatriates returning to the UK the position is (currently) different. Where foreign service exemption applies the potential tax relief allowed in respect of a qualifying termination payment could be far more substantial for an expatriate than for a local hire who has spent no time working abroad. However, the foreign service exemption will no longer apply to UK tax residents who have their employment contracts terminated on or after 6 April 2018.

16.38 Post termination restrictions may be less important for expatriates (see Chapter 11).

16.39 Historically, because of the foreign service exemption the potential financial impact of the lost tax relief might have been so great that the employer considered it inappropriate to include a PILON clause, regardless of the potential future effect on covenants. Loss of foreign service relief in 2018 removes the need for debate.

16.40 Note too that more than one country's tax rules and mandatory employment laws may apply at the same time. For example, there is no point in spending a lot of time worrying about the availability of tax relief in the UK if the remuneration is taxed in another jurisdiction anyway. This sometimes arises, for example, where UK-based employees are also US citizens subject to US tax and without available tax credits (see **16.81**).

Garden leave

16.41 It can be helpful to include a garden leave clause in the employment documents. The clause could allow the employer to control the employee's conduct whilst the employee is not required to work. An employee is still an employee during garden leave and usually continues to receive his normal remuneration. As for an ordinary employment, a garden leave clause can give a useful alternative to relying on post termination restrictions for an expatriate. Garden leave clauses may also be useful for expatriates because the arrangements may offer the employer some additional practical control over the termination process. For example:

- the employer may be able to keep the employee on garden leave whilst requiring return to the home country. This may effectively change the place of dismissal and, occasionally, the application of mandatory employment laws, or allow a period during which an alternative assignment could be identified before the employment ends; or

- there may be situations where garden leave helps the business manage conflicting timing requirements. For example, the interaction of immigration requirements (perhaps to leave the host country within a fixed period of time following termination of employment); the needs of the business (perhaps to ensure that the employee is not in the office once he is told he will be dismissed); and the needs of the expatriate (perhaps to allow a child to complete exams before he leaves a host country school).

16.42 It is worth bearing in mind that garden leave is not permitted in all countries and that the commencement of garden leave might have an immediate impact on immigration status. See also **11.23** on garden leave.

Arrangements for giving notice

16.43 The practical arrangements for giving notice of termination of employment should usually be made clear in the employment contract from the start. Normally the contract should confirm:

- the notice period to be given by both the employer and employee (taking account of any minimum, maximum or matching requirement set by mandatory laws, see **16.24–16.28**);
- if the notice period changes with length of service, whether a particular notice period will apply on service or expiry of notice (i e so the transition point is clear);
- that notice must be given in writing;
- who notice must be served on and where (eg notice on the home company might be served on the company at its registered office in the home country marked for the attention of the company secretary);
- the method by which notice can be given (eg whether notice may be served personally, by registered or ordinary post, by fax, courier, e-mail, etc). The method by which notice can be served is often governed by mandatory employment laws. For example, there may be a requirement for notice to be given in person or by registered post and notice may not be effective if served in another way. Even if there are no mandatory employment laws to be observed, some thought should be given to the method by which notice can be served, particularly if there is a home country arrangement and the employee and employer are based in different countries. For example, service by post may not be appropriate if the post is unreliable or the service date will be uncertain. Service by fax is only likely to be appropriate if the fax number is confidential and regularly checked. In practice, the notice provisions could require a combination of methods, for example, service in person or by post, and in each case a copy by email to a specified person. ('In person' may need clarification, as this may or may not cover delivery by a third party, eg a courier service. This is the

sort of language that can be unhelpful in an expatriate employment document that may need to be interpreted by someone with a different understanding of the phrase.)

16.44 Even if advice has been sought at the outset of the assignment, and the documents have been drafted to take that advice into account, it will still be worth checking that there have been no changes to mandatory laws relating to notice, and that the particular circumstances have not made the agreed arrangements for serving notice inappropriate. Checks should be made well before any steps to dismiss the employee are taken.

16.45 The place in which notice is given and/or where the employment ends could make a difference to whether mandatory employment laws apply. Flying the employee back to the home country to be given, or work out, his notice may not always be appropriate.

16.46 It can sometimes be helpful for a manager to fly to the host country in order to serve notice personally, manage the expatriate's departure, answer questions, arrange for conclusion of a severance agreement, etc.

Terminating both employment and assignment

16.47 One surprisingly common mistake is for those drafting the employment documents to fail to distinguish clearly between termination of the employment and termination of the assignment.

16.48 It is worth bearing in mind the following key points:

- if the assignment is to end the employment may or may not end as well;
- usually the employee is not given any power to terminate the assignment without terminating the employment: that is usually an option reserved for the employer; and
- if the employment is to end, both the assignment and the underlying employment will need to end.

16.49 It is important to bear in mind that arguments are usually harder to resolve on termination of employment when relationships tend to deteriorate; the financial stakes can be high for the employee; and the employer can quickly be drawn into incurring substantial legal and other professional expenses. Clear drafting is particularly important for terms dealing with termination.

16.50 For expatriate employment arrangements the issues become even more important. The opportunities for face-to-face meetings may be fewer; there is more potential for misunderstanding; and the legal requirements can be more complicated even without the ambiguity created by poor drafting. On the plus side the costs, uncertainty and practical difficulties associated with dispute will often encourage the expatriate to reach agreement too.

16.51 Documents that clearly set expectations can go a long way to reducing the risk of dispute.

Example – home country employer

16.52 If there is a home country employment arrangement, the employee will have a contract of employment with the home company, which should include a term specifying the arrangements for giving notice of termination of employment. Suppose though that there is an old employment contract with the home company, including a clause setting out arrangements for terminating the employment, and a separate assignment letter varying the terms of that contract for the duration of the assignment. The assignment letter includes a clause setting out arrangements for terminating the assignment and providing for return to the home country in that event. The home employer informs the employee in writing that the assignment will end on a particular date. The employee may know that no new assignment is being offered but still argue that notice to terminate the employment has not started to run.

16.53 Suppose the documents are in the form described above but the employer serves notice of termination of both the assignment and the employment. The employee may argue that the employer has given him a contractual commitment not to serve notice of termination of the employment until the assignment has ended. This could, in turn, lead to difficulties with dismissal and/or an increase to the size of any termination payment due. Even if the employer can technically defend his drafting, dealing with the arguments may involve time and money.

Example – host country employer

16.54 Suppose the employee is employed by the host company for the duration of the assignment. He also has a 'residual' employment agreement with the home company he worked for before the assignment began. The host company serves notice of termination of the employment with the host company. This does not terminate the residual employment agreement with the home company: a separate procedure would be needed to end that agreement. If no thought is given to this there is a possibility that the residual employment relationship with the home country will automatically revive at the end of the host company employment. Again, this may lead to increased expense.

Who should give the employee notice

16.55 It is worth emphasising that decisions to dismiss should be made by the employer and notice of termination of employment should be served by the employer. Care should be taken to ensure that decisions are taken and communicated by the right representative on behalf of the right company and that the correct headed paper etc is used. See Chapter 4 regarding the importance of supporting the identity of the correct employer and the potential consequences of failing to do so.

The inter-company expatriate supply agreement

16.56 There is also likely to be some arrangement between the home and host companies providing for supply of the employee's services (the inter-company expatriate supply agreement, see Chapter 6). In practice, because the home and host companies will usually be group companies that arrangement will often end by informal agreement. However, the employment documents should provide for the home and host companies to be able to serve notice on each other to terminate that arrangement too.

16.57 Ideally, the inter-company expatriate supply agreement should be managed correctly despite a co-operative relationship between the parties. If it is not there may, for example, be tax consequences.

16.58 If notice is served by the host or home company on the other, or the companies simply agree that the assignment should end on a particular date, this should not technically have an impact on the employee's employment. As the employee is not a party to the inter-company expatriate supply agreement that agreement should not be used to serve notice on the employee. However, service of notice between the companies may have an impact on whether mandatory employment laws can be complied with effectively (because, eg, the notice will probably provide good evidence that decisions have already been made in relation to termination of the employment). Extra care should be taken when there is no close connection between the home and host companies.

16.59 Where there is a host country employment arrangement there may also be a need to terminate the inter-company expatriate supply arrangements. However, this is likely to be less important than with a home country arrangement as the inter-company agreement is unlikely to provide for significant fees relating to remuneration costs. (This is because the host company should have been bearing salary costs during the assignment.)

MANDATORY EMPLOYMENT LAWS

When mandatory employment laws apply

16.60 Almost all countries have mandatory employment laws to protect employees on termination of employment. Different countries are likely to have different rules about when the mandatory employment laws apply. Host country mandatory laws are likely to be most significant but other countries' laws may be relevant too. (See **10.30–10.61** for a more detailed explanation.)

Effect of mandatory employment laws

16.61 Mandatory employment laws relating to termination of employment vary enormously between countries. In some countries notice must be given in a particular way, perhaps in a meeting with an explanation, or on a particular day of the month. In others there may be a need to obtain approval for the dismissal or severance terms from a works council, court or employment authority, in advance or after the dismissal has taken effect.

Severance pay

16.62 Most countries will provide for specific payments to be made in certain circumstances, for example, where the employment ends by reason of 'redundancy' (or for 'economic reasons'). Usually some form of financial redress is also available for the employee if he is dismissed for a reason that is not regarded as 'fair' or where required procedures are not followed. The payments to be made can be substantial, particularly in Europe.

16.63 As a minimum, severance pay is likely to need to take account of:

- payment in lieu of any period of unworked notice (calculated in accordance with the employment documents and/or mandatory employment laws);
- benefit arrangements (it will of course be helpful if the effect of termination on benefits, eg leased accommodation or bonus, has been clearly detailed in the employment documents);
- redundancy pay if the reason for termination is redundancy or additional compensation to take account of other mandatory requirements or breach of mandatory requirements (eg mandatory host country severance pay); and/or
- other contractual promises (eg in relation to company redundancy pay or repatriation expenses).

Reasons for termination

16.64 In many countries permitted reasons for termination are prescribed, but this may not be a problem if agreement can be reached with the employee on the severance terms. This can put an expatriate employee in a stronger position when negotiating severance terms, because he would be aware of the additional expense and time that would be incurred by the employer if his consent were not given to the proposed arrangements.

Void dismissal

16.65 It may come as a shock to the employer if it finds out 'too late' that failure to follow the correct procedures, or to dismiss for a valid reason or reach agreement, not only leads to substantial financial penalties but also to the dismissal itself being declared 'void'. This may mean that the employer is ordered to keep the employee in employment and continue to pay his normal remuneration until the employment can be terminated properly. The employer may even be obliged to continue to employ indefinitely if there are no valid reasons for dismissal. It is worth remembering that in some countries not every employment problem can be resolved with money.

Approval for dismissal

16.66 The dismissal and/or any severance agreement reached with the employee may also require approval. Seeking formal approval may take time, and the employee may be entitled to remain in employment and receive his remuneration until the approval is granted. If fall back arrangements will apply if agreement on termination and/or terms is not reached with the employee this will form the backdrop to any negotiations regarding the severance terms.

Consensual approach

16.67 Sometimes rules that may seem impossible to live with to employers from some jurisdictions (eg the US and UK) can in practice work quite well in the host country. For example, a requirement for approval by employee representatives such as a works council may seem like a hostage to fortune to those unused to the arrangement. However, in practice, this may be a formality where the employer and employees have clearly understood and co-operative ways of working together. These accepted practices can create difficulties for those who are not used to dealing with problems by consensus. An attempt to ride roughshod over established procedures may be possible technically but create unforeseen problems when the co-operation of the same people is required at a later date for something else. Host country employment law advice should always be sought not only in relation to legal requirements but also in relation to tactics for achieving the business objectives.

Before the assignment begins – employment documents

16.68 At the time employment documents are prepared (ie before the assignment begins) it is important to take host country advice not only about the law but also on what is 'normal' and 'expected' on dismissal. This means that enquiries should extend beyond the legal requirements that apply. If the law provides for a certain minimum severance payment but, in practice, employees will only agree to 'mutual termination' to avoid a court procedure if a larger package is offered then this should be known from the outset. The information may not be provided if it is not requested. The choice of governing law for the contract should also be considered carefully. It is particularly important for those from EU countries to remember this, as we are not used to the governing laws affecting the application of mandatory employment laws. In some countries the choice of law for the employment documents could make a difference to whether host country law needs to be complied with on termination of employment. (See **10.3–10.29** on governing laws.)

Timing

16.69 There is rarely a lot of time between a question about the possibility of dismissal and pressure to implement dismissal quickly. This, of course, means that some 'fair' reasons for dismissal will not be available.

16.70 For example, it may be possible to dismiss for poor performance in the host country only if there is some documentary evidence of the poor performance, and the steps taken to help remedy the situation, over a reasonable period of time. If the expatriate has never been given any negative feedback it may be difficult, or impossible, to demonstrate that any steps have been taken to improve the situation. This is, of course, a common problem for local hires too but with expatriates the issues can be exacerbated. For example, home country managers who will make a decision to dismiss may not be aware of the host country constraints and the importance of tackling things early. Managers may also find it more difficult to give negative feedback to an expatriate where communication is infrequent or where they are afraid of an employee response that they cannot easily manage from overseas. It can also take longer to source advice at the time of the dismissal. Access to documents and information may be limited and it may take more time to understand host country legal and tax requirements. Needless to say, the earlier enquiries are made about the employer's options, the more options there are likely to be.

Requests for host country advice on dismissal

16.71 The host country employment law specialist asked to advise on a potential dismissal may find the following information helpful:

- the number of employees likely to be affected;
- the likely reasons for the proposed dismissal;
- when it is proposed the employment should end, and any reasons for that;
- what has been said and done already (eg whether the problems or dismissal have already been discussed with the employee);
- the employee's role (job title, duties, seniority in the UK sense, authority, etc);
- details of any appointments held or 'powers' granted to the employee;
- the location of the employment and the industry (and any other information that may be relevant to whether a particular collective agreement applies);
- the employee's nationality and immigration status;
- the employee's date of birth;
- details of any special concerns, for example, recent complaints, pregnancy or illness;
- the employee's social security status (this may sometimes be important for determining whether particular severance payments are due);
- the employee's start date (for the assignment, for the employment and/or with the group);
- the employee's current remuneration package including bonus arrangements (basic salary may not be the only element taken into consideration when a compulsory termination payment is calculated);

- details of any host country representation arrangements that may apply (eg whether there is a works council and/or employee numbers);
- the notice period specified in the contract and whether there is any contractual right to pay in lieu of notice or require the employee to remain on garden leave;
- whether the employer would like to be able to enforce any existing post termination restrictions or introduce any new ones;
- copies of the employment documents.

(See Chapter 17 for some suggestions on approaches to seeking advice.)

Home country mandatory laws

16.72 Although host country mandatory employment laws are likely to be most significant on termination of an expatriate employment, other countries' mandatory laws may be relevant too. These might be the mandatory laws of the country from which the employee has been assigned or perhaps of his country of origin or his employer's country of registration.

UK

16.73 Suppose an employee is posted abroad by his English employer on a home country employment arrangement for the purposes of the home employer's business. The *Serco* 'posting' exception applies (see **10.59–10.60**) and the employee is therefore entitled to make an 'unfair dismissal' complaint in an English tribunal. He may also be subject to host country mandatory laws because he is working there (ie the employer needs to consider the impact of both home and host country mandatory laws). The solution may be a severance agreement that meets the technical requirements of both countries and that provides for sufficient compensation to make litigation in either country unattractive. The technical requirements might, for example, include both approval by the host country authorities as well as an agreement meeting the requirements of a formal UK 'settlement agreement' (see the Glossary at Appendix 3).

PROFESSIONAL COSTS

16.74 The costs of dealing with expatriate dismissals may be much higher than those associated with 'ordinary' dismissals.

16.75 The expatriate may not want the cost, inconvenience and delay that may arise from a protracted dispute. If the 'deal' is right expatriates will often agree to the proposed severance terms quickly. Attention to the human aspects of managing termination of employment can be well repaid.

16.76 In almost all cases there will be an increased need for comprehensive advice before any steps are taken to dismiss. As well as employment law concerns, there are also likely to be immigration, tax and social security matters to deal with. These issues are likely to be less straightforward than is usually the case for local hires. In some situations there may be unavoidable procedural requirements that must be dealt with, for example court or employment authority approval for termination or deregistration requirements. Host country professional assistance will almost always be required. In addition, a standard form severance agreement is unlikely to be appropriate and translations may need to be prepared.

16.77 Professional fees are likely to be higher than those that might be expected for a local hire. See Chapter 17 for some suggestions on how those costs might be managed.

TAX AND SOCIAL SECURITY IMPLICATIONS

Tax and social security relief on termination payments

16.78 Many countries offer tax and social security relief on termination payments, and in most cases the relief applies subject to strict rules. Those rules will typically specify both the types of payment that will qualify for relief and the maximum relief allowed.

Example – UK foreign service exemption or reduction

16.79 See 16.37.

Double tax treaties

16.80 If the employee's income is subject to tax and/or social security contributions in more than one country then both countries' rules will need to be considered. Although double tax treaties may generally help to prevent the same money being subject to tax in two countries, if the severance payment is not taxable in both countries covered by the tax treaty there will be no double tax. The country which taxes the severance payment may not have to apply treaty exemption because there is no tax to pay in the other country which is party to the double tax treaty. Alternatively, a tax saving in one country may lead to more tax being due in another.

Example – US national working in the UK

16.81 If a US citizen is working in the UK and is dismissed, he may qualify for UK tax relief on all or part of his termination pay, subject to strict conditions. His worldwide income may also be taxed in the US because he is a citizen, so the value of the UK tax relief will depend on how much is clawed back by US tax authorities.

Effect on remuneration already paid

16.82 Termination of employment may affect the tax treatment of remuneration already paid to the employee. For example, if the employee returns to the home country immediately after termination of his employment, this may mean remuneration accrued (or benefits provided) earlier in the home country tax year becomes subject to home country tax. This could be significant for the employer if, for example, the employee's remuneration is subject to tax equalisation or protection promises and there is additional tax to pay at the employer's expense. The employer may also be exposed to unexpected employer's social security contributions.

16.83 If this potential problem is anticipated at the outset it may be possible to provide the tax equalisation promise subject to a requirement that the employee remains out of a particular country for a specified period after termination. In practice, though this is rarely done, the employee may lose the right to live in the host country when his employment ends. He is unlikely to want to agree to roam the world to save his employer tax. A decision not to return to the home country immediately is more likely to be taken by an expatriate who would personally bear more tax if he returned.

Tax returns

16.84 As at the outset of the assignment, or on change of assignment, the employee's tax affairs are likely to be more complex when both the assignment and employment end. Termination is unlikely to coincide neatly with the end of the tax years for the home and host countries.

16.85 It will be in both the employee's and the employer's interests to ensure that tax returns are completed and submitted properly; that any tax equalisation or protection arrangements are applied correctly and that any opportunities to minimise tax are taken. The employer may need the employee's assistance after the employment ends to recover outstanding tax etc from tax authorities for the employer if tax equalisation or protection arrangements have been made or loans have been provided to the employee to protect cash flow.

16.86 See **7.90** and framework document **A2.4** at Appendix 2 for some suggestions regarding clauses that could be included in the original employment documents to make management of tax on termination easier. If those issues were not considered at the outset of the assignment it may be possible to insert terms in the severance agreement to facilitate recovery of overpaid tax from the relevant authorities for the benefit of the employer etc.

Timing of tax and social security advice

16.87 It usually makes sense for the employer to seek tax and social security advice early, before the severance package is agreed and documented. This is important in relation to most terminations, but is particularly important for expatriates because:

- tax equalisation or protection promises may mean that the employer, rather than the employee, bears the costs of additional tax and/or social security;

- the size of expatriate termination packages tends to be large;

- there is often scope for considerable saving where the practical steps that will be taken (eg return dates) have not yet been fixed;

- once the employer has taken some practical steps to manage the termination, the opportunities to make savings may be lost;

- changing the net 'deal' after the employee has been given an indication of what he may receive could have more serious consequences than might be the case for a local hire, for example because the expatriate's agreement to termination and the terms offered is needed;

- the employer may lose the opportunity to provide in the severance agreement for recovery of a sum likely to be reimbursed by tax authorities;

- the professional costs of dealing with disputes and mistakes tends to be higher; and

- the employer will often be paying for the advice at a later stage anyway, for example, because the employer will meet the costs of preparing tax returns.

IMMIGRATION

16.88 Termination of the employment may terminate the employee's right to work and/or live in the host country and the employee (and his family) may need to comply with strict time-limits for repatriation. The employer may have some responsibility to inform the immigration authorities, return papers and/or ensure that the expatriate's bills are paid. If the time-limits are tight a period of garden leave may help but this may not always be permitted.

16.89 If the expatriate is to be replaced, the employer should also think about the time that might be needed to secure immigration clearance for the replacement, to reduce the risk of an unexpected gap between the outgoing expatriate's departure and the incoming expatriate's arrival.

16.90 The issues are similar to those that arise in relation to termination of assignment (see **16.16**). However, where the employment is to end or has ended, co-operation is more likely to be agreed through a severance agreement, whereas this may be agreed more informally with an employee who will move on to another group assignment.

16.91 Care should also be taken when the severance agreement is prepared to ensure that the employer is not promising to provide benefits etc which conflict with immigration restrictions, for example provision of host country accommodation after permission to remain in the host country has expired.

COLLECTIVE DISMISSALS

16.92 Many countries, including EU countries, have additional rules that apply if it is proposed that a threshold number of employees should be dismissed for the same reason. This is rarely an issue for expatriate assignments where employments tend to be terminated individually. However, it is worth checking whether other employees have recently been dismissed and whether it is anticipated that any other employees may be dismissed so that any applicable laws can be checked.

EU

16.93 Directive 98/59/EC, the 'Collective Dismissals Directive' applies, broadly, where it is proposed that:

- at least 20 employees should be dismissed within 90 days at one establishment; or
- at least 10, 10% or 30 employees (depending on employee numbers at the establishment) should be dismissed within 30 days.

(UK employers and advisers should be aware that the Directive allows a choice of qualifying criteria. Although the first of the criteria above have been adopted in the UK other EU countries may have chosen to adopt the second criteria.)

16.94 If the qualifying threshold is reached collective information and consultation rights may arise. The penalties that apply if the employer fails to comply with information and consultation requirements can be severe and could include, for example, imprisonment, fines and void dismissals.

16.95 These EU obligations were bolted on to existing national arrangements and the practical requirements vary substantially from country to country. It is worth remembering that these may not be the only information and consultation obligations that apply. There may also be other obligations to inform or consult with employee representatives in accordance with local rules or practices.

16.96 If proposed dismissals are likely to affect employees in more than one country then the group may also be obliged to inform and/or consult with its European Works Council (EWC) if it has one (see the Glossary at Appendix 3).

US CONSIDERATIONS

16.97 Generally, US employment is 'at will', (ie either the employee or the employer may end the employment at any time for any reason, with or without giving notice). It is important that US employers understand that employment 'at will' is not possible in most other countries and that mandatory laws relating to severance can apply regardless of the contents of the employment documents. (See **21.2** on 'at will' employment.)

16.98 In practice, the basic 'at will' rule may not apply anyway if the employee has entered into a new contract with the employer (as is likely if the employee is on an expatriate assignment). A US employer may also be exposed to claims (particularly discrimination claims) in relation to termination of the employment. It is, therefore, usually sensible to ensure that the reasons for dismissal are clear and that a severance agreement is concluded when an expatriate employee is dismissed, whether the assignment is to or from the US. It can also be helpful to ensure that the severance arrangements are properly documented so that tax and social security implications and other terms are clear.

16.99 It is important for non-US advisers and employers to understand that laws do not apply uniformly across the US. For example, the employer may need to take account of both US Federal and State laws.

16.100 The following are areas to watch for when considering termination arrangements for employees with a US connection.

- *Age discrimination and cooling off periods*: US age discrimination laws generally apply to older rather than younger employees. Special rules may apply to the conclusion of severance agreements for employees who are over 40 years old. There may be a need to give an older employee a period to consider the proposed settlement terms before he is required to sign the severance agreement and to allow for a 'cooling off period' after signature during which the employee can withdraw his agreement to release claims. In practice, this opportunity for reflection is usually offered to younger employees too. Compliance may be facilitated by preparing two severance agreements, one settling US claims and one settling claims under other countries' laws, and by providing for conditional or later payment of compensation.
- *Language*: The release may need to be in simple and clear language. Given that US drafting style is different from UK drafting style, where both countries' laws are to be settled it may be helpful for the US release to be included in a separate document.
- *Comprehensive settlement agreements*: Generally, where there is a severance agreement covering release from both US and another country's claims it may be helpful to include the US release in a separate document. Inclusion of a comprehensive US-style release may not be helpful in respect of host country law.

- *Arbitration*: See **21.28**.

- *UK*: Where a severance agreement is to cover release of claims under US and UK laws it is almost always helpful to use two linked severance agreements. This is both for the reasons outlined above and also because for the UK settlement agreement to be effective a UK solicitor must confirm that he has advised on the terms and effects of the agreement. It may be easier to persuade the UK solicitor to do this if the relevant agreement only releases claims arising under laws with which he is familiar.

- *Future claims:* There may be restrictions under US law on release from future claims.

- *Right to consult a lawyer:* Under US law the employee may need to be informed of his right to consult a lawyer.

- *Group terminations:* Additional requirements may apply where there is a group termination.

- *Health cover*: Some employees with US connections may have a right to continue private health insurance cover at their own expense after the employment ends (see the Glossary at Appendix 3 under 'COBRA').

VULNERABLE EMPLOYEES

16.101 In many countries special protection against dismissal is given to vulnerable categories of employee, for example pregnant women and those on maternity leave, sick or disabled employees and trade union or works council representatives. In some countries, dismissal of an employee with special status leaves the employer exposed to additional claims. In others it is not possible to dismiss protected employees or employees during a protected period at all. Any special circumstances should be drawn to the attention of the host country employment law specialist at the earliest opportunity.

SEVERANCE AGREEMENTS

16.102   Please refer to the checklist at **A1.12** at Appendix 1 and the annotated home country framework severance agreement **A2.7** at Appendix 2.

16.103 Similar issues will need to be considered if there is a host country employment.

16.104   The severance agreement would have a similar scope as for a local hire. For example it would need to deal with termination of employment, settlement of claims, outstanding remuneration, holiday, termination payments, etc. However, expatriate severance arrangements are inevitably more complex. The following issues may be worth particular attention.

Identity of the employer

16.105 The severance agreement should confirm the intended employment structure. The correct entity should be identified as employer and the respective responsibilities of any other companies that are parties to the agreement or mentioned in it should be made clear. For example, severance pay should normally be paid by the employer. (See Chapter 4 regarding the importance of the identity of the employer for expatriate employment arrangements.)

Tax and social security

16.106 Advice should always be sought before proposed terms are communicated to the employee and the agreement should make the assumed tax and social security treatment clear, particularly if tax equalisation or tax protection promises apply or will apply to some or all of the payments to be made. Clear provision should be made for ongoing employee obligations, for example, in relation to recovery of overpayments, tax returns, etc.

Separate documents

16.107 If there is a host country employment arrangement it may sometimes be appropriate to document the termination of the host country employment and home country residual employment separately.

16.108 In some circumstances it may also be helpful to document settlement of claims under different countries' laws separately, either in separate sections of the same document or in two separate documents. (See **16.97–16.100** on settlement of US claims.) It may be helpful to choose different governing laws for each part, ie Country A's laws to govern the section settling claims under Country A's laws and Country B's laws to govern the section settling claims under Country B's Laws. (See **10.3–10.29** on governing laws.)

Form of the documents and conclusion

16.109 Both home and host country advisers should be asked to comment on the form of the documents. Many countries have special requirements about the content of documents or how they are concluded. For example, counterpart documents or conclusion by email/PDF may not be allowed; a cooling off period may be required; the employee may need to be independently advised first; the agreement may need to expressly confirm that host country termination payments have been made; the parties may not be free to choose the termination date; a translation may be required for filing with the local authorities, etc. (See **15.123–15.128** on legal privilege and 'without prejudice' negotiations.)

Benefits

16.110   Care should be taken to ensure that all relevant benefits are covered and the sums due, conditions, etc are clear. If the employee's co-operation is required in relation to something such as vacation of accommodation after the agreement is concluded then it may be appropriate to withhold certain payments until the co-operation has been secured. There may be a need to deal with exchange rate and payment arrangements. Even if the employment contract is vague on repatriation expenses, these should be detailed carefully in the severance documents.

Practical arrangements

16.111   The agreements should be detailed to reduce the risk for dispute or ongoing negotiation once the arrangements are concluded. As there is likely to be a need for some ongoing co-operation, even if only in relation to tax returns, it makes sense to require the employee to keep the employer informed of future contact details.

Timing of delivery of payments

16.112   Given that there may be practical difficulties with enforcing specific terms and that a relatively high degree of cooperation and flexibility is likely to be required going forward to make the administration easier, the employer should consider whether it is appropriate to deliver all payments and/or benefits 'upfront'. Delayed or split payments may offer greater incentive but can also create complexity, eg if the individual relocates before a second payment is made.

STRATEGY AND PREPARATION

16.113   As always, successful negotiation requires some preparation. This is particularly so with expatriate termination arrangements. The sums due can be high, there will be a number of complex compliance issues to deal with and the risk of disrupting colleagues and business relationships can also be higher. Careful consideration of each party's perspective, and the technical context, can often help the employer to identify creative solutions to problems that arise. There is often far greater scope for resolving expatriate disputes satisfactorily because the parties' objectives are not always precisely aligned. For example, potential disruption to family life may be a high priority for the employee but fixing that may not be very expensive.

Anticipating potential termination at the start, and drafting the employment documents with that in mind, can help enormously.

CHAPTER 17

GETTING THE JOB DONE

17.1 Most project managers look for commercial and accurate advice, given promptly and at an appropriate cost. These expectations are not always met. This chapter explores some of the techniques a project manager might use to try to secure the service he wants from advisers.

IDENTIFYING THE ADVICE NEEDED

17.2 Hopefully, this book will be helpful in giving guidance on the areas where advice might be useful. This might include, for example, advice on:

- corporation tax;
- sales tax (VAT);
- income tax;
- social security;
- immigration;
- employment law;
- pensions;
- data protection;
- intellectual property;
- share plans; and/or
- compensation and benefits.

17.3 There will also be a need to identify the jurisdictions that might be relevant. These will normally be the home and host countries but sometimes other countries will also be important, such as the country of which the employee is a national, or the previous host country.

17.4 It is usually helpful not only to identify the advice that would be useful but also to assess the commercial importance of that advice. For example, intellectual property advice could be very important if an engineer is to be sent to the host company to develop new technology. On the other hand, creation of intellectual property is unlikely to have much commercial significance if the employee is a salesman. An understanding of the likely length of the assignment and the value of the employee to the business would be useful. Some idea of the potential risks of failing to obtain proper advice in each area would also be helpful, but that is often difficult to assess before advice is sought, particularly if the employer has not done business in the host country before.

17.5 It makes sense to seek advice on critical and urgent issues first. For example, if immigration requirements cannot be met there is little point in spending money on detailed employment law advice (see Chapter 3 on viability of the assignment and checklist **A1.5** at Appendix 1).

FINDING THE RIGHT ADVISERS

17.6 Finding appropriate specialists is not always easy. There are international directories listing specialists in various jurisdictions and the internet can be helpful. However, many directories rely too heavily on information provided by the advisers themselves to provide a clear view of whether the adviser will be any good.

17.7 The following suggestions may help.

- A trusted adviser may be able to recommend someone they have worked with before. This approach is not fool proof but an adviser who values his client is unlikely to recommend someone who he thinks will do a bad job, and the introduction may help secure a better service. Advisers with the same area of specialism are more likely to be able to recommend appropriate advisers in other countries. It may be worth asking the adviser expressly whether they have used the recommended adviser themselves before, rather than just asking generally for the name of someone who might be able to help.

- If a host country adviser is required, a recommendation from people in the host country may help. It may be worth checking that the advisers used locally have some experience of international work, because, for example, those making the recommendations may work in the host country language with them.

- An introductory telephone call and email exchange can help to give a feel for the quality of service likely to be provided. For example, the quality of language skills and some idea of commercial focus and speed of response.

- Specialists in a neighbouring country with strong international links may be able to help. For example, a Hong Kong lawyer from a well-known firm should be able to recommend a good PRC lawyer.

- Do not assume that because one adviser in a firm is recommended that his colleagues will be equally as good. This is particularly the case for employment law.

- International networks of advisers do not always offer a consistent or better service than firms with a local focus, although they may deal with a higher volume of international work and they may be more likely to employ people with good language skills.

- Look after the people work is referred to. They are more likely to provide a good service next time. Make sure they get paid promptly and try to avoid unreasonable deadlines.

TIME

17.8 More time should be allowed to obtain advice from another jurisdiction. Cross-border advice should normally be checked more carefully to reduce the risk of misunderstanding (see below) and timescales that appear reasonable in one country may seem unreasonable in another.

17.9 The project manager needs to keep on top of timescales. For example, the availability of the adviser, time differences, normal 'weekend days' and public and religious holidays (try www.bank-holidays.com) should be checked. Requests for advice should always be made quickly. Other unexpected things are likely to cause delay, and delay with delivering the instructions is at least something that can be controlled.

17.10 For example, if a European adviser is asked to seek advice from Malaysia at 5pm CET it would make sense for the European lawyer to send an email to Malaysia before going home so that the Malaysian lawyer has time to consider the request before the European adviser gets in to work the next day. A decision by the European lawyer to wait until the morning may effectively mean a whole day is lost.

17.11 Conversely, if a European adviser is asked to seek advice from the US at 5 pm it would make sense for the European lawyer to check availability, and ideally have a call, before detailed emails are sent (if necessary an alternative adviser can be found the same day); the key issues can be discussed briefly; and, when the instructions are confirmed in writing, they will be more appropriate and are more likely to cover the required information. If definitive instructions are sent to the US by email without initial enquiry, the European adviser may spend a frustrating morning the following day wondering why a response has not arrived or may have to wait until lunchtime to respond to the basic questions the US lawyer needs answered before starting work.

17.12 When advice is not received at the promised time then this should always be followed up promptly.

17.13 A common source of avoidable problems is the adviser who is asked to source advice from another country and who then delays before asking the questions, thinking there is plenty of time. If more work is required than he has anticipated, then neither the client whose deadline is missed nor the overseas lawyer who works harder to make sure the deadline is achieved will be impressed.

17.14 If email instructions are to be given quickly, with the hope that the adviser receiving the instructions will turn the work around quickly, it is worth trying to anticipate the information that the adviser will need to get started. Unnecessary delay can also be caused if the person giving the instructions is not available to answer questions. Time differences and other commitments may limit the periods during which both advisers can speak, so it is worth being clear about availability from the outset so opportunities are not lost. The following minimum information should usually be provided:

- relevant background information, see further below;

- specific questions and clarity on what is required by way of answer, including some idea of the detail required or whether further advice will be sought later;

- the full name and address (and ideally VAT/sales tax number) of the client who will pay the bill and other relevant parties (this is particularly important if the questions are being asked of lawyers, who will probably need to be clear about the identity of their client and check for conflicts of interest before starting work);

- some clarity regarding fees, eg whether the overseas adviser is to (a) start work immediately before fees are agreed; (b) reach agreement on fees before starting; or (c) start work immediately unless he thinks a specified budget is insufficient;

- information about expected timescales, and why the work is urgent if it is urgent;

- a request for immediate confirmation that the instructions have been received and that the requested assistance can be provided within the required timescales/cost. If that confirmation is not received the project manager should follow up promptly.

17.15 Most importantly, additional time needs to be allowed for unexpected responses to queries. For example, if the business wants advice on dismissing an employee by the end of the week this may not be achievable if there is a host country requirement to obtain approval from an employment authority first and there is no good reason for termination. If more time is available after the advice is received, the range of potential solutions may be wider and less expensive to implement.

COST CONTROL

17.16 As with any project, costs can be managed by discussing and agreeing fee arrangements up front and keeping track of where time is spent.

17.17 Care with instructions will usually save professional fees, and may also help prevent the expensive mistakes that can arise from misunderstanding etc (see below). Professional costs are nearly always linked to time spent by the adviser on the project. If thought is given at the outset to things that might save the adviser time, then costs are likely to be lower. For example, if facts are provided in a confusing way or are later corrected then costs are likely to be higher.

17.18 It is usually a mistake to assume that by setting a low and rigid budget quality advice will be delivered at a lower cost, even if the project manager has the commercial negotiating position to demand this. Providing answers to the same questions will not take the same length of time in every country because the legal issues will vary. Hourly rates can also vary substantially between countries. Sometimes those with higher hourly rates can provide the advice at a cheaper overall cost. That may be because they need to do less research, because they have a better understanding of what is required commercially or because attitudes to time recording vary. Flexibility (and some trust) is needed to produce good results.

17.19 Sometimes other advisers are able to manage fees more effectively than project managers who have no previous connection with the adviser giving the advice. For example, a firm of solicitors that regularly supplies a large volume of corporate work to particular overseas advisers may be able to secure a better service for its clients on employment matters. An adviser in a similar technical area but from a different country may also be able to estimate the appropriate time required to undertake a particular piece of work more accurately than a project manager from a different background who may not appreciate what is involved.

17.20 The biggest challenges will usually be to decide which specialists are needed and what advice is required. Trying to understand every angle can be very expensive and time consuming. Managing cost with expatriate assignments involves managing risk. For example, it is may not be worth seeking extensive specialist pensions advice if a young expatriate is not interested in pension arrangements and there is no obligation on the employer to make pensions provision.

LANGUAGE AND COMMUNICATION

17.21 The biggest challenge with any international project is usually communication. This is not just a question of ensuring that both the adviser and the person seeking the advice speak the same language to a reasonable standard. There is also a need for everyone involved to manage communications in a way that reduces the risk of misunderstanding.

17.22 One particular problem that dogs international work is that the person seeking the advice will naturally ask the questions that would produce the right answers in their own country. What works well in one country does not always work well in another.

17.23   The following practical suggestions may help:

- *Orally and in writing*: Wherever possible, communications should be made both orally and in writing. For example, written instructions may be easier to follow (and save the adviser time preparing file notes) but a written response to questions should be discussed over the phone to ensure that the full picture is given. There will almost always be a need to ask supplementary questions.

- *Pro forma response*: Where an answer of a particular style or depth is required it can sometimes be helpful to provide a pro forma 'answer' to help the adviser understand what is required. This can be particularly helpful when the same advice is being sought from a number of different jurisdictions and presentation of the answers in the same format is likely to help those comparing advice from different countries.

- *Vocabulary*: Information should be provided in a way that avoids or clarifies vocabulary that could be interpreted in different ways in different countries. For example, if the employer proposes making an employee 'redundant', more information about the factual background could help the adviser to give more focused advice if the best dismissal process will depend on the reason for termination. A fuller explanation might be:

    'The business is planning to stop selling widgets in Country X. If that happens a widget salesman will not be needed in Country X. The business is thinking about dismissing Y for redundancy. Y is the only widget salesman in Country X and would not be replaced. There is no criticism of Y's performance and there are no other sales vacancies within the group in any country. Y is not yet aware of these plans.'

- *Background information for application of mandatory laws*: It will often be helpful to provide some information about the seniority (in the English hierarchical sense) of relevant employees; their roles; the industry they work in; and where they work geographically. The adviser may then be in a better position to determine which applicable laws or collective agreements are likely to apply, and so give more focused advice. Better still, a discussion with an adviser up front about the information that will be needed can save a lot of time. If the adviser has to consider every possible scenario the result is likely to be further questions or a response that reads more like a legal textbook than commercial advice, and a bigger bill.

- *Starting again*: It may sometimes be quicker (ie cheaper) to replace a document with a fresh draft using just the information contained in the original document, rather than to amend the original document. The options (ie amend or replace) should be discussed at the outset, bearing in mind where the document will be used, enforced etc. There is little point in paying a home country adviser to draft a 'perfect' document that then needs to be completely rewritten by a host country adviser because most of it will not work locally.

- *Closed questions*: It is usually helpful to ask specific questions to ensure that the answer that is wanted is provided. For example, 'What is the minimum notice period that an employer must give an employee in Country X?'. However, this approach will not always give the full picture. For example, the adviser might say '1 month' but may not mention that notice must always be worked out and that the contract must provide that the same period of notice must be given by the employee if he wants to leave. Including some open questions too can help reduce the risk of narrow questions limiting the answers. This is one of the areas where a follow-up conversation can really help.

- *Cost focus*: It is common in the UK to ask, 'How much will it cost and how long will it take?' to follow a best practice route and at the same time to assess the risks of other preferred approaches. Potential solutions are often assessed in terms of financial risk and commercial benefits. This approach does not work well in all jurisdictions. Sometimes there is simply no alternative but to comply with local laws and practices. For example, in some countries it is not possible to effectively dismiss employees until the relevant procedures have been followed. In other countries 'normal' practices may not mirror the mandatory rules and very specific questions about legal requirements and minimum costs may give misleading results.

- *Short-term outlook*: Another, particularly UK and US, tendency is to focus on the particular problem to be resolved whilst ignoring the longer-term picture. For example, a particular result may technically be achievable but may, in practice, have an adverse impact on relationships with employee representatives. In countries where the co-operation of employee representatives is essential to get things done, pushing for achievement of the short-term goal may have negative longer-term consequences.

- *Subjective interpretation*: Particular care should be taken with subjective interpretation. Both those giving and those receiving advice will naturally bring their existing experience to bear on interpretation. For example, a European adviser may inform an American adviser that four weeks' 'leave' should be offered. The American adviser may assume that this can include time off due to both sickness and holiday. The possibility of specifying a number of days' absence to cover time off for any reason might not occur to the European adviser who might, again quite reasonably, assume that 'annual leave' means annual holiday and that sickness and family leave are different things altogether.

- *Style*: Style can be very important and some discussion should take place about expectations before documents are prepared. For example, in the UK we expect documents to be very detailed because of our history of fairly low-level employment protection. In the past the contract typically specified the whole agreement and generally what the contract said was what applied. UK employment protection is more extensive now, but the contract terms are still critical and there is little employee resistance to longer documents. In a country where most terms are covered by mandatory collective agreements that cannot be varied, long documents may seem unnecessary, and can sometimes be unhelpful. In the US where 'employment at will' is still possible detailing all the employment terms at length may seem like overkill.

- *Common themes*: Although different countries have different employment laws and practices, the issues which arise in relation to hiring, managing and dismissing employees are very similar. This means that specialists from the same specialist area are more likely to be in a position to formulate appropriate questions in relation to a particular issue, even if they do not know all the answers.

- *Order in which things are done*: A lot of time and money can be saved if thought is given upfront to who should be involved and when. Employment lawyers should usually check that tax, social security and immigration advisers have been engaged at the outset.

17.24 Nobody can be an expert on every country's laws (or every technical issue). However, with a broad understanding of the areas where things are likely to be different (or similar) and a sensible process for ensuring all the bases are covered, it is possible to reduce the likelihood of things going wrong. Time spent preparing clear explanations of relevant facts and choosing the right questions will usually save both time and money.

CHAPTER 18

BREXIT AND GLOBAL MOBILITY

18.1 At the time of writing the UK is in the process of leaving the EU. Given the political uncertainty comments on the status quo and 'Brexit' process will probably date very quickly. Nonetheless, some attempt has made below to highlight some of the key themes affecting global mobility.

18.2 A key concern is the future relationship between the UK and Ireland and free movement of people between the two, see **18.15–18.24**.

18.3 It is predicted that Brexit may also trigger:

- tighter immigration controls both for overseas nationals wishing to live and work in the UK and British nationals wishing to live and work in other parts of Europe (see Chapter 19 on sending expatriates to the UK);

- Insolvency, and individual and collective redundancies (see Chapter 16 on ending assignments);

- domestic and international business growth;

- outsourcing, business sales, mergers and transfers;

- small and large-scale relocation of operations;

- increasing numbers of short-term business trips, international commuting and 'virtual' assignment arrangements (see Chapter 14);

- changes to roles, arrangements for engaging staff and employment terms;

- changes to arrangements for reciprocal recognition of qualifications;

- demand for 'expatriate' terms, including, eg, relocation and repatriation packages to mitigate employee uncertainty (see **18.11–18.12**);

- concerns about skills shortages and retention of staff;

- industrial relations and discrimination issues (see Chapter 12 on equality);

- currency movements (see **7.68-7.79**);

- increased focus on compliance (see **18.14**).

18.4 As economists know, expectation can be as powerful as reality in driving change. The impact of Brexit is already complex, with many businesses experiencing different effects at the same time. A business forced to relocate activities abroad for regulatory reasons may see redundancies and transfer issues at home, at the same time as new start up challenges and quick growth abroad. Not to mention a host of transitional arrangements, such as temporary cross-border working arrangements for senior executives, hiring of contractors to plug short term skills gaps or engagement of commercial agents to open new markets abroad.

Brexit will, inevitably, affect different businesses and employees differently.

UNCERTAINTY

18.5 For many employers and global mobility specialists, the key current concern is uncertainty.

18.6 Brexit is naturally having an impact on individual employees whose long-term immigration expectations are unclear. For example, uncertainty could lead to (and already has in some areas):

• fewer employees seeking employment in the UK;
• employees leaving the UK;
• employees seeking greater assurance before accepting employment in the UK.

REASSURANCE

Immigration

18.7 In order to mitigate potential retention issues, many employers have taken steps to reassure employees who are concerned about their immigration status, for example by meeting the costs of personal professional immigration advice or providing generic guidance by way of workshops. Some employees have opportunities to improve their position, for example they may qualify for an additional passport or have lived in the host country for long enough to be confident of a right to remain under local rules regardless of Brexit (see **18.19**). It may be helpful for the individual to take practical steps to secure their potential rights sooner rather than later.

18.8 Worry may also stem from concern about family members, eg partners of another nationality or elderly dependents who may need to reside with the family in the future.

18.9 The difficulty for employers it that they cannot always easily identify the employees who may be concerned or where practical assistance might help. It would be possible to request the information from employees directly, but there are a number of quite onerous data protection and discrimination constraints to be navigated. Also, direct enquiry can only pin down the information at a particular point in time. Setting up arrangements that would enable lawful ongoing monitoring is more challenging.

18.10 Many employers have taken a pragmatic approach to developing contingency plans, perhaps focusing closely and individually on key personnel, such as main board directors, and offering generic or voluntary support to other groups. For some areas where there will be skills, shortages have been clear since Brexit first became a reality.

Expatriate terms

18.11 See Chapter 22 on employee perspectives. It seems likely that some employees will need more persuasion before they accept new roles in the UK or abroad. Currently, many employees from other EU countries apply for jobs in the UK in the same way as UK nationals do. Their applications are typically managed in the same way and the individuals may deal with any necessary relocation arrangements themselves. They may purchase a house and choose to put their children into the UK schooling system.

18.12 Employees who do not have an expectation that they will remain in the UK for the long term may need to be encouraged to take up a role in the UK by offers of expatriate terms, such as:

- relocation and repatriation support;
- help with placing children in international schools;
- assistance with managing currency fluctuations to help them maintain their home abroad; and/or
- assistance with preparation of tax returns.

There is nothing very new here for global mobility specialists, but it does seem likely that a higher proportion of recruits to the UK from overseas will need more support.

ALTERNATIVE WORKING ARRANGEMENTS

18.13 Where employees resist relocation of their families, or the duration of the role is uncertain, employers may choose to bridge the gap by offering alternative international working arrangements. It does seem likely that there will be an increase in business visitor traffic and international commuter and virtual employee arrangements as a consequence of Brexit. It is worth bearing in mind too that there was a trend towards these sorts of temporary short-term international working arrangements before the Brexit vote (see Chapter 14).

COMPLIANCE

18.14 A trend towards increased compliance activity in global mobility was also noticeable before Brexit. It seems inevitable that this will accelerate in the years to come, eg because:

- politics may dictate that governments demonstrate increased focus on mobility compliance, particularly in jurisdictions that have experienced high levels of migration or where governments lean to the right;

- advances in technology make monitoring compliance easier;

- public agencies are increasingly communicating with each other and sharing information relating to non-compliance;

- there is pressure to increase tax receipts.

This is not, of course, all linked to Brexit, but there is certainly increased pressure in the UK on immigration and tax compliance. Potential penalties for failing to comply are also increasingly significant.

IRELAND

Context

18.15 The Republic of Ireland is an independent country. The United Kingdom consists of four countries and three legal jurisdictions, including Northern Ireland. (Please refer to the Glossary if an explanation is needed.)

18.16 In a sense, Irish citizens are no different from other EU nationals who can currently visit, live and work in the UK. But Ireland is the UK's closest neighbour and the UK is Ireland's biggest trading partner. Ireland will naturally be hardest hit by any trade tariffs between the EU and UK. Also, legally, the immigration status of Irish people is different from the status of other EU nationals. Brexit would affect Ireland, and Irish nationals, differently from other EU countries.

British and Irish passports

18.17 A very high proportion of UK residents hold passports issued by the Republic of Ireland, are already entitled to apply for Irish passports, or would consider themselves to be of Irish descent. (According to the Irish passport office 733,000 passports were issued in 2016. 66,000 of those were issued in London. The Republic's resident population was only 4.7 million.) The volume of business traffic between the two islands is exceptionally high.

18.18 Many Irish people hold both British and Irish passports, and Brexit is not expected to create any immigration problems for them. Many Irish citizens are also already eligible to apply for a British passport if they choose to, some because they met the criteria for being British at birth and some because they have lived here for long enough.

Irish citizens resident in the UK

18.19 It is worth taking a closer look at Irish nationals who have been in the UK a long time, but who are not technically British. Citizens of the Republic of

Ireland are also EU nationals and they can currently live and work in the UK just like any EU national. However, Irish nationals living in the UK for at least five years may apply for British citizenship provided they meet the qualifying criteria. All other EU nationals who have lawfully exercised their treaty rights for at least the previous five years must currently apply for 'permanent residence' in the UK and, following that, for UK citizenship, if they wish to become UK citizens.

18.20 As many Europeans are already finding out, living in the UK for five years does not automatically mean that treaty rights have been lawfully exercised for five years. After an initial three-month period, EU nationals must have been doing things that qualify (eg being employed, self-employed or studying). Being self-sufficient or a student may be OK, but the individual must be able to show that they had comprehensive medical cover during that period. At the time of writing the UK Government has published some material suggesting that they may waive the latter requirement for those EU citizens applying under the settled status scheme.

The Common Travel Area

18.21 All Irish passport-holders are automatically treated as 'settled' here in the UK from their date of arrival. They do not need to worry about periods without private medical cover or gathering detailed evidence of their working history. Special rules apply based on 'Common Travel Area' rules that applied long before the UK joined the EU in 1972. These rules recognise the special relationship and shared history of the UK and Ireland and are currently respected by the EU.

18.22 There is no guarantee that the Common Travel Area can be preserved post-Brexit. But, currently, it seems unlikely that any of the negotiators will aim to create unnecessary difficulty for Irish people living in the UK.

The border

18.23 After Brexit, the border between Northern Ireland and the Republic would be the UK's only land border with the EU. Thousands of people cross that border every day for work. Many live on one side of the border and work on the other and many businesses operate on both sides of the border. At the time of writing there is strong political commitment to keeping that border open. In addition, there remain high levels of migration from other EU countries into the Republic.

18.24 The practical arrangements for reconciling commitments to keep the border open and immigration control have not yet been articulated. This is clearly an area that global mobility specialists need to watch, and to which global mobility specialists may well be able to contribute constructively.

IMPACT OF BREXIT ON GLOBAL MOBILITY SPECIALISTS

18.25 Aside from the complexity, and worry, related to our relationship with Ireland, from the perspective of experienced global mobility specialists there is not much that is genuinely 'new' here. However, it does seem likely that businesses will need substantially more support going forward, and that 'domestic' HR specialists, even in very small businesses, will need to get up to speed with mobility relatively quickly.

18.26 Professional skills shortages may well develop and the increased importance of compliance may mean that businesses will need to engage directly with a wider range of specialists.

18.27 There may also be some positive consequences to the pressure on global mobility support. The UK has always led the way in offering specialist global mobility services, and many multinational global mobility functions are based here. Increased demands are likely to lead to quicker development and dissemination of best practice, both within the UK and across jurisdictions. We are already seeing huge steps forward in the development of supporting information technology and it is possible that in some respects compliance may become easier even if the bar is raised.

CHAPTER 19

SENDING EXPATRIATES TO THE UK

19.1 The most important issues for a business to consider when thinking about sending employees to work in the UK are likely to be immigration, tax and social security contributions.

19.2 Employment laws will be important when the employment documents are prepared but are unlikely to have a significant impact on the initial decision to go ahead with the assignment or on the identity of the employer or structure of the employment relationship (see also Chapters 3–6).

19.3 This chapter gives an overview of:

- Immigration (**19.4–19.31**).
- Corporation tax (**19.32**).
- Income tax (**19.33–19.56**).
- Social security contributions (**19.57**).
- Employment laws (**19.58–19.92**).
- Health (**19.93–19.95**).
- Pensions (**19.96–19.105**).
- Share plans (**19.106–19.111**).
- Data protection (**19.112–19.115**).

IMMIGRATION

19.4 The UK operates points-based immigration arrangements for those who wish to work or study in the UK and who are not European Economic Area (EEA) or Swiss nationals. (See **19.27** below on EEA nationals and see the Glossary at Appendix 3 for a list of EEA countries.) The arrangements are generally known as the 'points-based system' or 'PBS'.

19.5 Further information about the points-based system is currently available on the UK Visas and Immigration (UKVI) website at www.gov.uk. The Home Office is, generally, responsible for immigration. UKVI, part of the Home Office, is responsible for the issue of visas (entry clearance) to people who are overseas and for granting permission to remain to people who are already in the UK.

The five tiers

19.6 The points-based system currently provides for five 'tiers'. Each tier includes a number of types of immigration permission. They are:

- Tier 1 – high-value migrants such as investors and entrepreneurs;
- Tier 2 – skilled workers with a job offer to fill a gap in the UK workforce;
- Tier 3 – low skilled workers needed because there is a temporary shortage of workers in a specific area (suspended);
- Tier 4 – students;
- Tier 5 – youth mobility workers and temporary workers (people who are allowed to work in the UK for a limited period to satisfy non-economic objectives).

19.7 Criteria are set for each immigration tier and points are awarded for satisfying the criteria for the relevant permission. The expatriate will need the prescribed minimum number of points for the relevant immigration permission to enable him to submit an application.

19.8 Tier 3 is currently suspended and unlikely to be activated in the foreseeable future.

19.9 Tiers 1 (high-value migrants) and 2 (skilled workers with a job offer to fill gaps in the UK labour market) are the categories most likely to be relevant to those planning an expatriate assignment to the UK.

Tier 1 – high-value migrants

19.10 This replaced various other immigration categories, including the Highly Skilled Migrant Programme and the International Graduate Scheme. Within Tier 1 there are currently three types of permission:

- exceptional talent/promise;
- entrepreneurs (unlikely to be relevant for an expatriate assignment because of restrictions on being employed); and
- investors.

19.11 Tier 1 applicants do not need sponsorship (but see below on Tier 2) and make individual applications based on personal criteria (there are exceptions for entrepreneurs).

19.12 Some individuals who already have leave to remain in the UK may be able to apply for Tier 1 immigration permission to (UKVI) whilst they are in the UK. Applicants from outside the UK need to submit their application online and then attend a UK visa application centre in their home country.

19.13 The application forms and more detailed guidance are available on the website (www.gov.uk).

19.14 The Tier 1 (Exceptional Talent) visa is aimed at highly skilled individuals who have been endorsed by one of five Designated Competent Bodies in one of the following fields: science, humanities, engineering, medicine, digital technology or the arts, either as a recognised leader or as an emerging leader. For example: an individual in the digital technology sector will submit an application for endorsement to Tech City UK. If this is granted an application for leave to remain/enter must be submitted. This application is subject to a maintenance requirement. (The maintenance requirement cannot be satisfied by undertakings from an UK employer as they can with Tier 2 applications, see below.)

19.15 Leave under Tier 1 (Exceptional Talent) can be granted for a maximum period of five years.

19.16 Practically, Tier 2 applications (see below) are more likely to be appropriate for an expatriate assignment. However, Tier 1 (Exceptional Talent) may be helpful if the proposed assignee meets the qualifying criteria for Tier 1 and it is difficult for the employer and employee to meet the Tier 2 requirements, for example, because there is no entity able to issue a certificate of sponsorship (see **19.17–19.21**). Immigration permission granted under Tier 2 is not transferable to another employer, which may suit an employer concerned about staff retention, whereas Tier 1 (Exceptional Talent) permission allows the individual to work for different employers. The flexibility to work for more than one employer may sometimes be beneficial, for example, if the assignee will need to work for more than one group company in the UK.

Tier 2 – sponsorship

19.17 An applicant under Tier 2 (skilled workers with a job offer to fill a gap in the UK labour market) must have a certificate of sponsorship, issued by an approved sponsor with a presence in the UK, before submitting an application for immigration permission. This is the case whether he is making an application for entry clearance from overseas or an application for leave to remain from within the UK. (Note that there is also a separate option for a 'sole representative' of an overseas company planning to set up a UK branch or a wholly owned subsidiary of an overseas parent company. Restrictions apply but a sponsor license is not required.)

19.18 A UK-based employer must obtain a sponsor licence from UKVI before it can issue a certificate of sponsorship. There are conditions attached to the granting of a sponsor licence. For example, the sponsor must agree to comply with monitoring, reporting and other immigration compliance obligations. Applications for a sponsor licence must be submitted to UKVI. Once the application has been submitted, the employer may receive a visit from a compliance officer of UKVI. The compliance officer will carry out checks to help UKVI assess whether the employer is able to comply with the sponsorship duties. There is no right of appeal if the employer is refused a sponsor licence, although the employer can apply again provided the reason for refusal is not subject to a cooling off period. For example: a six month cooling off period will apply from the date of the refusal where the application was refused on the grounds that the employer did not have proper processes necessary to comply with their sponsor duties.

Tier 2 – qualifying for the certificate of sponsorship

19.19   Under Tier 2 points can be awarded if:

- the sponsor has completed a resident labour market test in accordance with the relevant code of practice for their sector (ie broadly, advertised the job) if applying under Tier 2 (General); or
- the position falls within a recognised shortage skilled occupation (a list of occupations is available on the UKVI website); or
- the certificate is being issued on the basis of an intra-company transfer (eg where the individual has been employed by a qualifying overseas group company for at least 12 months. The latter criterion is currently waived where the salary on offer is at least £73,900).

19.20   Points will also be awarded for the salary offered. The assignee must also satisfy a maintenance requirement (see **19.24**). The employment documents should confirm remuneration clearly.

19.21   A public list of current sponsors (and their ratings) can be viewed on the UKVI website at www.gov.uk.

Home and host company employment arrangements

UK host company employer

19.22   Obtaining approval from UKVI to act as sponsor can take time. So, if a proposed UK host employer is not currently approved, the need to obtain a licence to act as sponsor may delay the assignment. The UK host employer does not need to be a UK-registered legal entity (ie registered as a UK 'Limited' company, 'Plc' or 'LLP') but must have a 'presence' in the UK to act as sponsor.

Overseas home company employer

19.23   An overseas home company that is to remain the employer during the assignment is unlikely to be registered in the UK as a sponsor. If the employee is to be assigned by the home company to provide services to a UK host company (whilst the overseas home company remains the employer) then the UK host company may still be able to apply for immigration permission, notwithstanding that it will not be the employer. This would be done on the basis that there is an 'intra-company transfer'. (The terminology used by UKVI is slightly confusing as 'intra-company transfer' can apply even where employment is not actually transferred from one group company to another.) See the UKVI website for a more detailed explanation of when intra-company transfer arrangements are possible and the documentation that is required to support an application made on that basis (www.gov.uk).

Tier 2 and entry clearance

19.24 The expatriate himself (ie not the employer) will need to apply for entry clearance from his home country or country of residence before the assignment begins. The expatriate will need to:

- provide the certificate of sponsorship number issued by the sponsor (see above);

- provide some biometric data (photo and fingerprints) at a UK visa application centre;

- if applying under the Tier 2 (General) category, show that he or she has sufficient understanding of the English language. This might be done, eg, by demonstrating that the individual is a national of a country where English is the majority language; has completed a UK Bachelor's degree or overseas equivalent taught in English; or has passed a recognised English language test. Assignees being transferred to the UK by virtue of an intra-company transfer do not need to satisfy the English language test; and

- provide documents to demonstrate they meet the maintenance requirements. Currently, applicants applying under Tier 2 from outside the UK must show that they have held a minimum of £945 and £630 for each dependent family member who is to join them in the UK) for at least three months prior to the entry clearance application date. However, if the applicant is not able to satisfy this criterion, and the sponsor has an 'A' rating, the sponsor will instead be able to give an undertaking that it will maintain the assignee and any dependants without recourse to public funds for their first month in the UK.

Tier 2 – duration of immigration permission

19.25 Certificates of sponsorship can be issued for an initial period of up to five years. Under the Tier 2 (Intra-company Transfer) category an extension application can be made for a further four years, if the salary package is at least £120,000.

Timing and Tier 2 applications

19.26 Once the proposed employer has a sponsor licence, issue of a certificate of sponsorship to a potential assignee should be relatively quick, provided the employer is satisfied that the potential assignee meets the relevant criteria. The employer can issue the certificate of sponsorship itself using an online facility provided by UKVI, called the 'Sponsorship Management System'. There is no requirement to seek UKVI's or any other specific approval before issuing a certificate of sponsorship to a potential assignee, although UKVI staff will review the assignee's entry clearance application and may at that stage look at the issue of the certificate of sponsorship.

EEA nationals

19.27   EEA nationals (with the exception of Croatian nationals) and Swiss nationals currently have an automatic right to work in the UK. They can travel to the UK and work here without first seeking entry clearance or applying for a work permit. (See **18.15-18.22** on nationals of the Republic of Ireland). Croatian nationals must first obtain authorisation to work in the UK, unless they are exempt from doing so.

19.28   Schengen visas issued by other EU countries are not accepted in the UK (see **3.19–3.23**).

Families

19.29   Dependent family members of Tier 1 and Tier 2 applicants, including spouses, civil and unmarried partners and children under the age of 18 years, can join the expatriate in the UK. They must submit separate entry clearance applications. For consistency and ease of administration all the applications, including the expatriate's, should normally be submitted together. The number of dependent family members will affect the evidence of maintenance funds required (see **19.24**). Dependent family members who are granted entry clearance have the right to work in the UK.

Employment documents

19.30   Employment documents should confirm remuneration, absence reporting arrangements and other terms that must be confirmed under English law (see s 1 of the Employment Rights Act 1996).

Termination of employment

19.31   Tier 1 immigration permission will not be affected by termination of a particular UK employment as it relates to the individual and not the job. Tier 2 immigration permission relates both to a particular employee and their employment and is not transferable between employees, jobs or employers. If the employee's employment ends and he holds Tier 2 immigration permission then he will either need to obtain alternative immigration permission (such as Tier 1 Exceptional Talent) which permits him to remain in the UK or make immediate arrangements to leave the UK. UKVI may impose bans from the UK of up to 10 years for individuals who break UK immigration rules, including overstaying.

CORPORATION TAX

19.32 See general comments on corporation tax at **4.39–4.48** and **13.8–13.18** (regarding corporation tax residency, permanent establishment, transfer pricing and the availability of corporation tax deduction). The arrangements for a UK assignment should always be checked with a corporation tax specialist before they are implemented.

INCOME TAX

UK terminology

19.33 The following terms come up frequently when tax and social security advice is sought in relation to employees with a UK connection: 'tax resident', and 'domicile'. ('Ordinarily resident' has been superseded by new tax legislation.) See the Glossary at Appendix 3 for broad-brush explanations, but note that the meaning of these terms in the UK is complex and advice from a specialist tax adviser is usually recommended if the relevant category is important for tax purposes.

19.34 The same terms may be used for different things in different countries and sometimes for different purposes in the same country. For example 'domicile' has one meaning for UK tax purposes and a different meaning where jurisdiction (ie where claims can be made) is being considered.

Payroll arrangements

19.35 Payroll services may be purchased from third parties (eg specialist payroll service providers) who can manage the UK payroll on the employer's behalf, or may be administered by the business itself. Payment is normally made in 12 equal monthly instalments in arrears. The employee must be issued with an itemised payslip which, amongst other things, must confirm the payments and deductions made and the identity of the employer. The employer is likely to be obliged to make deductions from pay in respect of Pay-As-You-Earn (PAYE) income tax and employee's social security contributions (National Insurance contributions or NIC) if due and to pay those amounts over to Her Majesty's Revenue and Customs (HMRC) together with employer's NIC if due.

19.36 Decisions on the preferred identity of the employer must be made before the payroll arrangements are set up. Both employer and employee will be given unique PAYE reference numbers/codes. It is not appropriate to simply include a home company employee on the host company payroll even if this, at first blush, seems convenient.

19.37 Specialist tax advice should always be sought before payroll arrangements are set up, as the requirements are complex, penalties for failure to comply can be severe and there may be more opportunity to save expense if the issues are considered before practical arrangements are implemented.

Length of assignment

19.38 A form may be submitted to HMRC to confirm the intended length of assignment. The intended length of assignment is important for determining the employee's tax status ('resident', 'ordinarily resident', 'domiciled', etc) and may also affect tax relief available in respect of expenses, benefits and allowances. The intended length of assignment may also be confirmed in the employment documents.

Overseas workdays

19.39 An employee who is tax 'resident' in the UK will be subject to UK income tax on earnings for UK duties. However, he will only be subject to UK income tax on earnings for non-UK duties to the extent that those earnings are paid to him or remitted by him to the UK. If the employee has only one employment and performs duties partly inside and partly outside the UK his earnings will usually be apportioned between UK and non-UK duties, pro rata to the number of 'workdays' spent performing duties in the UK and overseas to determine the income tax due. The UK employer must operate PAYE on the employee's entire earnings unless the apportionment of 'workdays' is agreed with HMRC in advance. Specialist tax advice should be sought before the assignment begins in relation to overseas workdays, and remittance arrangements if these may be relevant and the employment documents should properly record relevant facts, administrative arrangements and duties to co-operate. See 7.93–7.97.

UK day counting

19.40 See 5.8–5.13 for a general explanation of the way that 'day counting' works for the purpose of determining tax status, and framework document **A2.4** at Appendix 2 on dealing with day counting in the employment documents.

19.41 Day counting rules change from time to time and may be different for immigration and tax purposes. Any day on which the employee is present in the UK at the end of that day (ie at midnight) must currently be 'counted' to determine UK tax status. This has an impact on employees who work part of the week in the UK and part of the week in another country as travelling days can count to meet the threshold number of days for UK tax residency (183 days). (Spending 183 days or more in the UK in one tax year is just one of the ways in which an employee might qualify as 'tax resident' in the UK, see Glossary.)

19.42 Employers should seek income tax advice and ensure policies, contract terms and instructions to employees on record keeping are updated to take account of changes. Any practical changes to working arrangements as a consequence of new rules should be properly documented.

See **14.28–14.34** on tracking employee movements more generally.

Tax returns

19.43 Some UK employees are required to file tax returns. This is done on a self-assessment basis. If the employee is sent a tax return he must complete the return and submit it to HMRC by the deadline. (The deadline is currently 31 January after the end of the relevant 6 April to 5 April tax year, although there may be advantages to earlier submission.) Almost all senior expatriates assigned to the UK will need to complete a tax return. Both employer and employee will have an interest in ensuring that tax returns are completed properly and on time. Normally, the employer will meet the costs (or some of the costs) of professional advice relating to tax returns. See **7.93-7.98** on tax return support.

19.44 The employee's spouse or partner may need to submit a separate tax return and both may need to seek advice in relation to the tax treatment of personal wealth and any planning opportunities. (See Chapter 22 on employee perspectives.)

19.45 The employment documents should normally confirm any limits on the assistance provided and the employee's obligations to co-operate, provide relevant information promptly etc (see **7.93–7.97**). Tax refunds may be paid directly to the individual so it can be helpful to include clauses in the employment documents requiring the employee to pass the relevant sums on to the employer if there is a tax equalisation or protection promise (ie so the employee must repay the employer). Note that the timing and wording of agreement may have an impact on recoverability due to the way UK 'deductions from wages' legislation works (see s 13 of the Employment Rights Act 1996). (See also Chapter 22 on claw-back.)

Dual employments

19.46 (See employer; **6.58** on dual employments; and the Glossary at Appendix 3 for an explanation of the meaning of 'domicile'.) Note that it is difficult to establish dual employments in the UK, as the arrangements are frequently challenged.

Detached duty relief

19.47 Normally, travel expenses between the employee's permanent workplace and his home will not attract UK income tax relief: the employee simply has to meet the expenses out of his net income. However, the employee's UK place of work will not be regarded as a 'permanent workplace' if the employee expects to be working there for 24 months or less. This means the journey from the employee's home to the workplace and back would not be treated as ordinary commuting and the employee may be entitled to UK income tax relief for the cost of the journey. Employers should not assume that tax relief will be available for the first 24 months of every assignment, regardless of the actual assignment length. What matters is how long the employee *expects* to be at the particular workplace. If the employee expects to work there for more than 24 months from the outset then the workplace will be a permanent workplace from the first day and no relief will be available. If the employee expects to work there for less than 24 months from the outset but he later expects to be there for more than 24 months then relief will be lost from the date his expectation changes.

19.48 In addition, if the employee qualifies for detached duty relief, UK housing, utility and subsistence expenses may qualify for relief even where the expenses are not reimbursed by the employer. This relief can be very valuable for the expatriate (and his employer if he has been given a tax equalisation or protection promise). Housing can be one of the most expensive benefits likely to be offered to an expatriate who is sent to work in the UK, particularly if he is assigned to work in London.

19.49 Qualifying criteria include the following:

- new hires do not qualify: the expatriate must be temporarily assigned from his permanent workplace;
- the assignment must be expected to last for less than 2 years; and
- documentary evidence of the expenses incurred will be required.

19.50 If detached duty relief may be available tax advice should be taken early and, where appropriate, HMRC clearance should be sought.

19.51 The employment documents should accurately record key facts, such as the anticipated length of the assignment.

Housing expenses

19.52 See above in relation to assignments expected to last for less than two years and detached duty relief.

19.53 Expatriate tax advisers may also be able to recommend ways to structure the arrangements that reduce the potential expense if a longer-term assignment is anticipated. Note **20.23** and **4.114** on tax evasion.

Relocation expenses

19.54 The first £8,000 of relocation expenses incurred by an expatriate in moving to the UK to take up a UK assignment may be paid free of UK tax, subject to certain conditions. These include for example:

- only certain expenses qualify for relief;
- the expenses must be incurred within a particular time frame;
- documentary evidence will be required; and

- the new residence must be within reasonable commuting distance of the new UK place of work.

19.55 Expatriate relocation expenses may, of course, exceed £8,000 and so some of those expenses may be subject to tax. Care should be taken to ensure that any related tax equalisation or protection promise is clear. If repayment provisions are included (eg providing for repayment in the event that the employee terminates his employment voluntarily within a certain period) then the effect on tax should be considered. This is because the repayment clause is unlikely to allow recovery of any tax due, or already paid, in respect of the expenses.

Tax equalisation and UK company directors

19.56 Employers used to be prohibited under s 311 of the Companies Act 1985 from promising to pay a UK statutory director remuneration free of income tax or varying by reference to income tax. This effectively meant that if the expatriate was to be a UK director he could not be offered a tax equalisation or tax protection promise. The restriction no longer applies and it is possible to offer a tax equalisation or protection promise in relation to directors' pay.

SOCIAL SECURITY CONTRIBUTIONS

19.57 See **19.35, 4.34–4.36** and **5.21–5.25.** EU regulations apply (see Regulation 883/2004).

EMPLOYMENT LAWS

Sources of UK employment law

19.58 England and Wales, Scotland and Northern Ireland are 'common law' jurisdictions. Laws are found in legislation (statutes and regulations) and in case law (court and tribunal decisions). (See the Glossary at Appendix 3 for an explanation of the meanings of 'UK', 'Great Britain', etc.) Although England and Wales (together), Scotland and Northern Ireland are technically separate jurisdictions and there are some minor differences between the laws of each jurisdiction from an employment law perspective, the vast majority of employment laws are the same in all three jurisdictions and, for convenience, can be loosely described as 'UK' laws.

19.59 The UK is currently a member state of the EU and has implemented employment-related directives. Private sector employers (ie organisations that are not considered to be an 'emanation of the state') are not required to comply with EC directives directly but instead with the UK laws implementing them. They must, however, comply directly with the Treaty article relating to equal pay for men and women, Article 157, and will be required to comply with the GDPR (data protection regulation) directly. See Chapter 18 on the potential impact of Brexit.

Collective agreements

19.60 England's industrial relations system is different from most other European countries' arrangements. Collective agreements are not normally considered to be a source of law, or used to implement employment laws. Collective agreements are generally non-binding agreements negotiated between a trade union (or trade unions) and an employer (or employers or employers association). Some terms of a collective agreement may be incorporated in an employment contract where the terms are appropriate, and provided this has been agreed by the particular employer and employee. (Contrast **10.42–10.46.**)

19.61 For historic reasons, collective bargaining typically applies to public sector workers and employees in larger/older businesses. The agreement may set basic terms such as minimum pay rates for factory workers. Collective agreements rarely apply to senior employees in the private sector. The key point is that incorporation of the terms of a collective agreement into an employee's contract of employment does not happen by accident. There is no central mechanism for extending collective agreements made with one employer to another employer's employees or to a particular sector or region. There is, however, a mechanism by which a sufficient proportion of employees can insist that the employer conducts collective bargaining, although it is not often used.

19.62 Practically, senior expatriates working for commercial organisations in the UK will rarely be covered by collective agreements. In any case, that type of expatriate is likely to enjoy far better terms than those that are usually set by collective bargaining.

Directors and 'managing executives'

19.63 Employment laws in the UK do not generally distinguish between 'blue collar' and 'white collar' workers or between junior and senior employees. There is no special category of '*cadre*', '*dirigenti*' or 'managing executive' to whom different employment laws may apply. Executive directors will hold an 'office' as director as well as being employees. No special employment laws apply to them (or do not apply to them) simply because of their status as director, although they will have additional obligations etc because of their separate office as director. Typically, UK statutory directors who are also employees are known as 'executive' directors. UK directors who provide services but are not employed are usually known as 'non-executive' directors.

Registration requirements

19.64 Employment laws will, typically, apply to employees working in the UK in the same way, whether the employee is employed by a UK-registered legal entity or by a company registered overseas. See **10.50–10.55** on the Posted Workers Directive.

19.65 There is normally no additional requirement to formally register as an employer with any labour authority in the UK. (See comments above in relation to tax, social security and immigration. See also gla.gov.uk for information on the Gangmasters & Labour Abuse Authority though this will not usually be relevant to senior expatriates.)

Employers liability and other insurance

19.66 Employers are required to take out insurance to cover the risk of personal injury claims from employees. This is known as 'employers' liability insurance'. Failure to comply with the relevant legislation may potentially lead to financial and criminal penalties, including for company directors personally.

19.67 In addition, the employer may consider taking out:

- key man insurance; and/or
- permanent health insurance (also known as PHI or long-term disability cover) in respect of employees; and/or
- insurance in relation to the cost of employment claims.

19.68 Introduction of a new PHI (long term disability) plan may not be helpful for the employer particularly where the employer has limited resources in the UK. In practice, the benefit is quite expensive to provide; the employer's obligations if a claim needs to be made can be quite onerous and the existence of a PHI policy could potentially lead to complex legal dispute with the employee.

19.69 Insurance cover is available to help employers manage financial risks associated with employment claims. However, this will not usually be appropriate in an expatriate context. The cover is usually provided subject to conditions, including usually compliance with the insurer's guidance on management of a claim or potential claim. Given the complexity of expatriate arrangements; the importance of issues outside the scope of employment law unlikely to be covered by the insurance (eg tax and social security contributions); and the reality that most expatriate claims are settled rather than litigated, the employer is likely to want a free hand to deal with any dispute as it sees fit at the time.

Hours of work

19.70 The employer and employee can agree on the hours of work that will apply, subject to limits. For example, the employee must be given minimum daily and weekly rest breaks. The EC Working Time Directive 2003/88/EC has been implemented in the UK and restrictions largely mirror the minimum requirements of that Directive. It is currently possible for an employee to 'opt' out of the limit on average maximum working time (the '48-hour week') subject to conditions. Currently there are no proposals to alter the current UK protection following Brexit, although it currently does seem unlikely that the UK will adopt the enhanced protection currently being considered by other EU member states.

19.71 A typical working pattern for an office worker might be normal hours of work of 9 am to 5 pm Monday to Friday with an expectation that the employee will also work outside these core hours without additional pay if needed. Employees may make flexible working requests, eg to request flexible hours to accommodate childcare commitments.

Holiday

19.72 Under legislation based on the Working Time Directive, full-time employees are, broadly, entitled to a minimum of four weeks' paid holiday per year, in addition to bank and public holidays on which the employee is allowed to take paid leave. (Further information is available at www.gov.uk.)

19.73 In England there are currently eight bank and public holidays. These are New Year's Day, Good Friday, Easter Monday, two May bank holidays, one August bank holiday, Christmas Day and Boxing Day (ie St Stephen's Day). Note that public holidays are not consistent across UK jurisdictions. See, eg, www.publicholidays.co.uk.

19.74 Most employers offer 20 to 30 days' annual holiday per year to full time office workers in addition to paid time off on bank and public holidays to full time employees. 25 days' holiday may be appropriate for a senior executive.

Illness

19.75 Employers must pay Statutory Sick Pay (SSP) to qualifying employees. However, the standard rate for SSP is currently (2017) only £89.35 a week. Most employers voluntarily offer a period of full pay, to include the minimum statutory entitlement, though the period during which this is paid varies considerably between employers. (It is also usually more convenient from an administrative perspective to provide for a period of company sick pay as it is not then necessary to make special payroll arrangements for short absences.)

Minimum wage

19.76 Employees are entitled to receive a minimum wage although this is unlikely to be significant for the sort of expatriate we are considering in this book. (The national minimum wage for most employees has been £7.50 per hour from April 2017.)

Benefits

19.77 Benefit packages for senior office workers vary but a typical local hire might be offered:

- salary;
- bonus/incentive arrangements;
- pension (with employee's and employer's contributions subject to minimum levels);
- life assurance cover (usually to assure a sum equal to three or four times basic salary);
- private medical insurance cover (dental cover is rare for locals);
- sometimes PHI (also known as long-term disability cover), although if this is not already in place introduction may not be helpful for the employer;
- sometimes a car or, more often, a car allowance.

19.78 An expatriate might in addition be offered:

- assistance with housing (usually the most valuable expatriate benefit);
- more comprehensive private medical cover (but PHI is rarely offered to expatriates);
- assistance with education, for example to allow the child to attend an international school;
- assistance with relocation and repatriation expenses;
- flights for home leave;
- a cost of living allowance;
- tax equalisation or protection; and
- assistance with tax return preparation.

Notice of termination of employment

19.79 The employee and employer may agree on the notice period that must be given to terminate the employment, provided the period agreed is at least as long as the 'statutory minimum notice' period. Statutory minimum notice from the employer is, broadly, one week for each completed year of service, subject to a maximum of 12 weeks' notice after 12 years. In practice, the notice period to be given by the employer and the employee is nearly always the same but this is not required.

19.80 Employment 'at will' cannot apply in the UK. If employment at will were agreed the agreement would be overridden by the statutory minimum requirements anyway. If no notice period is agreed at all then a period of notice that is longer than the statutory minimum may be implied, depending on the circumstances.

19.81 A contractual right to pay in lieu of notice may be retained by the employer. 'PILON' clauses are usually included in the employment contract for senior local hires. (See **16.29–16.40**.)

Termination of employment and severance agreements

19.82 As in most countries, there are UK laws that protect employees on termination of employment. For example, employees may be able to claim that they have been 'unfairly dismissed' if they are dismissed for an unfair reason or an unfair procedure is followed.

19.83 There is no requirement to obtain the approval of an employment authority, court or other public body either in advance of dismissal or subsequently. Formal approval is not required for 'settlement agreements' either although, if they are to effectively prevent employees from making certain claims, certain strict requirements must be complied with. For example, the agreement must confirm certain information and a qualified person (eg an appropriately qualified solicitor) must advise the employee before he enters into the agreement.

19.84 If the employee makes a complaint that he has been 'unfairly dismissed' and is successful with his claim then (at 1 October 2017) he may be awarded compensation of up to £95,211 (in ordinary circumstances; there are some exceptions). Reinstatement and re-engagement can be ordered but the employer can generally pay additional compensation rather than comply with the order.

19.85 Employees who are dismissed by reason of 'redundancy' and who satisfy various qualifying criteria will be eligible for statutory redundancy pay. This is calculated using a formula on the basis of the employee's age, length of service and a 'week's pay'. The amounts are generally not high, the maximum payment from April 2017 being £14,670.

Discrimination

19.86 As with other EU countries, the UK has legislation protecting employees against discrimination on grounds of sex, marital or civil partnership status, race, disability, age, religion or belief, sexual orientation and fixed-term or part-time status. Special protection is offered in relation to maternity and to trade union officials, employee representatives and employees who make 'whistleblowing' or health and safety complaints or assert statutory rights. Compensation for discrimination is not capped. (See also Chapter 12 on equality.)

Family-related rights

19.87 The UK has implemented various European directives relating to family rights and has, in addition, more extensive national protection in place. (See also Chapter 12 on equality.) Family-related rights include the following:

- a right to maternity leave of up to one year;
- a right to Statutory Maternity Pay (SMP) consisting of 6 weeks' maternity pay at a rate equal to 90% of 'normal weekly earnings' followed by up to 33 weeks' lower rate SMP paid (from 6 April 2017) at the rate of £140.98 per week (but note this will depend on whether the employee is paying UK national insurance contributions) – see also the example at **12.25–12.34**);
- a right to up to two weeks' paid paternity leave (but note pay is at the level of lower rate SMP) and to take 'shared parental leave';
- a right to request flexible working arrangements (the employer has a corresponding duty to follow certain procedures and consider the request);
- well-developed sex discrimination laws;
- a right to time off for domestic emergencies to care for dependants (adults and children are covered);
- a right to up to 18 weeks' unpaid parental leave per child (not more than 4 weeks to be taken per year in ordinary circumstances).

Continuous employment

19.88 In the UK 'continuous employment' is a technical term that is used to determine whether an employee has sufficient length of service to be entitled to make statutory claims, most importantly the statutory rights to make an unfair dismissal complaint and receive statutory redundancy pay. UK statutory rules will determine the relevant period of continuous employment. An employee who arrives on assignment in the UK is unlikely to be particularly concerned about continuity of employment at the outset of his assignment. Nevertheless, the employer is required to confirm certain core terms in writing (see **19.91**), including the date statutory continuous employment begins and it is worth checking that the period confirmed in the documents is correct.

19.89 The employee may also be concerned about continuity of employment for the purposes of his employment rights and benefits in his home country when he returns, in which case the answer will be determined by the relevant home country or plan rules. Some countries will take account of earlier service with another group company or related business and some will not. The employer may be able to offer some contractual comfort that the employee will not lose out.

19.90 See **20.41–20.54** for a more detailed explanation of the way that the UK statutory period of continuous employment is determined.

Documents

19.91 All employees working in the UK must be issued with a written statement confirming certain core terms of employment and this information is normally given in the employment contract. (See s 1 of the Employment Rights Act 1996.) Similar requirements apply in other EU countries, although the UK legislation pre-dates the relevant EC Directive. (See **8.37** on the Employment Particulars Directive.) There are a number of additional matters that the employer is not required to document but which can be helpful for the employer.

19.92 Please refer to Chapter 6 on the employment documents needed and Chapters 7 and 8 on content of the documents.

HEALTH

Health and safety

19.93 The UK has extensive health and safety laws. The practical requirements will vary considerably depending on what the employee is required to do and specialist advice is recommended even if the employee is to be an ordinary office worker and there is generally a low risk of accident or injury at work. For example, requirements relating to office workers may include communication of emergency procedures, provision of free eye tests, workstation/VDU assessments and special arrangements for pregnant women and those returning from maternity leave.

The National Health Service (NHS)

19.94 The NHS, broadly, provides free treatment to people who are resident in the UK, regardless of their nationality. This means that some employees who are assigned to the UK may have to pay for NHS treatment. See the Glossary at Appendix 3 on benefits available to EEA and Swiss nationals who hold a European Health Insurance Card (EHIC). Note that Brexit may have an impact on EHIC arrangements.

Private health insurance

19.95 Employers of expatriates working in the UK usually offer private health insurance as a benefit to expatriates and their families, regardless of whether they are entitled to free NHS treatment. Private health insurance is a benefit that is also enjoyed by many UK 'local hires', particularly senior employees, although this rarely includes private maternity pay. Provision of private medical cover can offer some advantages, eg:

- it will be essential if the employee, or an accompanying family member, is not eligible for treatment under the NHS;

- the employee is likely to have access to quicker medical care (eg NHS waiting lists for minor operations may be avoided);
- the employer may benefit, for example, because the employee may be able to return to work more quickly;
- the treatment offered may be more comprehensive than that offered under the NHS;
- employers are typically able to offer cover at a lower cost than that which might be available to an individual employee on the open market;
- the employer may be able to offer medical cover without account being taken of the particular employee's (or family member's) state of health, any 'pre-existing conditions' etc;
- special considerations may apply to US nationals.

Note that private medical services are not always superior to services provided by the NHS and that, in practice, there is overlap both in the relevant hospitals and medical practitioners treating private and NHS patients. A key advantage of private medical care in the UK for employers is speed of treatment.

PENSIONS

Employee joins UK plan

19.96 There is no prohibition under UK law on an overseas national joining a UK pension plan, although joining the plan for a short period may have some disadvantages for the employee. For example:

- the employee may not be a member of the UK plan for long enough for the benefits to vest;
- if the pre-assignment home country pension plan is a final salary pension plan then the employee's salary for determining pension entitlement under that plan will be 'frozen';
- similarly if the UK pension plan is a final salary pension plan, when the assignment ends the pension benefits will be 'frozen' based on salary during the assignment and will not take account of future salary increases;
- the employee may be more exposed to exchange rate fluctuations than if he had participated in a plan based in the country in which he will retire and draw his pension benefits.

The employee wishes to remain in his overseas home country pension plan

19.97 Whether the employee may remain in his overseas home country pension plan will depend on that plan's rules and the pension laws of his home country.

Tax relief on pension contributions

19.98 When an employee comes to work in the UK and wishes to continue to contribute to his home pension plan, tax relief on contributions made by the employee or in respect of him are governed by the 'migrant member relief' (MMR) rules.

19.99 An overseas pension plan falls within the MMR rules if it is a 'qualifying overseas pension scheme' (QOPS), subject to various conditions. The employee must also be a 'relevant migrant member'. (Amongst other things the employee must not have been UK tax resident when he first became a member of the QOPS.)

19.100 Tax relief on contributions may also be available under the terms of a double tax treaty.

Drawing benefits

19.101 Where eg:

- contributions to an overseas pension plan have received UK income tax relief under MMR;
- contributions to an overseas pension plan have received UK income tax relief under a double tax treaty; or
- in certain other circumstances,

certain UK tax charges may apply where a benefit is paid from the overseas scheme, subject to conditions. Potential tax charges should be kept under review.

Executive joins plan in country other than the UK or his home country

19.102 The issues will be similar to those that apply if an employee is assigned from the UK overseas (see **20.84–20.85**).

19.103 The employee may consider making contributions to a plan based in another country (ie in neither the UK nor the home country). This may offer some potential advantages:

- the plan can be based in a country with favourable tax etc laws;
- the employee can potentially remain in the plan through subsequent assignments to other countries;
- more flexibility may be available in relation to the drawing of benefits. For example, laws on the minimum age at which pension can be drawn may be avoided.

19.104 However, the current host country, and/or future host countries may not allow income tax relief on contributions to the plan. Depending on relevant location(s) there may be further adverse tax consequences.

Transfer payments

19.105 The employee will probably only want to make a transfer payment from an overseas pension plan to a UK pension plan if he intends to retire in the UK. A transfer payment offers some potential advantages:

- the UK pension plan may offer more flexibility in taking benefits (though this is unlikely);
- the UK pension arrangements may be subject to more favourable tax treatment (this would of course also depend on the tax treatment that applies in the country from which the transfer payment is made).

SHARE PLANS

19.106 Employees who are offered an assignment to the UK may be concerned about the impact of the assignment on existing incentive arrangements and also about any new arrangements that may apply to them during the assignment. See **15.9–15.19** for an overview of issues relating to these concerns.

19.107 It may be tempting simply to offer the expatriate the opportunity to participate in the normal incentive arrangements for UK local hires. However, that may not be appropriate where the arrangements involve shares or share options. For example:

- the plan rules may not allow participation by employees who are employed by their home company rather than the UK host company or may have eligibility criteria restricting participation by employees who do not have the appropriate tax status;
- if the assignment is a relatively short-term host country assignment (ie where the UK entity will employ the expatriate for a short period of time) the employee may have no prospect of achieving sufficient service to benefit from 'vesting' of shares or 'exercise' of share options in the normal way before the UK employment ends. The practical impact of termination of employment is likely to be determined by the plan rules and reasons for termination;
- for some employees, for example those assigned from the US, the standard UK arrangements may not offer the same tax benefits as they might to local hires (and participation may potentially result in negative consequences for both employer and employee); and
- the point(s) at which tax or social security contributions might become due (grant, vesting, exercise, etc) are likely to vary depending, for example, on the type of share plan, the employee's tax status at the time shares or

options are granted, vest, exercised, etc; the home country from which the expatriate has been assigned; where the expatriate might be assigned to next (and the timing of that move); and whether he will have any overseas duties during the UK assignment.

19.108 Consideration should be given to the employee's current arrangements (eg any home country incentive plan the employee may already participate in) as well as any new arrangements that will apply during the UK assignment. For example:

- a change to the expatriate's employer from the host to the home company may trigger termination provisions in the pre-assignment plan; and

- the start of a new UK assignment may not mean that share options already granted are taxable but if, for example, those options are exercised whilst the employee is resident here an unexpected UK tax charge may be triggered.

19.109 Specialist share plans advice should be sought before the assignment begins in relation to the tax treatment and the likely effect of the plan rules on the particular individual both during and on termination of the assignment and/or employment.

19.110 Care should be taken to ensure that the scope of any tax equalisation or protection promise offered is clear and that the employer has some understanding of the potential financial costs of the promises made.

19.111 More detailed information on the tax treatment of share and share option arrangements for an employee sent to the UK is available on the HMRC website at www.hmrc.gov.uk/manuals/ersmmanual/ERSM160000.htm.

DATA PROTECTION

19.112 As other EU countries, the UK is obliged to comply with the Data Protection Directive. (See **15.73–15.99** for further detail, particularly on transfer of personal data and sensitive personal data outside the EU.)

19.113 Further information is available from the UK Information Commissioner's Office (ICO) website at www.ico.gov.uk.

19.114 Normally, the UK-based host company will need to register as a 'data controller' if it has not done so already. A list of registered data controllers is available on the ICO website.

19.115 If personal information regarding the expatriate is provided to third party 'data processors' (eg to a relocation agent finding accommodation for the family) then the data controller will need to ensure that that data is treated properly. This will include due diligence on the information security procedures of the third party and where necessary suitable contractual terms. If the data processor manages the personal data outside the EEA then it is mandatory to have an approved contact in place using the EC model clauses on transfers from a data controller to a data processor.

CHAPTER 20

SENDING EXPATRIATES FROM THE UK

20.1 This chapter gives an overview of issues relating to:

- immigration (**20.2**);
- corporation tax (**20.3**);
- VAT (**20.4–20.5**);
- income tax (**20.6–20.13**);
- social security contributions (**20.14–20.22**);
- tax evasion (**20.23**);
- share plans (**20.24–20.25**);
- inheritance and personal wealth (**20.26–20.33**);
- employment law (**20.34–20.54**);
- cultural awareness training (**20.55–20.56**);
- data protection (**20.57–20.60**);
- health (**20.61–20.65**); and
- pensions (**20.66–20.90**).

IMMIGRATION

20.2 UK immigration permission is unlikely to be a concern when an employee working in the UK is sent on an overseas assignment. However, it may be worth bearing the following in mind:

- generally there will be no restriction on leaving the UK but an employee who has custody of children, eg following divorce, may be subject to restrictions on travel abroad with his children;
- a period of work abroad may affect the employee's longer-term personal immigration status in the UK, eg the employee may experience difficulties on return;
- if the employee is already an expatriate and has been assigned to work in the UK from overseas he may currently hold a particular type of UK immigration permission. A gap between the end of the current UK assignment and departure for the new assignment abroad may cause problems and care should be taken with timing.

Particular care should be taken with employees who are assigned from the UK and who are not UK citizens given the uncertain impact of Brexit.

CORPORATION TAX

20.3 The key concerns are likely to be:

- the availability of a corporation tax deduction in relation to employment-related costs (eg remuneration, severance pay, etc); and
- whether a 'permanent establishment' is created in the host country for a UK-registered company (see **13.12–13.15**).

SALES TAX

20.4 The key issues are likely to be whether sales tax is:

- due on any inter-company payments; and
- recoverable.

20.5 If a UK home company employer receives a fee from the host company for the employee's services abroad, sales tax may be due. It is usually sensible for the two companies to enter into an inter-company expatriate supply agreement to record the relevant arrangements (see **8.73–8.83**, checklist **A1.10** at Appendix 1 and framework document **A2.6** at Appendix 2 on inter-company expatriate supply agreements more generally).

INCOME TAX

20.6 The primary concern where an employee is assigned abroad from the UK is likely to be tax due in the host country, rather than tax due in the UK. However, UK income tax may be relevant even after an assignment abroad has begun. For example:

- if the assignment is short the employee may still be treated as UK tax resident for the whole UK tax year (Eg if a UK tax resident employee, Amanda, is sent on a three-month assignment from the UK to the United Arab Emirates (UAE) and no income tax is payable there, income tax may nevertheless be due in the UK in respect of the whole tax year, including in respect of Amanda's UAE assignment income. The short assignment may not be long enough to 'break' Amanda's UK tax residence);
- UK income tax may be due in respect of the first and last years of a longer assignment, in addition to any income tax due in the host country (relief may be available through a double tax treaty);

- a UK tax return is likely to be needed in respect of the first year of the assignment (employees' UK tax returns must normally be submitted by 31 January after the end of the relevant UK tax year on 5 April);
- the employee may have assets or income of his own that will remain subject to UK tax during the assignment regardless of the treatment of his employment income, eg UK rental income on his UK home (see 20.26–20.33);
- the employee may retain some UK duties after the assignment begins, eg, he may be required to attend board meetings in the UK and receive fees for those duties or he may undertake some minor 'incidental' duties in the UK that relate to his host country employment.

20.7 The date on which the employee leaves the UK may make a difference to whether the employee remains tax resident during the last tax year in which he works in the UK. Timing can make a particular difference if the overseas assignment is due to start around the start of the UK tax year (April).

20.8 When assessing tax due in the host country, specialist advice should be sought, for example in respect of:

- income tax rates in the host country;
- whether a double tax treaty between the UK and the host country applies (which will typically provide that employment income should be taxed in the host country, perhaps with some exceptions for short-term assignees);
- whether any tax relief is potentially available in the host country, for example, in relation to expatriate benefits such as housing or relocation expenses (Expenses relating to relocation from the UK to the host country and back again may attract tax relief under UK law but this may not benefit the employer or the expatriate if the expenses are taxed in the host country instead. Similarly, it may be possible for the UK employer to provide medical insurance cover to an employee sent abroad free of UK tax but this may be of no value if the benefit is instead taxed in the host country).

It may be worth asking about potential relief on termination of employment too as this may affect the way the employment documents should be drafted.

Withholding obligations

20.9 As well as understanding whether UK income tax is due, it is important for the UK employer and any new host company employer to understand whether they have any UK withholding obligations. That is, whether the employer is required to operate 'Pay-As-You-Earn' (PAYE) and pay over any tax to Her Majesty's Revenue and Customs (HMRC).

20.10 For example, suppose an employee, Humphrey, is recruited in the UK on the open market by the host company to undertake a short-term assignment in the Middle East. No duties will be performed in the UK. Suppose no income tax or social security contributions are due in the host country. The new host country employer may assume that it has no income tax-related obligations. However, suppose Humphrey is resident in the UK and UK income tax is due in respect of income for the tax year in which Humphrey does the work in the host country. The taxable income includes his salary for the Middle East assignment, even if Humphrey is paid in the host country in cash. The host company will need to understand whether it must pay over the income tax due to HMRC or whether Humphrey will be responsible for that. The answer to that question may depend, amongst other things, on the host company's (and other group companies') presence in the UK. It would be sensible for the host company to check its obligations with a UK tax specialist so that it can make any necessary payroll arrangements. Even if there is no employer PAYE obligation Humphrey could be forewarned so that he does not feel he has been misled if he is faced with an unexpected income tax bill or claims from HMRC for interest and penalties on tax not paid.

Tax equalisation and UK directors' pay

20.11 It is now possible to offer a tax equalisation or protection promise to an employee who holds office as a statutory director of a UK-registered company. Section 311 of the Companies Act 1985 no longer applies.

Relocation expenses and home leave

20.12 The home and host companies should consider whether UK tax relief may be available in relation to home leave and/or relocation expenses at the start or end of the assignment.

Payroll arrangements

20.13 As well as understanding the income tax and social security contributions that should be paid and which country's or countries' authorities it should be paid to, the employer will need to make practical arrangements for managing the payroll. Host country requirements should be checked. These may, for example, include registration requirements for the employee and employer, the need to grant 'powers' to authorise the payroll (see **13.26–13.29**), the need for the employer to arrange for funds to be available, and for the employee to set up a bank account in the host country to receive his pay.

SOCIAL SECURITY CONTRIBUTIONS

20.14 See also **4.31–4.38** and **5.21–5.22** for broad-brush descriptions of issues relating to participation in a home country social security scheme for a period of time after the employee leaves the home country to work in the host country.

20.15 UK employer's social security contribution rates can be substantially lower than the rates that apply in other EEA countries. It may therefore reduce costs if the UK-based employer remains the employer during the assignment and an application is made to allow the employee to remain in the UK social security scheme, at least initially. It may be possible for the employee to remain in the UK social security scheme for up to five years provided host country requirements are met and permissions are granted.

20.16 Some countries outside the EEA may also have agreements with the UK regarding the treatment of social security contributions for expatriates.

20.17 There may be no agreement at all with other countries, in which case social security contributions will normally be determined separately in accordance with the rules of both the UK and the overseas country. Contributions may potentially be due in both home and host countries.

20.18 Some countries do not require payment of social security contributions at all, so if a UK employee is sent abroad it may be cheaper if he does not remain within the UK social security scheme. However, if the employer has a place of business in the UK and the employee was resident in the UK before the assignment began the employer may be required to pay UK National Insurance contributions for at least the first 52 weeks of the assignment.

20.19 It is worth bearing in mind though that payment of UK National Insurance contributions does not just affect costs for the employer and employee. Whether contributions are paid can also affect the benefits that the employee is eligible to receive.

20.20 Where the contributions to be made may change during the assignment, for example, because the employee is no longer able to stay in the UK social security scheme, care should be taken with tax equalisation and protection promises so that the net effect is clear from the outset.

20.21 International social security advice should always be sought from a specialist before the employment structure for the assignment is determined. The technical issues are complex, vary considerably between countries and the best approach to dealing with them is likely to depend on the employee's personal circumstances (eg his nationality) and the proposed assignment arrangements (eg its anticipated length) too. The costs of getting it wrong can be substantial.

Child benefit

20.22 Rules relating to child benefit may depend on the host country for the assignment. These should be checked so that the employee is clear about his entitlements. Tax equalisation and protection clauses in the employment documents may clarify the treatment of child benefit. In practice, senior expatriates would often be ineligible for child benefit even if they were in the UK because remuneration is too high.

TAX EVASION

20.23 The UK has stringent laws relating to tax evasion and active enforcement authorities. The Criminal Finances Act 2017 recently came into force. This legislation allows for prosecution of a company for failing to prevent its employees and other 'associated persons' from facilitating tax evasion in the UK and abroad. See also **4.114** on tax evasion more generally.

SHARE PLANS

20.24 Employees who are offered an assignment overseas may be concerned about the impact of the assignment on existing incentive arrangements and also about the arrangements that may apply to them during the assignment (see also **15.9–15.20** and **19.108–19.113**). These need to be addressed, for example, because:

- both employer and employee should be clear about the tax treatment of pre-assignment UK incentive plans and of any new assignment-related plan;
- any tax equalisation or protection clauses in the employment documents should be clearly drafted to reduce the risk of dispute over who should meet any additional income tax, capital gains tax or social security obligation; and
- the employee may be able to control the timing of some actions that may have tax implications (eg when a share option is exercised).

20.25 More detailed information on the tax treatment of share and share option arrangements for an employee sent abroad from the UK is available on the HMRC website at https://www.gov.uk/government/organisations/hm-revenue-customs.

INHERITANCE AND PERSONAL WEALTH

20.26 See **15.68–15.71** regarding the potential effect of death of the expatriate or a member of his family, or inheritance by the expatriate or his family, whilst he is abroad. (See also Chapter 22 on employee perspectives generally.)

20.27 If the employee dies during the assignment UK inheritance tax will normally apply if the employee is domiciled in the UK. However, another country may also require payment of inheritance tax. Host country tax may be offset against UK liability but the general effect may be that the employee's estate is subject to the worst of the two tax regimes.

20.28   The expatriate's attention should be drawn to the need to check any existing will or make a new one (and to encourage his partner to do so). This is particularly important for expatriates assigned from the UK as they may not be aware that host country laws could lead to a change to beneficiaries, as well as having tax implications.

20.29   If the employee is no longer eligible to participate in his home country pension arrangements he may also be unable to participate in life assurance arrangements linked to the pension plan. If the employer does not provide alternative life assurance cover the expatriate should be encouraged to make his own provision.

20.30   The expatriate and his family members may have personal assets that may, for example, be subject to capital gains tax on disposal, or generate income that is subject to income tax. The employee's UK home may be let during the assignment; he may have savings accounts or money invested in other financial products; his wife may wish to take her car to the new host country; or he may own shares or benefit from a family trust. The assignment may have an effect on the UK tax due in respect of personal assets or income.

20.31   UK income tax is deducted from some interest and dividend payments before they are paid over. There may be practical difficulties with recovery of the tax deducted if, for example, there is no helpful double tax treaty to facilitate that. Similarly, the letting agent or tenant for the employee's UK home may be obliged to deduct tax before paying rent to the expatriate once he is overseas. It may be appropriate for the expatriate to transfer investments to different investment vehicles or to dispose of an asset before the assignment begins. There may also be opportunities for capital gains tax planning if the expatriate is able to dispose of an asset at a particular time before, during or after the assignment.

20.32   It is not usual for the employer to take responsibility for meeting the costs of financial and tax planning advice in relation to personal wealth and the employment documents should normally make this clear (see **7.86–7.90** and framework document **A2.4** at Appendix 2). However, the employee should be encouraged to seek independent tax/financial advice at his own expense, particularly if he considers the value of his UK assets or income is significant. UK tax returns may be required for every year of the assignment, for example, if the employee wishes to seek relief in relation to personal wealth. The employment documents should make clear that the costs of preparing tax returns will not normally be met by the employer if they relate solely to personal wealth.

20.33   The employee may also want to consider the impact of the assignment on any covenants or other arrangements to make charitable gifts.

EMPLOYMENT LAW

Selection for an assignment and discrimination

20.34　The opportunity to undertake an international assignment is likely to be seen as a positive advantage by many employees. To reduce the risk of allegations of discrimination the employer should apply objective non-discriminatory business criteria when selecting the most suitable employee for the assignment.

20.35　There is currently UK legislation protecting employees against direct and indirect discrimination on grounds of sex, marital and civil partnership status, sexual orientation, race, disability, age, religion or belief, fixed-term and part-time status.

20.36　The following are examples of challenges that may arise in the context of an expatriate assignment, see Chapter 12:

- women may find it difficult to work effectively in some Muslim countries or may be more exposed at an insecure location;
- homosexual activity may attract criminal penalties, including in some countries the death penalty;
- race and religion may affect the likelihood that the employee will be accepted by the local population and his commercial success in the role;
- immigration rules may be different for different nationalities, for example, employees who are nationals of countries at war or experiencing problems with terrorism may find it difficult to obtain immigration permission;
- religious employees may not be willing to work on the days normally worked in the host country (eg Christians may not be willing to work on a Sunday or Muslims on a Friday);
- some countries may not accept unmarried partners, civil partners or children that are not born within marriage;
- it may be difficult to find appropriate educational facilities for children with disabilities.

(See also Chapter 3 and Checklist **A1.3** at Appendix 1 regarding initial enquiries to try to identify (and resolve) potential challenges at the outset.)

20.37　There may be potential conflict between the employer's obligations to comply with UK discrimination legislation and the employer's views on the most suitable employee for the assignment. In practice, if there is a genuine business reason for not selecting an employee for a particular role selection is unlikely to cause a legal problem and, most likely, the employee, if he becomes aware of it, will accept the reason too.

20.38   Care should be taken though to ensure that decisions are not based on stereotypical assumptions about host country requirements or what the expatriate is likely to agree to. For example:

*   strict host country laws on homosexuality may not, in practice, prevent a homosexual employee from doing the job in the host country. An unwillingness to offer the job to the employee simply on the grounds of his homosexuality may amount to sexual orientation discrimination;

*   failure to consider the parent of a disabled child for an assignment on the assumption that the assignment would not be compatible with care for the child may amount to disability discrimination, particularly if the child could be cared for equally well in the host country.

Application of mandatory UK employment laws

20.39   Generally, an employee must be employed in Great Britain in order to benefit from statutory employment protection. This may mean that the employee often loses the protection of mandatory British employment laws once his assignment to the host country begins. (See **10.30–10.61** on the application of mandatory employment laws, particularly the *Serco v Lawson* 'posting exception' described at **10.59–10.60**.)

20.40   The fact that the employee may lose the protection of mandatory UK employment laws is unlikely to have a bearing on the structure of the assignment. The structure is far more likely to raise concern about immigration, tax or social security (see Chapter 6). The employee himself is unlikely to raise concerns either, though he may look for some comfort through his employment documents, for example, regarding what will happen at the end of the assignment.

Continuity of employment

20.41   If a UK employee asks about the effect of an overseas assignment on his continuity of employment the employer will need to understand the purpose of the question to answer it properly.

Continuity for internal/benefit purposes

20.42   The employee may be concerned about continuity for internal purposes, for example, the effect of the assignment on his ability to continue to participate in his current company benefit arrangements, either during the assignment or on his return to the UK when the assignment ends. See **20.66–20.85** below on pensions and **15.9–15.20** on share plans.

20.43   In practice, continuity is unlikely to be a significant concern for most other benefits as few will be based on length of service, particularly now that age discrimination legislation is in force in the UK. It may be relatively easy to provide comfort contractually in respect of most concerns, for example, in relation to the rate at which annual holiday accrues or company redundancy pay.

Statutory continuity of employment

20.44 UK employees who are assigned abroad may be concerned about continuity of employment for statutory purposes.

20.45 Suppose an English employee, Sarah, works for three years in England and then discusses a proposed two-year assignment to France with her UK-registered employer. Sarah wants to know how her continuity of employment will be affected by the assignment. Sarah asks whether she will 'lose out' and whether her employer will 'put her right' if she does.

20.46 In the UK, as in many other countries, some employment rights are subject to qualifying periods of employment. For example, an employee normally needs two years' 'continuous employment' to make a complaint of 'unfair dismissal' or receive Statutory Redundancy Pay (SRP). The amount of SRP to be paid also depends on the period of continuous employment.

20.47 Legislation sets out the way that 'continuity of employment' is determined for these purposes. See Chapter I of Part XIV of the Employment Rights Act 1996 (ERA 1996), particularly s 215 (employment abroad etc).

20.48 Transfer of employment from one employer to an 'associated employer' will not 'break' continuity of employment (see ERA 1996, s 218(6) generally and s 231 for a definition of 'associated employer').

20.49 A period of employment abroad with the same employer or an 'associated employer' (ERA 1996, s 215) will not break continuity. Service will accrue during the overseas assignment, ie it will 'count' as continuous employment, for the purposes of determining whether an employee has been employed for long enough to make an unfair dismissal complaint.

20.50 However, the standard rule for determining SRP entitlement is different. Any week in which both (a) the employee is employed outside Great Britain for any part of the week and (b) where secondary class 1 National Insurance contributions are not due does not 'count' towards the period of continuous employment. Although SRP is not usually high even if it is due, many UK company redundancy schemes offering more generous redundancy pay are based on the SRP formula. (Exceptions apply to those that are 'ordinarily resident' in Great Britain and to some seamen. Whilst the employee is 'ordinarily resident' in Great Britain weeks abroad will count towards continuous employment for SRP purposes.)

20.51 See 10.56–10.61 for an explanation of when the employee might be able to make other statutory claims whilst on assignment, or in connection with termination of an assignment. Eligibility to make a claim is different from accrual of continuous employment. The employee may accrue continuous employment during an assignment but still not be eligible to make a claim for SRP or unfair dismissal purposes whilst he is working abroad.

20.52 These are statutory rules. If the employee does not have the qualifying period of continuous employment for unfair dismissal or SRP purposes he will not be eligible to make claims to an English Employment Tribunal in that regard. The employer cannot give the employee back these statutory rights during the assignment or following return to the UK: he is either entitled to those rights in accordance with the legislation or he is not. The employer can, of course, always offer additional financial compensation, for example, by offering an expatriate severance pay that is broadly equivalent to a company redundancy scheme offered to UK-based employees who qualify for SRP. Care should be taken to ensure that the tax treatment of any payments to be made is clear. Typically tax equalisation or protection arrangements are not applied to expatriate severance arrangements and tax benefits equivalent to those available to ordinary UK-based employees are not promised. It may also be useful to ensure that the expatriate arrangements only provide for payments and do not include any promises related to procedures designed for UK employees that may conflict with host country mandatory laws.

20.53 In practice, expatriates rarely ask questions about qualifying service for UK statutory employment rights. Even if they do, the answers to those questions are unlikely to discourage an English employee from accepting an overseas assignment. Qualifying service for unfair dismissal purposes is not broken and continues to accrue. The employee's SRP would not be a large figure and the employer can easily provide comfort by making contractual promises in respect of payment on redundancy (ie company redundancy pay) to ensure the employee does not lose out substantially.

20.54 It will be important, though, to deal with the issues relating to benefit entitlements, particularly share plans and pension arrangements.

CULTURAL AWARENESS TRAINING

20.55 See 12.35 and 15.29–15.32 on cultural awareness generally.

20.56 Although the UK is a multi-cultural society and most employees are used to working with employees from different backgrounds, cultural awareness training is particularly important for employees sent from the UK. It is easy to wrongly assume that flexible or relaxed attitudes are the norm in other countries or that employees in the host country will have similar expectations about 'normal' behaviour as employees with a similar background working in the UK. Good manners can be important for ensuring that the business operates effectively and it will be difficult for the expatriate to behave appropriately if he does not know what people in the host country think is appropriate. See also Chapters 12 and 15 on cultural awareness more generally.

DATA PROTECTION

20.57   As an EU member state, the UK has been obliged to implement the Data Protection Directive. See **15.73–15.99** regarding the requirements of the Directive.

20.58   Implementation in the UK is through the Data Protection Act 1998 (further information is available at www.ico.gov.uk). UK compliance issues will always arise in relation to an expatriate assignment from the UK because the UK home company will inevitably need to process personal data (and probably sensitive personal data too) and send that data outside the UK.

20.59   If the home country also has data protection laws (as will be the case with assignments to EEA countries) there will also be a need to comply with that legislation.

20.60   At the time of writing we are anticipating introduction of the EU Data Protection Regulation (see Chapter 15). This could technically cease to apply on Brexit. However, currently it is anticipated that UK data protection laws will be maintained post-Brexit.

HEALTH

20.61   All employers have a duty to use reasonable skill and care to protect the safety of their employees. That obligation applies in relation to employees assigned to work abroad, as well as those employed to work in the UK in the ordinary way.

20.62   See **15.59–15.67** on health and safety more generally. Those concerns and practical suggestions apply to employees sent from the UK as well as to employees assigned from other countries.

20.63   There is quite a lot of UK-specific case-law in relation to death or injury suffered by employees assigned abroad. Employers must do what they reasonably can to identify and prevent or minimise risks to an employee's health and safety.

20.64   Employers should also be wary of pressing an employee to accept an apparently dangerous assignment, or an assignment that the employee himself considers dangerous. UK legislation offers special protection to employees who are dismissed or suffer a disadvantage because they have made health and safety or 'whistleblowing' complaints. If the relevant criteria are satisfied compensation for dismissal can be uncapped and a qualifying period of continuous employment will not be required.

20.65 See the Glossary at Appendix 3 on benefits of obtaining a European Health Insurance Card (EHIC). The potential impact of Brexit on EHICs is not clear.

PENSIONS

The employee wishes to remain in his UK pension plan

20.66 Employees who are sent from the UK to work abroad would often like to remain in their pre-assignment UK employer's pension plan. This may, for example, be for one or more of the following reasons.

- the plan offers substantial benefits. For example, the pre-assignment employer may offer a generous final salary pension plan. Equivalent pension arrangements may not be offered by the host company or other group companies;
- the UK pension plan is closed to new members. The employee may be concerned about whether he will be able to rejoin the UK pension plan if he has to leave it to take up the assignment abroad; and/or
- the employee may intend to retire and take his pension in the UK, and UK pension arrangements may be more convenient for him than overseas arrangements.

Abolition of the old '10-year rule'

20.67 A member of a UK pension plan who was sent to work abroad used to be able to stay in his UK pension plan (subject to conditions) for a maximum period of ten years. This old '10-year rule' has been removed and an expatriate can now potentially remain in a UK pension plan whilst working abroad for any length of time.

Key concerns for an employee who wants to stay in a UK pension plan

20.68 An employee who wishes to remain in his UK pension plan, and his employer, should take care to ensure that:

- he remains eligible to participate in the UK pension plan under the plan rules (see **20.69–20.71** below);
- the implications of the 'cross-border activities' provisions have been considered (see **20.72–20.75** below); and
- tax implications have been considered (see **20.79–20.81** below).

Plan rules

20.69 Every pension plan has its own rules, normally attached to a Trust Deed. Those rules will include criteria that should be used to determine whether an employee is eligible to participate in the pension plan. For example, an employee is only likely to be able to participate in an occupational pension plan if he is an employee of a particular employer, or specified employers (usually specified group companies). This means that if the employee is assigned to work abroad, the identity of his employer during his assignment may be critical to whether he is able to continue to participate in the UK pension plan.

20.70 This is unlikely to be an issue where there is a home country employer as the employee's employer will not change during the assignment. However, the position may be different if the employee is to be employed by the host company during the assignment. If host company employees are not permitted to join the UK plan, and it is not possible or cost effective to amend the plan rules to allow them to participate, it may not be possible for the employee to remain in his current UK home company scheme.

20.71 Sometimes, if the employee also maintains a 'residual employment' relationship with his home company the residual contract may confirm the arrangements to apply at the end of the current assignment such as pension augmentation. Alternatively, and this may be more efficient, the host company may be able to adhere to the UK pension plan.

Cross-border activities

Assignment to an EEA country

20.72 If the employee is employed by a 'European employer' during his assignment then the plan may only be able to accept pension contributions from the European employer if various procedural requirements are met. A 'European employer' is, broadly, an employer who employs people in a non-UK EEA country (see the Glossary at Appendix 3 for a list of current EEA countries) and wishes to make contributions to the UK plan. UK defined benefit plans that accept contributions from a European employer are also subject to strict funding requirements.

20.73 However, it may be possible to avoid stringent conditions if the employee falls into an exemption that applies to 'seconded workers'. An employee will only be a seconded worker if he:

- is posted abroad for a 'limited period'; and
- expects afterwards either to return to the UK to work for his pre-assignment employer or to immediately retire.

20.74 If it is intended that the employee should be a 'seconded worker' then it is usually helpful to confirm facts that demonstrate that the qualifying conditions are satisfied. This could be done either in:

- the employment contract (or assignment letter confirming variations to a previous contract) if the pre-assignment UK employer will continue to employ the employee during the assignment (ie if there is a home country employment arrangement); or
- a residual employment agreement with the home company if the employer will be another entity registered in a non-UK EEA country (ie if there is a host country employment arrangement).

In either case, specialist pensions advice would be needed before the documents are drafted.

Assignment to a non-EEA country

20.75 If the employee is assigned to a non-EEA country different rules will apply. Whether the employee may participate in the UK plan will depend on the plan rules and stricter (rather than the normal) funding requirements will not apply.

Who should make pension contributions

20.76 Pension contributions may be made by the employee.

20.77 Additional pension contributions are normally made by the employee's employer. This means that pension contributions should normally be made by the UK home company if it is to remain the employer during the assignment or by the host company if there is a host country employment arrangement. If pension contributions are made by another entity (eg the home company if the host company is to be the employer during the assignment) then the costs of the pension contributions should be recharged to the employee's employer. The arrangements for recharging those costs should be confirmed in an inter-company expatriate supply agreement and should be reflected in the companies' accounts.

20.78 Decisions regarding the company to make the payments to the plan and any recharging arrangements should be made in the light of specialist pensions advice.

Tax implications of remaining in the UK plan

Tax relief on pension contributions

20.79 If the employee is assigned from the UK to work in another EU country, arguably the EU host country tax authorities should allow tax relief on pension contributions made to the UK plan by the employer or employee. However, the legal position is not entirely clear, especially where the UK pension plan does not meet the requirements that pension plans in the host country are required to meet. In practice, the host country may not allow the tax relief.

20.80 If the employee is assigned from the UK to work outside the EU it may be more difficult to obtain tax relief, although it may sometimes be possible to obtain tax relief under a double tax treaty.

Tax on drawing benefits

20.81 Tax should also be considered in relation to drawings from pension. This is because the host country may seek to charge tax on drawings, even if the employee has left the host country before he draws his pension.

Employee joins plan in host country

20.82 Whether the employee can join a host country pension plan will depend on the plan rules and the laws of the host country. This is unlikely to be a problem in the EU. However, the vesting period under the plan rules should be considered carefully (ie the period during which the employee must remain a member of the plan before his benefits will vest).

Potential disadvantages

20.83 The plan may not offer the same benefits as the UK plan the employee participated in before his assignment began.

20.84 Even if the host country plan is as or more favourable than the employee's pre-assignment UK plan:

- the employee's UK plan benefits will be frozen (ie if the pre-assignment UK plan was a final salary plan the benefits will not take account of future pay increases);
- if the Host Country plan is a final salary plan, the future benefits under that plan after the employee leaves the Host Country will not take account of future pay increases.

Income tax

20.85 The employee is likely to find it possible to obtain host country tax relief in respect of contributions to the plan but that will, of course, depend on the tax laws that apply to the assignment and those that apply when benefits are drawn.

Employee joins plan in country other than the UK or the host country

20.86 The employee may consider making contributions to a plan based in another country (ie in neither the UK nor the host country). This may offer some potential advantages:

- the plan can be based in a country with favourable tax etc laws;

- the employee can potentially remain in the plan through subsequent assignments to other countries;
- more flexibility may be available in relation to the drawing of benefits (eg the strict laws in the UK on the minimum age at which pension can be drawn may be avoided);
- a stable currency for the plan can normally be chosen.

20.87 However, the current host country, and/or future host countries may not allow income tax relief on contributions to the plan. Depending on the relevant location(s) there may be further adverse tax consequences.

Transfer payments

20.88 The employee will probably only want to make transfer payments from a UK pension plan to an overseas pension plan (known as the 'Receiving Scheme') if he intends to retire abroad. He might then wish to make a transfer payment to a plan based in the host country or in some other country. There are some potential advantages to making a transfer payment out of a UK pension plan, for example:

- the Receiving Scheme may allow more flexibility regarding the drawing of benefits;
- there may be tax advantages, for example, if the employee retires abroad, it might be difficult for him to draw benefits from the UK pension plan without UK income tax first being deducted;
- the employee may be less vulnerable to currency fluctuations when the benefits are drawn.

20.89 Transfer from a UK-registered pension plan to a Receiving Scheme abroad will incur heavy UK tax penalties unless the Receiving Scheme is a 'qualifying recognised overseas pension scheme' (QROPS). Note proposed changes to tax laws may make this option very expensive going forward. Specialist up to date pensions advice is strongly recommended in respect of all proposed transfers including to QROPS.

20.90 A transfer payment even to a QROPS may incur a significant tax charge going forward.

OVERVIEW

20.91 Considerations to apply to employees assigned to the UK are in many ways similar to those applicable to employees assigned abroad from other jurisdictions. The above is intended to highlight some UK-specific concerns.

CHAPTER 21

US PERSPECTIVES

INTRODUCTION

21.1 This chapter is written especially for US employers sending US employees abroad, and their advisers. Experienced US mobility specialists may wish to skip this chapter as it is primarily intended to highlight some potential differences that may take US professionals who are new to international HR by surprise. Please note that the author has no US law expertise, this chapter is not a substitute for independent, up to date, US law advice and that this chapter is not intended to cover the US legal aspects of international assignments.

EMPLOYMENT 'AT WILL' AND EMPLOYMENT CONTRACTS

21.2 Employees working overseas will almost always have an employment contract and are likely to be protected against 'unfair' dismissal and changes to employment terms. Most jurisdictions do not accept that an employee can be employed without an employment contract. It is worth bearing the following in mind:

- Outside the US, even where there is no employment contract document, an employee will generally still have an employment contract. The terms of that employment contract will just be less clear if they are not written down.

- 'At will' employment is not generally recognised outside the US. If documents are drafted to confirm 'at will' employment for employees working outside the US, a notice period will typically be imposed automatically by law. Minimum notice periods are rarely something that an employer can 'contract out' of.

- Most expatriate benefits are likely to be regarded as 'contractual' regardless of whether they are documented.

- Employment contracts offer an opportunity to set employee expectations, reduce employer risk and retain some flexibility. If the default position is an undocumented employee-friendly contract it is usually better, from the employer's perspective, to document the preferred terms and expressly reserve some discretion.

- In many cases an employment contract will be required for submission to public authorities, eg, with an application for immigration clearance. Employees assigned to or from the US will, naturally, expect to see their entitlements confirmed in writing before they commit to relocation.

- The Employment Particulars Directive, see **8.37**, has been implemented in all EU member states and requires that certain employment terms be documented for employees working in the EU. In practice, these obligations are not particularly onerous as the terms that must be documented are terms that most employers would naturally choose to document for an employee travelling overseas anyway, such as salary, place of work etc.

MANDATORY EMPLOYMENT LAWS

21.3 'Mandatory' employment laws will typically apply to employees who physically work in a particular jurisdiction, and there will usually be little that an employer can do to avoid that, even if it wants to. Mandatory host requirements might include, for example, laws covering mandatory sick pay, maternity leave and pay, overtime, holidays, pension provision, contribution to an unemployment fund, or medical cover. The principle will not be a surprise but the range of mandatory terms that could apply might be, for example, compulsory '13th month' payments may be required. Host requirements may also sometimes be imposed in unexpected ways, eg, by 'collective agreement'.

COLLECTIVE AGREEMENTS AND WORKS COUNCILS

21.4 Watch out for jurisdictions where an employee may be automatically covered by a collective agreement even where no trade union is recognised. The way collective agreements work varies substantially across jurisdictions. A collective agreement may sometimes impose compulsory minimum employment (or severance) terms without the employer even knowing that it exists.

21.5 It is usually best to check for collective agreements at an early stage. The host country adviser will usually need some explanation of business activity, the employee's job title and status and location of the place of work.

21.6 It is important to understand that mandatory laws imposed by collective agreement do not typically apply to all staff in the same way, even within the same organisation. By their nature they can be patchy in application, eg applying only to senior managers in the chemical industry in a particular state. They can also change without the employer's knowledge. Those changes may fall out of line with a static employment contract, so checking that assumed terms are up to date can be important, eg prior to termination.

21.7 Please also refer to the Glossary at Appendix 3 for a more detailed explanation of the differences between types of 'works council' and other arrangements for employee representation. It is also worth highlighting that very different expectations regarding cooperation and consensus can apply in different places. Failure to seek guidance on local 'norms' in addition to minimum legal requirements can have a very significant impact on outcomes, not just at the time but also, for example, when cooperation is needed from the same representatives in the future. See Chapter 15 on ongoing management and Chapter 16 on ending the assignment.

APPLICATION OF US LAWS TO INTERNATIONAL ASSIGNEES

21.8 Just because an employee is covered by one country's laws that does not mean that the employee will not be covered by another country's laws. The legal rules on applicable laws are complicated and vary between jurisdictions. Employees sometimes enjoy no protection at all or the best of both Worlds. This is something that should be checked for the particular jurisdictions before documents are finalised.

21.9 There is a tendency for overseas employers to prefer to choose their own country's (or State's) laws to govern a contract. In practice, this may not be the best choice (see Chapter 10 on applicable laws).

21.10 Some US laws may have extraterritorial application, eg laws relating to bribery and corruption, modern slavery, equality etc may potentially apply to US businesses and nationals overseas. Even though local Host Country mandatory employment laws may apply, see **21.3** above, that will not automatically release a US employer from compliance with US laws. Employers should take care to seek US Home Country legal advice in addition to Host Country advice. Familiar laws can apply in unfamiliar ways to US employees working overseas.

BARGAINING POWER AND DISCRETION

21.11 Employment contracts are not commercial contracts. In most jurisdictions, as with the US, the unequal bargaining power of employer and employee is recognised and there are many areas where public policy will override employer preferences. What an employer offers will not necessarily be what the employer is required to deliver.

21.12 Particular care is needed with discretion in some jurisdictions. For example, making clear that a benefit such as bonus or a particular kind of medical cover is discretionary may not be effective in some jurisdictions. In addition, some types of discretion commonly permitted abroad may have adverse consequences for US employees, eg it may not be appropriate for US tax payers to participate in some overseas long-term incentive plans.

TERMINATION OF EMPLOYMENT, NON-COMPETES ETC

21.13 Restrictions on the way employees can be treated on and after termination of employment are a common theme across jurisdictions. It is worth checking, for example, to see whether there are any special restrictions on the non-competes that are permitted (see Chapter 11 on competition) and whether payments must be made to retain them. See also Chapter 16 on severance, particularly comments on freedom to dismiss.

21.14 It is important to appreciate that getting termination processes wrong (eg failing to obtain approval of a severance package by a labour court where this is required) and/or not having sufficient reason for dismissal could have very significant consequences. In some circumstances, the employee may be compulsorily reinstated or a dismissal may be treated as void. Getting this wrong can be very expensive.

US employers should check exit costs particularly carefully to reduce the risk of nasty surprises.

TAX

21.15 Unlike domestic employees, internationally mobile employees will typically be subject to income tax obligations in more than one jurisdiction. This is not something that is peculiar to US citizens, but the way that this happens for US nationals (and green card holders) is different as US tax payers are, in principle, taxed on their Worldwide income regardless of residence.

21.16 US employees, and their employers, will need to be particularly conscious of compliance obligations when working internationally. US tax payers who are assigned abroad should consider seeking independent tax advice *before* they leave the US, as relocation can have adverse effects, eg on US investments or trusts, from departure even if the employee starts work at a later date.

21.17 Some jurisdictions do not have the same tax year as the US, eg the UK tax year runs from 6 April, and not 1 January, each year.

SOCIAL SECURITY

21.18 Social security rates applicable outside the US, particularly Continental European employer rates, can be very high. Rate differentials may also prompt greater attention by public authorities to compliance.

21.19 The financial impact of additional social security contributions on both employers and employees should not be underestimated, nor should the value attributed to the benefits that social security contributions afford.

POTENTIAL PENALTIES

21.20 Taking time to think about the history and cultural expectations of a given location may help make sense of many of the differences in legislation. For example:

- freedom of association and trade unionism may be strongly associated with democracy;
- using anonymous 'whistleblowing hotlines' may not be acceptable in a country that has experienced occupation;
- attitudes to 'neutrality' at work may vary widely;
- criminal penalties may potentially apply to some compliance failures, including sometimes, personally, to directors.

GET THE EMPLOYER RIGHT

21.21 The identity of an expatriate's employer can make a huge difference to assignment costs. Make sure that the practical benefit arrangements and the way they are documented support the identity of the preferred employer. As a rule of thumb, US employers often prefer to retain US employees in the employment of a US employer rather than transfer employment to a local company. Please refer to Chapter 4 for more discussion of factors that may be relevant to this.

BENEFITS

21.22 Benefits for expatriates are expensive. Be clear about why they are being offered so that costs can be assessed appropriately. For example:

- for compliance, eg, paid vacation, sickness or maternity leave;
- to persuade the employee to go, eg, by paying American school fees;
- to reduce uncertainty about the value of remuneration, eg, by offering tax equalisation, exchange rate protection or cost of living allowances (see Chapter 7);
- for security, eg, by providing a car and driver and forbidding use of public transport;
- to 'put the employee right', eg, by covering relocation and repatriation or additional housing costs;
- to reduce distraction from the job, eg, by providing home search support.

Sometimes employers decide that cash is a better alternative, eg, because it encourages the right attitude. (See Chapter 7 on documenting expatriate reward). Arrangements for medical cover may be worth more attention.

Medical cover

21.23 Typically, expatriates to be assigned abroad from the US will be offered international medical cover, and adequate medical cover may be a host country immigration requirement. Care should be taken to ensure that employees are clear about the extent of cover, particularly whether the insurance provided will cover them on home leave in the US or if they wish to return home to the US to have a baby. This may be a particular issue for US assignees because of the cost and quality of US healthcare – in practice more expensive cover may be required. US nationals may also potentially be covered by host country state medical care options, which can sometimes be of high quality. Care should be taken on termination of the assignment or employment to ensure that cover applicable on the employee's return home to the US is managed appropriately.

Vacation

21.24 US nationals are often delighted by the additional holiday entitlement they may enjoy outside the US, eg a minimum of four weeks' holiday per year in the EU, sometimes longer. The way in which holiday is used may often differ too. For example, in Europe holiday should not be used for absence due to illness or vice versa. US employers are sometimes surprised too by European attitudes to taking substantial holiday, ie most will expect to take their full entitlement each year and not to work during their holiday.

DON'T FORGET THE FAMILY

21.25 For example, schooling, housing and flights home may be critical. Never underestimate the importance of 'buy in' from the employee's family or the real value of relatively low cost or informal benefits, like assistance with obtaining a work permit for a partner or social support from colleagues. International assignments frequently fail – sometimes expensively – because families' needs cannot be met. For example, American families are often keen to ensure that their children attend American schools even in English-speaking host countries to minimise disruption to their studies. This may affect choice of accommodation. There are many commercial and voluntary organisations who support US nationals abroad, see for example 'American in Britain' magazine.

EQUALITY

21.26 Expatriate benefits are typically linked to 'home' country and family. See Chapter 12. Make sure equality, and potential mitigation strategies, are properly considered before the package is finalised, as exposure to potential US litigation may present greater risk.

THE FUTURE

21.27 Sometimes the most valuable thing a lawyer can do is to focus minds on the future, including 'worst case scenarios'. What happens if host laws change; if benefit costs increase, when the assignment ends? Anticipation can make a difference to the financial outcome. Who will bear the costs of breaking a long-term lease? Does the reason for termination of the assignment make a difference? It is important to consider the impact on the expatriate personally. For example, does a broad tax equalisation policy cover the employee for the impact of surprise future inheritance, relocation post termination or the detrimental impact of the assignment on the employee's rights under a previous employer's share plan? If not, is it worth making the scope of the promise clear from the outset? This is not just about managing potential exit costs or reducing the risk of dispute. It is about supporting a positive and trustful employment relationship. For US employers this should not be a surprise at all but anticipating change, potential disputes etc becomes a more commercially significant issue in jurisdictions where dismissal, and changing contract terms, is more difficult.

ARBITRATION

21.28 It is common for US employment documents to provide for arbitration and other similar dispute resolution arrangements. Documents prepared for use in other jurisdictions rarely include such clauses. Arbitration clauses are commonly included in commercial and other agreements to help make dispute resolution quicker, cheaper and/or more certain. However, inclusion of this type of clause in expatriate employment documents typically has the opposite effect from that intended. For more precise analysis of the pros and cons it is best to look at the specific jurisdictions. However, it may be worth bearing in mind that:

- many non-US jurisdictions have relatively cheap, quick and sure public mechanisms for resolving employment disputes, and these are often much cheaper to engage with than US-style arbitration arrangements;

- many non-US jurisdictions may have laws that ensure that local employment legislation, and access to local dispute resolution processes, cannot be ousted by contract provisions (effectively making arbitration decisions non-binding);

- many non-US jurisdictions (including the UK) impose restrictions on the way that severance agreements can be effectively concluded (requiring, eg, advice to be given to employees in a particular way, approval by a labour court or public authority, a particular form of document or conclusion of the agreement in a particular way) and this may sometimes be difficult to achieve through arbitration;

- the uncertain impact of arbitration clauses may make resolution by informal negotiation more, rather than less, difficult.

AMERICAN ENGLISH

21.29 English is used in a variety of different ways in different jurisdictions. For example, English is commonly used to prepare legal documents in Canada, England, Ireland, Australia, India and America but different vocabulary may be used in each, or more confusingly the same vocabulary may be used to mean different things. The Glossary set out at Appendix 3 is intended to assist.

In addition, writing styles can be quite different. Anyone who has read Steinbeck or Hemmingway and then a document prepared by an American lawyer can appreciate that these differences can be apparent within jurisdictions as well as between them.

21.30 From a UK perspective, the key drafting style differences between US and UK lawyers are that:

• US lawyers tend to use much longer sentences than UK lawyers;

• US lawyers tend to include multiple examples and lists intended to cover different scenarios whereas UK lawyers tend to avoid this approach; and

• US employment documents tend to focus on different things, for example benefits and proprietary interests are likely to receive more attention in the US.

Overseas lawyers can be reluctant to comment on differences of style and will instead tend to focus on specific legal points and the specific questions asked. Direct discussion can, however, help keep costs down. Sometimes it will be better to retain the US drafting style and sometimes it will be cheaper, or safer, to start afresh using host country drafting as the base. (For example, starting afresh will usually work better if US post termination restrictions (non-competes) are to be adapted for use in the UK but US confidentiality terms will often work well in the UK with minor tweaks.) The important thing is to make an appropriate decision on the best starting point at an early stage.

GETTING THE DOCUMENTS RIGHT

21.31 Expatriates generally need detailed employment documents, not just to protect employer and employee, but because public authorities in a variety of jurisdictions may refer to them, eg, labour inspectorates, immigration officials, tax, social security or pension authorities. Clear documents will naturally help with those interactions. More importantly, clear documents help manage employee – and family – expectations, and increase the likelihood of a happy and successful new assignment. This is, of course, the same for all international assignments, not just assignments from the US.

CHAPTER 22

EMPLOYEE PERSPECTIVES

INTRODUCTION

22.1 When negotiating any contract, it is important to understand the other party's position. The issues that employers and employees must deal with when settling the terms of a domestic employment contract are generally two sides of the same coin. In practice, most domestic contract terms are consistent between employees within an organisation (or between employees at a certain level within the organisation). Substantial negotiation tends to revolve round a few key 'movables', like salary or 'on target' bonus levels, where the employer and employee typically have opposing commercial interests.

22.2 With expatriate contracts the value attributed to terms by the parties is generally less symmetrical, and less closely linked to the commercial cost of delivering remuneration and benefits. There are more variables and expatriate employees often have more bargaining power than 'local hires' – and higher expectations that their demands will be met. 'Special deals' are common.

22.3 This gives more opportunity for creative negotiation, and advisers who are aware of the options, and of what is 'normal' and achievable in a particular context can help their clients get a better deal.

22.4 Those advising employees should, ideally, also read the more detailed earlier chapters focusing on the employer's perspective. (Similarly, those advising employers would do well to consider the employee perspectives highlighted below.) This chapter is not intended to repeat the detail set out in earlier chapters but highlights some things that employees, and their advisers, may wish to focus on particularly.

WHY THIS HOST COUNTRY AND WHY THIS ROLE?

22.5 It is worth reflecting on why the employee wants to do this role in this particular place. Does he want to join family or friends, enhance career progression, or simply to earn more money? How long will it take to achieve those goals? What are the employee's other options? The employee's motivation will, naturally, have an impact on the employment terms he is prepared to accept. It would also be helpful for the employee to understand the business objectives outlined in Chapter 2, and particularly whether he is the best, or only, candidate for the role.

FAMILY

22.6 A decision to accept a new role abroad typically has greater impact on family members than a domestic role change. Does the employee have a partner who wants to work, a child about to take exams or dependent parents? What will happen to their home? What sort of accommodation will the employee need in the host country, and how much will that cost? Does the employee already have financial commitments, eg to a home country mortgage or school fees, and, if so, what currency are those commitments tied to?

22.7 Ideally, the employee should think carefully about family circumstances and the real financial and practical impact of the proposed move on all family members as early as possible. It is helpful to differentiate between family 'deal breakers' such as children's schooling or a partner's career, and family preferences where concessions could be made, eg in relation to housing. As always, prioritising goals upfront can help ensure that the key objectives are achieved.

22.8 When trying to identify and prioritise preferences, it makes sense, where possible, to ask everyone who will be affected for their views. The priority given by family members to different needs can sometimes be surprising. Family 'buy in' (particularly a partner's buy in) to compromises made is also likely to be much more important for an expatriate assignment – and ideally this should endure through the assignment.

22.9 The employee should take time to try to identify personal and family circumstances that the employer may not initially focus on. For example, issues relating to marital status, potential relationship breakdown, health, pregnancy or custody of children that may have a bearing on whether the assignment can happen or may make things difficult.

22.10 It is important to think ahead, eg, the employee's family circumstances are likely to change over time, if only because children grow older.

22.11 Things that an employer might do to help with family circumstances include, eg, provision of:

- immigration support for family members;
- accommodation suitable for the family, and related support;
- health cover for the whole family;
- support for education (pre-school, school and/or tertiary education);
- contribution to 'home leave' expenses;
- support for a 'trailing partner', eg assistance with local job search;
- help with settling in, eg with expatriate networking, club memberships, language training etc.

See also Chapter 7 on expatriate benefits.

22.12 While family may be of great importance to the employee, employers are sometimes limited in their ability to help directly. (See further below and Chapter 12 on equality.)

NET PAY

22.13 Net remuneration and tax are key issues for expatriates to focus on. Expatriates should be clear about the real impact of any tax-related promises and these should ideally be clearly confirmed in writing. See Chapter 7. Whilst tax equalisation commitments may not always be offered by employers, all expatriates are likely to have cross-border tax compliance obligations and will require specialist support. It is normal for the employer to recognise common interest in the employee's compliance and to contribute to the costs of securing relevant tax advice, eg the costs of preparing tax returns for relevant jurisdictions. This may be particularly important for the first and last tax years of the assignment when tax compliance is likely to be more complicated.

22.14 Note that, from an employee's perspective, tax equalisation is only likely to be beneficial if the employee requires certainty on net income or the employee is moving to a higher tax jurisdiction. If the employee is moving to a jurisdiction where tax rates are lower, tax equalisation may, in practice, mean lower net pay. It is not always helpful to ask for tax equalisation.

22.15 Currency movements and cost of living differentials will also have an impact on the net value of remuneration. See 7.68–7.75 for explanation of some of the employee's options for securing comfort from the employer.

22.16 Where the employer is less sophisticated, or less willing to accommodate special or complex arrangements, it may still be possible to negotiate increased remuneration to ensure that the risk of negative currency movements etc is reduced sufficiently. Note that if net pay comfort is rigid the risk of future changes, eg to currency or tax rates, falls on the employee.

HOW WILL THE FUTURE LOOK?

22.17 Taking account of the needs of the job, and the employee's personal situation, how is the future likely to look? How easy would it be to find another job when the assignment is over, or if things don't work out? Would a big currency shift change the employee's perspective? How are the expatriate's family circumstances likely to change? Is another child likely and will educational needs change during the assignment? It is worth weighing up both the risk of the event occurring and the likely impact if it does.

22.18 For example, death of the expatriate might be an unlikely event but should be planned for if there is dependent family. Typically, employers will not meet the costs of reviewing wills, but it would be prudent for the employee to seek his own independent specialist advice if residence will change. It would be sensible to review tax implications and to consider practicalities like the appointment of guardians and interim arrangements to assist the family. At a very basic level, ensuring that appropriate contact information and documents are easily accessible to dependents may help.

(See also below on anticipating the end of the assignment.)

PERSONAL FINANCIAL SITUATION

22.19 Employers of expatriates will usually consider the financial impact of an assignment on a 'typical' expatriate. However, they are unlikely to have insight into the employee's detailed personal financial circumstances. The employee should consider his own circumstances more carefully and seek advice from appropriately qualified people. For example:

- joining an overseas pension or incentive plan could potentially have an impact on US tax obligations;

- moving overseas may have an impact on trust funds or taxation of existing personal investments;

- incentives awarded by a previous employer might vest whilst the employee is overseas;

- the employee, or a family member, may anticipate inheriting money from a relative during the assignment.

Independent financial advice should be sought from properly qualified advisers as early as possible and, in any case, before the assignment begins or the individual or family members relocate. Ideally, financial affairs would be considered broadly to include, eg, wills, any pre-nuptial agreement and other related personal matters. (See **15.68–15.71**.)

IMMIGRATION AND OTHER CHECKS

22.20 Employers in most jurisdictions must make immigration checks, and most prudent employers will insist on additional checks, eg of qualifications, references or criminal records. Employees should expect to be required to produce original documents to the employer, and to third parties in order access some essential services. Employees should also be aware that some jurisdictions insist on more intrusive health checks, eg HIV testing.

UK and Brexit

22.21 EU employees accepting new employments in the UK should consider whether they are likely to meet UK immigration criteria if the employee's EU passport is no longer sufficient post Brexit. If the employee cannot continue to meet immigration conditions he will not be able to live and work in the UK. However, the end of a right to work in the UK on the basis of EU nationality alone would not necessarily mean an end to working in the UK. Many nationals of non-EU countries already work in the UK. Immigration laws are changing rapidly but it might be worth checking to see whether the employee could meet other current criteria, eg because of role, family circumstances or investor status. The employee might be able to take steps now to improve his position. For example, is the employee eligible to apply for an additional UK passport, and if so should the employee apply now? The employee could also ask the employer to make contractual commitments to make things easier if immigration status is lost. Employers who have already secured an UK immigration 'sponsor license' may find it easier to help. (See Chapter 18 on global mobility and Brexit.)

HOW CAN THE EMPLOYER HELP?

22.22 Some employers will help, but this may depend, eg on the employer's scale, the employee's seniority and value to the business, the employer's experience of managing mobility and whether there is a big pool of candidates. Ie, this very much depends on the employee's bargaining power. A highly paid senior employee who has been recruited for unique fit is much more likely to secure concessions.

22.23 'Expat terms' designed to give comfort to those accepting overseas roles might include those highlighted above, for example:

- terms designed to reduce the impact of currency fluctuations;
- contractual tax equalisation promises, cost of living allowances etc designed to protect net pay;
- assistance with immigration and tax compliance;
- benefits to help mitigate the impact of a move on personal life, such as help with schools, accommodation or health cover; or
- reimbursement of relocation (and perhaps more importantly) repatriation expenses.

UK

22.24 With Brexit looming, it seems likely that negotiating positions will shift for employees accepting new roles in the UK, particularly where there are skills shortages. Some EU nationals who might previously have been happy with UK 'local terms' may be able to secure more comfort.

WHAT IS THE EMPLOYER REALLY OFFERING?

22.25 Employment terms are usually initially discussed informally, but the reality will not be clear until proposed terms are confirmed in writing. The employee should check the employment documents provided carefully. The employee will need to understand the employment terms that will apply if he accepts. The employee will also need clarity about pre-conditions, e g immigration, reference and other checks. Normally it is better not to give up a current role until the employee has a signed contract in hand and is confident that any outstanding conditions can be met. Senior employees, particularly those in bonus-driven roles, should take particular care to check incentive terms. All employees should check terms relating to termination carefully, see further below.

WHAT WILL HAPPEN AT THE END?

22.26 The most important piece of advice lawyers can usually give on a new contract is often to focus on what happens at the end, before the contract is signed. Not just at the natural end, but if things go wrong before that time.

22.27 What will happen if the project is completed early? If the employee can no longer rely on an EU passport to work in the UK? If school doesn't work out for the employee's children? If the employee needs to end a rental agreement relating to host country accommodation prematurely? If the employee or his partner becomes pregnant?

22.28 What could the employee do now to make the outcome better? Should the employee check the employee's lease for early termination penalties? Would a long 'notice period' in the employee's employment contract help? Should bonus goals be adjusted? Would private medical cover help? Does the employee's contract confirm that repatriation expenses will be paid or that the employee will be offered another job if he loses host country immigration permission? Will those promises really 'put the employee right'?

22.29 Typically repatriation expenses for a 'fair' long term assignment will mirror those offered on relocation. The contract should clarify the detail of the repatriation package, bearing in mind that the employer may be less willing to help at that time. See 7.57–7.64.

CLAW-BACK

22.30 If assignments fail, financial consequences can be severe for employer and employee. For example, there may be long-term commitments to accommodation that the employee can no longer occupy. Relocation and repatriation expenses, and the costs of immigration and tax advice, may be 'wasted'. Employers are increasingly seeking to recover lost costs from employees whose assignments end prematurely. They may seek to do so by including 'claw-back' clauses in the employment documents. Even if the principle is accepted, and lawful, employees should check the terms of repayment carefully. For example:

- What are the potential figures?

- Do the sums to be repaid genuinely reflect costs and losses to the employer or do they amount to a (potentially unenforceable) penalty?
- How would any disputes be dealt with?
- Is there any legal protection available under applicable laws?
- When would the employee be required to return the money?
- Is there provision for 'pro-rata' reduction of the sums to be repaid to reflect the period already spent in the host country and what are the trigger dates?
- What happens if the assignment ends unfairly or the employee is 'constructively dismissed'?
- Will currency movement have an impact?
- Will any tax already paid on amounts to be repaid be recoverable?

COULD THE JOB BE DONE ANOTHER WAY?

22.31 Other options might work better for the employee, his family and the employer. Where there is more than one group company, which should employ the employee? Could the employee stay in the employee's home country and work remotely? Could the employee's family stay at home whilst the employee commutes for work? (See Chapter 14.) Could the business itself, or part of it, be relocated to the host country?

HOW EASY WOULD IT BE FOR THE EMPLOYER TO GIVE THE EMPLOYEE WHAT THEY ARE LOOKING FOR?

22.32 Extra comfort and alternative arrangements could be more difficult and expensive for the employer than may immediately appear to be the case. For example:

- The employer may be constrained by discrimination rules: it may not be possible to accommodate personal circumstances lawfully, eg to give the employee better benefits than a 'local hire' in the same role just because the employee needs to relocate family (see Chapter 12 on equality).
- Some alternative employment structures can be surprisingly expensive to implement. For example, doing some kinds of work 'remotely' in the employee's home country instead of the UK might expose the employer to additional corporation tax or social security bills (see Chapter 14 on business visitors, international commuters and virtual assignees).
- Many larger employers have policies designed to promote consistency, contain costs or help with efficient management. It is usually much easier to secure concessions that do not entail a breach of established 'policy'. (See Chapter 9 on assignment policies.)

- It is often easier to secure an increase to 'less visible' remuneration, such as a bonus, than to secure additional benefits, such as a car. (See Chapter 7 on expatriate reward.)

FIXING THE CONTRACT AND MANAGING COST

22.33 Typically, it is best to let the employer incur the time and expense of structuring the employment relationship and documenting proposed terms, or at least to do the bulk of the work first.

22.34 Those advising individuals will normally wait for documents to be produced before commenting on any problem areas. However, there are often key personal 'deal breakers' that are worth raising early, before the employer has expended too much time and expense on preparing documents. For example, if the employee will not relocate unless an accompanying partner can work in the host location it is usually worth pointing this out at an early stage so that immigration constraints can be checked first. It is important that the employee takes the initiative in raising this sort of personal issue early as in many cases employers will either be reluctant to ask intrusive personal questions or will not think to ask.

22.35 It may be possible for the employee to secure a contribution from the employer towards the costs of independent advice and in many cases advice is offered directly by advisers engaged by the employer. It is important that the employee understands who an adviser's client is so that he can decide whether additional independent comment is appropriate. The basis on which expatriate tax and immigration advice is provided may be unclear, although most professionals will provide a proper engagement letter clearly identifying the client and clarifying fee responsibilities on request.

TIPS FOR THOSE ADVISING INDIVIDUALS

22.36 See also the checklist at **A1.4**.

22.37 Time spent by the employer and employee anticipating and exploring each other's needs is likely to lead to arrangements that work better for everyone. The party who prepares best for negotiation usually gets the better bargain.

APPENDIX 1

CHECKLISTS

INTRODUCTION

A1.1 The following checklists are intended to help the person preparing the employment documents to gather together information that is likely to be needed to draft the documents.

A1.2 The following checklists are included in this Appendix:

- quick review of employment documents for employers (**A1.3**);
- quick review of employment documents for employees (**A1.4**);
- request to host country adviser for preliminary advice on viability (**A1.5**);
- issues to consider before drafting expatriate documents (**A1.6**);
- information for short-term home employer assignment letter (assumes the underlying home employment contract is satisfactory) (**A1.7**);
- information for long-term home employer employment contract (assumes the pre-assignment home employment contract will be replaced) (**A1.8**);
- information for residual contract with home company (where host company will be employer) (**A1.9**);
- information for inter-company expatriate supply agreement (**A1.10**);
- information for commuter assignment (**A1.11**); and
- information for severance agreement (**A1.12**).

See also **8.57** for suggestions about special terms for dual employment contracts.

QUICK REVIEW OF EMPLOYMENT DOCUMENTS FOR EMPLOYERS

A1.3

- **Employer:** Who is the intended employer? Is the correct name and registered address given? Is the paperwork consistent with the assumed employment status? Are the facts consistent?

- **Documents:** Do you have the right documents with the right parties? Is there an inter-company agreement? Are there any more contract documents, policies, letters or emails?

- **Advice:** Have the documents been checked by relevant advisers, including from income tax, social security, immigration and employment law perspectives?

- **Corporation tax:** Have the job title and role been checked with corporation tax advisers?

- **Mandatory laws:** Are any applicable collective agreements clearly identified? Has the contract been checked by a host country employment law specialist?

- **Benefits:** Are the arrangements clear? Are they compatible with the assumed employment status? Is there sufficient flexibility? Has adequate medical cover been provided?

- **Notice:** Does the notice period relate to termination of the assignment or the employment or both? Are the administrative arrangements practical? Do the notice provisions work?

- **Covenants:** Are any post termination restrictions included and, if so, do they meet local requirements for enforcement (eg a need to make payments or to specify liquidated damages)?

- **Tax:** Are practical tax obligations and any tax equalisation arrangements clear?

- **Future:** How will future changes to immigration or tax laws, family size, termination etc affect the employment? How much will it cost to terminate the assignment early and are clauses to assist with mitigation to be included, eg claw back arrangements? Does any lease for accommodation contain a break clause and who will bear any early termination costs?

- **Cooperation:** Is there anything the employee can do to make things easier and if so should this be confirmed in the documents?

QUICK REVIEW OF EMPLOYMENT DOCUMENTS FOR EMPLOYEES

A1.4

- **Conditions:** Is the contract subject to any pre-conditions, or is the employment subject to conditions continuing to be met, eg immigration clearance or regulatory approval? Can/have you met the conditions? Is the risk acceptable?

- **Immigration:** Are there any special immigration concerns, eg a partner who wants to work, children that are adopted or a custody agreement with a divorced spouse? How have these issues been dealt with?

- **Net pay:** Is the gross and net remuneration clear? Have any adjustments been made to reflect cost of living, hardship etc? Can you ask for more cash?

- **Currency:** Are the currency, and place, in which remuneration will be set and delivered and any applicable exchange rates clear? How would currency movements affect you financially and has anything been done to mitigate the impact?

- **Benefits:** Are the benefits to be provided clear? Including incentives?

- **Health:** Has adequate international health cover been confirmed, for you and your family? Do any of you have pre-existing conditions? Are host country medical services adequate?

- **Accommodation:** How much assistance will be provided with accommodation etc? What will it be like?

- **Tax:** Will assistance with tax returns, tax equalisation or cash flow problems be provided?

- **Relocation:** Are any relocation and repatriation expenses to be reimbursed to you clearly confirmed?

- **Personal financial position:** How will relocation affect you personally outside work eg your pension, investments, a share plan from a former employer etc. Is any help given? Will the employer pay for any advice for you?

- **Other change:** What would happen if there were other changes, eg birth of another child, illness, change to schooling needs as children grow, divorce, safety concerns, or if the role or location are not as anticipated?

- **Termination:** Are the terms that will apply on termination of employment, particularly the notice period, clear? How will termination of your assignment or employment affect any incentive arrangements? Are there any early termination claw back clauses? Who would be responsible for any accommodation-related early termination penalties? If you leave will you be subject to post termination restrictions and are they likely to be enforceable? How easy will it be to get another job from overseas and have any promises been made to you about return to work for the home company?

REQUEST TO HOST COUNTRY ADVISER FOR PRELIMINARY ADVICE ON VIABILITY

A1.5 Before considering the detailed technical issues that may be relevant to the structure of the employment arrangements and content of the documents, it is usually worth asking some questions of host country advisers. The answers can be used to help decide whether the assignment is viable in principle, and whether it is worth spending further time and incurring further expense. The following checklist highlights some of the information and questions that could be included in the initial enquiry (see also Chapter 3).

Background information to be provided

- Brief explanation of purpose of assignment
- Home and host countries (and the country where the employee is working now if this is not the home country)
- Names of home company and host company, if there is one, and countries of registration
- Description of any operations the group already has in the host country (eg a company, branch, representative office, premises) and location within the host country
- Number of employees to be assigned
- Whether the assignee will be a new recruit or a current employee (and, if the latter, which company employs him now)
- Employee's current and proposed roles including title/description, salary and start dates
- Nature of the home and host company businesses
- Employee's nationality, and nationalities and relationships to the employee of any family members to accompany the employee
- Whether the employee's partner wants to work in the host country too
- Initial thoughts assignment length

Advice requested

- Whether residence, work permits or other immigration permission will be required for the employee and his family
- Whether immigration permission is likely to be obtained and how long this is likely to take
- Whether expatriates or family members from a particular background are likely to encounter special difficulties (eg because of sex, marital status, legitimacy, sexual orientation, nationality, ethnic origin, religion)
- Whether there are any restrictions on who can employ the employee in the host country (eg the place the relevant company is registered), including whether the home company (or preferred employer if known) could employ
- Whether there are any employer registration requirements and any preconditions for registration (eg whether the employer must have premises in the host country)
- Brief explanation of the consequences of failing to comply, for employer and employee
- Whether there are any potential timing problems (eg time taken to obtain work permit)

Practical things

- Some indication of the detail of response required
- Identity of the adviser's client, including the client's billing address, and VAT number if applicable
- When the advice is needed, and why it is needed at that time if it is urgent
- Fees, including whether the adviser should start work before fees are agreed
- Sender's contact details and availability to answer questions
- Request for confirmation of safe receipt of request for advice and whether the adviser is willing to advise (within the timeframe, budget, etc)

ISSUES TO CONSIDER BEFORE DRAFTING EXPATRIATE DOCUMENTS

A1.6 The following checklist makes some suggestions about some of the things that should be considered before drafting of the expatriate employment documents begins.

- What are the business objectives for the assignment?
- Which legal entity currently employs the employee?
- Which legal entities could potentially employ the employee during the assignment?
- Is corporation tax advice required (eg will a permanent establishment be created, will a corporation tax deduction be available in respect of the employee's remuneration, are any restrictions on employer identity, duties, etc needed)?
- Is sales tax advice required (eg will VAT be due and will it be recoverable)?
- Is income tax advice required (eg where will the employee pay income tax, can any savings be made, are there any restrictions on assignment length, type of benefit, etc)?
- Is social security advice required (eg can the employee stay in his home country scheme and, if so, for how long, any restrictions on employer identity, assignment length, etc)?
- Is immigration advice required (eg any restrictions on employer identity, assignment length, duties, will the expatriate's partner be able to work, etc)?
- Are there any host country restrictions on which entity can employ the employee in the host country (eg place of registration, premises, etc)?
- Are there any employer-registration requirements in the host country?
- Is employment law advice required (eg applicable mandatory employment laws, potential termination costs, etc)?

- Is pensions advice required (eg can the employee remain in his home country plan, any restrictions on employer's identity, etc)?

- Are there any share plans, bonus or long-term incentive plans that may be affected by the assignment (eg effect on eligibility, tax, targets, etc)?

- Is intellectual property likely to be important and, if so, who should own it?

- Which entity should employ the employee during the assignment?

- How long will the assignment be for?

- What documents are needed for the assignment?

- Are the existing employment documents satisfactory or are they out of date, poorly drafted or confusing?

- Should the existing documents be amended, suspended or replaced? (Check termination provisions particularly carefully.)

- Should any home, host or group wide employee policies apply to the employee during the assignment? Are there any particular policies that should be expressly disapplied (eg in relation to severance pay)?

- Does the assignment team have any management guidelines/policies regarding benefits etc that should be taken into consideration to ensure consistency between expatriates?

- What language must the documents be issued in and what languages do likely users, eg home company, host company, employee and relevant authorities, work in?

- If there is a dispute, where is any employment claim likely to be made?

- What are the employee's and managers' expectations about the format, style and level of detail to be included in the documents?

INFORMATION FOR SHORT-TERM HOME EMPLOYER ASSIGNMENT LETTER (ASSUMES THE UNDERLYING HOME EMPLOYMENT CONTRACT IS SATISFACTORY)

A1.7 The following checklist lists information that the adviser is likely to find helpful before he starts to prepare a short-term assignment letter for a home country employment (ie where the identity of the employer will not change during the assignment).

Home employer

- What is the home country?
- What is the home employer's name?
- What is the home employer's registered address?
- Are there any other group companies?

Host company

- What is the host country?
- Will the employee provide services to the home employer or a separate host company during the assignment?
- If the employee will provide services to a separate host company during the assignment, what is the host company's name and registered address?
- What is the relationship between the home company and the host company?

Employee and family

- What is the employee's name?
- What is the employee's current home address?
- In which country does the employee currently work?
- Will the employee be accompanied or visited by any family members during the assignment (names, ages and relationships to the employee to be provided)?

Assignment start date and duration

- When will the assignment begin?
- How long will the assignment last, or be expected to last?
- Will the employer be able to end the assignment and, if so, will any period of notice be required from the employer?
- Will the employee be able to end the assignment and, if so, will any period of notice be required?
- Will the employee return to the same pre-assignment job on his pre-assignment terms when the assignment ends?

Immigration

- What is the employee's nationality?
- Is the employee entitled to live and work in the host country for the assignment or will immigration permission be required?
- Will there be any restriction on duties in the host country?
- Will there be any limit on the length of stay in the host country?
- Will immigration permission be required to allow family members to accompany or visit the employee in the host country?

Job title, duties and reporting lines

- Has any immigration application specifying job title or duties already been submitted?
- Will there be any change to the employee's pre-assignment job title or duties and, if so, what will the changes be?
- Who will benefit from the employee's work (eg the home employer or the host company)?
- Who will the employee report to in the home country (name and job title)?
- From whom will the employee receive day-to-day instructions in the host country (name and job title)?
- Are there any special codes of conduct or regulations that the employee will need to comply with during the assignment?

Place of work

- Where will the employee normally work in the host country (address)?
- Will the employee be required to travel? (If so, where to and are there any restrictions on length of time or destinations?)

Hours of work

- What will the employee's normal days and hours of work be (including breaks)?
- Will there be any change to overtime arrangements? Will any new host restrictions apply?

Remuneration

- Will there be any change to salary?
- Will there be any change to payment arrangements (eg to currency, place of payment, timing)?
- How will exchange rates be dealt with?
- Are there likely to be any problems with banking arrangements for the employee?
- Will the employee receive any special bonus or allowance for the assignment?

Tax and social security

- Have income tax implications been considered?
- Have social security implications been considered?
- Have corporation tax implications been considered?

- Have VAT implications been considered?
- Will tax protection be expressly confirmed?

Travel and accommodation

- Will the employer meet or reimburse the employee's travel expenses between the home and host countries at the start, during and at the end of the assignment (how often, any limits, is there a policy)?
- Will any travel expenses be paid for family members (eg if they visit the employee at the weekend rather than the employee going home)?
- How will the employee travel within the host country? (Will he be provided with a hire car or will he use public transport and claim travel expenses? Is there a policy document?)
- Will the employee be provided with hotel or other temporary accommodation in the host country?
- Will the employee be reimbursed meal expenses or paid a subsistence allowance?
- What will the arrangements for reimbursement of expenses be (currency, timing, authorisation and is there a policy document)?

Health and insurance

- Will any additional private medical insurance cover be provided?
- Will the employee need a European Health Insurance Card (EHIC)?
- Will any additional accident or travel insurance cover be provided?
- Will the home employer's employers' liability insurance (or similar cover against claims from the employee in the event of personal injury) apply?
- Will the employer make any special security arrangements?
- Have any special health and safety arrangements been made by the employer or host company?

Pension and life assurance

- Will pension and life assurance arrangements be affected by the assignment?

Holiday

- Will the employee take home or host country public holidays during the assignment?
- Will any extra days be given at the beginning or end of the assignment?
- Will there be any restrictions on taking holiday during the assignment?

Business expenses

- Will expenses be reclaimed in the usual way or will the host company be involved (and, if so, how)?
- Where and in what currency will expenses be reimbursed?
- Will a float or company credit card be provided?

Confidential information, intellectual property and data protection

- Will the employee be required to sign any agreements directly with the host company (eg regarding intellectual property, confidentiality, competition)?
- Is any intellectual property likely to be created? If so, what and who will it belong to?
- Are the home company and host company already compliant with applicable data protection laws?
- What arrangements are already in place to allow transfer of personal data outside the home and host countries and to third parties?

Miscellaneous

- Is there a need to comply with 'posted worker' laws or are there other laws or collective agreements requiring minimum terms during the assignment?
- Will the employee be required to keep any records (eg for immigration or tax purposes)?
- Will the employee be provided with any equipment for use during the assignment?
- Will the application of any of the home employer's policies change or be suspended during the assignment (eg equal opportunities, redundancy, expenses, absence policies)?
- Will any collective agreements or mandatory laws apply to the employee during the assignment?
- Who will sign the assignment letter for the home employer (name, job title)?
- Are there any home or host requirements regarding evidence of the signatory's authority, given that the assignment letter forms part of the employment contract?

Existing documents

- Are there any existing documents relating to the assignment (eg current employment contract, draft assignment letters, email correspondence with the employee, advice provided by specialists, etc)?

INFORMATION FOR LONG-TERM HOME EMPLOYER EMPLOYMENT CONTRACT (ASSUMES THE PRE-ASSIGNMENT HOME EMPLOYMENT CONTRACT WILL BE REPLACED)

A1.8 The following checklist lists information that the adviser is likely to find helpful before he starts to prepare a 'home employer' employment contract for a long-term assignment. (This may also be referred to as an 'assignment letter'.)

Home employer

- What is the home country?
- What is the home employer's name?
- What is the home employer's registered address?
- Are there any other group companies?

Host company

- What is the host country?
- Will the employee provide services to the home employer or a separate host company during the assignment?
- If the employee will provide services to a separate host company during the assignment, what is the host company's name and registered address?
- What is the relationship between the home employer and the host company?

Employee and family

- What is the employee's name?
- What is the employee's current home address?
- In which country does the employee currently work?
- Will the employee be accompanied to the host country by any family members (names, ages and relationships to the employee to be provided)?

Start dates and duration

- When did/will the employment begin?
- Is there any relevant period of earlier employment with another employer (eg a group company)?
- Will there be a probationary period (unlikely)? (If so, how long will the probationary period be, what is its purpose and are there any host country advantages/constraints?)
- Is the employment to be for a fixed term (if so, how long) or for an indefinite period?
- When will the assignment begin?
- How long will the assignment last, or be expected to last?
- What notice period will the employee be required to give to end the employment?
- What notice period will the employer be required to give to end the employment?
- Can the employee give notice to end the assignment (unlikely) and, if so, what notice period will be required and will the employment end automatically on termination of the assignment?
- What notice period will the employer be required to give to end the assignment?
- Should a payment in lieu of notice clause be included? If so, how will compensation be calculated? (Is this allowed in the host country?)
- Is a garden leave clause required? (Is this allowed in the host country?)
- Should the contract allow for transfer of employment to any related company? (Eg if a new employing entity will be established in the host country shortly.)
- Will employment be offered in the home country, or another country, at the end of the assignment?
- Will any additional/redundancy payment be offered if no employment is offered at the end of the assignment (or if the employee declines any offer made)?

Immigration

- What is the employee's nationality?
- Is the employee entitled to live and work in the host country or will immigration permission be required?
- Will there be any limit on length of stay in the host country?
- Will immigration permission be required to allow the family to accompany the employee and/or allow the employee's partner to work in the host country? What are their nationalities and are there any special issues to consider?

Job title, duties and reporting lines

- Has any immigration application specifying job title or duties already been submitted?
- What will the employee's job title and duties be?
- Who will benefit from the employee's work (eg the home employer or host company)?
- Will the employee be allowed to undertake other work (eg for another employer or group company)?
- Who will the employee report to in the home country (name and job title)?
- From whom will the employee receive day-to-day instructions in the host country (name and job title)?
- Are there any special codes of conduct or regulations that the employee must comply with?
- Will the employee be a director or hold another appointment or be given any 'powers'? (If so, will the home employer have discretion to require resignation or withdraw?)

Place of work

- Where will the employee normally work in the host country (address)?
- Will the employee be required to travel? (If so, where to and are there any restrictions on length of time or destinations?)
- Is the normal place of work likely to change within the host country during the assignment? (If so, where to?)

Hours of work

- What will the employee's normal days and hours of work be (including breaks)?
- Will the employee be required to work overtime?

Salary and bonus

- What will the employee's annual gross basic salary be?
- In what country will salary be paid?
- In what currency will salary be paid?
- How will exchange rates be dealt with?
- At what intervals will salary be paid (monthly in arrears?)?
- Is there any requirement to make a 13th month or similar payment?
- Will the home employer pay salary itself or will another entity make payments on the home employer's behalf?

- When will salary be reviewed by the employer?
- Is overtime paid?
- Will the employee receive a bonus or commission?
- If so, will there be a plan setting targets etc, or is this intended to be discretionary?
- Does the employee currently participate in any bonus or commission arrangements?
- Will a notional or reference salary be used (and, if so, what for)?

Allowances

- Will a cost of living adjustment (COLA) be applied? (If so, could this be a negative figure?)
- Will a hardship allowance be paid?
- Will a disturbance allowance be paid?
- Will a subsistence allowance be paid?
- Will a housing allowance be paid?
- Will any offset in relation to rental of the employee's property in the home country be applied?
- Will a car allowance be paid?
- Will any other allowances be paid?

Other benefits

- Will pre-visit expenses be reimbursed or paid (for the employee and/or his family, any conditions, limits or policies)?
- Will relocation expenses be reimbursed or paid (ie from the home country to the host country). If so, will the following be covered (any limits, conditions or policies)?
  - Expenses relating to home country property (eg letting agents' fees)?
  - Temporary accommodation in home country prior to departure?
  - Flights?
  - Temporary accommodation in host country on arrival?
  - Transporting personal possessions by air or sea?
  - Insurance for personal possessions?
- Will accommodation in the host country be provided? (If so, specify any limits, conditions or policies):
  - Will the lease be taken out by the employer or the employee?
  - Will rent be paid or reimbursed?
  - Will assistance with a deposit be provided?
  - Will any utility or similar expenses be reimbursed or paid (eg gas, electricity, landline, mobile phone, local taxes, service charges)?
  - Who should take out contents insurance?
  - Responsibilities of employer and employee for damage, default etc?

- Will the employee be required to vacate the host country accommodation on termination of employment?
- Who will meet any early termination penalties? Any minimum stay? Voluntary termination?

- Will a car be provided?
- Will any domestic assistance be provided (eg chauffeur, security guard, cleaner, cook, gardener) and if so who will employ and pay wages?
- Will school fees be paid or reimbursed (any limits, conditions or policies)?
  - Annually/termly?
  - In the home or host country?
  - Flights home for children at boarding school?
  - Names/age/dependency restrictions?
  - To cover nursery and/or tertiary education?
  - Extra lessons, books, exam fees, etc?
  - What happens when costs increase, eg on transfer to secondary school?
  - Will payment be made to the end of the school year if employment ends during the school year?
  - Who pays deposit?
- Will flights for home leave (between home and host country) be provided or reimbursed?
  - How many times a year?
  - Who for?
  - Limits on class of travel or cost?
  - Reimbursed or paid?
  - Impact of termination part way through the year?
- Will language training be provided? (If so, who for and when?)
- Will cultural awareness training be provided? (If so, who for and when?)
- Will repatriation expenses be reimbursed or paid (ie from the host country to the home country)? If so, will the following be covered (any limits, conditions or policies?):
  - Expenses relating to wait to reoccupy home country property (eg hotel accommodation in the home country)?
  - Flights?
  - Transporting personal possessions by air or sea?
  - Insurance?
  - Any conditions (eg time-limit for return, no new job in the host country)?

Tax and social security

- Have income tax implications been considered?
- Have social security implications been considered?
- Have corporation tax implications been considered?
- Have VAT implications been considered?

- Will any tax equalisation or protection arrangements apply (if so, which payments will the promise apply to)?
- Will any record keeping or other administration requirements be specified?
- Will help with tax returns be provided? (Any limits on cost or scope?)
- Will any loans be made, eg to cover double taxation cash flow problems?
- Will the employee be independently advised?

Health and insurance

- How long will company sick pay be paid for (subject to host country mandatory laws)?
- Will private medical insurance cover be provided for the employee and/or his family?
- Will the employee, and any family, need a European Health Insurance Card (EHIC)? What will be the impact of Brexit on entitlement to EHIC?
- Will any additional accident, travel or emergency (SOS) cover be provided?
- Will the home employer's employers' liability insurance (or similar cover against claims from the employee in the event of personal injury) apply?
- Will any special security arrangements be made (and will the employee be required to comply with any restrictions)?
- Will any special health and safety arrangements be made?
- Will the employer require the employee, or his family, to submit to a medical examination before or during the assignment?
- Will the employer be able to require the employee to return to the home country in the event of ill-health?
- Will permanent health insurance cover (PHI)/long-term disability cover be provided?

Pension and life assurance

- Does the employee currently participate in a home employer pension plan?
- Can the employee stay in the plan during the assignment?
- Will any international or alternative pension arrangement be provided?
- Will the pension plan be a defined contribution (money purchase) pension plan or a defined benefit (final salary) plan?
- What contributions will be made by the employer?
- What contributions will be made by the employee?
- Is life assurance cover provided? If so, what is the assured sum?
- If the employee cannot participate in his chosen plan throughout the assignment will the employer offer him an alternative benefit?

- Has the assignment been discussed with the employer's pensions advisers?

Holiday

- How many days' annual holiday will the employee be entitled to?
- Will any transitional arrangements apply to take account of a change to annual holiday entitlement at the beginning or end of the assignment?
- Will the employee be entitled to additional time off on host country public holidays, or will annual holiday be expressed as an aggregate figure?
- Will any special arrangements be made, for example, for Easter or Christmas?
- When will the holiday year begin and end?
- Can holiday be carried forward? If so, how many days and when must it be taken by?

Business expenses

- Will expenses be reclaimed in the usual way or will the host company be involved (and, if so, how)?
- Where and in what currency will expenses be reimbursed?
- Will a float or company credit card be provided?
- How will exchange rates be dealt with?

Confidentiality, intellectual property and data protection

- Will the employee be required to sign any agreements directly with the host company (eg regarding intellectual property, confidentiality, competition)?
- Is any intellectual property likely to be created? If so, what and who will it belong to?
- Are the home company and host company already compliant with applicable data protection laws?
- What arrangements are already in place to allow transfer of personal data outside the home and host countries, and to third parties? Has account been taken of family members' privacy rights?

Miscellaneous

- Will the employee be required to keep any other records (eg for immigration purposes)?
- Will the employee be provided with any equipment for use during the assignment?

- Will any of the employer's policies apply during the assignment (eg equal opportunities, redundancy, expenses, absence, etc)?
- Will any collective agreements or mandatory laws apply to the employment? (If unknown, any information that may be helpful to determine this, eg industry sector, location of business, employee numbers, etc.)
- Who would sign the contract for the home employer (name, job title)?
- Are there any home or host formalities, eg regarding evidence of authority, place of signature, language?

Existing documents

- Are there any existing documents relating to the assignment, eg current employment contract, draft assignment letters, email correspondence with the employee, advice provided by specialists, etc.

INFORMATION FOR RESIDUAL CONTRACT WITH HOME COMPANY (WHERE HOST COMPANY WILL BE THE EMPLOYER)

A1.9 The following checklist lists information that the adviser is likely to find helpful before he starts to prepare a 'residual contract' with the home company where there is a host employment arrangement. This would not be an employment contract. (See figure 6.3.)

Home country residual employer

- What is the home country?
- What is the home country residual employer's name?
- What is the home country residual employer's registered address?
- Are there any other group companies?

Host country assignment employer

- What is the host country?
- What is the host country assignment employer's name?
- What is the host country assignment employer's registered address?
- What is the relationship between the home country residual employer and the host country assignment employer?

Purpose

- What is the purpose of the residual contract (eg to clarify what will happen at the end of the assignment, to clarify arrangements for provision of benefits by home country residual employer during assignment)?

Pre-assignment contract

- Will the pre-assignment employment contract with the home company be suspended during the assignment and revive when it ends, or will the pre-assignment employment contract terminate immediately before the assignment begins and be replaced with this document?

Reporting lines

- Who will the employee report to at the residual home country employer (name, job title)?

Benefits

- Will the residual home country employer continue to provide any pension benefits or allow continued membership of its pension plan? If so, what is the name of the pension plan?
- Will pension be based on a notional salary or on the actual salary paid by the host country assignment employer during the assignment?
- Are there any limits or constraints that should be confirmed to the employee (eg a maximum period during which the employee can work overseas/for the host company and remain a member of the pension plan)?
- Will any other benefits be provided by the residual home country employer during the assignment?

Notional salary

- What will the notional salary be at the start of the assignment?
- At what intervals will the residual employer review notional salary?

Termination and re-employment

- What notice period does the host country assignment employer have to give the employee to terminate the employment with the host country assignment employer?
- Will the employee be required to inform the home country residual employer if he serves or receives notice of termination of his employment with the host country assignment employer?

- Will the home country residual employer promise to offer re-employment with the home country residual employer when employment with the host country assignment employer ends? (If so, does this promise cover termination of the host employment by the employee or only termination by the host employer; and will the notional salary apply to the new employment with the home company, or will the final salary with the host country employer apply to the post-assignment employment?)
- Will the pre-assignment employment terms with the home country residual employer be revived?
- Will the home country residual employer or the host country assignment employer bear repatriation costs at the end of the assignment? If the residual employer will bear those costs what will they include?
- Will the home country residual employer be able to terminate the residual employment contract at any time, even during the assignment, and, if so, what notice must be given?
- What will happen to the employee's continuity of employment during the assignment and after it ends?

Signature

- Who would sign the contract for the home country residual employer?
- Is any apostille, power of attorney or other evidence of authority of signatory required?

Existing documents

- Are there any existing documents relating to the home country residual employment (eg current employment contract, email correspondence with the employee, advice provided by specialists, etc (request copies))?

INFORMATION FOR INTER-COMPANY EXPATRIATE SUPPLY AGREEMENT

A1.10   The following checklist lists information that the adviser is likely to find helpful before he starts to prepare an inter-company expatriate supply agreement. (See figures 6.1 and 6.3.)

Home company

- What is the home country?
- What is the home company's name?
- What is the home company's registered address?
- Are there any other group companies?

Host company

- What is the host country?
- What is the host company's name?
- What is the host company's registered address?
- What is the relationship between the home company and the host company?

Employer and employee(s)

- Will the home or host company employ the employee(s)?
- Will the supply agreement relate to one employee or several employees?
- What is/are the employee(s) name(s)?

The Services

- What will the employee(s) do for the host company?
- Will the home company supply people or specific services?

Responsibilities

- Which company will be responsible for discipline, dismissal, grievances, approving expenses, appraisal, pay reviews, etc in relation to the employee(s) (should be the employer)?
- If the home company is the employer will the host company's treatment of employee(s) be restricted and will there be any obligation to keep the employer informed (eg of information relevant to salary review or a decision to take disciplinary action)?
- What insurance cover must the host company provide?
- What insurance cover must the home company provide?
- Will any warranties or indemnities be provided by either company?
- Should any specific health and safety responsibilities be confirmed?

Confidentiality, intellectual property and data protection

- Will a confidentiality clause be required?
- Will the employee be required to sign any agreements directly with the host company (eg regarding intellectual property, confidentiality, competition)?
- Is any intellectual property likely to be created? If so, what and who will it belong to?

- Are the home company and host company already compliant with applicable data protection laws?
- What arrangements are already in place to allow transfer of personal data outside the home and host countries and to third parties?

Payment arrangements

- At what rate will fees be charged?
- Will fees be paid in advance or in arrears?
- Will VAT be charged on top?
- At what intervals will invoices be submitted?
- What periods will the invoices cover (eg the previous calendar month)?
- When must the invoices be paid?
- If the home company will be the employer, will the host company pay any remuneration or reimburse any expenses to the employee on behalf of the home company, and if so how will that remuneration be reimbursed?
- What arrangements are there between the two companies regarding reimbursement of disbursements between each other?
- How will exchange rates be dealt with?

Termination arrangements

- What notice must the host company give the home company to end the supply of an employee?
- What notice must the home company give the host company to end the supply of an employee?
- What notice must the host company give the home company to end the supply agreement?
- What notice must the home company give the host company to end the supply agreement?

Signature

- Who will sign the agreement for the home company (name, job title)?
- Who will sign the agreement for the host company (name, job title)?
- Is any evidence of authority or apostille required for signatories?

INFORMATION FOR INTERNATIONAL COMMUTER AGREEMENT

A1.11   The following checklist lists information that the adviser is likely to find helpful before he starts to prepare an international commuter agreement.

Rationale

- Who proposed this arrangement? The employee or the employer?
- Why?

- Will this be a transitional or permanent arrangement?

- Is this the home employer's first international commuter arrangement or do other home employees already work this way? Do other employees commute between these locations?

Home company

- What is the home country?
- What is the home company's name?
- What is the home company's registered address?
- Are there any other group companies?

Host company

- What is the host country?
- Is there an existing host company and, if so, will the employee provide services to that company?
- What is the host company's name?
- What is the host company's registered address?
- What is the relationship between the home company and the host company?

- Will the employee be employed by a separate host entity or by the home company or both?

Employee and family

- What is the employee's name?
- What is the employee's current home address in the home country?
- In which country does the employee currently work?
- Will the employee be accompanied by any family members (names, ages and relationships to the employee to be provided) or will they remain in the home country?

Start dates and duration

- When did/will the employment begin? Is there any relevant period of earlier employment with another employer (eg a group company)?
- When will the commuter arrangement begin?
- How long will the commuter arrangement last, or be expected to last?
- Will there be a formal trial period?
- What notice period will the employee be required to give to end the employment?
- What notice period will the employer be required to give to end the employment?
- Can the employee give notice to end the commuter arrangement and, if so, what notice period will be required and will the employment end automatically on termination of the commuter arrangement?
- What notice period will the employer be required to give to end the commuter arrangement?
- Should a payment in lieu of notice clause be included? If so, how will compensation be calculated? (Is this allowed in both countries?)
- Is a garden leave clause required? (Is this allowed in both countries?)

Immigration

- What is the employee's nationality?
- Is the employee entitled to live and work in both home and host countries or will immigration permission be required for either?
- Will there be any time limits on that immigration permission?
- Will any immigration permission be required for family members or will they remain in the home country?

Job title, duties and reporting lines

- Has any immigration application specifying job title or duties already been submitted?
- What will the employee's job title and duties be in each country?
- Are there any immigration restrictions on the activities that can be carried out in each country?
- Who will benefit from the employee's work in each company (eg the home employer or host company)?
- Will the employee be allowed to undertake other work (eg for another employer or group company)?
- Who will the employee report to at the home employer (name and job title)?

- From whom will the employee receive day-to-day instructions in the host country (name and job title)?
- Are there any special codes of conduct or regulations that the employee must comply with?
- Will the employee be a director or hold another appointment or be given any 'powers' in either home or host country? (If so, will the home employer have discretion to require resignation or withdraw?)

Place of work

- Where will the employee normally work in home and host countries (address)?
- Will the employee work at home?
- If he employee will work at home will he use his own equipment?
- Will the employee be required to travel outside the home and host countries? (If so, where to and are there any restrictions on length of time or destinations?)
- Is the normal place of work likely to change within the host country during the assignment? (If so, where to?)

Hours of work

- What will the employee's normal days and hours of work be (including breaks)?
- How will time be split between work in home and host countries?
- Will the employee be required to work overtime?

Salary and bonus

- What will the employee's annual gross basic salary be?
- In what country will salary be paid?
- In what currency will salary be paid?
- How will exchange rates be dealt with?
- At what intervals will salary be paid (monthly in arrears?)?
- Is there any requirement to make a 13th month or similar payment?
- Will the home employer pay salary itself or will another entity make payments on the home employer's behalf?
- When will salary be reviewed by the employer?
- Is overtime paid?
- Will the employee receive a bonus or commission?
- If so, will there be a plan setting targets etc, or is this intended to be discretionary?

- Does the employee currently participate in any bonus or commission arrangements?
- Will a notional or reference salary be used (and, if so, what for)?

Allowances

- Will any allowances be provided, eg a subsistence allowance in the host country?

Other benefits

- Will accommodation in the host country be provided? If so will this be hotel accommodation, a serviced apartment or a long lease?
- Will a car be provided in the home or host country?
- Will flights and other travel expenses be reimbursed?
  - How often?
  - Who for?
  - Limits on class of travel or cost?
  - Reimbursed or paid directly by the employer?
  - Is there a policy?
- Will language training be provided? (If so, who for and when?)
- Will cultural awareness training be provided? (If so, who for and when?)
- Will repatriation expenses be reimbursed or paid (ie from the host country to the home country)? Eg transporting personal possessions by air or sea?

Tax and social security

- Have income tax implications been considered?
- Have social security implications been considered?
- Have corporation tax implications been considered?
- Have VAT implications been considered?
- Will any tax equalisation or protection arrangements apply (if so, which payments will the promise apply to)?
- Will any record keeping or other administration requirements be specified? Eg 'day counting' obligations?
- Will help with tax returns for both home and host tax authorities be provided? (Any limits on cost or scope?)

- Will any loans be made, eg to cover double taxation cash flow problems?

- Will the employee be independently advised?

Health and insurance

- How long will company sick pay be paid for (subject to host country mandatory laws)?
- Will international private medical insurance cover be provided for the employee and/or his family?
- Will the employee, and any family, need a European Health Insurance Card (EHIC)? What will be the impact of Brexit on entitlement to EHIC?
- Will any additional accident, travel or emergency (SOS) cover be provided?
- Will the home employer's employers' liability insurance (or similar cover against claims from the employee in the event of personal injury) apply?
- Will any special security arrangements be made (and will the employee be required to comply with any restrictions)?
- Will any special health and safety arrangements be made?
- Will the employer require the employee, or his family, to submit to a medical examination before or during the assignment?
- Will the employer be able to require the employee to return to the home country in the event of ill-health?
- Will permanent health insurance cover (PHI)/long-term disability cover be provided?

Pension and life assurance

- Does the employee currently participate in a home employer pension plan?
- Can the employee stay in the plan during the commuter assignment?
- Will the pension plan be a defined contribution (money purchase) pension plan or a defined benefit (final salary) plan?
- What pension contributions will be made by the employer?
- What pension contributions will be made by the employee?
- Is life assurance cover provided? If so, what is the assured sum?
- If the employee cannot participate in his chosen plan throughout the assignment will the employer offer him an alternative benefit?

- Has the assignment been discussed with the employer's pensions advisers?

Holiday

- How many days' annual holiday will the employee be entitled to?
- Will the employee be entitled to additional paid time off on home or host country public holidays, or will annual holiday be expressed as an aggregate figure?

- Will any special arrangements be made, for example, for Easter or Christmas?
- When will the holiday year begin and end?
- Can holiday be carried forward? If so, how many days and when must it be taken by?

Business expenses

- Will expenses be reclaimed in the usual way or will the host company be involved (and, if so, how)?
- Where and in what currency will expenses be reimbursed?
- Will a float or company credit card be provided?
- How will exchange rates be dealt with?
- Will commuting expenses be taxed and, if so, will the employee be protected against the impact?

Confidentiality, intellectual property and data protection

- Will the employee be required to sign any agreements directly with the host company (eg regarding intellectual property, confidentiality, competition)?
- Is any intellectual property likely to be created? If so, what and who will it belong to?
- Are the home company and host company already compliant with applicable data protection laws?
- What arrangements are already in place to allow transfer of personal data outside the home and host countries, and to third parties? Has account been taken of family members' privacy rights?

Miscellaneous

- Will the employee be required to keep any other records (eg for immigration or tax purposes)?
- Will the employee be provided with any equipment for use during the assignment?
- Will any of the employer's policies apply during the assignment (eg equal opportunities, redundancy, expenses, absence, etc)?
- Will any collective agreements or mandatory laws apply to the employment? (If unknown, any information that may be helpful to determine this, eg industry sector, location of business, employee numbers, etc.)
- Who would sign the contract for the home employer (name, job title)?

- Are there any home or host formalities, eg regarding evidence of authority, place of signature, language?

Existing documents

- Are there any existing documents relating to the assignment, eg current employment contract, draft assignment letters, email correspondence with the employee, advice provided by specialists, etc.

INFORMATION FOR SEVERANCE AGREEMENT

A1.12 The following checklist lists the information that the adviser is likely to find helpful before he starts to draft an international severance agreement, ie an agreement to provide for payments and settle claims that may arise on termination of the expatriate's employment.

Home company

- What is the home country?
- What is the home company's name?
- What is the home company's registered address?
- Are there any other group companies?

Host company

- What is the host country?
- What is the host company's name?
- What is the host company's registered address?
- What is the relationship between the home company and the host company?

Employment arrangements

- Does the home company or the host company employ the employee?
- What documents are currently in place between the home company, the host company and the employee?
- Is the identity of the employer clear and undisputed?

Employee and family

- What is the employee's name?
- In which country does the employee currently work?

- What is the employee's host country address?
- Will the employee repatriate to the home country or another country?
- What is the employee's home country address?
- Are there any relevant family members?

Role

- What is the employee's current role?
- Does the employee hold any directorships or other appointments?
- Does the employee have any powers of attorney, bank mandates or similar in his name?
- Are there any role-related timing constraints?

Termination

- What are the reasons for proposed termination of the employment?
- Will termination be on notice, on less than full notice or by mutual agreement?
- When is the employment expected to end/did the employment end?
- Has notice already been given, if so, when was it given and what end date was specified?

Immigration

- What is the employee's nationality?
- Are the employee's (and his family's) immigration papers in order?
- Do the immigration papers correctly reflect the identity of the employee's employer?
- Will the employee be required to leave the host country within a fixed period after the employment ends or active duties cease?
- Does the host company or the home company have any obligations (eg to report the end of the employment or return papers to the immigration authorities)?

Remuneration

- What remuneration accrued to the termination date is outstanding?
- How will termination affect bonus and/or long-term incentive plans?

Benefits

- Is the employee provided with accommodation and, if so, what rent has been paid and what early termination penalties or other costs will apply?
- Is the lease in the employer's or the employee's name?
- Who paid any deposit in respect of the accommodation and how much is it?
- Will the employee be required to vacate the accommodation (and, if so, when)?
- Are all utilities in the employee's name?
- Does the employee have any children in school and, if so, when do the relevant terms end and are there any early termination/deposit issues to consider? Are there any pending examinations to be taken into consideration?
- Has the employee been provided with a company car and, if so, are there any early return penalties?
- Has the employer engaged any domestic employees or a driver to assist the employee and/or his family and, if so, what arrangements will be made in that regard?
- What other benefits does the employee receive?
- Is the employee or any family member currently undergoing medical treatment?

Repatriation arrangements

- Will the employer pay for the costs of flights for the employee and his family from the host country to the home country?
- Are there any limits (eg on timing of travel, costs, class, carrier, etc)?
- What arrangements will be made for air freight/shipment of the employee's, and his family's, personal possessions (any limits on cost, volume etc)?
- Will the costs of any temporary accommodation needed in the host or home company be met?
- Are the relevant terms or policies clearly documented?

Business expenses

- Have all expenses been claimed and reimbursed?
- If not, what are the time-limits for making claims and reimbursement?

Severance payments

- Is there any home or host company severance policy that must be applied?

- Must any severance pay due under mandatory laws be specified?
- Will any payment in lieu of notice be made? (Is PILON permitted?)
- What severance payments will be made?
- When will they be paid?
- Where will they be paid?
- In what currency will they be paid?
- Will the payments be subject to any conditions?

Tax

- Has the employee been given any promises in relation to tax equalisation or tax treatment of any termination payment?
- Is the employee's co-operation required in relation to any tax/social security issues (eg to recover overpaid tax for the benefit of the employer, submit tax returns promptly)?
- Will any tax advice be provided in relation to the severance agreement and/or final payments due and/or final tax returns?
- Will immediate return to the home country prejudice any tax and/or social security arrangements (eg by changing tax residency)?
- Will the employer or employee provide a tax indemnity in relation to remuneration or severance payments?
- Is 'foreign service' or a similar tax exemption or reduction likely to be available in respect of any severance pay?

Confidentiality, garden leave and post termination restrictions

- Will any period of garden leave apply? (Is this permitted?)
- Will the existing contractual terms apply (eg re confidentiality or competition)?
- Will any new post termination restrictions be introduced (if so, what are they to cover)?
- Do any additional payments need to be made?
- What laws will govern any new restrictions?
- Will additional confidentiality provisions be required in relation to the circumstances of termination, existence and terms of the agreement, etc?
- Is there any requirement to take action in relation to covenants etc before termination takes effect?

Miscellaneous

- Will the employee be required to provide contact details going forward?
- Where will any disputes arising from the severance agreement be resolved?

- What country's laws will govern the severance agreement?
- What language must the severance agreement be in and are any translations required?
- How should the rights of third parties be dealt with?

Conclusion

- Are separate severance agreements required to settle claims under home and host country laws?
- Are separate severance agreements required to settle claims against each of the home and host companies or can a severance agreement with the employer cover other relevant parties (the host company, group companies, officers and employees, etc) too?
- Is approval required from any employment authority or court to make the severance agreement effective or is there any filing or similar requirement?
- Can counterpart documents be used or do the parties need to sign the same document?
- Can the agreement be concluded by fax or email or do the parties need to sign the same document or be in the same place at the time of signature?
- Who will sign the agreement for the home company (name, job title)?
- Who will sign the agreement for the host company (name, job title)?
- Is any evidence of authority or apostille required?
- Is evidence that the employee has been advised required?
- Is any cooling off period required before the agreement can become effective?

APPENDIX 2

FRAMEWORK EMPLOYMENT DOCUMENTS

INTRODUCTION

A2.1 The following framework documents are intended to help identify the key issues that should be covered by the expatriate documents, and to provide a starting point for drafting. Because the appropriate terms to be included in expatriate employment documents vary so widely these framework documents should not be treated as 'precedents' in the traditional sense. Drafts should always be reviewed and amended by appropriate specialists from the relevant countries before they are issued to employees.

A2.2 The following framework documents are included in this Appendix:

- short-term home employer assignment letter (assumes the underlying home employment contract is satisfactory) (**A2.3**);
- long-term home employer assignment letter (**A2.4**);
- home company residual contract (where the host company will be the employer) (**A2.5**);
- inter-company expatriate supply agreement (**A2.6**);
- home employer severance agreement (**A2.7**); and
- granting or removal of 'powers' (including apostille) (**A2.8**).

SHORT-TERM HOME EMPLOYER ASSIGNMENT LETTER (ASSUMES THE UNDERLYING HOME EMPLOYMENT CONTRACT IS SATISFACTORY)

A2.3 [*NB: See 5.31–5.47 on the special features of short-term assignments and checklist A1.5.*]

[*to be typed on the home country employer's headed notepaper (should include registered address)*]

Private & confidential – addressee only

[*Name of employee*]

[*Home address of employee at date letter issued*]

By [*Delivery method*]

[*Employer's reference*]

[*Date*]

Dear [*Name of employee*]

Your assignment to [*Host Company/Host Country*]

I am pleased to confirm the terms of your short-term assignment to [[*host company, registered address*] (the 'Host Company') in] [*Host Country*].

I confirm that during your assignment you will remain an employee of [*home employer*] (your 'Employer').

Your assignment will begin on, and these assignment terms will apply to you from, [*date assignment begins*]. Your assignment [will end on [*assignment end date*]/[is expected to continue until approximately [*date assignment expected to end*]. However, this date is indicative and is not intended to create a fixed term.] Your assignment may [start later or end earlier] in accordance with the terms of this assignment letter.

Your current terms and conditions of employment, as set out in your contract of employment dated [*date*] [as amended] (your 'Pre-Assignment Contract'), will continue to apply to you during your assignment, except as set out in this assignment letter. At the end of your assignment the assignment terms set out in this assignment letter will no longer apply, you will return to your pre-assignment role and your Pre-Assignment Contract terms will apply to you.

During your assignment the following assignment terms will apply to you.

1. Immigration

The start and continuation of your assignment will be subject to you obtaining appropriate documentary evidence of your entitlement to reside and work in [*Host Country*] for the duration of the assignment and to you remaining entitled to do so. Your Employer will, at its expense, where appropriate apply for or assist you to obtain any necessary immigration permission, including any work or other permits or visas, required for your assignment. You are required to co-operate with and assist your Employer, and to comply with any conditions or limits imposed by your Employer, in this regard.

[*NB: any other conditions to be satisfied before the assignment can begin?*]

2. Job title, duties and reporting lines

Your job title and normal reporting arrangements will remain unchanged. [The Host Company's [*job title*] (currently [*name*]), will be your day-to-day contact at the Host Company in [*Host Country*].]

[*NB: Any change to job title or home company reporting lines and any substantial changes to duties that should be mentioned?*]

3. Place of work

(a) You will be based at [the Host Company's premises at] [*address*] in [*Host Country*]. However, you may be required to travel to or work at other locations within [*specify area*] from time to time for the proper performance of your duties. [It is not anticipated that you will spend more than [ ] days inside/outside [*area*] – *specify restrictions if appropriate.*]

(b) You are required to maintain accurate records of time spent in [*Host Country*] and [*Home Country*] and any other country you may travel to during the assignment in such manner as your Employer may direct from time to time and to provide such records to your Employer immediately on demand, whether before, on or for the period of [3 years] following termination of your assignment.

4. Hours of work

[The Host Company's/the following] normal hours of work will apply to you during your assignment: [9 am] to [5 pm] [Monday] to [Friday] with [1 hour] for lunch. [*NB: Any change to overtime arrangements?*]

5. Remuneration

(a)   Your Employer will continue to pay you your salary in [*Home Country*] in [*Home Country currency*] at your current rate and into your nominated bank account in the usual way. [*NB: Normal deductions? Any portion paid in Host Country?*]

(b)   [*NB: Any additional pay? Eg* In addition to your normal salary you will receive an [*assignment*] allowance at the rate of [*currency and rate*] per [week/month] payable in [*Home/Host Country*] [weekly/monthly] in [advance/arrears] in [*Home/Host Country currency*]]

(c)   [*NB: Will any comfort regarding tax and social security contributions be given in the agreement or will this be dealt with practically 'behind the scenes'? A simple 'you will be no worse off etc' promise may be appropriate*]

6. Transport and accommodation

(a)   Your Employer will reimburse you in respect of the costs of [one] return [economy] class flight for yourself between [*Home Country*] and [*Host Country*] both at the start and at the end of the assignment, subject to your Employer's policy in force from time to time.

(b)   [*NB: Specify transport arrangements and consider whether these are to be treated as expenses or benefits, eg* [You will be provided with a car [and driver] for your [business and personal] use in [*Host Country*].]/[Whilst in [*Host Country*] you should use taxis and public transport for business travel, and should reclaim business travel expenses in the usual way, subject to your Employer's usual policy in force from time to time. For the avoidance of doubt, you may claim business expenses in respect of travel between your hotel and [*normal place of work*].]

(c)   Your Employer will reimburse you in respect of accommodation and subsistence expenses in [*Host Country*], subject to its policy in force from time to time.

7. Additional assignment benefits

In addition to the benefits to which you are entitled under the Pre-Assignment Contract you will be eligible for the following.

(a)   Your Employer will [reimburse you in respect of] the costs of [one] return [economy] class flight for yourself [or a family member] between the [*Home Country*] and [*Host Country*] per [week/month], subject to your Employer's policy in force from time to time.

(b)   [*NB: Any additional benefits?*]

8. Health and insurance

Health and safety

(a)   You must comply with [the Host Company's] reasonable health and safety policies and directions. [*Name, job title*] will contact you separately to discuss health and safety issues relating to your assignment. If you have any additional concerns or questions regarding health and safety during your assignment please let [*name, job title of home employer's representative*] know. [Please read your Employer's 'travel safety' policy carefully.]

Sick pay etc

(b)   Your usual sickness and absence arrangements will continue to apply save as follows. In addition to complying with your Employer's normal sickness and absence procedures, if you are unable to attend for work due to sickness or injury you should inform [*name and job title of the Host Company representative*] [promptly]. [*NB: Specify any exceptions.*]

Medical insurance

(c)   You are eligible to participate in your Employer's [international] medical insurance plan, subject to your Employer's policy in force from time to time. The policy is currently with [*provider*] and currently covers treatment in [*Host Country*], subject to conditions. Please ensure that you read the policy document carefully before you travel.

[EHIC

(d)   You are required to apply for a European Health Insurance Card (EHIC) immediately if you have not already done so, and to produce the card to [*name, job title*] as soon as possible. A photocopy may be retained on your personnel file.]

Travel and accident insurance

(e)   You are eligible to participate in your Employer's travel and accident insurance policies, subject to your Employer's policy in force from time to time.

9. Pension and life assurance

[For the avoidance of doubt, your pension and life assurance arrangements will continue on the terms confirmed in your Pre-Assignment Contract. *NB: Check this is possible.*]

10. Holiday

(a) Your usual holiday arrangements will continue to apply save as follows.

(b) You must take [*Host Country*] public holidays that fall during your assignment in lieu of [*Home Country*] public holidays that fall during your assignment.

(c) [Your Employer will need to reach agreement regarding any annual holiday you wish to take with the Host Company. It would therefore be helpful if you could give [*name, job title of home employer representative*] as much notice as possible and at least [ ] weeks' notice of proposed holiday plans.]

[Your annual holiday entitlement will accrue in the normal way during your assignment. However, your Employer is unlikely to consent to annual holiday being taken during the first [*period*] of your assignment.]

[*NB: Specify any other changes.*]

11. Business expenses

[You should follow your Employer's normal procedures for claiming expenses. You must not submit claims to the Host Company.] / [During your assignment you must submit any expense claims to your Employer. Expenses approved by your Employer will be reimbursed by the Host Company on behalf of your Employer, subject to your Employer's expenses policy in force from time to time.]

12. Confidentiality, intellectual property and data protection

(a) You will continue to owe a duty of confidentiality to your Employer during your assignment and must comply with [*refer to terms*] of your Pre-Assignment Contract. In addition, it is a condition of your assignment that you sign the Host Company's confidentiality agreement, a copy of which is enclosed with this assignment letter.

(b) [*NB: Confirm whether home or host company will own any intellectual property created during the assignment and ensure any appropriate agreements are concluded between the employee and host company and the home and host companies.*]

(c) By signing this letter you consent to the reasonable provision of personal information to the Host Company in [*Host Country*] for the purpose of the assignment. [*NB: Consent may not be sufficient to allow lawful transfer of personal data to some countries. (See* **12.72–12.91***) A copy of an appropriate data protection policy explaining the purposes for which the data will be used and requesting more explicit consent should normally also be provided. Note that in some countries it may not be appropriate to deal with this in the assignment letter.*]

13. Termination/notice etc

(a)   Your Employer may terminate the assignment at any time and for any reason, whether on or before [*anticipated end date – NB: Consider tax, social security, immigration restrictions, etc*] at its absolute discretion. [Your assignment will not continue beyond [*date*] without your consent.] Any decision by your Employer to end your assignment, or agreement with you to continue the assignment beyond [*date*], will be confirmed to you in writing. [You will be given at least [ ] days' written notice of termination of your assignment.]

(b)   [For the avoidance of doubt, arrangements regarding termination of your employment, as set out in your Pre-Assignment Contract, will continue to apply to you during your assignment. Notice of termination of your employment may be served by you or by your Employer to expire during, on or after your assignment ends, and your assignment will automatically end on termination of your employment. – NB: *this sort of confirmation may alarm the employee unnecessarily, a short assignment notice period may be more appropriate for this type of assignment*]

14. Equipment

You will be provided with the use of [*specify equipment, eg mobile, laptop*] for the performance of your duties, for the duration of your assignment. Such equipment will remain the property of your Employer and you may be required by your Employer to return such equipment at any time. [*NB: Specify any conditions, eg compliance with relevant policies.*]

15. Miscellaneous

Notices

(a)   [*NB: Specify arrangements for service of notice, if different from those in the Pre-Assignment Contract or refer to the Pre-Assignment Contract.*]

Policies

(b)   [*NB: Make clear whether home country policies will apply or not during the assignment.*]

Collective agreements

(c)   [*NB: Reference to applicable collective agreements or confirm that none apply.*]

Whole agreement

(d)   This assignment letter and your Pre-Assignment Contract together record the whole agreement between you and your Employer in respect of your employment and assignment and supersede any prior agreements in that regard. [*NB: Any exceptions?*]

Language

(e)   This assignment letter has been prepared in [English] and a translation has been prepared in [*Host Country language*]. In the event of any conflict the [*Host Country/English language*] version shall apply.

Third party rights

(f)   [Other than the Group Companies, as defined in your Pre-Assignment Contract] only you and your Employer shall have the right to enforce this assignment letter. Only the consents of you and of your Employer are required to vary the terms of this assignment letter.

Applicable laws

(g)   This assignment letter shall be governed and construed in all respects by [the laws of England and Wales] and you and your Employer irrevocably submit to the [non-exclusive jurisdiction of the Courts of England].

[*NB: Consider whether there is any opportunity to expressly contract out of host country employment laws.*]

[*NB: Consider whether governing law in relation to non-contractual obligations should be specified.*]

Please would you sign, date and return the duplicate copy of this assignment letter to me to confirm that you have read, understand and agree to its contents. The additional copy of the assignment letter is for you to keep.

Yours sincerely

[*Name of authorised signatory for home company*]

[*Job title of authorised signatory for home company*]

Duly authorised for and on behalf of [*home company*]

[*NB: Consider whether any apostille or evidence of authority of signatory is required (unlikely)*]

I confirm that I have read, understand and agree to be bound by the contents of this assignment letter.

Employee's signature: Date signed: ....
....

[*Employee's name*]

LONG-TERM HOME EMPLOYER ASSIGNMENT LETTER

A2.4 *[NB:*

- *This assignment letter will not be appropriate if the individual is to be employed by the host company. In that case there should be a new employment contract with the host company and a 'residual' agreement with the home company may also be required, covering, eg, return to the home country following termination of the assignment.*

- *An inter-company expatriate supply agreement dealing with the relationship between the home and host companies, particularly regarding fees, will usually also be appropriate.*

- *Consider whether any collective agreements, eg requiring minimum notice or salary, will apply during assignment.*

- *Consider whether the pre-assignment employment contract with the home country employer should be suspended, replaced or amended by the assignment letter. For example, consider the quality of the drafting and whether the pre-assignment contract would be easily understood in the host country. Pay particular attention to the termination arrangements.*

- *Consider whether it would be appropriate to include new post termination restrictive covenants.*

- *See also 6.12–6.39 on home employer arrangements generally; Chapter 7 and 8.7–8.[] on the content of a home employer assignment letter; and checklist A1.8.]*

[*to be typed on the home country employer's headed notepaper (should include registered address)*]

Private & confidential – addressee only

[*Name of employee*]

[*Home address of employee at date letter issued*]

By [*Delivery method*]

[*Employer's reference*]

[*Date*]

Dear [*Name of employee*]

Your assignment to [Host Country/Host Company name]

This letter is to confirm the terms which will apply to you during your assignment to [*Host Company*] [*registration number and registered address*] (the 'Host Company') in] [*Host Country*] (your 'Host Country').

[*NB: If the assignment is to provide services to a separate legal entity, consider whether restrictive covenants, confidentiality arrangements etc should be entered into directly with the host company as well.*]

Your assignment will begin on, and the Assignment Terms set out below will apply to you from, [*date*] and [is expected to/will] continue until [*date*], subject to earlier termination (see paragraph 5 below). [Your assignment may continue beyond, or finish earlier than on [*date*]/Your assignment may be extended if both you and your Employer agree to this.]

[*NB: Decide whether the employment is to end automatically on a fixed date if no further action is taken. Check, eg, possibility of restrictions on fixed-term contracts; notice requirements; tax/social security/pension implications of proposed assignment length for particular host country etc. There may be problems if the assignment is too long as well as if it is too short. See Chapter 5.*]

During your assignment you will remain in the employment of [*Home Company*] (your 'Employer') [under the terms of your employment contract with your Employer dated [*date*] as amended from time to time prior to the date of this letter (your 'Pre-Assignment Contract'), except as varied by the terms set out below (your 'Assignment Terms'). [*NB: Will any of the existing terms be retained? Any subsequent (ie since the Pre-Assignment Contract was concluded) variations to record, eg pay reviews? Obtain copy of Pre-Assignment Contract and check it, particularly notice provisions. If the Pre-Assignment Contract is unsatisfactory, or unsuitable for use during the assignment, provide for the Pre-Assignment Contract to be terminated and replaced, or suspended for the duration of the assignment.*]

The [*Name of Employee Handbook*] and other policies developed for your Employer's and Host Company employees working in [*Home Country*] (your 'Home Country') or your Host Country, including for example [*eg company redundancy policy or incentive arrangements*], will not apply to you during your assignment. [*NB: specify any relevant exceptions.*]

Your Assignment Terms will be as follows.

1. Job title, duties etc

(a)   Your job title will be '[*job title*]'.

(b)   [*NB: Specify any relevant change to duties. Consider consistency with any application for immigration permission, corporation tax consequences, impact on application of mandatory laws, etc. For example, ability to conclude commercial contracts in the Host Country may need to be restricted.*]

(c)   [*NB: Specify any relevant appointments, eg as director or General Manager, and related terms. Include appropriate terms to facilitate removal from appointment.*]

(d)   You should refer to [*job title of appropriate host company representative*] (currently [*name*]) (your 'Local Contact') for day-to-day instructions related to your work in Host Country during your assignment.

(e)   You will, however, report to your Assignment Manager [*job title of appropriate home country employer representative*] (currently [*name of Assignment Manager*]) for the duration of your assignment. All consents and authorisations which you are required to obtain from your Employer should be sought from your Assignment Manager unless you are instructed otherwise by your Employer.

(e)   If there is any conflict between any instruction given to you by your Local Contact and any instruction given by your Assignment Manager, you must comply with the instruction given by your Assignment Manager.

2. Place of work

Your normal place of work will be at [*location including address*] in your Host Country. However, you may be required to travel to or work at other locations within [*specify area NB: tax implications?*] from time to time for the proper performance of your duties. [It is not anticipated that you will spend more than [ ] days per [ ] [in/outside] [*area*] – *specify if appropriate*], subject to any applicable laws.

3. Hours of work

Your normal hours of work will be [the Host Company's normal office hours at [*location*], currently] [*time*] am to [*time*] pm [Monday to Friday]. You are required to work such additional hours as are necessary for the proper performance of your duties, subject always to any applicable laws.

[*NB: check Host Country working time and overtime rules.*]

[*NB: any additional holiday or transitional arrangement for the start and end of assignment?*]

4. Holiday

Your holiday entitlement will be determined in accordance with your Pre-Assignment Contract, except that you must take Host Country public holidays in lieu of Home Country public holidays.

[*NB: Any variations to reflect host country requirements, eg regarding holiday pay?*]

5. Duration and termination

(a) The start and continuation of your assignment will be subject to the immigration conditions set out in paragraph [].

(b) During your assignment the provisions of your Pre-Assignment Contract relating to termination of your employment with your Employer will continue to apply.

   [*NB: Check that these are appropriate – eg check well drafted; local procedural requirements, eg date on which notice can expire, whether payment in lieu of notice (PILON) is possible, whether any local minimum/maximum notice period must apply. If the arrangements are to be varied ensure that it is clear whether the new/old arrangements will apply from the date of service or date of expiry of notice.*]

(c) For the avoidance of doubt, and subject to paragraph 5(b), notice of termination of your employment with your Employer may be given by you or your Employer at any time (ie whether before, on or after termination of your assignment) and your assignment will end automatically on termination of your employment.

(d) Your assignment may be terminated by your Employer giving you not less than [*notice period*] months' notice in writing (or otherwise in accordance with this letter).

[*NB: it is not usual to offer the employee the option to terminate the assignment without terminating the employment.*]

(e) At the end of your assignment these Assignment Terms will cease to apply (and provided your employment with your Employer is not terminated) you may be offered (and if offered would be expected to accept) employment with your Employer (or with any Group Company) at [*the same or a more senior grade*] and at a salary which would not be less than your Notional Salary (at the rate applicable on the date your assignment ends). (Please note that this may be lower than your then applicable Assignment Salary). [For the avoidance of doubt, if such a position is offered to you with your Employer you would not be entitled to receive any redundancy pay from your Employer (or any other Group Company) whether or not you decide to accept the position offered to you.] Please note that neither the Host Company nor your Employer has any obligation to offer new or continued employment to you at the end of your assignment.

(f)   For the purposes of this assignment letter 'Group Company' means [*insert appropriate definition*].

(g)   [Alternatively, you may be offered employment with your Employer (or any Group Company) in any country outside your Host Country (ie a new expatriate role) subject to new terms and conditions of employment which your Employer (and/or the relevant Group Company) considers are appropriate for the new expatriate role offered to you. Your salary for the new expatriate role would not be less than your then Notional Salary.]

(h)   [*NB: Consider whether it is appropriate to offer any assurance regarding redundancy pay at all, eg:* Should you decide not to accept any new expatriate role offered to you, and no alternative employment is offered to you in Home Country, you may be eligible for a redundancy payment. [We are pleased to confirm that, notwithstanding that your Employer's redundancy policy (including procedures) for employees based in Home Country does not apply to you, the amount of any redundancy pay would be calculated in the same way as for your Employer's employees working in Home Country, subject to applicable laws. Your Employer offers you no assurance regarding the treatment of any redundancy pay for tax or social security purposes and any such payment would not be Tax Equalised. The amount of any Company redundancy payment would be reduced by the amount of any [severance payment (or similar payment) – *NB: Use right terminology*] due to you under any applicable laws.]

(i)   [*NB: Will the reasons for termination affect the benefits to be provided? Eg:* If your employment is terminated by you before [*date*] or if your employment is terminated by your Employer [following your refusal of an offer of employment in Home Country in accordance with paragraph 5(e) above or] by reason of your gross misconduct or other serious breach of your employment contract by you, this would be regarded as 'Voluntary Termination' for the purposes of this assignment letter, see further below.]

6. Remuneration

Salary and COLA

(a)   Your Notional Salary will be at the rate of [*Notional Salary in figures*] ([*Notional Salary and currency in words*] [*NB: This is not the same as the currency for payment*]) per year.

Your Assignment Salary will be at the rate of [*Assignment Salary in figures*] ([*Assignment Salary in words*] [*currency*]). [Your Assignment Salary will be Tax Equalised, see paragraph 7(a) below.]

Your Cost of Living Allowance ('COLA') is currently at the rate of [*COLA in figures*] ([*COLA in words*] [*currency*]) per year [and will be paid in addition to your Assignment Salary]. Your COLA will not be Tax Equalised. The applicable COLA will be determined by your Employer from time to time at its absolute discretion [*NB: Take care if COLA can be a negative figure*].

Incentives

(b)   [*NB:*
  * *Specify or refer to relevant incentive arrangements.*
  * *Ensure that any earlier plans are properly accommodated/replaced.*
  * *The home employer should be responsible although incentive awards may reflect host country duties, targets etc.*
  * *Does the incentive plan itself make clear whether payment will be due if the employment or assignment terminates part way through the plan year, or after the plan year ends and before delivery?*
  * *Are the provisions relating to variation and/or withdrawal adequate?*
  * *Are incentives determined by reference to Assignment Salary or Notional Salary?*
  * *Any currency issues?*
  * *Does tax equalisation apply to incentives?*
  * *Take particular care with long term incentive plans*]

Please note that your assignment could affect the tax and/or social security contributions due in respect of any incentive and/or share or share option plan in which you may participate. Eg the timing of your assignment could affect your rights and obligations on grant, vesting or exercise of shares or share options including, eg, arrangements offered by a previous employer. It is your responsibility to ensure that you understand the relevant tax and social security treatment. Your Employer offers you no assurance in that regard.

Additional Allowances

(c)   In addition to your Assignment Salary and COLA you will receive the following allowances (together your 'Assignment Allowances'):

Disturbance allowance

You will receive a one-off, [Tax Equalised], lump sum payment of [*disturbance allowance and currency in figures*] ([*disturbance allowance and currency in words*]) (your 'Disturbance Allowance'). This sum is intended to cover 'out of pocket expenses' associated with your relocation to your Host Country, such as [provision for pets, small electrical goods, clothes, mail redirection, utility reconnection charges, etc].

Hardship allowance

You will receive a hardship allowance at the rate of [*hardship allowance and currency in figures*] ([*hardship allowance and currency in words*]) (your 'Hardship Allowance').

Payment arrangements

(d)   [Unless otherwise specified in writing in this assignment letter, all payments referred to in this assignment letter/*or specify*] shall be delivered as follows.

Payment will be made in twelve equal instalments monthly in arrears on or about the [ ]th day of the month by credit transfer to your nominated bank account(s) [in the places specified below].

Payment shall be made subject to appropriate deductions in respect of any Home Country and/or Host Country income tax and/or Home Country and/or Host Country social security contributions, [any pension contributions due] and other lawful deductions.

[*NB: any exceptions? Any 13th month payments due?*]

A proportion of your Assignment Salary (and COLA) will be paid by your Employer in Home Country in [*Home Currency*].

A proportion of your Assignment Salary (and COLA) and [] will be paid by [your Employer/Host Company on your Employer's behalf] in Host Country in [*Host Country Curren*cy].

Your Employer may, at its absolute discretion, agree to vary the proportion of your Assignment Salary (and COLA) paid in each country. Requests for variation to payment arrangements should be made to your Assignment Manager.

Unless expressly confirmed in writing, all other payments will be made by your Employer in the [Home Country/Host Country] in [Home/Host Currency].

(Please note that payments to a Home Country bank account may be subject to income tax and social security contributions in another country or countries, and payments to a bank account in another country may be subject to income tax and social security contributions in Home Country and/or other countries.)

[NB: *Is a provision confirming the method by which exchange rates will be determined required?*]

[NB: *Payment arrangements for allowances may vary. The assignment letter should specify currency of payment, intervals at which payment is made, whether payment is made in advance or arrears, place of payment, etc.*]

Review

(e) Your Notional Salary, your Assignment Salary, your COLA [and relevant Assignment Allowances] will be reviewed by your Employer from time to time at its absolute discretion. Currently, these are reviewed [annually in [*month*] – NB: *In practice timing may be different for different allowances*]. Following review, your Notional Salary and Assignment Salary may be increased but will not be reduced. [The applicable COLA [and Assignment Allowances?] may be increased or decreased but will not be negative amounts.]

[NB: *Consider any host country requirements, eg for additional holiday pay; requirements of any applicable collective agreements etc.*]

7. Tax and social security

Tax Equalisation

(a) Your Employer will 'Tax Equalise' your Assignment Salary and any other remuneration and/or benefits identified as 'Tax Equalised' in this assignment letter (the 'Tax Equalised Amounts').

For the purposes of this assignment letter the 'Tax Equalised Amounts' include [*specify*].

Any sum not expressly identified as 'Tax Equalised Amount' shall not be treated as such. For the avoidance of doubt, the following shall not be Tax Equalised: [social security contributions, personal non-employment income, inheritance, corporation tax gains, incentive plans, severance pay, pension].

Your Employer will estimate the [*Home Country – national/Federal/local/ State*] income tax [and social security contributions] which would be due in respect of the Tax Equalised Amounts if you were working in Home Country in the ordinary way (eg disregarding the effect of any [*NB: specify as appropriate eg, inheritance, non-employment income*]) (your 'Hypothetical Tax').

The Tax Equalised Amounts will be increased or reduced such that, after deduction of any Home Country and Host Country income tax and social security contributions that actually apply to the Tax Equalised Amounts, the sums due to you will be equal to the sums which would have been due if Hypothetical Tax had been deducted instead.

[*NB:*
- *Make sure the clause used is consistent with any illustrations provided to the employee and that it is checked by both employment lawyers and expatriate tax advisers. The applicable arrangements vary considerably and the above wording is indicative of the type of clauses that might be used only.*
- *If COLA, or any other adjustment, can have the effect of reducing salary then the tax equalisation clause may need to be more complex.*
- *Tax equalisation may not be provided at all. Tax protection (ie along the lines of 'you will not receive less than...') or a broad 'net pay' promise may be given instead. Note that employees may sometimes lose out when pay is Tax Equalised, eg if they move to a lower tax jurisdiction.*
- *Sometimes more than one type of tax comfort will be provided to the employee, eg salary may be tax equalised whilst some benefits are paid to the employee 'free of tax' (ie the employer covers the costs), ie so a number of clauses will be required.*]

If any overpayment is made to you by your Employer as a result of Tax Equalisation your Employer reserves the right to recover all or part of any sum(s) overpaid from you by making deductions in accordance with paragraph 8, and without prejudice to your Employer's other rights and remedies.

Tax returns and record keeping

(b) You are required to maintain accurate records of time spent in Host Country and Home Country and any other country you may travel to during the assignment in such manner as your Employer may direct from time to time. You must provide such records to your Employer immediately on demand, whether before, on or within [3 years] following termination of your assignment, whether or not your employment also ends.

It is your responsibility to comply with Host Country and Home Country tax requirements [*NB: Any other relevant countries, eg US or previous Host Country?*] and to ensure that your tax returns are properly submitted within the appropriate deadlines.

[It is also your responsibility to promptly recover any overpayment of tax or social security contributions made to any relevant authority for the benefit of your Employer and to pay over any such sums recovered to your Employer promptly. If you fail to do so your Employer reserves the right to recover all or part of any sum(s) from you by making deductions in accordance with paragraph 8, and without prejudice to your Employer's other rights and remedies. For the avoidance of doubt this obligation shall continue after your assignment and/or employment ends for so long as such sums remain outstanding.]

Any penalties or interest charges incurred because you fail to provide information or documentation requested by the nominated tax adviser promptly will be your responsibility. Your Employer will not reimburse you in respect of any such costs.

You are eligible to receive tax advice at your Employer's expense, from tax advisers nominated by your Employer from time to time (and subject to such financial and/or other conditions as your Employer may from time to time impose), in respect of both Home Country and Host Country [and US] tax returns relating to any period of your assignment.

[*NB: your Employer may want to assist with tax returns relating to the assignment period even if the employment has ended.*]

Such advice will be provided in relation to remuneration from your employment only. Your Employer will not pay for additional tax planning advice, for example in relation to personal investments or inheritance.

For the avoidance of doubt, your Employer shall take no responsibility for any advice given at its expense and may impose financial limits on its contribution, at its absolute discretion from time to time.

It is a condition of the provision of Tax Equalisation and the tax assistance set out in this paragraph 7 that you take all reasonable steps to assist your Employer in keeping related costs to a minimum. For example, if you fail to keep documentary evidence of your expenditure or proper travel records, or to make claims for reimbursement of tax promptly or your employment ends on Voluntary Termination before [*date*], and in each case as a consequence additional Home Country or Host Country income tax and/or social security contributions, interest or penalties become due any such additional payments will be your responsibility.
Your Employer reserves the right to recover all or part of any sum(s) due from you in respect of your failure to comply with this paragraph 7 by

making deductions in accordance with paragraph 8, and without prejudice to your Employer's other rights and remedies.

[NB: *consider including terms to facilitate recovery of loans made to the employee to reduce cash flow disadvantage to the employee where there is a consequence of double taxation.*]

8. Deductions

By signing this assignment letter, you authorise your Employer to deduct from your remuneration or any other sums owed to you by your Employer (whether during, on or after termination of your employment) all (or part of) any sum(s) due from you to your Employer, and without prejudice to Company's other rights and remedies.

[NB: *consider including specific terms relating to recovery of deposits.*]

9. Business expenses

You will be reimbursed in respect of expenses incurred wholly and necessarily in the proper performance of your duties in accordance with your Employer's policy from time to time in force. Your expenses will be reimbursed by your Employer by direct credit transfer into your nominated [Home Country/Host Country] bank account in [*currency*] monthly in arrears, subject always to your compliance with your Employer's expenses policy in force from time to time including your provision in good time of evidence satisfactory to your Employer that the expenditure has been properly incurred.

Please note that failure to comply with your Employer's expenses policy and requirements, eg failure to retain receipts, could have a significant impact on your income. Please refer to [] in this regard.

[NB: *If the host company reimburses expenses the assignment letter should make clear that it does so on behalf of the home company.*]

10. Confidentiality, intellectual property [and data protection]

(a) You will continue to owe a duty of confidentiality to your Employer during your assignment as set out in [your Pre-Assignment Contract]. In addition, it is a condition of your assignment that you sign the Host Company's confidentiality agreement, a copy of which is enclosed with this letter.

(b) [NB: *Confirm whether home or host company will own any intellectual property created during the assignment and ensure any appropriate agreements are concluded between the employee and host company and the home and host companies.*]

(c) By signing this letter you consent to the reasonable provision of your personal data to the Host Company in Host Country (and from the Host Company in the Host Company to your Employer in the Home Country) for the purpose of the assignment. [*NB: Consent here is unlikely to be sufficient to allow lawful transfer of personal data to some countries from the EU (see **12.72–12.91**). A copy of an appropriate data protection policy explaining the purposes for which the data will be used and requesting more explicit consent should ideally be provided separately. Separate consents are likely to be required in respect of Family members.*]

11. Pension

[During your assignment you will continue to be eligible to participate in [*name of home country pension plan*] (the 'Pension Plan'). Your Notional Salary [*NB: Check this is possible*] will be used for the purposes of calculating [your Employer's pension contributions/your pension entitlement – *NB: Is this a final salary/defined benefit or money purchase/defined contribution plan?*], subject to any applicable limits. Your pension contributions will be deducted from your Assignment Salary. Your participation will remain subject to the terms of the Pension Plan from time to time in force and applicable laws. Please note that if you are no longer entitled to participate in the Pension Plan because, for example, you have spent too long outside Home Country, your participation will be discontinued and, in that event, no substitute pension arrangement, pension contributions or compensation will be offered to you.]

Your Employer gives you no assurance regarding the tax or social security treatment of pension. You should be aware that relocation (eg at the start or end of your assignment or in the future) may have a substantial impact on your pension, for example, on the tax treatment of contributions, accumulation of funds and/or drawn down of pension and you are encouraged to seek independent financial advice in that regard.

[*NB: Pensions clauses should always be checked by appropriate pensions advisers who are familiar with home and host country requirements and the relevant trust deed and rules.*]

OR:

[There will be no pension plan applicable to your employment, and no pension contributions will be made by your Employer, in respect of the period of your assignment.]

[*NB: will cash payments be made instead?*]

12. Health

Health and safety

(a)   You must comply with the Host Company's reasonable health and safety policies and directions. [*Name, job title*] will contact you separately to discuss health and safety relating to your assignment. If you have any additional concerns or questions regarding health and safety during your assignment please let [*name, job title of home employer's representative*] know.

Medical cover

(b)   Your 'Family' for the purposes of this assignment letter means your partner and your children under the age of 18 years (your 'Children') if any.

[*NB: Make thorough enquiries regarding the nature of the employee's family. The family may include civil partners, co-habitees, parents, stepchildren, children that do not reside with the employee, etc.*]

[[*EEA/EU*] COUNTRY NATIONALS: You may be eligible to receive treatment under the national health system of other [*EEA/EU*] countries. If so, you are required to apply promptly for a European Health Insurance Card for yourself and each member of your Family. You [and your Family] are expected to use the Host Country state health plan for treatment wherever possible.]

AND/OR:

[You and your Family will be eligible to participate in your Employer's [international] medical insurance plan in force from time to time.]

Fitness to work

(c)   Your Employer may from time to time (whether before or during your assignment) require you to submit to a medical examination by medical practitioner(s) nominated by your Employer at its absolute discretion, and at your Employer's expense. You consent to the disclosure of the results of any such examination to your Employer and the Host Company, in so far as they relate to your fitness to perform your duties and/or eligibility to receive benefits, and subject always to applicable laws. Your Employer may cease payment of your remuneration and discontinue the provision of benefits to you if it is advised by such medical adviser that you are fit to return to work (and you do not do so immediately) or if you fail to attend any such examination without good reason and without prejudice to your Employer's other rights and remedies.

[*NB: any requirements in relation to family members, eg as a condition of provision of cover?*]
[*NB: required examinations may not be permitted or appropriate in all jurisdictions.*]

Your Employer reserves the right to withdraw any offer of assignment or terminate any assignment and/or require you to return to Home Country without notice (or on short notice) if, in your Employer's opinion, you are not fit to perform your duties or unlikely to return to work within a reasonable time period or if, in your Employer's reasonable opinion, you [or a member of your Family] should undergo medical treatment in Home Country.
[*NB: consider including terms relating to evacuation*]

13. Car

You will be provided with a car for your business and personal use in Host Country, subject to approval by your Assignment Manager.

[*NB: Any terms relating to fuel costs/insurance/licensing requirements/road tax/company driver/Family members driving/fines? Reference to any separate policy?*]

14. Education

Your Employer will pay the costs of school fees for sending your Children [over the age of 5 years] to appropriate schools (in [Host Country/Home Country]) during your assignment and until the end of any school term in which your assignment ends. Payment will be made directly to the school on production of an appropriate invoice from the school addressed to your Employer and subject to the approval of your Assignment Manager and to a maximum cost of [*amount and currency in figures*] ([*amount and currency in words*]) per Child in respect of each school year. No reimbursement will be made in respect of the costs of university, or other tertiary, education. [*NB: Is a deposit required and if so who will pay the deposit? What will happen to the deposit on termination? Who will pay any early termination fees if the child leaves part way through the school year? Any policy relating to other school-related expenses, eg exam fees, books, etc?*]

15. Immigration

The start and continuation of your assignment are subject to you obtaining appropriate documentary evidence of your entitlement to live and work in Host Country and to you remaining entitled to live and work in Host Country, lawfully.

Your Employer will, at its expense, where appropriate apply for (and where appropriate assist you to obtain) any necessary immigration permission, including any work, residential and other permits or visas, required for yourself [and your Family] for the assignment. You are required to assist your Employer, provide all reasonable cooperation, information and documentation and to comply with any conditions or limits imposed by your Employer in this respect.

You must inform your Employer promptly of any potential or actual change of circumstances that may have an impact on your immigration status [and/or that of any member of your Family].

[You must return your work permit and all related documentation to your Employer immediately on termination of your assignment. You will be permitted to keep copies for your personal records, subject to applicable laws.]

[NB: *any requirement to keep company informed or refrain from particular activities?*]

16. Language and cultural awareness training

Your Employer will provide you [and your Family] with such language and cultural awareness training prior to and during your assignment as your Employer at its absolute discretion considers appropriate. Approval for language training should be sought from your Assignment Manager. [*NB: Is this a benefit or a business requirement? Offered on a Net basis?*]

17. Accommodation

Your Employer will meet the cost of [furnished/unfurnished] accommodation for you [and your Family] in Host Country considered suitable by your Employer and subject always to the prior written approval of your Assignment Manager [and to a maximum monthly rental cost of [*maximum monthly rent*]].

[NB: *Consider:*

- *conditions attached to any available tax relief*
- *suitability, eg family size, pets, status*
- *whether the employer or the employee will be responsible for the lease and payment of rent to the landlord*
- *damage to property*
- *payment and return of deposit*
- *utility bills*
- *local taxes*
- *insurance for the property and personal belongings*
- *assistance of relocation agent*

- *responsibility for any early termination or similar costs at the end of the assignment*
- *rental income from employee's property in the home country*]

[It is a condition of your assignment that you must not purchase any property in Host Country and you must procure that no member of your family does so.]

[*Offered on a 'Net' basis?*]

18. Relocation and repatriation expenses and home visits

Subject to Company policy in force from time to time (including applicable financial limits and the prior written approval of your Assignment Manager), and as follows, your Employer will reimburse you the costs of the following:

- one economy class one-way flight, for yourself and each member of your Family, between Home Country and Host Country on or about the start of your assignment and within [*period, consider any immigration restrictions*] following the end of your assignment [(provided that your employment does not end on Voluntary Termination)) between Host Country and Home Country (or the location of any subsequent expatriate assignment by your Employer); and
- flights for yourself and each member of your Family, between Home Country and Host Country during your assignment subject to a maximum aggregate annual cost of [*annual limit and currency*]; and
- transporting a reasonable amount of your, and your Family's, personal belongings at the start and within [*period*] following the end of your assignment between Home Country and Host Country or the location of any subsequent expatriate assignment by your Employer. The costs of the air freight of [*weight*] per person and a [*volume*] sea freight container, would normally be paid for by your Employer [provided that your employment does not end on Voluntary Termination].

[No costs shall be borne by your Employer in respect of transporting any belongings or your Family or you back to Home Country in connection with the termination of your assignment if your employment ends on Voluntary Termination.]

If you let your home in Home Country, you may have items which you do not wish to leave in your home while overseas. Your Employer will pay for storage and insurance costs in respect of that property subject to a maximum aggregate cost of [*specify limit and currency in figures*] ([*specify limit and currency in words*]) plus VAT per year for the period of your assignment.

[*NB: Are any other benefits offered, eg assistance with temporary accommodation in the host and home countries at the start or end of the assignment, letting agency's fees for home country property?*]

[19. Grievances and discipline

If you have any grievance relating to your assignment or your employment you should raise it with your [Assignment Manager] in writing. You should make it clear that you wish to raise a formal grievance. If the grievance is not resolved to your satisfaction you may raise the matter with [*job title*] of your Employer in writing whose decision will be final.

For the avoidance of doubt, any disciplinary action in respect of your assignment shall be taken by your Employer and not the Host Company. You may appeal against any disciplinary decision to [*job title*] currently [*name*].

Your Employer's disciplinary and grievance policies for Home Country based employees and the Host Company's disciplinary and grievance policies for Host Country based employees shall not apply to you during your assignment.

This paragraph shall not confer any contractual rights upon you. [*NB: check with Host Country employment lawyers to see if this is helpful.*]

20. Miscellaneous

Notices

(a)   [*NB: Specify arrangements for service of notice, bearing in mind that postal services may be slow or unreliable. Ensure that the notice arrangements are consistent with the identity of the employer.*]

Policies

(b)   [*NB: Make clear whether home country policies will apply or not during the assignment.*]

Collective agreements

(c)   [*NB: Reference to applicable collective agreements or confirmation that none apply.*]

Whole agreement

(d)   This assignment letter and your Pre-Assignment Contract together record the whole agreement between you and your Employer in respect of your assignment [and employment] and supersede any prior agreements in this regard. [*NB: Any exceptions eg share plans? Termination by mutual agreement? Stronger terms re representations etc?*]

Language

(e) This assignment letter has been prepared in [English] and a translation has been prepared in [*Host Country language*]. In the event of any conflict the [*Host Country /English language*] version shall apply.

Third party rights

(f) [Other than the Group Companies,] only you and your Employer shall have the right to enforce this assignment letter. Only the consents of you and of your Employer are required to vary the terms of this assignment letter.

Applicable laws

(g) This assignment letter shall be governed and construed in all respects by [the laws of England and Wales] and you and your Employer irrevocably submit to the [non-exclusive jurisdiction of the Courts of England].

[*NB: Consider whether there is any opportunity to expressly contract out of host country employment laws.*]

[*NB: Consider whether governing law in relation to non-contractual obligations should be specified.*]

Please would you sign, date and return the duplicate copy of this assignment letter to me to confirm that you have read, understand and agree to its contents. The additional copy of this assignment letter is for you to keep.

Yours sincerely

[Name of authorised signatory for Employer]

[Job title of authorised signatory for Employer]

Duly authorised for and on behalf of *[Employer's name]*

[NB: Consider whether any apostille or evidence of authority of signatory is required (unlikely)]

I confirm that I have read, understand and agree to be bound by the contents of this assignment letter.

Employee's signature: Date signed: ....

....

[Employee's name]

HOME COMPANY RESIDUAL CONTRACT

A2.5 [*NB: Consider the purpose of this agreement, and related specialist advice, carefully before starting to draft. Check carefully to ensure this agreement is consistent with the employment contract with the host company and any inter-company expatriate supply agreement between the home and host companies. See also* **6.40–6.54** *regarding the purpose of a residual contract and Chapter 8 regarding the content of a residual contract.*]

[*to be typed on the home country employer's headed notepaper (should include registered address)*]

Private & confidential – addressee only

[*Name of employee*]

[*Home address of employee at date letter issued*]

By [*Delivery method*]

[*Employer's reference*]

[*Date*]

Dear [*Name of employee*]

Your employment with [*Home Company*] (the 'Company') and assignment to [*Host Company*] (the 'Host Company') in [*Host Country*]

This letter is to confirm the terms that will apply to you in relation to your assignment to the Host Company in [*Host Country*] (your 'assignment').

During your assignment you will be employed by the Host Company on terms agreed between you and the Host Company (your 'Assignment Employment Contract'). [*NB: Insert precise reference to Host Company contract?*] Your current employment with the Company will [end/be suspended] immediately before your employment with the Host Company begins.

1. Assignment Start Date

The Company understands that your assignment to the Host Company will begin on [*assignment start date*] (your 'Assignment Start Date'). [*NB: is the start date clear or likely to change?*]

2. [Termination/suspension] of current employment with the Company

(a) The [termination/suspension] of your employment with the Company [and your employment contract with the Company dated [*date*] (your

'Pre-Assignment Contract')] prior to your Assignment Start Date is by mutual agreement. You acknowledge and agree that you have received adequate consideration for [termination/suspension]; that you have no claims arising from such [termination/suspension]; and that you will receive no additional compensation in connection with such [termination/ suspension].

(b) [*NB: Record any practical arrangements relating to termination/ suspension of employment, eg in relation to accrued but untaken holiday, if no separate severance agreement is entered into.*]

3. Notional Salary

(a) Your Notional Salary for the purposes of this Agreement is at the rate of [*currency*] [*rate*] per year. For the avoidance of doubt, your Notional Salary is a hypothetical salary and is used for reference purposes only. The Company shall be under no obligation to pay any salary to you during your assignment.

(b) Your Notional Salary may be reviewed by the Company from time to time at its absolute discretion. The Company may decide not to increase your Notional Salary but will not reduce it during your assignment.

4. Confidentiality, intellectual property and data protection

(a) You will continue to owe a duty of confidentiality to the Company during your assignment. In addition, it is a condition of your assignment that you sign the Host Company's confidentiality agreement, a copy of which has been provided to you separately by the Host Company.

(b) [*NB: Confirm whether home or host company will own any intellectual property created during the assignment and ensure any appropriate agreements are concluded between the employee and host company and the home and host companies.*]

(c) By signing this letter you consent to the reasonable provision of personal information to the Host Company in [*Host Country*] for the purpose of the assignment. [*NB: Consent may not be sufficient to allow lawful transfer of personal data to some countries. (See 12.72–12.91) A copy of an appropriate data protection policy explaining the purposes for which the data will be used and requesting more explicit consent should be provided.*]

[*NB: consider including more detailed cooperation and provision of information clauses eg to assist with tax and immigration compliance, including for a sufficient period after termination of employment.*]

5. Pension and other benefit arrangements during your assignment

(a) [Notwithstanding that you will not be employed by the Company during your assignment,] you will remain eligible to participate in the following benefit arrangements during your assignment, subject to the terms of such plans in force from time to time:

(b) [*NB:*
  - *Specify any relevant arrangements, terms and conditions, maximum period of participation etc.*
  - *Ask relevant specialists (eg pensions advisers) to check conditions are consistent with the wording of this Agreement.*
  - *Refer to Notional Salary if appropriate.*]

6. Arrangements on termination of assignment

(a) It is the Company's intention that immediately following termination of your assignment you will return to the employment of the Company in [*Home Country*].

[*NB: OR provide for automatic revival of employment with the Company on termination of assignment.*]

(b) As your employer during your assignment, the Host Company may terminate your employment with the Host Company in accordance with your Assignment Employment Contract. You are required to inform the Company immediately in writing of receipt of any notice of termination of employment by the Host Company whether such notice is given in accordance your Assignment Employment Contract or otherwise ('Notice of End of Assignment').

(c) Following receipt of any Notice of End of Assignment from you or notification given by the Host Company to the Company of termination of your employment by the Host Company, the Company shall make reasonable efforts to find alternative employment for you in [*Home Country*] with the Company. Any such employment available may be offered to you on [such terms as the Company shall at its absolute discretion consider appropriate].

[*NB: OR could provide for revival of earlier Pre-Assignment Contract*]

(d) [You are currently regarded as a [Grade X] employee by the Company and it is anticipated that any employment offered to you in [*Home Country*] to commence after termination of your assignment will be at that level or at a higher [grade].]

(e) [It is anticipated that any employment offered to you in [*Home Country*] to commence after termination of your assignment will be at a salary equal to [or greater than] your Notional Salary.]

[*NB: Confirm whether any severance pay will be offered by the Company if alternative employment cannot be found?*]

7. Continuity of employment

(a) [*NB: Clarify dates on which employment with the Company and group began and effect of assignment on any statutory continuity of employment.*]

(b) [*NB: Clarify effect of assignment on continuity of employment for benefit purposes, eg if a qualifying period of service is required for participation in any benefit arrangements discontinued for the duration of the assignment.*]

8. Notice of termination of residual contract

(a) Either you or the Company may terminate this residual contract by [giving the other not less than [*notice period*] months' written notice]. For the avoidance of doubt, notice of termination of this residual contract may be given by the Company at any time and for any reason, whether before, on or after termination of your assignment to and employment with the Host Company.

(b) For the avoidance of doubt, the Host Country shall have no power to terminate this residual contract.

9. Post termination restrictions

(a) [*NB: Will any post termination restrictions apply during the assignment or continue to apply on termination of the residual contract?*]

(b) [*NB: Consider whether a period of garden leave or temporary role on termination of the assignment might be helpful, for example to give an opportunity for the Company to look for alternative employment for the employee.*]

10. Miscellaneous

Notices

(a) [*Specify arrangements for service of notice, bearing in mind that postal services may be slow or unreliable. Ensure that the notice arrangements are consistent with the identity of the employer.*]

Policies

(b) [*NB: Make clear whether home country policies will apply or, more likely, not during the assignment.*]

Collective agreements

(c)   [NB: *Reference to applicable collective agreements or confirmation that none apply.*]

Whole agreement

(d)   This residual contract records the whole agreement between you and the Company and supersedes any prior agreement between you and the Company regarding your employment with the Company.

[NB: *Amend if Pre-Assignment Contract is to be suspended rather than replaced.*]

Language

(e)   This residual contract has been prepared in [English] and a translation has been prepared in [*Host Country language*]. In the event of any conflict the [*Host Country/English language*] version shall apply.

Third party rights

(f)   [Other than the Group Companies, as defined in []] only you and the Company shall have the right to enforce this residual contract. Only the consents of you and of the Company are required to vary the terms of this residual contract.

Applicable laws

(g)   This residual contract shall be governed and construed in all respects by [English law] and you and the Company irrevocably submit to the [non-exclusive jurisdiction of the Courts of England].

[NB: *Consider whether governing law in relation to non-contractual obligations should be specified.*]

Please would you sign, date and return to me the duplicate copy of this letter to confirm that you have read, understood and agree to its contents. The additional copy is for you to keep.

Yours sincerely

[*Name of authorised signatory for home company*]

[*Job title of authorised signatory for home company*]

Duly authorised for and on behalf of [*home company*]

[*NB: Consider whether any apostille or evidence of authority of signatory is required*]

I confirm that I have read, understand and agree to be bound by the contents of this residual contract.

Employee's signature: Date signed: ....
....

[*Employee's name*]

INTER-COMPANY EXPATRIATE SUPPLY AGREEMENT

A2.6 [*NB: This framework document has been prepared on the basis that the home company is the employer. See also* **8.70–8.80** *on the contents of an inter-company expatriate supply agreement and checklist* **A1.8** *at Appendix 1*]

THIS AGREEMENT IS MADE ON [*date*]

BETWEEN:

[*HOME EMPLOYER*] [*registered number*] the registered office of which is at [*registered address of home employer*] (the 'Employer'); and

[*HOST COMPANY*] [*registered number*] the registered office of which is at [*registered address of host company*] (the 'Host Company').

WHEREAS:

The Host Company and the Employer have agreed that the Employer shall provide the services of the Employee [or Employees] to the Host Company on the terms of this Agreement.

IT IS AGREED AS FOLLOWS:

1. Definitions etc

(a)   In this Agreement:

Authorised Representative(s)

mean(s) [*job title(s)*] for the Host Company and [*job title(s)*] for the Employer or such other people as either party may notify to the other in writing.

Employee

means [*name*]. [Those people whose names are listed at Schedule [ ]] [and such other people as the Host Company and the Employer may agree from time to time in writing.]

Services

means [*description*]. [For the avoidance of doubt, the Services are for the purposes of the business of the Host Company and not for the purposes of the business of the Employer.]

[*NB: A detailed description of the services may be important, eg for VAT, corporation tax or immigration purposes.*]

(b)   The headings in this Agreement are for convenience only, do not form part of this Agreement and shall not be taken into account in its construction or interpretation.

(c)   References to clauses and schedules in this Agreement are to clauses of and schedules to this Agreement unless otherwise indicated.

2. Duration

The provision of the Services will start on [*date provision of Services begins*] and will continue [until [*date*]]/[until terminated on the expiry of not less than [ ] months'] notice given by either the Host Company or the Employer to the other in writing (the 'Term'). [For the avoidance of doubt, the Term is not expected to continue beyond [*date*].]

[*NB: Implications for, eg, social security, income tax, immigration.*]

3. Location

The Employer will provide the Services at the Host Company's premises at [*address*] [or at such other place within [*Host Country*] as the Host Company may reasonably direct from time to time].

[*NB: Implications for, eg, corporation tax, income tax, social security, immigration.*]

4. The Employer's obligations

Hours of work

(a)   The Employer shall procure that:
  •   the Employee's normal hours of work during the Term shall be [9 am to 5 pm] [Monday to Friday] each week;
  •   the Employee shall be obliged to work such overtime as may be required for the proper performance of the Services (subject to applicable laws); and
  •   public holidays applicable in [*Host Country*] shall apply to the Employee.

Conduct of the Employee

(b)   The Employer shall, and shall procure that the Employee shall:
  •   provide the Services in a professional manner, using all reasonable skill and expertise; and
  •   comply with any reasonable targets or time-limits set by the Host Company in relation to the Services.

Use of facilities

(c)   The Employer shall, and shall procure that the Employee shall, use any facilities provided by the Host Company only for purposes authorised by the Host Company.

Provision of information

(d)   The Employer shall and shall procure that the Employee shall:
- maintain such records as the Host Company may reasonably require of time spent providing the Services [and of the country or countries in which the Services are provided]; and
- provide the Host Company with such information (and in such form) regarding the Services as the Host Company may reasonably request from time to time; and
- subject to clause 9, provide the Host Company with such information regarding the Employee as the Host Company may require from time to time in order to comply with its legal obligations including, inter alia, obligations relating to immigration status, income tax and social security and other tax liabilities.

Training

(e)   The Employer shall, at its own expense, ensure that the Employee undertakes any training necessary to ensure the Employee has the relevant up-to-date skills and expertise to provide the Services properly.

Obligations as employer

(f)   The Employer will fulfil its legal obligations as employer of the Employee, including, inter alia, its obligations to:
- pay the Employee's remuneration;
- issue appropriate employment documents;
- allow the Employee to take paid holiday at the Employer's expense;
- make any appropriate payments in respect of absence; and
- reimburse the Employee in respect of expenses incurred by the Employee in providing the Services.

For the avoidance of doubt, the Host Company will not provide salary, holiday pay or any other absence pay or any other employment benefit to the Employee.

[NB: *Will the host company make any salary or other payments to the employee on the employer's behalf?*]

Representations

(g)   The Employer shall procure that the Employee represents himself as an employee of the Employer, and shall not represent himself or hold himself out as a representative of the Host Company.

Health and safety

(h)   The Employer will comply with, and shall procure that the Employee complies with, relevant laws and other requirements relating to the health and safety of the Employee.

Professional indemnity or other insurance

(i)   The Employer accepts that it has a legal risk in respect of [employer's liability and professional indemnity] and will arrange and maintain, at its own expense, appropriate insurance cover in relation to these matters at all times in respect of the provision of the Services, subject always to such minimum standards as the Host Company may from time to time reasonably request. The Host Company may from time to time require the Employer to provide the Host Company with documentary evidence that such cover is in place. The Employer shall promptly comply with any such request.

5. The Employer's warranties

The Employer warrants that:

- in entering into this Agreement, and in providing the Services the Employee will not be in breach of any obligation to any third party; and
- the Employee is not currently engaged on any other contract that conflicts with the best interests of the Host Company; and
- no documents or other information will be provided by the Employee for use in the provision of the Services that infringe any third party intellectual property rights and any documents or other materials created by the Employee in the provision of the Services for use by the Host Company will be original and created specifically for the Host Company; and
- the Employee has the following qualifications: [ ]; and
- the Employee may lawfully live and provide the Services in the [*Host Country*]; and
- the personal details regarding the Employee provided to the Host Company by the Employer from time to time are accurate and not misleading.

6. The Host Company's obligations

Facilities

(a)   The Host Company will, to the extent reasonably required to enable the Employer to provide the Services efficiently, allow the Employee access to the Host Company's premises, facilities and information systems, subject to the Employer ensuring that the Employee complies with any reasonable workplace rules or regulations for contractors that the Host Company may notify to it.

Health and safety

(b)   The Host Company will comply with relevant laws and other requirements relating to the health and safety of the Employee.

Insurance

(c)   The Host Company shall take out all appropriate insurance cover relating to the Employee.

Information and co-operation, discipline and dismissal

(d)   The Host Company shall give the Employer all reasonable co-operation, information and assistance regarding the Employee and the Services to enable the Employer to manage the employment of the Employee effectively. In particular, but without limitation, the Host Company shall provide the Employer with all appropriate information and assistance in relation to any performance assessment, pay review, disciplinary or grievance procedure or dismissal. For the avoidance of doubt, the Host Company has no authority or delegated responsibility regarding discipline or dismissal of the employee.

[NB: *Will the host company provide any services to the employer, eg payroll services?*]

7. Fees and disbursements

Fees

(a)   The Host Company will pay the Employer fees for providing the Services at the rate of [*currency and rate*] [inclusive of/plus] [Value Added Tax] if applicable.

Disbursements

(b) The Host Company shall reimburse the Employer in respect of disbursements wholly and necessarily incurred in the proper provision of the Services subject to the provision by the Employer to the Host Company of appropriate documentary evidence that such disbursements have been properly incurred.

[*NB:*
- *Are prior approval or a list of qualifying disbursements required?*
- *Will the host company reimburse expenses to the employee on behalf of the employer? If so, specify the relevant recharging arrangements etc.*]

Payment arrangements

(c) On or before the [ ]th day of each month the Employer shall submit invoices to the Host Company for fees and disbursements due in respect of the Services provided during the previous calendar month showing any [Value Added Tax] separately. Fees shall be specified in [*currency*].

[For the avoidance of doubt, no payment will be made in respect of any period during which the Services are not provided (eg due to the Employee's illness).]

The Host Company will pay the fees and disbursements due plus any applicable [Value Added Tax] to the Employer in [*currency*] within [28] days of receiving any such invoice.

8. Confidential information

(a) The Employer will procure that the Employee will keep secret and confidential and will not use, disclose or permit to be used or disclosed any trade secrets or confidential information relating to the Host Company's business affairs or finances or any such information relating to a subsidiary, supplier or customer of the Host Company which may come into its or their possession in providing the Services. Such obligations will apply during the Term and for so long after the Term as such information remains confidential.

(b) The Employer will deliver immediately on demand by the Host Company and, in any event, when the provision of the Services ceases for any reason, to the Host Company all working papers and other materials and any copies provided to or obtained by the Employee in providing the Services.

(c) The Employer shall procure that the Employee signs such confidentiality agreements with the Host Company, and any clients or customers of the Host Company, as the Host Company may reasonably require.

(d)   This clause shall not apply to any documents or other materials and data or other information which are already in the public domain, other than through a breach of this clause, and shall cease to apply to the extent that either party is required by law to make a disclosure.

(e)   The Employer will, and will procure that the Employee will, only use Confidential Information provided by the Employer for the proper provision of the Services.

9. Data protection

The Employer and the Host Company shall comply with [*reference to relevant contract, policy etc relating to data protection*].

10. Restrictive covenants

The Employer will and will procure that the Employee will sign the Host Company's [*post termination restrictions*] in the form of the document set out at Schedule [ ] to this Agreement. [For the avoidance of doubt, notwithstanding any other term of this Agreement, [*Country*] laws will govern the terms of any such agreement.]

11. Intellectual property

(a)   The Employer will, and will procure that the Employee will, promptly disclose to the Host Company all works in which copyright or design rights may exist which the Employee may make or originate either solely or jointly with others in the course of providing the Services. Any such copyright works or designs created by the Employee in the course of providing the Services shall be the property of the Host Company, whether or not the work was made at the direction of the Host Company or was intended for the Host Company or any customer of the Host Company and the copyright in it and the rights in any design shall belong to the Host Company.

(b)   In order to give effect to the provisions of clause 11(a) above, the Employer shall, and shall procure that the Employee shall, hereby irrevocably assign to the Host Company with full title guarantee and free from all encumbrances all copyright or design rights (both present and future throughout the world for the whole term of such rights in all languages, including any extensions or renewals) in all copyright works or designs referred to in clause 11(a) including for the avoidance of doubt all rights whether known at the date of this Agreement or otherwise.

(c)   The Employer will, and will procure that the Employee will, execute or sign any documents and do all other acts as the Host Company may reasonably require to vest in the Host Company the entire title to and benefit of the works referred to in clause 11(a). The Employer hereby irrevocably appoints, and confirms that it shall procure that the Employee irrevocably appoints, the Host Company as its (or their) attorney to do all acts and execute all documents as may be required to secure such vesting if the Employer or the Employee fails to comply with any request under this clause [ ] within seven days of the request being made.

[*NB: Signature as deed? Requirements regarding power of attorney?*]

(d)   The Employer will, and will procure that the Employee will, give the Host Company all reasonable assistance to enable it to defend any claim action or proceedings brought against the Host Company as a result of an alleged infringement of any of the rights assigned to it under this clause 11.

[*NB: Will moral rights be waived?*]

12. Immediate termination

[Without prejudice to [ ]] The Host Company or the Employer may terminate the provision of the Services with immediate effect if:

(a)   the Employee is no longer entitled to live and/or work in [*Host Country*]; and/or

(b)   the other party materially breaches any of the terms of this Agreement; and/or

(c)   the other party goes into liquidation, makes a voluntary arrangement with its creditors or has a receiver or administrator appointed.

The Host Company may also terminate the provision of the Services with immediate effect if:

(d)   the Employee is incompetent;

(e)   the Employer is seriously or persistently negligent in relation to the Services; and/or

(f)   the Employer fails or refuses, after written notice, to provide some or all of the Services properly required of it.

13. Exclusive services

The Employer shall not provide the services of the Employee to any person other than the Host Company during the Term.

14. Intention of the parties

The Employer and the Host Company agree that this Agreement is a contract for services in respect of services to be provided by the Employer to the Host Company. In entering into this Agreement the parties do not intend to create at any time any employment or worker relationship between the Employee and the Host Company and the parties acknowledge and agree that the Employee is an employee of the Employer.

15.   Miscellaneous

Notices

(a)   Any notice to be given by either the Employer or the Host Company to the other must be in writing. Any notice shall be served [by post or delivered by hand] to the last known registered office of the other party and marked for the attention of the Company Secretary. [A copy of any notice shall be delivered to the other party by fax. [*specify fax numbers etc*]] [*NB: Or specify alternative arrangements*]

Whole agreement

(b)   This Agreement cancels and is in substitution for all previous arrangements (whether oral or in writing) in relation to the provision of services of the Employee(s) by the Employer to the Host Company.

Language

(c)   This Agreement has been prepared in [English] and a translation has been prepared in [*Host Country language*]. In the event of any conflict the [*Host Country /English language*] version shall apply.

Third party rights

(d)   Only the Employer and the Host Company shall have the right to enforce this Agreement and only the consents of the Employer and the Host Company shall be required to vary the terms of this Agreement.

Amendment

(e)   No modification or amendment to this Agreement shall be valid unless it is made in writing and signed on behalf of the Employer and the Host Company.

Waiver

(f)   Failure or delay by the Employer or the Host Company in exercising or enforcing any of its rights, in whole or in part, under this Agreement, or at law, shall not be deemed to be a waiver of such right nor operate to bar its exercise or enforcement at any future time or times.

Applicable laws

(g)   This Agreement will be governed by and construed in accordance with [English law] and both parties submit to the exclusive jurisdiction of the [English] courts in relation to any dispute arising under it.

[NB: *Consider whether governing law in relation to non-contractual obligations should be specified.*]

Conclusion of this Agreement

(h)   This Agreement may be executed as one document or in any number of counterparts and provided that at least one counterpart document has been executed on behalf of each party this Agreement shall be deemed concluded.

SIGNED by

[*Name*]

[*Job title*]

duly authorised for and on behalf of

[*the Host Company*]

date signed ....

SIGNED by

[*Name*]

[*Job title*]

duly authorised for and on behalf of

[*The Employer*]

date signed ....

[*NB: Is signature as a deed or any evidence of authority or apostille required?*]

HOME EMPLOYER SEVERANCE AGREEMENT

A2.7 [*NB: Specialist advice should always be sought in relation to severance terms to apply on termination of employment. This framework agreement is intended to provide some suggestions regarding issues to be considered. See also Chapter 13 on ending the assignment and/or employment.*]

Private & confidential

Without prejudice and subject to contract

THIS AGREEMENT IS MADE ON [*date*]

BETWEEN:

[*NAME OF EMPLOYER*] [*registered number*] the registered office of which is at [*registered address of employer*] (the 'Employer'); and

[*HOST COMPANY*] [*registered number*] the registered office of which is at [*registered address of Host Company*] (the 'Host Company'); and

[*NAME OF EMPLOYEE*] (the 'Employee') of [*home address of employee at date of signature*].

[*NB: Consider whether it is necessary or appropriate for the host company, or any other companies, to be party to the agreement, e g to benefit from any release offered by the employee.*]

WHEREAS:

(a)   The Employee's employment with the Employer began on the Employment Start Date.

(b)   The Employer supplies the services of the Employee to the Host Company in the Host Country.

(c)   The Employee's assignment to the Host Company in the Host Country began on the Assignment Start Date.

(d)   This Agreement sets out the terms on which it has been agreed that [the Assignment and the Employment will end, and on which claims related to the Assignment and Employment, and their termination, will be waived and settled.]

IT IS AGREED AS FOLLOWS:

1. Definitions

(a)   In this Agreement:

Assignment

means the assignment of the Employee by the Employer to provide services to the Host Company.

Assignment Start Date

means [*Assignment Start Date*].

Claims

means [*specify relevant claims*].

Company Car

means [*make, model, registration number*] provided to the Employee by the Employer.

Contract of Employment

means the contract of employment made between the Employer and the Employee dated [*date*][, as amended by an assignment letter dated [*date*]].

Employment

means the Employee's employment by the Employer.

Employment Start Date

means [*Employment Start Date*].

Exchange Rate

[*insert definition if appropriate*].

Family

[*insert definition or name them*].

Group Company

means [*insert definition*].

Home Country

means [*home country*].

Host Country

means [*host country*].

Person

means any company, corporation, partnership, limited liability partnership, individual or any other legal entity, registered in any jurisdiction.

Released Parties

means [the Employer, each Group Company and each of their employees, officers, agents and shareholders].

Termination Date

means [*termination date*] / [the date of this Agreement].

(b)   The headings in this Agreement do not form part of this Agreement and shall not be taken into account in its construction and interpretation.

(c)   Unless otherwise indicated references to legislation are to the legislation of [*Country*] in force from time to time.

(d)   Unless otherwise indicated references to clauses and schedules in this Agreement are to clauses of and schedules to this Agreement.

2. Termination of Employment and Assignment

The Employment and the Assignment [will terminate/ended] on the Termination Date [by reason of redundancy/for economic reasons/by mutual agreement between the Employer and Employee/by reason of the Employee's resignation].

[*NB: Consider specified reasons for termination of employment and terminology carefully, taking particular account of host country laws, impact on incentive entitlements etc.*]

3. Resignation from appointments

(a)   The Employee hereby confirms that it is his intention to resign from each and every appointment (whether [as director or secretary or otherwise]) to the Employer, the Host Company or any other Group Company, or otherwise held in the course of the Employment, with effect from the [Termination Date/date of this Agreement/*specify date*].

(b)   The Employee shall deliver to [the Employer] not later than on the day this Agreement is concluded [a] duly signed and dated letter[s] of resignation (in the form of the draft letter[s] set out at Schedule [ ] from his appointment[s] as [director/secretary] of [*specify companies*].

(c) The Employee warrants that he does not hold any other appointment with [or hold any power of attorney for] the Employer, the Host Company, any other Group Company or any other company by virtue of his Employment.

(d) The Employee hereby irrevocably authorises any director of the Employer to be his authorised attorney to do all things and to execute all documents in his name and on his behalf as may be necessary to effect each such resignation on [the Termination Date/the date of this Agreement/*specify date*] or, at the Employer's absolute discretion, any time thereafter. A letter signed by any director of the Employer or document executed under the authority conferred by this clause will be conclusive evidence of the same.

[*NB:*

- *Appointments may include offices as director or secretary and also other appointments that may have been granted in the host country or elsewhere to facilitate operations of the host company.*
- *Consider any local requirements regarding resignation, eg the need to appoint an alternative representative first.*
- *Consider whether it would be appropriate to conclude the Agreement in the form of a Deed and the appropriate form of any Power of Attorney or other authority, and whether this is effective in the Host Country.*
- *Consider whether it may be appropriate to specify any required future co-operation.*
- *Consider whether it would be possible or appropriate to withhold all or part of the compensation until after the necessary actions have been taken.*]

4. Immigration

[The Employee shall provide the Employer with all original papers relating to [his] right to [work] in Host Country on [*date*], unless the Employer (at its absolute discretion) agrees in writing to a later delivery date, any such later date to be on or prior to the Termination Date. The Employee will be permitted to retain photocopies of such papers for his own purposes.]

[*NB:*

- *Is the employee obliged to leave the Host Country within a specified period of time after termination of employment?*
- *Would a period of garden leave help? Is that permitted?*
- *Will the employer be exposed to any penalty if the employee fails to leave the host country at the appropriate time or pay his bills?*
- *Is the employer required to return any immigration papers or report the termination of the employment to the host country immigration authorities?*

- *Will any benefits or payments be linked to future co-operation with immigration requirements?*
- *Consider whether it would be possible or appropriate to withhold all or part of the compensation until after key conditions have been met.]*

5. References

Subject to any obligation to comply with any legal or regulatory requirement regarding references and to the Employer's right not to include any statement which is misleading or false the Employer shall, within 28 days of a written request being made to the Employer's [*job title*] (or such other person as is nominated by the Employer from time to time for the purpose and notified to the Employee in writing) by the Employee, provide a written reference in the form of the draft reference set out at Schedule [ ] to any prospective employer. The Employee shall not approach (or encourage any other Person to approach) any other employee of the Employer, the Host Company or any other Group Company other such nominated person with a view to obtaining a written or oral reference.

[*NB:*

- *It may not always be necessary or appropriate to agree the terms of a reference.*
- *Check whether there are any mandatory requirements regarding provision of references.*
- *Additional provisions may be required, eg in relation to announcements or oral enquiries.]*

6. Remuneration and benefits

Subject to deduction of such income tax and social security contributions as may be appropriate, the Employer shall continue to provide the Employee with the salary and benefits to which he is entitled under the terms of the Contract of Employment in respect of the period up to and including the Termination Date.

The Employee accepts that he is not entitled to and shall not be paid any further remuneration by or receive any further benefits from the Employer or any other Released Party save as specified in this Agreement [(including at Schedule [ ] to this Agreement)].

[*NB: Consider, and if appropriate clarify, tax equalisation and protection arrangements, see further below.*]

Pension

(a)　[For the avoidance of doubt, no further pension contributions shall be made by the Employer in respect of any period after the Termination Date in respect of any pension for the Employee.]

　　[*NB:*
　　•　Is pension provided by the employer?
　　•　Are money purchase or defined benefit arrangements provided?]

[Shares/share options]

(b) The Employee's entitlements regarding [shares/share options] shall be determined in accordance with the relevant plan rules.

> [NB:
> * *Describe plans and entitlements, eg, number of vested shares, more precisely?*
> * *Check interaction with tax equalisation and protection arrangements.*
> * *Consider whether any remuneration committee or other approval may be required.*
> * *Consider tax implications of vesting, exercise etc carefully in the light of the employee's likely change of country of residence.*
> * *Consider the impact of the specified reason for termination on entitlement, particularly if the terminology appropriate for the host country more generally is not consistent with that used in the plan documents.*]

[The Employee warrants that he holds no shares on behalf of the Employer, the Host Company, any other Group Company or any other company by virtue of the Employment.]

Bonus

(c) [NB: *Clarify any outstanding cash bonus issues. Ensure that tax treatment, currency issues etc are clear.*]

Company Car

(d) The Employee shall return the Company Car in satisfactory condition (together with the keys and all documents relating to it) to [*job title of Host Company representative*] at [*place*] at [*time*] on or before the Termination Date.

Private medical insurance

(e) The Employee and his Family will continue to be covered under the Employer's private medical plan subject to the current terms until [the Termination Date/[*date to allow for cover till return home*]].

[NB: *Consider whether cover should be continued for longer to allow the employee to return to the home country before the cover ceases. There may be additional issues to consider if the employee wishes to continue US medical cover.*]

Accommodation and utilities

(f)   The Employee will be reimbursed in respect of the reasonable costs of [rent, gas, electricity and management/service charges] relating to the accommodation provided to the Employee by the Employer (the 'Accommodation') in respect of the period up to and including [the Termination Date] or the date on which the Employee vacates the Accommodation, if earlier. The Employee is responsible for all other expenses in relation to lease of the Accommodation, including for the avoidance of doubt, any rent relating to any period of occupation after the Termination Date and any early termination fees or other penalties.

[NB:

- *Is the lease in the employer's name or the employee's?*
- *Has the employer paid any deposit that should be recovered?*
- *Will the employer bear the costs of penalties/the rent for any period after the termination date?*
- *Does the employer have any exposure relating to damage to the property?*
- *Will the lease be terminated or transferred to the expatriate's replacement or to the expatriate's own name?*
- *Does the employer wish to withhold any portion of the severance pay until the accommodation issues have been resolved, eg vacation of the property and settlement with the landlord?*
- *Is the employee's property in the home country leased out and will any transitional arrangements apply pending the expiry of that lease?*]

Education

(g)   The Employee's children's school fees have been paid [by the Employer] in respect of [*specify period*]. The Employee will be responsible for any further payment of school fees in respect of his children and the Employer will not pay or reimburse the Employee in respect of any further fees.

[NB:
- *Is the employer or the employee responsible to the school for the payment of fees?*
- *Has the employer paid any deposit that it wishes to recover?*
- *Will the employer bear the costs of penalties for early termination/fees for any period after the termination date, eg to the end of the school year?*]

Repatriation

(h)   [The Employee understands that he is required to leave the Host Country on or before [*date*].]

[The Employee hereby agrees that, following his departure from [*Host Country*] he shall not enter [and remain for longer than [ ] days in] [*Home Country*] before [*date*].]

Subject as follows, the [Employer/Host Company] will reimburse the Employee in respect of the following expenses to assist him with repatriation:

- up to [*amount in figures and currency*] ([*amount in words and currency*]) in respect of flights for the Employee and his Family between the Host Country and Home Country;
- the costs of air and sea freight of the Employee's and his Family's personal belongings between Host Company and Home Country, subject to the following limits [ ].

(i)   These sums will be reimbursed to the Employee on condition that the Employee and his Family leave Host Country within [3 months of the Termination Date] and that the Employee provides the Employer with such documentary evidence that such expenses have been properly incurred and of such departure as the Employer may reasonably require on or before [*date*] and provided that the Employee shall not have not accepted an offer of employment or commenced employment with any third party in Host Country.

[*NB:*

- *Will any temporary accommodation in the home or host country be provided?*
- *The employer may wish to limit the reimbursement of repatriation expenses in the event that the employee secures alternative employment in the host country or does not return to the home country.*
- *The employer may control expenses by making the relevant arrangements for flights, removals etc directly.*
- *The way in which these expenses are dealt with may affect the tax treatment of the expenses and/or there may be limits on the relief allowed.*]

7. Business expenses and repayment of sums due from the Employee

(a)   Provided the Employee submits claim(s) in respect of all outstanding business expenses within 7 days following the Termination Date, the Employer will reimburse the Employee within 28 days following the Termination Date [in [*currency*] into the Employee's nominated bank account in [*Country*]] all expenses wholly and necessarily incurred in the proper performance of his duties, subject to the Employer's current expenses policy.

(b) The Employee acknowledges that he owes the following sums to the Employer: [*specify any outstanding amounts*]. The Employee confirms that the Employer may deduct such sums from any sum due to Employee from the Employer, whether under this Agreement or otherwise, without prejudice to its other rights and remedies.

[*NB: Take care to ensure that expatriate/personal expense reimbursement is clearly differentiated from reimbursement of business expenses. If possible the actual sum should be agreed.*]

[*NB: Are any allowances paid in advance and if so will they be recovered?*]

8. The Severance Payments

(a) Subject to [ ], the Employer shall without admission of liability within [28] days following the Termination Date pay to the Employee:
 • [*amount in figures and in words and currency*] in respect of the termination of the Employee's employment [to include [*any mandatory requirements?*]] (the 'Termination Payment');
 • [*amount in figures and in words and currency*] as [payment in lieu of notice of termination of employment made under the terms of the Contract of Employment/damages in respect of the Employer's failure to give due notice of termination of employment];
 • [*amount in figures and in words and currency*] in lieu of [ ] days' accrued but untaken holiday

together the 'Severance Payments'.

[*NB: Check contractual obligations and mandatory employment laws.*]

(b) Subject to clause 8(d) the Severance Payments shall be paid to the Employee by the Employer within 28 days following the Termination Date in [*currency*] into the Employee's nominated bank account in [*Country*].

(c) The Employee acknowledges that the Severance Payments and other benefits to be provided under the terms of this Agreement are substantially greater than the Employee's entitlements under the terms of his contract of employment and any applicable laws.

(d) [Payment of the [Termination Payment/Severance Payments] is conditional on the Employee's compliance with [the terms of this Agreement, including for the avoidance of doubt] [his co-operation in relation to compliance with immigration requirements, vacation of his accommodation and delivery of a letter of resignation from his appointments as [*specify appointments*] before the Termination Date in accordance with clauses [*specify relevant clauses*]]

[*NB: Check that a clause along these lines is permitted as there may be mandatory rules regarding the payment of severance payments and the extent to which the parties can contract out of those obligations or apply conditions. What would be the effect of breach of warranty?*]

9. Outplacement

(a) The Employer shall pay for outplacement services [in accordance with its policy for expatriates in force at the date of this Agreement] for the Employee, provided that:

- the Employee advises the Employer in writing that he wishes to use such services within 3 months following the date of this Agreement (any such request should be sent to the Employer at its above address marked for the attention of [*job title*]); and
- the cost of such services shall not exceed [*amount in words and currency*] ([*amount in figures and currency*]) (including VAT); and
- such services shall be provided by a third party nominated by the Employer at its absolute discretion; and
- such payment in respect of outplacement fees will be made directly to [the providers nominated by the Employer] [within [28] days of the Employer receiving a copy of an invoice addressed to the Employee and marked payable by the Employer showing the fees due].

10. Legal advice

The Employee confirms that prior to accepting the terms of this Agreement he had the opportunity to seek independent legal advice on the terms and effects of this Agreement and its effect on his ability to pursue his legal rights in relation to the Employment and Assignment and termination of the Employment and Assignment.

The Employer will make a contribution towards the legal fees incurred by the Employee in respect of advice regarding termination of the Employment of [*amount in figures and currency*] ([*amount in words and currency*]) including VAT.

[*NB:*

- *If the UK extra statutory tax concession regarding direct payment of solicitors' fees to the solicitor is likely to offer any benefit this clause should be amended to reflect the requirements of the concession.*
- *If the agreement is intended to be a UK settlement agreement then the agreement will need to be amended, eg to include a solicitor's certificate, reference to the relevant legislation, and confirmation that the required conditions have been satisfied.*]

11. Warranties

(a)   The Employee warrants that to the best of his knowledge, information and belief he has not done any act or omitted to do any act which if it had come to the Employer's attention prior to the date of this Agreement would have entitled the Employer either to terminate the Employment summarily and without compensation if the Employee had still been employed or, if it had been done after the date this Agreement had been entered into, would have been in breach of any of its terms.

(b)   The Employee warrants that, at the date of this Agreement, he is not employed or self-employed in any capacity other than by the Employer nor is he in discussions which are likely to lead to, nor has he received, such an offer of employment or self-employment.

(c)   The Employee warrants that to the best of his knowledge, information and belief at the date of this Agreement he is not aware of any circumstances that may give rise to a claim by the Employee against the Employer or any Released Party in respect of any personal injury and/or industrial disease.

12. Settlement

(a)   [The terms of this Agreement are without any admission of liability and shall be in full and final satisfaction of all and any claims or rights of action (including inter alia the Claims) that the Employee may have arising under the Contract of Employment, [or any other agreement between the Employee and the Employer, the Host Company or any Group Company], Host Country laws, Home Country laws or the laws of any other relevant jurisdiction against the Employer or any other Released Party in connection with or arising out of the Employment, the Assignment or the termination of the Employment or the Assignment, or any other matter whatsoever and the Employee agrees to irrevocably waive any such claims or rights of action which he may have, save:
   - that he may bring a claim or claims for damages for personal injury arising out the Employment (save to the extent that the Employee is aware or ought reasonably to be aware that he has sustained such personal injury on the date of this Agreement);
   - [that he may bring a claim or claims in respect of accrued pension rights;]
   - any claims or other rights of action which, if included in this clause would render this clause void (whether in whole or in part); and
   - any claim to enforce the terms of this Agreement

together the 'Excluded Claims'.]

(b)   The Employee accepts that the Employer is entering into this settlement for the benefit of itself and, as trustee, for the benefit of each Released Party.

(c)   The Employee agrees not to institute or pursue any proceedings (save in respect of any Excluded Claim) in a court of relevant jurisdiction for any remedy arising from the Employment, the Assignment or its or their termination.

(d)   It is a condition of the payment of [the Severance Payments] that no proceedings in any forum in the Home Country, the Host Country or any other country have been commenced by the Employee against the Employer or any other Released Party.

[*NB:*
- *The terms of any release should be checked with Home Country and Host Country lawyers.*
- *Do mandatory employment laws allow a provision for repayment in the event claims are commenced?*
- *Is release needed in relation to any appointments, offices or 'powers'?*]

13. Confidentiality, garden leave and post termination restrictions

Acknowledgements

(a)   The Employee acknowledges that he continues to be bound by the terms of the Contract of Employment that govern his conduct after the Termination Date.

Consideration

(b)   The [Employer] shall pay the Employee the sum of [*amount in figures and currency*] ([*amount in words and currency*]) as consideration for the Employee's agreement complying with the terms of this clause 13 and the restrictions set out at Schedule [ ].

[*NB:*
- *In some countries mandatory employment laws require that a specific payment or continuing payments (eg linked to salary for the period of the restrictions) be made in respect of post termination restrictions.*
- *There may also be a need to expressly release the employee from post termination restrictions, eg if the employer is not concerned about restrictions and it wishes to avoid making payments to the employee.*]

Confidentiality

(c)   The Employee acknowledges that he will continue to owe a duty of confidentiality to the Employer, the Host Company and to each other Group Company after termination of the Employment.

The Employee undertakes to keep confidential the existence and terms of this Agreement and not to disclose the same to any other Person unless expressly authorised by the Employer in writing save for the purposes of:

- seeking professional advice in relation to its terms (provided that prior to doing so the Employee imposes upon any such Person a like condition of confidentiality);
- disclosing the same to the proper authorities as required by law;
- disclosing the same to his spouse or partner (provided that prior to doing so the Employee imposes upon any such Person a like condition of confidentiality);
- disclosing to any actual or prospective employer that his employment with the Employer terminated by agreement upon terms which remain confidential;
- disclosing the terms of Schedule [ ] [*post termination restrictions*] to any prospective employer.

The Employee undertakes not to make or publish or cause to be made or published to anyone in any circumstances any disparaging, untrue or misleading remarks concerning the Employer or any other Released Party. [*NB: Consider whether such a clause is appropriate or enforceable in the relevant countries.*]

Co-operation

(d) The Employee shall promptly provide such co-operation as the Employer may reasonably request from time to time in connection with any matter, claim, demand or proceeding made against the Employer, the Host Company (or any other Group Company) or in which the Employer, the Host Company (or any other Group Company) is involved with respect to which his knowledge, actions or conduct may have or may have had relevance.

Such co-operation shall include, without limitation, promptly providing relevant information and documents and answering questions with care and attention and in good faith. The Employer shall promptly reimburse the Employee in respect of reasonable expenses incurred by the Employee in providing such co-operation, subject to the production of appropriate documentary evidence that such expenses have been properly incurred.

[*NB: Is this permitted? Any other co-operation required? Tax and immigration requirements etc*]

Garden leave

(e) [*NB:*
   - *Garden leave (see the Glossary at Appendix 3) may not be possible under mandatory employment laws.*

- *Garden leave may give the employee more time to pack up his belongings and leave the Host Country if immigration permission will terminate when the employment ends or shortly afterwards.*]

The Employee shall remain on garden leave until the Termination Date. The following terms shall apply in respect of the Employee's garden leave period.

- The Employee acknowledges that during this period of garden leave the Employer may require that the Employee does not attend his normal place of work and that the Employee may be required to work and/or make himself available at his home address in [*Host Country*] as the Employer may from time to time direct.

- The Employee shall take all his outstanding holiday entitlement, subject to approval of the Employer, during garden leave and before the Termination Date.

- Save as may be expressly agreed in writing between the Employee and the Employer (and at the Employer's absolute discretion) and subject to any immigration restrictions, the Employee is required to *remain in Host Country until* after the Termination Date, including for the avoidance of doubt during any holiday period.

- The Employee shall not perform his normal duties but must co-operate fully with the Employer and provide the Employer and the Host Company with such assistance as the Employer may reasonably require.

- The Employee accepts that his powers and responsibilities have been withdrawn and shall no longer hold himself out as [*job title*] of the Employer or as a representative of Host Company.

- The Employee shall not contact or communicate with any employees, clients, customers or suppliers of the Employer, the Host Company or any other Group Company about any aspect of the business of the Employer or any Group Company save as instructed by or agreed by the Employer in writing save that if any such individual contacts the Employee then he may say that he is leaving the Employer and the Host Company and that they should contact [*job title*]. [For the avoidance of doubt he may communicate with such individuals for purely social purposes provided that he does not initiate such communications and that he does not discuss any [commercial] matter relating to the Employer, the Host Company or any other Group Company.]

- The Employee shall not enter into any premises of the Employer, the Host Company or any Group Company without the Employer's consent.

- The Employee shall not be employed by, or do any work, whether paid or unpaid for, any third party.

- Save in accordance with this clause the Employee shall not make any comment to any person about the change to his duties, except to confirm that he is on Garden Leave.

- The Employee acknowledges that he will remain employed by the Employer on the terms of the Contract of Employment during the Garden Leave period except as varied by this Agreement.

14. Return of property

To the extent not already delivered [(and save as set out below or otherwise agreed)] the Employee will return to [*job title*] of the Host Company at the Host Company's premises (or if appropriate delete) within 7 days following the date of this Agreement all [*list relevant property*] property belonging to or relating to the business of the Employer, the Host Company or any other Group Company and its or their clients and suppliers which the Employee has in his possession or which is under the Employee's control.

[Within 10 days of the date of this Agreement the Employee shall provide to the Employer written confirmation that he has complied with his obligations under this clause 14.]

15. Taxation and payment arrangements

Payment arrangements

(a) Unless otherwise expressly stated in this Agreement:
   - all payments to be made under the terms of this Agreement will be made by the Employer to the Employee in [*currency*] into the Employee's nominated bank account in [*country*] within [28] days following the Termination Date; and
   - the Exchange Rate shall be applied where appropriate to determine the appropriate amount to be paid.

Tax treatment

(b) [The Employer gives no warranty or other assurance to the Employee regarding the appropriate treatment of any payment made or benefit provided to the Employee by the Employer for income tax or social security contribution purposes. – NB: *This will not always apply*]

Subject to the foregoing, the Employer and the Employee understand that [*specify understood tax treatment of payments referred to in this Agreement if appropriate*].

Tax returns

(c)   The Employee acknowledges that it is his responsibility to comply with Host Country and Home Country tax requirements [*NB: Any other relevant countries, eg US or previous Host Country?*] and to ensure that his tax returns are properly submitted within the appropriate deadlines.

[The Employee shall take all reasonable steps to promptly recover any overpayment of tax or social security contributions made to any relevant authority for the benefit of the Employer and shall pay over any such sums recovered to the Employer promptly.]

The Employee is eligible to receive tax advice at the Employer's expense, from tax advisers nominated by the Employer from time to time (and subject to such financial and/or other conditions as the Employer may from time to time impose), in respect of Home Country and Host Country [and US] tax returns relating to the period of the Assignment]/[the [*date*]/[*date*] [*Home Country*] tax year and the [*date*]/[*date*] [*Host Country*] tax year.] Any penalties or interest charges incurred due to the Employee's default (for example because the Employee fails to provide information or documentation requested by the nominated tax adviser promptly) will be the Employee's responsibility.

Tax indemnity

(d)   The Employee is responsible for any income tax [and employee's social security contributions] due in respect of [payments and benefits referred to in this Agreement] and the Employee hereby agrees to indemnify the Employer, the Host Company and any relevant Group Company and to keep the same indemnified on a continuing basis against all and any such liabilities (including any interest, penalties, reasonable costs and expenses) that any such company may incur in respect of or by reason of such payments or the provision of such benefits.

[*NB: A tax indemnity may not be enforceable and may not be appropriate, for example where the employer has been responsible for providing tax advice and there is a tax equalisation arrangement in place.*]

Tax equalisation

(e)   [No tax equalisation or tax protection arrangements shall apply to any payment referred to in this Agreement. The Employee hereby confirms that no further payment is due to him from the Employer in respect of tax equalisation or tax protection of any remuneration or other payments made to him by the Employer whether before or after the date of this Agreement, and whether referred to in this Agreement or not.]

[Payment of any remuneration due or benefits to be provided under the Contract of Employment in respect of the period up to the Termination Date shall be made subject to the current tax equalisation/protection arrangements in accordance with the Contract of Employment. Such tax equalisation/protection arrangements shall not apply to the Severance Payments/any payment under this Agreement, save [ ].]

[*NB: If there is a tax equalisation or protection policy ensure that the severance agreement clarifies the payments to which that policy will apply. Check the policy itself is clear if, instead of documenting the arrangements here, the arrangements confirmed in another document are referred to in this agreement.*]

16. Miscellaneous

Notices and contact details

(a) Any notices or other documents may be delivered or served on the Employee by the Employer at the Employee's address for service, currently the address specified at the top of this Agreement.

The Employee shall inform the Employer of an address, telephone number and email address for such other communications as the Employer may consider appropriate in connection with the Employment after the Termination Date. The Employee shall ensure that the Employer is kept promptly informed of any change to such address for service and contact details for the period of [24 months] following the Termination Date.

Whole agreement

(b) This Agreement records the whole agreement between the Employee, the Employer [and the Host Company] in respect of the termination of the Employment and the Assignment and supersedes any prior agreements in this regard.

[*NB: Are there any other arrangements or separate severance agreements that should remain in place?*]

Language

(c) This Agreement has been prepared in [English] and a translation has been prepared in [*Host Country language*]. In the event of any conflict the [*Host Country/English language*] version shall prevail.

Third party rights

(d)   The Employer and each Released Party are expressly provided with the right to enforce the waiver given by the Employee pursuant to clause 12 together with the right to enforce the benefit of all other clauses in this Agreement conferring rights on third parties including (but not limited to) the undertakings at clause 13. Only the consents of the Employee and the Employer are required to vary the terms of or terminate this Agreement even if that variation or termination affects the benefits conferred in this Agreement on a third party.

Applicable laws

(e)   This Agreement is governed by the laws of [*Country*] and any dispute is subject to the [non] exclusive jurisdiction of the Courts of [*Country*].

The Employee acknowledges and agrees with the Employer that the laws of [*Home/Host Country*] do not apply to the Employee's Employment with the Employer or the Contract of Employment and that such laws do not apply to this Agreement.

[*NB: Consider whether governing law in relation to non-contractual obligations should be specified.*]

17. [Condition precedent and] conclusion of this Agreement

[*NB: Insert any appropriate condition precedent, eg a requirement for employment authority or Court approval or for a cooling off period.*]

Notwithstanding that this Agreement is marked 'without prejudice' and 'subject to contract', when this Agreement has been dated and signed on behalf of each party to it [and the conditions set out in [ ] have been satisfied] it will be open and binding.

This Agreement may be executed as one document or in any number of counterparts and provided that at least one counterpart document has been executed on behalf of each party this Agreement shall be deemed concluded.

[*NB:*

- *Counterpart documents are generally more convenient but cannot be used in all countries. It may be better in some cases for all parties to sign the same document.*
- *Consider whether it would be prudent to conclude the Agreement in the form of a Deed, eg if powers of attorney are to be granted.*

- *Consider whether any claims should be dealt with in a separate agreement or agreements.*]

Signed by

Name............................

Job title............................

duly authorised for and on behalf of

[*NAME OF EMPLOYER*]

Date of signature:

In the presence of:

Name:

Address:

Occupation:

[Signed by

Name............................

Job title............................

duly authorised for and on behalf of

[*NAME OF HOST COMPANY*]

Date of signature:

In the presence of:

Name:

Address:

Occupation:]

[*NB:*

- *Consider whether it is necessary for the host company to be a party or whether the host company may benefit from the terms of the severance agreement without being a party to it.*
- *Consider whether some evidence of authority or apostille is required.*]

Signed by [*EMPLOYEE'S NAME*]

Date of signature:

In the presence of:

Name:

Address:

Occupation:

Schedule A
Resignation letter

The Directors

[*name of company*]

[*registered address of Company*]

[*date*]

Dear Sirs

[*name of company*]

I hereby resign from my appointment as [director] of [*name of company*] with [immediate effect/effect from [*date*]].

Yours faithfully

[*Name of employee*]

Schedule B
Confidentiality and post termination restrictions

References to clauses in this Schedule are to clauses of this Schedule unless otherwise indicated.

Confidentiality

The Employee will not use or disclose, directly or indirectly, any trade secrets or Confidential Information belonging to the Employer, the Host Company or any other Group Company except [to allow him to carry out his duties properly or] as required by law.

Confidential Information includes, inter alia, any confidential information relating to [*specify appropriate confidential information*] any document marked 'Confidential' or 'Secret', or any information which the Employee has been told is confidential or which he might reasonably expect the Employer, the Host Company or any other Group Company to regard as confidential, or any information which has been given to the Employer, the Host Company or any other Group Company in confidence by customers, suppliers or other persons.

The obligations contained in this clause [ ] will continue to apply to the Employee after his Employment ends, for so long as the information referred to in this clause [ ] remains confidential.

Post termination restrictions

[*NB: The appropriate terms are likely to vary substantially depending on the home and host countries.*]

[*NB: Ensure main body of Agreement includes appropriate cross references etc.*]

[*NB: Consider whether different governing laws should apply to the post termination restrictions.*]

Schedule C
Draft reference

[*Draft to be discussed/provided by* [*employee/employer*]]

[In accordance with our normal practice] this reference is provided for the benefit of the addressee only and is given without liability on behalf of the writer, [the Company] or any Group Company or any of its or their officers or employees. In particular, the Company expresses no opinion on the suitability of [*Employee*] for the post applied for.

[*name, job title, signature, date of signature*]

[NB: *Any mandatory laws regarding provision of references?*]

GRANTING OR REMOVAL OF 'POWERS' (INCLUDING APOSTILLE)

A2.8 [*NB: In many countries documentation should be in place to ensure that a senior manager has the authority he needs to represent the business or perform particular duties. These 'powers' may need to be registered with public authorities in the host country. The requirements for providing evidence that the powers are in place may be quite detailed and the form of the appropriate documents may vary considerably from country to country. (Please refer to 11.26–11.29 for a more detailed explanation of why powers of attorney or an apostille might be required and the Glossary at Appendix 3 on obtaining an apostille in the UK.) The bundle of documents required by the host country might include the following:*

- *a power of attorney granting authority (or resolution removing those powers) or appointment to (or removal of) the employee from a specific role with inherent power;*
- *an extract from board minutes to confirm the resolution of the legal entity to grant a power of attorney;*
- *company documents, eg to confirm the identity of the signatory to the board minutes or power of attorney;*
- *a solicitor or notary public's certificate confirming the identity of relevant signatories;*
- *an apostille.*]

Draft board minutes re removal and appointment

[*date*]

DECISION OF THE SOLE MEMBER OF [*HOST COMPANY SUBSIDIARY*]

[*Name of Home Company Parent*] [*registered number*] with its registered office at [*registered address*] duly organised and existing under the laws of [*Country*], in its capacity as [sole] member of [*Name of Host Company Subsidiary*] [*registered number*] with its registered office at [*registered address*], has RESOLVED AS FOLLO

WS:

(1) [*Name of employee to be removed from appointment*] [*date of birth*] residing at [*home address*] is removed from appointment as [*appointment*] of [*Host Company subsidiary*]; and

(2) [*Name of replacement employee*] [*date of birth*] residing at [*home address*] is appointed as [*appointment*] of [*Host Company subsidiary*]

with [*immediate*] effect from [*time and date*].

At [*place*] on [*date*] at [*time*]

....
[*Name of Home Company parent*]
represented by [*name and job title of authorised signatory*]

In the presence of:

Name of witness: ....   Solicitor and Notary Public

Of ....   (name of firm)

of..............................

....   (address of firm)

[NB: *the above is offered as a starting point: this document must meet the requirements of the relevant jurisdiction(s) and specific company constitution etc.*].

Documents to confirm the identity of a director who has signed a document on behalf of a UK company

[NB: *The bundle of documents might, for example, include the following:*

- *a copy of the up-to-date Memorandum and Articles of Association of the company obtained from Companies House;*
- *a copy of the form confirming the appointment of the relevant director as a director;*
- *a copy of the most recent Annual Return confirming the company's directors at that date;*
- *a signed statement from the Notary Public who is certifying the documents as set out below;*
- *an apostille.*]

I, [*Name of Notary Public*] [Notary Public] of [*Name and address of firm*]

hereby certify that the attached documents are true copies of documents registered at Companies House as at [date] and that such documents confirm the appointment of [*name*] as Director of [*Name of Company*].

Employee's signature: Date of signature:
....

Draft letter requesting apostille

Private & Confidential

[The Legalisation Office – *check current address*]

[*Date*]   [*reference*]

Dear Sir

Documents for legalisation

We enclose an original power of attorney granted by [*name of subsidiary*], to [*name*] together with [Notary Public's] certificate, extract from board minutes and company documents. We should be grateful if you would arrange for the documents to be legalised.

We also enclose a cheque for £[*check current fee*] made out to the '[]'. We should be grateful if you would provide a receipt for the fee of £[ ].

Any questions regarding the enclosed documents should be addressed to [*name*] (direct line [*telephone number*], [*email address*]).

For your convenience we enclose a self-addressed envelope for you to use to return the documents.

Yours faithfully

[*Name etc*]

Encs

APPENDIX 3

GLOSSARY

A3.1 This glossary gives brief general explanations of terms that are commonly used by those preparing expatriate documents. Care should be taken because technical terms can be used in different ways in different countries, and also within the same country in different contexts.

A3.2 For example, a simple word like 'consult' may mean many different things depending on where it is used.

A3.3 Another useful reference point for those dealing with assignments in and out of European countries is the European Union website at http://europa.eu, particularly the 'eurojargon' guide at http://europa.eu/abc/eurojargon/.

A1

A3.4 This is a certificate supplied by an EU country (and certain other participating countries) confirming that the employee may remain in his home country social security scheme during an assignment to another country. (See also **5.20–5.22**.) The A1 form replaced the E101 form.

ACCOMMODATION OFFSET

A3.5 Sometimes an employer who provides a housing allowance or accommodation in the host country will adjust the employee's remuneration to take account of income that the employee may receive, or be deemed to receive, from renting out his own home country property. The adjustment may be referred to as an 'accommodation offset'. Arrangements, and terminology used, may vary between employers (see **7.113–7.130** on accommodation generally).

ACQUIRED RIGHTS DIRECTIVE (ARD)

A3.6 Directive 2001/23/EC relating to transfers of undertakings is usually known in the UK as the 'Acquired Rights Directive'. The Directive requires that EU member states offer protection to employees when an undertaking, or part of an undertaking, that they are assigned to is transferred to a third party (the 'transferee'). The Directive can apply, for example, where there is a change of contractor as well as where all or part of a business is sold. The required protection includes:

- automatic transfer of the employee's employment with the undertaking to the transferee on the same terms and condition of employment (special arrangements apply to pensions);

- automatic transfer of trade union recognition and collective agreements to the transferee;

- a requirement for the transferor and transferee to inform, and sometimes also consult, representatives of their own affected employees;

- restrictions on changes to terms and conditions of employment post transfer;

- additional protection against dismissal; and

- special arrangements in relation to insolvency.

In the UK the Transfer of Undertakings (Protection of Employment) Regulations 2006, known as 'TUPE', implement the Acquired Rights Directive (see 'TUPE' below).

ACQUIS COMMUNAUTAIRE

A3.7 These are rights and obligations that EU countries share, including, amongst other things, the EU's treaties, directives, regulations, declarations and resolutions, international agreements on EU affairs and the judgments of the European Court.

AFFILIATE

A3.8 US employment documents often refer to a company's 'affiliates' or 'associates'. The term is usually used to describe companies or other legal entities within the same 'group' of companies. The term is generally defined in the relevant document. See the explanation for similar UK terms, 'associated company' and 'group company' below.

ALLOWANCE

A3.9 An allowance is a payment made to an employee for a particular purpose. The allowance could consist of one payment of a fixed amount, or of regular payments paid at a certain rate. Allowances do not usually vary (at least directly) with actual cost or expenditure incurred by the employee (compare 'expense' below).

A3.10 Allowances paid to an expatriate should usually be delivered by, or on behalf of, the employer.

A3.11 Expatriates may, eg, receive an assignment allowance, car allowance, cost of living allowance (or adjustment), disturbance allowance, education or schooling allowance, hardship allowance, housing allowance, relocation allowance, repatriation allowance, subsistence allowance, travel allowance or utility allowance (see Chapter 7 and below for some further explanation of different types of allowance). Terms describing allowances tend to take on different meanings within different businesses. The names given to allowances are not terms of art.

A3.12 Expatriate documents should clearly differentiate between reimbursement of expenses, payment of allowances and direct provision of benefits to an employee. The documents should also clearly state if receipts are required. Different arrangements may attract different tax treatments and may have different implications on termination of the assignment.

APOSTILLE

A3.13 Many countries are concerned about the authenticity of legal documents and many have arrangements by which documents can be certified in some way.

A3.14 An apostille (or 'legalisation') is the official confirmation that a signature, seal or stamp on a document is genuine. UK documents which have been 'notarised' by a notary public or 'certified' by a solicitor (and certain other documents) and then certified with an apostille are accepted for legal use in the countries that are party to the 1961 Hague Convention Abolishing the Requirement of Legalisation for Foreign Public Documents.

A3.15 Practically, if documents are prepared in one country for use in another it is sensible to check both the requirements of the country where they will be used and the requirements of the country where the apostille must be issued before the documents are finalised or an apostille is sought.

Apostille in the UK

A3.16 In the UK an apostille can be obtained from the Legalisation Office. The fact that a document is 'legalised' does not mean that its contents are accurate, and grant of an 'apostille' does not confirm official approval of the document.

A3.17 An explanation of the process for obtaining an apostille in the UK is available at https://www.gov.uk/get-document-legalised. The process is reasonably quick and not expensive.

ARTICLE

A3.18 The 'EU Treaty' (see explanation below) contains a number of 'Articles' that are directly binding on individuals and companies in EU 'member states' (see below). From an employment law perspective the Article most likely to be relevant is Article 157 of the current EU Treaty which provides for equal pay between men and women.

A3.19 Europeans sometimes refer to the clauses or paragraphs of employment contracts as 'articles'. The meaning of 'article' is in that case usually obvious from the context. The word 'article' is rarely used in that way in UK employment documents.

ASSIGNEE

A3.20 An assignee is a person who is sent on an 'assignment' (see below).

ASSIGNMENT

A3.21 The word 'assignment' is frequently used in an expatriate context, has a number of different meanings and can be the source of misunderstanding.

A3.22 'Assignment' is used loosely in this book to mean a period of employment in another country, regardless of whether the employee is technically employed by the same employer or a different employer during the period of employment in the host country.

A3.23 Sometimes the word 'secondment' is used instead of 'assignment'. This can cause confusion, especially where, between a particular group of people, the word 'assignment' is used to cover some kinds of arrangement and the word 'secondment' is used to cover others. Assignment and secondment are not terms of art and the two words can generally be used interchangeably.

A3.24 It is worth being aware that, in a domestic context, both 'assignment' and 'secondment' are typically used to describe circumstances where an employer provides an employee's services to another company. They can also be used to cover circumstances where the expatriate's employment is transferred to the host country employer temporarily (see 'host country employment' below).

A3.25 Misunderstanding cannot be avoided simply by using 'secondment' or 'assignment' consistently. It is usually helpful to provide a broader description of the arrangements to make the assumed meaning clear. Advisers should take care to ensure that they understand the meaning attributed to these expressions by clients.

ASSIGNMENT ALLOWANCE

A3.26 Sometimes the employer pays the employee additional remuneration solely because he will be working on assignment. This may be paid in addition to, or instead of, more specific allowances such as a cost of living allowance or disturbance allowance. A lump sum or fixed-rate assignment allowance is more likely to be paid without other allowances in respect of a short-term assignment.

ASSIGNMENT MANAGER

A3.27 A term typically used within organisations to describe a person responsible for administrative and practical arrangements related to the assignment. The assignment manager will typically be based in the home country and is usually not the line manager. The title can mean different things to different people/organisations so context is important.

ASSOCIATED COMPANY

A3.28 An 'associated company' is usually a company within the same 'group' of companies. For example, a parent company, sister company or subsidiary. The employment documents should usually include precise definitions of terms used to describe relationships between group companies (see also 'affiliate' above, and 'group' and 'group company' below). This may be done by reference to legislation.

UK – generally

A3.29 The term 'associated employer' is used at s 218(6) of the Employment Rights Act 1996 (ERA 1996), in the chapter relating to 'continuity of employment'. (The ERA 1996 is the main piece of UK employment legislation.) For that purpose ERA 1996, s 231 gives the following definition:

'For the purposes of this Act any two employers shall be treated as associated if –

(a) one is a company of which the other (directly or indirectly) has control, or
(b) both are companies of which a third person (directly or indirectly) has control;

and "associated employer" shall be construed accordingly.'

A3.30 In practice though, definitions used in employment documents for the purposes of describing the employee's obligations to group/associated companies in relation to, for example, post termination restrictions and confidentiality, will usually be drafted by reference to particular sections of companies or tax legislation.

'AT WILL' EMPLOYMENT

A3.31   A US term normally used to describe a situation where an employee can be dismissed by his employer without a period of notice and, in the US, without giving any reason. Note that employment 'at will' does not equate to 'no employment contract' and that employment protection legislation may still apply on termination of employment. See Chapter 21 on US perspectives.

BANK HOLIDAY

A3.32   A UK term used to describe certain public holidays. (Confusingly, some UK public holidays, eg Good Friday, are not technically 'bank' holidays.)

BOARD

A3.33   'The Board' is often used loosely in the UK and US to describe the Board of Directors of a company, ie individuals formally appointed as such and with prescribed authority and duties. Companies registered in other countries may have other arrangements, eg a 'two tier board' including a 'supervisory' board that may include employee representatives.

BREXIT

A3.34   A colloquial term used to describe the UK's proposed separation from the EU.

BRITAIN

A3.35   See 'Great Britain' below.

BRITISH ISLES

A3.36   See 'Great Britain' below.

BRUSSELS CONVENTION

A3.37   The Brussels Convention on Jurisdiction and the Enforcement of Judgments in Civil and Commercial Matters 1968 is usually known as the 'Brussels Convention'. This international convention has now been largely superseded by the 'Recast Brussels Regulation', referred to as the Judgments Regulation in this book, Regulation (EU) 1215/2012 (see 'Judgments Regulation' below and **10.62–10.74**). (NB the potential impact of Brexit on the application of the Judgments Regulation to the UK.)

BRUSSELS PROTOCOL

A3.38 This is a protocol to the Rome Convention (on choice of governing laws) that gives the European Court authority to make decisions on interpretation of the Rome Convention. Note that the Rome Convention was superseded in December 2009 by an EC Regulation known as 'Rome II'. (See also Chapter 10 and 'European Court, 'Rome I', 'Rome II' and 'Rome Convention' below.) (NB the potential impact of Brexit on the application of EC regulations to the UK.)

BRUSSELS REGULATION

A3.39 Also known as the 'recast' Brussels Regulation. See 'Judgments Regulation'.

BUILD UP

A3.40 A 'build up' (or 'home country') approach to determining remuneration for an expatriate is usually aimed at providing a lifestyle that is broadly similar to the lifestyle the expatriate might expect to enjoy in his home country in a similar role. Salary is adjusted to take account, eg, of differences in cost of living, tax and social security contributions (see 'cost of living allowance' and 'tax equalisation' below). The phrase is sometimes also used to describe calculations prepared by assignment managers or tax advisers to determine how much money the expatriate will actually receive. This is not a term of art and different organisations will prepare these calculations in different ways, See 7.80–7.92 on tax equalisation.

BUSINESS VISITOR

A3.41 The term 'business visitor' is typically used to describe a person who makes one or more short-term trips to a country for business purposes, for example, to attend occasional business meetings. Special immigration rules may apply if relevant criteria are fulfilled, for example, it may not be necessary to obtain an ordinary work permit. (See 3.5–3.10 and 3.13–3.16 for descriptions of some of the risks associated with making business trips without appropriate immigration permission.) These short-term visits may also have income tax implications. 'Business visitor' may not have exactly the same meaning in a tax context. (See Chapter 14 on business visitors generally.)

CADRE

A3.42 A French term used to describe a senior executive. See 'top executive' below.

CAR ALLOWANCE

A3.43 An expatriate may receive an allowance to cover the costs of buying, hiring or running a car. The appropriate terms, and tax treatment, of such arrangements may vary considerably.

CIVIL PARTNER

A3.44 In some places relationships between adults that do not qualify as 'marriage' are recognised in law. Eg, in the UK it is possible for a same-sex couple to enter into a legally binding 'civil partnership'. This contractual relationship is offered protection by law and, generally, under UK law, civil partners should be treated no less favourably than married partners. Civil partnerships may not be recognised in other countries as equivalent to marriage, eg for the purposes of immigration laws. See also 'marriage'.

COBRA

A3.45 The US Consolidated Omnibus Budget Regulation Act 1985, known as 'COBRA', is a piece of US legislation that gave some employees a right to continued health care cover for a period of up to 18 months after their employment ends. The employee must pay the relevant insurance premium and an administrative fee of up to 2% of the premium. A severance agreement with an employee assigned from the US may need to offer the opportunity for the employee to elect to take continued cover. It is worth noting too that the reasons for termination of employment may affect the employee's rights under COBRA. US advice should be sought on the form of the severance agreement if COBRA may be relevant.

COLLECTIVE AGREEMENT

A3.46 A collective agreement is, broadly, an agreement made between a trade union (or unions) and an employer (or employers). Industrial relations have developed in different ways in different countries and the role of trade unions and status of collective agreements varies considerably between them. This is an area where it is important not to make assumptions (particularly for UK and US advisers who may not be aware of the importance of collective agreements in some European countries).

A3.47 Key points to understand are as follows.

*   In the UK collective agreements are not usually contractually binding between the employer and union, although they are normally followed in practice. Some terms of a non-binding agreement can, however, bind the employer and employee if incorporated into the individual employee's contract of employment by agreement between the employer and

individual employee. This can only apply to certain terms. A typical example might be a severance policy negotiated by non-binding collective agreement between the employer and union and then incorporated automatically into individual employees' contracts of employment because of their existing contract terms.

- In practice, UK collective agreements do not often apply to inbound or outbound expatriates.

- In many European countries collective agreements can apply automatically to employees, regardless of whether the particular employer and employee agree otherwise. 'Mandatory employment laws' are often implemented in Europe by means of collective agreement. (See **10.42–10.47**.)

- The qualifying criteria for determining whether a particular collective agreement applies can vary enormously. Collective agreements might, for example, apply to employees working in a particular geographical region, sector (pharmaceuticals, IT, etc), to a particular company's employees, or to employees with a particular level of seniority or undertaking a particular role.

- Collective agreements in some European countries can apply to surprisingly senior employees.

- The priority to be applied between legislation, case-law, collective agreements and individual contracts varies between countries.

- Sometimes it is possible to 'derogate' from the requirements of a collective agreement. If this is possible there are likely to be rules about how this may be done.

- The importance, status and role of trade unions also vary considerably.

COLLECTIVE DISMISSAL

A3.48 Many countries, including EU countries, have additional rules that apply if it is proposed that a threshold number of employees should be dismissed for a reason that is not connected to the individual employee's personal circumstances. The rules usually apply to 'collective redundancies' or dismissals for 'economic reasons' (see 'redundancy' below). The relevant EU directive is Directive 98/59/EC, the 'Collective Dismissals Directive'. The Directive provides, amongst other things, for consultation with employee representatives over contemplated collective dismissals. In practice, this sort of legislation is rarely relevant in an expatriate context but if more than one employee may be affected by a particular decision, for example if a number of expatriates may be dismissed, collective issues should be considered. (See also 'European Works Council' below.)

COLLECTIVE DISMISSALS DIRECTIVE

A3.49 Directive 98/59/EC, see 'collective dismissal' above.

COMMERCIAL AGENTS DIRECTIVE

A3.50 Directive 86/653/EEC, the 'Commercial Agents Directive', requires EU member states to provide protection for self-employed commercial agents who receive payments linked to sales, ie those paid through commission arrangements. Generally, this book deals with employment relationships and the Commercial Agents Directive does not apply to employees. See **6.12**.

COMMUTER ASSIGNMENT

A3.51 A term used to describe an arrangement under which an employee works as an 'international commuter'. See further below and Chapter 14.

COMPANY REDUNDANCY PAY

A3.52 Companies often have policies providing for enhanced redundancy pay, ie payments over and above the minimum amounts set by law, mandatory collective agreement etc. Sometimes enhanced 'company' redundancy pay is offered as a 'one-off' benefit to a particular group of employees or in respect of a particular round of redundancies.

UK

A3.53 In the UK, a company redundancy policy will typically be based on the formula for statutory redundancy pay (SRP), perhaps with the usual statutory cap on 'a week's pay' removed and replaced with actual pay or a greater number of weeks' pay for each year's service. Often the employer will have sought 'tax clearance' from the UK tax authorities that payment under the policy will attract tax relief. Any clearance given would, of course, only apply to UK income tax and will relate to a particular request. Clearance is unlikely to apply to expatriates working outside the UK. A UK company redundancy policy is unlikely to be appropriate for expatriates. However, sometimes an expatriate policy is developed by reference to an existing UK policy or the expatriate may have a contractual right to payment under the UK policy.

COMPROMISE AGREEMENT

A3.54 See 'severance agreement' below.

CONSULT

A3.55 Consultation requirements frequently arise in an employment context. For example, the 'social partners' may be consulted in relation to new legislation or an employer may consult with employee representatives or works councils and/or individual employees over redundancies.

A3.56 Care should be taken because 'consultation' can mean different things in different contexts and the differences can have significant consequences. For example, collective consultation over redundancies in EU countries should, as a minimum, be 'with a view to reaching agreement'. In some contexts there can be a requirement to actually reach agreement. It may be critical that certain decisions or communications have not been made before consultation begins. It is important to take local advice on what the local requirements are before any required period of consultation begins, documents are prepared, or communications are made.

CONSULTANT

A3.57 This term can also mean different things in different contexts. For example, this may be the job title given to an employee who provides advice or professional services either to the employer or a third party (eg the title 'IT Consultant' is frequently applied to those providing information technology services to clients). The term may also be used to describe an individual providing services as a self-employed contractor (see **6.2–6.13**). Sometimes the term may imply a particular level of seniority (eg in the UK health service a 'consultant' is generally a very senior doctor and a 'consultant' at a firm of solicitors may be a former partner whose expertise is particularly valued). From a technical perspective, the term 'consultant' is probably best avoided in expatriate documents. This is because it can be misleading and the employee's role and status within the business may be critical to other issues such as immigration, tax or social security or the application of collective agreements. See also 'contractor' below.

CONTINUITY

A3.58 See 'continuous employment' below.

CONTINUOUS EMPLOYMENT

A3.59 Many employment benefits and employment rights depend on length of service.

A3.60 Length of service is often referred to as 'seniority' in Europe. This can be a bit confusing for English or US advisers who are more likely to use the term 'seniority' to describe the level or status of the employee's role within the business, for example whether he is a senior manager or not, regardless of age or length of service. (See **19.88–19.90** and **20.41–20.54** on 'continuous employment' for UK statutory purposes.)

UK

A3.61 In the UK 'continuous employment' is a technical term that is used to determine whether an employee has sufficient length of service to be eligible to make certain statutory employment claims, most notably the statutory right to make an unfair dismissal complaint. (See **19.88–19.90** and **20.41–20.54**).

CONTRACT FOR SERVICES

A3.62 A contract for services is typically an agreement between two companies for the provision of services. The contract for services could also be with a self-employed individual. A contract for services is not an employment contract. A contract for services should not be confused with a 'service agreement' (a UK term typically used to describe a senior executive employment contract).

CONTRACTOR

A3.63 The term 'contractor' is generally used to describe a self-employed individual who provides his services to a third party.

A3.64 Confusingly though, the term is also often used to describe an individual who is employed by a company that then supplies the individual's services to a third party. (This is common, eg, in the IT sector.)

A3.65 Employment status is important in an expatriate context so the term 'contractor' should be used with particular care. For example, the term 'self-employed contractor' may be clearer if the contract is with an individual rather than a company. (See also 'consultant' above and **6.2–6.13**.)

COOLING OFF PERIOD

A3.66 Sometimes after an agreement is signed (eg a severance agreement) one or both of the parties to it will have a right to withdraw from the agreement, provided this is done within a specified period. This may, for example, affect the appropriate timing for payment of termination payments.

US

A3.67 For example, where there is a US connection there may be a requirement for a cooling off period to be incorporated into a severance agreement for an older employee (see **16.100**).

COST OF LIVING ALLOWANCE OR ADJUSTMENT (COLA)

A3.68 It costs different amounts of money to buy the same things in different places. Many employers adjust expatriate pay by applying a cost of living allowance where things are more expensive, or reducing pay through a cost of living adjustment where things are cheaper. Data can be purchased from third party providers to help the employer determine the appropriate size of the adjustment.

A3.69 It is important to think carefully about how these adjustments will work in practice. For example, how the arrangements will interact with exchange rate changes; how and when they will be updated; how they will affect any tax equalisation or protection arrangements; whether the COLA may be a negative figure; and interaction with other payments and allowances (see 7.40–7.47 for a more detailed explanation).

COURT OF JUSTICE OF THE EUROPEAN UNION (CJEU)

A3.70 See 'European Court' below.

CRITICAL ILLNESS COVER

A3.71 A term typically used in the UK to describe an insurance policy that provides lump sum payments to employees who contract specific illnesses, whether or not they are able to continue working. Critical illness cover should not be confused with 'permanent health insurance' or 'long term disability' cover, see below.

DEFINED BENEFIT PENSION PLAN

A3.72 See 'final salary pension plan' below.

DEFINED CONTRIBUTION PENSION PLAN

A3.73 See 'money purchase pension plan' and '401K plan' below.

DEROGATION

A3.74 This is a term often used in the context of treaties, or European directives or collective agreements, to describe an opportunity for a party to 'opt out' or 'derogate' from minimum standards that would otherwise apply. There are usually conditions that must be satisfied if the derogation is to be effective.

DESTINATION SERVICES

A3.75 Services linked to the host location, such as help with finding a house or schools and provision of cultural awareness or language training. Destination services are often provided to expatriates to help them settle in quickly.

DETACHED DUTY RELIEF

A3.76 This is a UK income tax relief (see **19.47–19.51**).

DEVELOPMENT ASSIGNMENT

A3.77 An assignment intended to develop the assignee's skills and experience. (See **2.11–2.12.**)

DIRECTIVE

A3.78 Member states of the EU (see 'European Union' below) are required to implement the terms of 'directives' in their own country. Implementation of employment directives may take effect through legislation or by means of collective agreement. The European Court is able to make decisions that guide the courts and tribunals of EU member states on interpretation of directives (see 'European Court' below).

DIRECTOR

A3.79 A formal company appointment. Confusingly, the term is often also used to describe individuals who do not hold a formal appointment but who are quite senior: they would typically have a title like 'Sales Director' but are sometimes just called 'Director'.

UK

A3.80 The following are not terms of art and the management structure of a particular company will be set out in its Articles (constitution). Normally:

- A director who has been formally appointed to the Board is sometimes known as a 'statutory' director in the UK.
- An 'Executive Director' is an employed director, engaged under a contract of employment (also known as a director's service agreement). There may also be non-executive directors who are appointed as director in accordance with the Articles but who are not employed. Non-executive directors will be typically be engaged under contracts for services.
- A 'Managing Director' (MD) or 'Chief Executive Officer' (CEO) is usually an employee who has been appointed to the Board (ie an executive

director) and who takes day-to-day responsibility for managing the company. The MD or CEO will normally be the most senior employee in the company and subject to decisions made by the Board.

- In the UK a Chairman (if there is one) is typically also appointed as a director but does not take on day-to-day management responsibilities. The Chairman typically takes on corporate governance responsibilities, often provides services on a part time basis and is usually engaged under a contract for services.

DISBURSEMENT

A3.81 See 'expense' below.

DISTURBANCE ALLOWANCE

A3.82 Disturbance allowances are often confused with relocation expenses. 'Disturbance allowance' is usually used to describe a small 'one-off' allowance to cover the costs, for example, of repurchasing small household goods such as an iron or kettle at the outset of the assignment. Tax advice should be sought before the allowance is offered. (See also 'allowance' above.)

DOMICILE

A3.83 This term has different meanings in different contexts.

A3.84 For example, the term 'domicile' is used in the Judgments Regulation and in a tax context.

UK

A3.85 In a UK tax context 'domicile' is a term used, broadly, to describe the employee's tax 'home'. The employee's domicile is normally determined at birth. The employee will normally have his father's domicile if he is born to married parents and his mother's if his parents were not married when he was born. Domicile may change subsequently, for example, domicile could change where a minor's parents separate, very occasionally by choice or because the employee has been tax resident in the UK for at least part of 15 out of 20 tax years. If domicile is critical to tax planning, specialist advice should always be sought.

A3.86 The term 'domicile' may also arise in the context of litigation, where the term does not have the same meaning as for tax purposes (see the English Civil Procedure Rules).

DOUBLE TAXATION

A3.87 This term is used to describe the situation where the same income is taxable in two countries. A double tax treaty may provide relief for the employee (see also **5.14**).

DUAL EMPLOYMENTS

A3.88 This term is used to describe the situation where one person has two separate employments. The employments can be with different companies within the same group as long as the employers are separate legal entities. These arrangements are frequently subject to challenge. (See also **6.58** and figure 6.4 for a description of the structure of dual employment arrangements and **8.57–8.61** on terms that may be consistent with dual employments.)

ECONOMIC REASONS

A3.89 See 'redundancy' below.

EDUCATION OR SCHOOLING ALLOWANCE

A3.90 An expatriate may be given an allowance towards the costs of educating his children. It is more common though for education-related expenses to be reimbursed against receipts subject to conditions, limits etc (see **7.137–7.139**).

EMPLOYEE LEASING COMPANY

A3.91 This is a term sometimes used to describe a company that employs staff and 'leases' them to do work for another entity. In some countries restrictions on 'employee leasing' arrangements apply. (See also 'global employment company'.)

EMPLOYERS LIABILITY INSURANCE

A3.92 In some countries, for example the UK, employers are legally required to take out insurance cover in relation to accidents at work or other illnesses or injuries that may be the employer's responsibility. The employer's potential liability for claims from the employee in respect of work-related injuries or industrial disease is unlikely to end just because the employee is sent abroad. A home country employer should check that its insurance policy covers claims when the employee is away from the home country. There may also be a requirement for the host company to take out cover. The host company may also be exposed to potential claims even if it is not the employer. (See **19.66–19.69** on insurance cover for UK assignments.)

EMPLOYMENT PARTICULARS DIRECTIVE

A3.93 Directive 91/533/EEC on an employer's obligation to inform employees of the conditions applicable to the contract or employment relationship. (See **5.38–5.40** and **8.37**.)

END OF SERVICE GRATUITY

A3.94 A term used in some jurisdictions (not the UK) to describe a payment to be made on termination of employment.

E101

A3.95 See 'A1'.

ERISA

A3.96 The Employee Retirement Income Security Act of 1974 (ERISA) is a US federal law that sets minimum standards for most voluntarily established pension and health plans in private industry to provide protection for individuals in these plans.

EU

A3.97 See 'European Union' below.

EU CUSTOMS UNION

A3.98 The EU has agreed customs unions with three countries: Andorra, Turkey and San Marino. In principle, there are no customs duties within the custom unions: goods circulate freely within the customs union area, whether they are made in the EU or imported from outside.

EURO AREA

A3.99 The 'Euro Area' or 'Eurozone' EU member states that have adopted the euro as their currency. The Euro Area currently includes Austria, Belgium, Cyprus, Estonia, Finland, France, Germany, Greece, the Republic of Ireland, Italy, Latvia, Lithuania, Luxembourg, Malta, the Netherlands, Portugal, Slovakia, Slovenia and Spain. The UK has never been part of the Euro Area.

EU TREATY

A3.100   The Treaty between EU member states on which the EU is based, currently the 'Treaty on the Function of the European Union', 'TFEU' or Lisbon Treaty. The 1957 Treaty of Rome had previously been amended by the Maastricht Treaty and the Lisbon Treaty. The Lisbon Treaty was signed at Lisbon on 13 December 2007.

EUROPEAN COURT

A3.101   The European Court of Justice ('ECJ'), based in Luxembourg, is now known as the 'Court of Justice of the European Union' ('CJEU'). This is the Court of the European Union (see 'European Union' below). Tribunals and courts of the EU member states can refer specific questions to the European Court. European Court decisions give explanations of the way that European directives, recommendations and EU Treaty articles should be interpreted. European Court decisions should be applied by the national courts of EU member states. This may lead to change to national laws and in some cases European Court decisions can be applied directly to employees in EU countries. The Court of Justice of the European Union should not be confused with the 'European Court of Human Rights', which is a different court (see below).

EUROPEAN COURT OF JUSTICE (ECJ)

A3.102   See 'European Court' above.

EUROPEAN COURT OF HUMAN RIGHTS (ECHR)

A3.103   This is the Court set up to make decisions relating to the European Convention on Human Rights (see below). The European Court of Human Rights is based in Strasbourg and should not be confused with the Luxembourg-based CJEU (see 'European Court').

EUROPEAN ECONOMIC AREA (EEA)

A3.104   The EEA includes the EU countries and the EFTA countries, except Switzerland, ie the EU member states and Iceland, Liechtenstein and Norway. (See 'European Union' and 'European Free Trade Association' below).

EUROPEAN FREE TRADE ASSOCIATION (EFTA)

A3.105   The following four countries are members of EFTA: Iceland, Liechtenstein, Norway and Switzerland.

EUROPEAN HEALTH INSURANCE CARD (EHIC)

A3.106 Most residents of participating countries, currently EEA countries and Switzerland, may apply for an EHIC (see 'European Economic Area' above for the EEA countries). An EHIC gives an employee who travels temporarily to another participating country access to state healthcare on the same basis as residents of the country they travel to. This is usually at reduced cost or free of charge. If there is a charge it may sometimes be possible for the employee to reclaim all or part of the cost in the country where treatment is given or following return home. The EHIC can be used by employees who travel on business, as well for holidays. The EHIC is normally valid for up to 5 years and can be renewed. Additional insurance cover will usually still be needed as the cover provided by an EHIC is not comprehensive. An EHIC may be an insurance requirement.

UK

A3.107 See the EHIC website at www.gov.uk for further information about current arrangements. Note the potential impact of Brexit.

A3.108 Where the employee undertakes an assignment to an EEA country evidence of continued payment of UK National Insurance contributions is normally required (normally an A1 where the assignment is expected to last for less than a year) to qualify for treatment, as well as the EHIC. Applications should be made to HMRC (see 'A1' above and 'Her Majesty's Revenue and Customs' below).

EUROPEAN UNION (EU)

A3.109 The following 28 countries are currently members of the EU: Austria, Belgium, Bulgaria, Croatia, Cyprus, Czech Republic, Denmark, Estonia, Finland, France, Germany, Greece, Hungary, Republic of Ireland, Italy, Latvia, Lithuania, Luxembourg, Malta, the Netherlands, Poland, Portugal, Romania, Slovakia, Slovenia, Spain, Sweden and the UK.

A3.110 Various countries have applied to join the EU but have not been accepted yet, eg, Former Yugoslav Republic of Macedonia and Turkey.

EUROPEAN WORKS COUNCIL (EWC)

A3.111 Directive 2009/38/EC (the 'recast' 'European Works Council Directive') requires multinationals with at least 1,000 employees in the EU and at least 150 employees in each of two EU member states to set up arrangements for transnational information and consultation of employees, if sufficient employees request this. The arrangements are usually referred to as 'European Works Councils' or 'EWCs'. If an EWC exists there should be an EWC agreement that explains the way that the EWC operates, its goals, etc. These may include, for example, information and consultation in relation to redundancies that may affect employees in more than one country. Note the potential impact of Brexit on EWCs.

A3.112   An EWC is unlikely to be concerned with an individual expatriate employment assignment or its termination. However, if the proposed changes are part of a bigger project affecting employees in more than one country then it is worth checking to see whether there may be any EWC implications that should be taken into consideration.

A3.113   There are various other works council arrangements in Europe, see 'works council' below.

EXPATRIATE (EXPAT)

A3.114   An expatriate is a person living in a country that is not their 'home country'. The term is used loosely to cover people who are working abroad and those who are living abroad for other reasons. Expatriates may be living abroad temporarily or may have permanently relocated to a new country.

EXPENSE

A3.115   When an employee buys something he incurs an expense. Expenses incurred in the performance of duties for the employer (business expenses) are usually reimbursed to the employee by his employer. Expatriates may be reimbursed by their employer in respect of other more personal expenses too (eg utility bills for their home or relocation expenses) (see also 'Allowance' above and 7.27–7.39). It is important to distinguish between allowances (usually 'one-off' fixed sums or regular payments at a set rate) and reimbursement of expenses (usually payments against receipts for money actually spent). Significant tax consequences may flow from this.

A3.116   Expenses are sometimes referred to as 'disbursements', though in the UK the term 'disbursements' is usually used to describe an expense incurred by a business or self-employed contractor, rather than an employee. In an expatriate context disbursements paid by the home or host company may be recharged to the other in accordance with an inter-company expatriate supply agreement. For example, the home country employer may reimburse business expenses of the expatriate incurred in providing services to the host company (under the terms of the employee's employment contract). The home company may then seek reimbursement of the disbursements from the host company (under the terms of the inter-company expatriate supply agreement).

FINAL SALARY PENSION PLAN

A3.117 Final salary pension plans (or schemes) are sometimes referred to as 'defined benefit' pension plans. These are, broadly, pension arrangements that provide for a pension based on length of service and salary at the end of the employment. A typical final salary plan might provide for accrual of pension rights at one-sixtieth of 'final salary' for each year of service. 'Final salary' might be determined by averaging, say, the last 3 years' remuneration. Because a final salary pension plan can be a valuable benefit, and particularly because many plans are closed to new members, an assignee may want to remain in his home country final salary pension plan during his assignment.

FISCAL YEAR

A3.118 A term used to describe a tax year or a company's financial year.

FOREIGN SERVICE RELIEF

A3.119 This is a UK term used to describe additional income tax relief that is currently available on termination payments if all or part of the payment relates to a period of service abroad. This relief will be abolished from April 2018 (see 16.37).

401K PLAN

A3.120 This is a term used to describe a type of US defined contribution retirement plan that allows employees to make voluntary contributions from remuneration to an employer-sponsored account ('401K' is a reference to a specific section of the US tax code). The fund can eventually be used to buy an annuity or otherwise. Expatriates with a US home country may wish to remain in their US 401K plan whilst they are assigned outside the US.

409A

A3.121 A reference to a section of the US tax code that sometimes causes concern in relation to expatriate remuneration.

GARDEN LEAVE

A3.122 'Garden leave' is a UK expression that describes an employee who is still employed during his notice period but who is not required to perform normal duties for the employer. His activities may be subject to additional constraints during the garden leave period, eg not contacting customers. In many countries a period of garden leave is used to protect the employer's business after active employment ends. Garden leave is not always allowed and may be subject to legal restrictions. (See **11.22–11.23** and **16.41–16.42** on garden leave.)

GENERAL MANAGER

A3.123   A term used, particularly in some European countries such as Italy, to describe a senior manager with a particular function. Typically, a company will have only one general manager who is likely to be (though not always) appointed to the Board. The commercial/employment laws that apply to general managers are typically different to those applicable to 'ordinary' employees.

GLOBAL EMPLOYMENT COMPANY (GEC)

A3.124   One of many terms used to describe a 'service company' established to employ expatriates.

GLOBAL MOBILITY

A3.125   A term used to describe people relocating to another country for work. Global mobility specialists advise on global mobility, including, for example, immigration, tax and HR specialists. However, the term is sometimes (particularly in the US) used to describe immigration work more narrowly.

GLOBAL NOMAD

A3.126   An informal term for a career expatriate who has taken a series of assignments in different countries.

GOVERNING LAW

A3.127   These are broadly the laws that are used to interpret a contract (see 10.3–10.29 and 10.78–10.82 and 'Rome Convention', 'Rome I' and 'Rome II' below).

GREAT BRITAIN

A3.128   Great Britain (sometimes abbreviated to 'Britain') technically consists of three countries. These are England, Scotland and Wales. Northern Ireland is not part of Great Britain.

A3.129 The United Kingdom (UK) consists of Great Britain and Northern Ireland.

A3.130 Sometimes reference is made to the 'British Isles'. This is a geographical description sometimes used in England to include the UK and the Republic of Ireland. Use of this term should be avoided in expatriate employment documents as it is confusing.

A3.131 There are three main legal jurisdictions within the UK. These are: England and Wales (ie the two countries together); Scotland; and Northern Ireland. Most employment legislation applies in the same or a similar way in all three jurisdictions (though laws may be introduced through different Acts or Statutory Instruments in each jurisdiction). Generally, the same employment documents will work well in any of the three jurisdictions but this should ideally be checked because some of the differences could have an impact. If claims are to be made then care must be taken to ensure those claims are made in the correct jurisdiction. Any severance agreement should take the jurisdiction into account.

A3.132 Some of the smaller islands around the UK have different legal and tax arrangements etc, for example, Jersey, Guernsey and the Isle of Man. These jurisdictions are sometimes chosen as places of registration for service companies supplying employees to work abroad. Although employment documents will be similar in form, employment laws are not always the same as those applicable in England.

GREEN CARD

A3.133 This refers to lawful permanent residence status in the US for foreign nationals and provides the foreign national with the right to work in the US permanently. This type of immigration permission can affect an individual's US income tax obligations, regardless of whether he actually works inside or outside the US.

GREENWICH MEANTIME (GMT)

A3.134 The time applicable in the UK in the winter. In the UK in summer British Summer Time applies (which is one hour ahead of GMT).

GRIEVANCE

A3.135 An internal complaint made by an employee to his employer. Grievance procedures vary widely and might, for example, be governed by collective agreements, legislation or company policies.

GROUP

A3.136 See 'group company' below.

GROUP COMPANY

A3.137 A group of companies is generally linked through share ownership. There is no standard definition of 'Group Company'.

A3.138 As expatriate assignments are usually arranged between companies within the same group it will usually be convenient to include a definition of 'Group Company' in each employment document. For example, the employment contract may make it clear that obligations, such as a duty of confidentiality, are owed to 'Group Companies'.

UK

A3.139 In the UK an appropriate definition is usually taken from tax or company law legislation, to reduce the risk of dispute arising later over the meaning of the definition.

HARDSHIP ALLOWANCE

A3.140 Sometimes additional allowances are offered to recognise the difficulties faced by employees working at a particular location. For example, a hardship allowance might be paid to an employee where social facilities are limited; his family cannot accompany him; there are issues with security; or the climate is 'bad' (see also 'Allowance' above and **7.48–7.51** for a more detailed explanation).

HER MAJESTY'S REVENUE AND CUSTOMS (HMRC)

A3.141 HMRC is the UK tax and social security authority that deals with PAYE ('Pay-As-You-Earn' employer obligations to withhold income tax from an employee's pay); National Insurance contributions (UK social security contributions); value added tax (VAT); corporation tax; etc. The HMRC website at www.hmrc.gov.uk offers useful information but is not an adequate substitute for specialist tax advice.

HOME COMPANY

A3.142 This is a term usually used to describe a company based in the employee's home country with which the assignee has a relationship. Typically, the employee works for the home company in his home country and the home company later decides to send the employee to work abroad. The home company may be the assignee's employer during the assignment, in which case the home company may be referred to as a 'home country employer' or 'home employer' or 'home company employer'.

HOME COUNTRY

A3.143 In this book the 'home country' generally refers to the country from which the employee is sent on assignment.

A3.144 For example, an Australian employee is working in Australia for a company registered in Australia and is assigned to work in Malaysia. The home country will be Australia.

A3.145 The term is sometimes also used to refer to the employee's country of origin, which can be a bit confusing if that is not the country from which the employee has been sent on assignment.

A3.146 For example, an Australian national works for 20 years in the UK and is sent by his UK employer to work in Malaysia. In this book we would generally refer to the home country as the UK. Some businesses and advisers might refer to Australia as the home country.

A3.147 It is important for those drafting expatriate employment documents to know if the employee's country of origin is not the country from which he has been assigned as this may, for example, affect benefit arrangements, immigration permission, tax and social security status, etc.

HOME COUNTRY EMPLOYMENT

A3.148 This term is used to describe an employment arrangement whereby the employee is employed by the 'home company' (see above) during the assignment (see **6.14–6.42** and figure 6.1).

HOST COMPANY

A3.149 This is a term usually used to describe a company in the host country to which an employee is sent to work abroad. The host company may also be the assignee's employer in which case the host company may be referred to as the 'host country employer' or 'host employer' or 'host company employer'.

HOST COUNTRY

A3.150 This term is used to describe the country to which the employee is sent on assignment, ie where he will work.

HOST COUNTRY EMPLOYMENT

A3.151   This term is used to describe an employment arrangement whereby the employee is employed by the 'host company' (see above) during the assignment (see **6.43–6.57** and figure 6.3).

HOUSING ALLOWANCE

A3.152   Employers of expatriates often pay allowances in respect of accommodation costs. This might be referred to as a 'housing' or 'accommodation' allowance (see **7.65–7.67** and **7.113–7.130**).

HYPOTHETICAL TAX

A3.153   When an employer applies 'tax equalisation' or 'tax protection' (see explanations below) to all or part of an employee's remuneration package, the employer will often refer to 'hypothetical tax' or 'hypo' tax. Hypothetical tax is not real tax, just a figure used to work out how net remuneration should be calculated to give effect to a tax equalisation or protection promise.

A3.154   The term is slightly confusing as it can mean different things to different employers, depending on how they make their own calculations.

A3.155   For example, the employee may have been promised that his net pay will be the same as if he were an ordinary employee working in his home country and paying tax and social security contributions in his home country. To work out the gross pay that would need to be paid to achieve this, the employer might calculate the tax and social security contributions that would have been due in the home country on that basis and that amount might be referred to as the 'hypothetical tax'.

IMMIGRATION PERMISSION

A3.156   This is a loose term used to describe the approval or clearance needed from an immigration authority to allow the employee to live or work in the country. Permission might be granted, for example, in the form of a work permit or visa (see **3.3–3.26** on immigration permission generally and **19.4–19.31** in relation to the UK).

INDEMNITY

A3.157   This is a good example of a 'false friend', an English word that seems familiar and clear but, in fact, can mean something different.

UK

A3.158 In the UK lawyers typically use the word 'indemnity' to describe the situation where one party promises to put the other party right financially if a particular eventuality arises. For example, in the UK a severance agreement will typically include a 'tax indemnity' so that if the tax authorities decide that the employer has taxed the termination payment incorrectly, the employer can recover additional tax and associated costs from the employee. In the context of a business sale the buyer and seller of the business may agree to 'indemnify' each other in particular circumstances (eg breach of warranty).

Europe

A3.159 In some European countries the word 'indemnity' is used to describe a termination payment that an employee will receive. If the term is used some enquiry should be made as to its precise meaning as the 'indemnity' might include, for example, redundancy pay, compensation for 'unfair dismissal' and/or payment in lieu of notice.

INJUNCTION

A3.160 This is a court order (in the UK now referred to as an 'interim order') that prevents the employee or employer from doing something. For example, an injunction may be sought to prevent a former employee from using confidential information or breaching post termination restrictive covenants (see **11.27** on UK interim orders and Chapter 11 generally on injunctions and post termination restrictive covenants). In some countries, for example the Republic of Ireland, an injunction can be sought to preserve the employment when the employer wishes to dismiss.

INTER-COMPANY EXPATRIATE SUPPLY AGREEMENT

A3.161 This is used in this book to describe a contract between the home and host companies regarding the employee (see **6.26–6.30**, **8.73–8.83**, checklist **A1.10** at Appendix 1 and framework document **A2.6** at Appendix 2).

INTERIM ORDER

A3.162 See the explanation for 'injunction' above.

INTERNATIONAL COMMUTER

A3.163 An employee who lives in one country and works in another. For example, an employee who spends Monday to Friday working in London but flies home to family in Dublin for the weekends. (See **14.43–14.51**.)

INTERNATIONAL LABOUR ORGANISATION (ILO)

A3.164 The ILO is an organisation based in Switzerland and linked to the United Nations that sets international labour standards. Countries may choose to ratify the standards but ratification does not necessarily mean that employers or employees must comply with the standards directly. In practice, standards set by the ILO are of little direct relevance to those drafting expatriate employment documents.

INTERNATIONAL PENSION PLAN

A3.165 Sometimes it is not possible and/or desirable for an employee to participate in a home or host country pension arrangement. The employee may be offered an 'international pension plan' instead. (See **19.102–19.104**.)

IRELAND

A3.166 References to 'Ireland' can be confusing. From a legal perspective, the 'Republic of Ireland' (also known as 'Eire') is an independent country within the EU. The term 'Ireland' is usually used by lawyers to refer to that country, but can sometimes be used to cover Northern Ireland too. From a legal perspective Northern Ireland is part of the UK, and is currently also within the EU. Expatriate documents should ideally refer to either the 'Republic of Ireland' (or 'Eire') or 'Northern Ireland', rather than to 'Ireland' to reduce the risk of misunderstanding.

JOB DESCRIPTION

A3.167 This is a short or long written explanation of the work that the employee actually does, or may be required to do. The job description may be important in an expatriate context, for example because of the potential effect on corporation tax, the application of collective agreements, etc (see **8.29–8.31**, **8.38** and **13.8–13.15** and 'collective agreement' above).

JOB TITLE

A3.168 This is the title or label that is given to the employee's role, such as 'General Manager' or 'Sales Manager'. The job title will usually give an indication of 'seniority' (in the UK sense) as well as the type of work done. Some job titles may imply authority to represent or bind the company or that the employee has particular responsibilities, for example 'Director' (see also 'job description' above).

JOINT EMPLOYMENT

A3.169 This is a term sometimes used to describe the situation where two companies, individuals, or other entities, employ the same person for the same job. This might be theoretically possible, for example, where a husband and wife jointly employ a nanny to look after their children. In practice, joint employment is not usually a good idea and is unlikely to be appropriate for an expatriate (see Chapter 4, **6.70–6.77** and figure 6.5).

A3.170 Joint employment should not be confused with 'dual employments' (where the employee has two separate employers, two employment contracts and two jobs) or 'split contract' or 'split payroll' arrangements (where the employee has one employer but two discrete sets of duties remunerated through two different payroll arrangements). See 'dual employments' and 'split contract' and 'split payroll' arrangements above and below.

JUDGMENTS REGULATION

A3.171 Council Regulation 44/2001/EC of 22 December 2000 on jurisdiction and the recognition and enforcement of judgments in civil and commercial matters (the 'Judgments Regulation') can apply to EU countries (see 'European Union' above). The Judgments Regulation may sometimes be referred to as the 'recast' 'Brussels Regulation' or the 'Jurisdiction Regulation' (see **10.62–10.74**). Note the potential impact of Brexit on EU regulations.

JURISDICTION

A3.172 When a particular court is able, under the relevant rules, to hear a particular legal claim it is said to have 'jurisdiction' to hear the claim (see **10.62–10.74**).

LABOUR COURT

A3.173 In some jurisdictions specialist tribunals and courts may deal with individual employment disputes. These courts will have local titles, often loosely translated as 'Labour Court'. This term may be confusing for a US audience, see 'labour law' below.

LABOUR LAW

A3.174 In Europe, including in the UK, 'employment law' and 'labour law' may be used interchangeably to mean the same thing.

A3.175 For advisers from a US background that can be a bit confusing as in the US laws that apply to individual employees are often referred to as 'employment laws' and laws that apply to trade unions and collective issues are often referred to as 'labour laws' or, using US spelling, 'labor laws'.

A3.176 In Europe we sometimes refer to 'individual' employment laws and 'collective' labour laws. However, 'collective' labour laws in Europe do not correspond precisely to 'trade union' or 'industrial relations' laws. The phrase is used more broadly to encompass laws that apply to groups of people rather than individuals. For example, there is a requirement to consult with employee representatives where there are 'collective' dismissals. (See 'collective dismissal' above.)

LEGAL ENTITY

UK

A3.177 In the UK an employee must be employed by an organisation that has 'separate legal personality'. This might, eg, be a company (a private company styled 'Ltd' or a public company styled 'Plc'), a traditional partnership, a limited liability partnership (LLP), a governmental organisation, or an individual human person. Entities registered abroad, for example an American corporation, can also employ. A branch or representative office of a company does not have separate legal personality and in that case the branch or representative office will not be the employer. The employer will be the company.

Elsewhere

A3.178 Other countries do not necessarily apply the same principles as the UK. Some countries, for example, may allow employment by a branch or representative office and some host countries may not allow employment by a company that is not registered in the host country. Care should be taken to understand the home and host country requirements so that the employer can be described clearly in the documents and so that related registrations, immigration permits, etc are taken out in the correct name.

LEASE PREMIUM

A3.179 This term may be used to describe an unusual arrangement whereby an upfront lump sum is paid instead of regular monthly rental payments.

LEGALISATION

A3.180 See 'apostille' above.

LEGAL PRIVILEGE

A3.181 See the explanation for 'privilege' below. (See **15.123–15.128** on disclosure.)

LISBON TREATY (TFEU)

A3.182 See European Treaty above.

LOCAL HIRE

A3.183 A term often used to describe employees who are recruited from the local population in the country where they will work. (Ie an employee who is not an 'expat'.)

LOCALISATION

A1.184 This is a term that is often used to describe a transition from 'expatriate' to 'local' (usually less favourable) terms of employment. Typically, the employer attempts to 'localise' terms if the assignment lasts longer than expected because of the employee's personal preferences (see **15.114–15.119**) or if a period prescribed in an assignment policy has been exceeded (eg three or five years). Localisation might, for example, entail of loss of housing or education assistance or withdrawal of tax equalisation.

LOCAL PLUS

A3.185 A term used to describe a remuneration and benefits package based on that which would be offered to a host country 'local hire', but with some expatriate 'extras', eg assistance with tax return preparation. (See **12.21–12.23**.)

LONG-TERM DISABILITY COVER

A3.186 See 'permanent health insurance' below.

LONG-TERM INCENTIVE PLAN (LTIP)

A3.187 This is a term generally used to describe arrangements that provide for benefits to be delivered over a relatively long period of time. Usually the intention is to align the employee's interests with the interests of shareholders. (See **11.31–11.41** on LTIPs and restrictive covenants and **15.9–15.20** on share plans generally.)

LUGANO CONVENTION

A3.188 This is an international convention relating to jurisdiction and the enforcement of judgments in civil and commercial matters (see also 'Judgments Regulation' and **10.62–10.74** on jurisdiction).

MANDATORY EMPLOYMENT LAWS

A3.189 The Rome Convention refers specifically to 'mandatory rules of law' and similar concepts are described in Rome I. 'Mandatory employment laws' is used more loosely in this book to cover employment laws that must be applied to employees. The parties cannot normally decide which mandatory employment laws will apply. They will usually apply automatically and override any conflicting terms in the expatriate employment documents. A country's mandatory employment laws usually apply to employees working in the relevant country. This means that host country, rather than home country, mandatory employment laws are most likely to be relevant to an expatriate assignment. Home country and other countries' mandatory employment laws may also apply. (See **10.30–10.61** for a more detailed explanation and 'Rome Convention' and 'Rome I' below.)

MANDATORY RULES OF LAW

A3.190 See 'Mandatory employment laws' above.

MARRIAGE

A3.191 Marital and/or partnership status is determined in different ways in different jurisdictions. Same sex partnerships are not always recognised and unmarried partners may be treated differently in different locations and for different purposes.

MEMBER

A3.192 A term typically used to describe a 'partner' in a limited liability partnership (LLP). Members will typically be self-employed but may be treated as employees in some jurisdictions.

MEMBER STATES

A3.193 See 'European Union', 'European Economic Area' and 'European Free Trade Association' above.

MONEY PURCHASE PENSION PLAN

A3.194 Money purchase pension plans are often referred to as 'defined contribution' pension plans. This is a pension plan where the pension the employee receives depends on the contributions paid by employer and employee, and how those invested contributions perform prior to retirement. There is no guaranteed pension amount but the employer will usually promise to make contributions to the plan at a fixed rate (say 5% or 10% of basic salary) (compare 'final salary pension plan' above).

MUTUAL AGREEMENT

A3.195 See 'termination by mutual agreement' below.

NATIONAL INSURANCE CONTRIBUTIONS (NIC)

A3.196 This is the term used for UK employers' and employees' social security contributions.

NON-COMPETE AGREEMENT

A3.197 This is a US expression used for what in the UK we might call 'post termination restrictive covenants' or 'post termination restrictions'. These are agreed restrictions on the employee's conduct after his employment ends (and sometimes also during the employment). They might include promises not to work for a competitor, or not to solicit custom or employees or interfere with supplier arrangements for a limited period of time after the employment ends. The objective will usually be to protect confidential information, trade connections or the stability of the employer's workforce (see 'Restrictive covenants' below and Chapter 11 generally).

NOTARY PUBLIC

A3.198 A 'Notary Public' is a public officer appointed under authority of state law with power, for example, to administer oaths, certify affidavits, take acknowledgments, depositions or testimony and record notarial protests. Some documents used in an expatriate context require certification by a Notary Public. An apostille may also be required (see 'apostille' above).

NOTICE OF TERMINATION OF EMPLOYMENT

A3.199 Most countries have rules on the appropriate period of notice to be given by the employer or employee to terminate the employment. These 'mandatory' rules will usually, but not always, take precedence over any agreement between the parties on notice.

A3.200 For example, in the UK the notice of termination to be given to the employee by the employer will be the longer of contractual notice (ie the agreed period) and statutory minimum notice. Statutory minimum notice is set by legislation and the notice period cannot be less than that.

A3.201 Most other countries have minimum or maximum periods of notice set by legislation and/or collective agreement(s). The US is of course a notable exception where employment 'at will' is generally permitted.

A3.202 When asking questions about notice it is important to understand any difference between the notice to be given by employer and employee; how any legal minimum or maximum applies; whether notice has to be given in a particular way or at a particular time; and whether notice must be worked (ie whether a 'payment in lieu of notice' can be made or 'garden leave' can be taken, see further below and above).

A3.203 It is important not to make assumptions in this regard. For example, if notice must be served personally or sent by registered post it may be ineffective if given by email. If notice must be given on a particular day of the month the notice period that will actually apply may be longer than the documents imply.

A3.204 A common error is for expatriate employment documents to fail to differentiate between the notice period to end the assignment and the notice period to end the employment. The assignment and the employment do not of course always end at the same time. (For more information on notice see **16.24–16.59.**)

NOTIONAL SALARY

A3.205 This is the term that is usually used to describe hypothetical salary, used as a reference point for a particular purpose.

A3.206 For example, actual pay may be determined by applying a cost of living allowance or adjustment (COLA) to notional salary (see 'cost of living allowance or adjustment' above).

A3.207 Notional salary may be used as a base for determining pension contributions or bonus payments.

A3.208 Notional salary may also be used to determine the basic salary that should apply if/when the expatriate returns to the home country (see also **7.10–7.12.**)

OFFER LETTER

A3.209 This term can be quite confusing because it means different things to different people.

UK

A3.210 In the UK the offer letter is normally an informal covering letter designed to be delivered with a longer and more formal contract of employment. Normally the offer letter and contract will be delivered together.

US

A3.211 In the US the document setting out key employment terms will often be in letter format and may be referred as the 'offer letter'. Sometimes 'offer letter' is used in this way in the UK too.

ORDINARILY RESIDENT

A3.212 In the UK 'ordinarily resident' had a particular meaning, and consequences, in an income tax context.

A3.213 The term is no longer used. A statutory definition of 'tax residence' now applies, see 'tax resident'.

A3.214 Specialist expatriate tax advice should always be sought in relation to 'tax resident' status as the rules can be complex and the financial consequences significant.

OVERSEAS

A3.215 In the UK, when we talk about an 'overseas' assignment or 'overseas' employer we are usually talking of an assignment to work outside the UK or for an employer registered outside the UK. In this book the term has been used loosely to mean 'any other country'.

PAY-AS-YOU-EARN (PAYE)

UK

A3.216 This is the UK term to describe an employer's obligation to withhold income tax from an employee's pay and account for the tax to HMRC (see 'Her Majesty's Revenue and Customs' above). In an expatriate context it is usual to refer more generally to tax 'withholding obligations'.

PAYMENT IN LIEU OF NOTICE (PILON)

A3.217 If the employee's employment ends before the appropriate notice period has expired then a payment may be due in respect of the remainder of the notice period.

A3.218 So, for example, suppose a UK-based employee is entitled to 4 weeks' notice but is allowed to work only 2 weeks of the notice period. A payment may be made 'in lieu' of the remuneration that would have been earned if the employee had worked out the remaining 2 weeks' notice.

A3.219 A payment in lieu of notice is often referred to as a 'PILON' for convenience.

A3.220 In some countries the employer is not permitted to make a PILON and the employee must be permitted to work throughout the notice period and receive salary and benefits in the ordinary way in respect of that period. In others a PILON can only be paid if agreement is reached with the employee or appropriate representatives.

A3.221 The method by which the appropriate PILON is calculated may vary considerably from country to country. For example, there may be rules about which benefits should be taken into consideration. (See also **16.29–16.40** on PILONs.)

PERMANENT ESTABLISHMENT

A3.222 Countries need to decide when to subject non-resident organisations that have operations in their country to corporation tax. Often the non-resident company will not have to pay corporation tax if it can show that it does not have a 'permanent establishment' in the host country. 'Permanent establishment' may typically be defined in relevant tax treaties as 'a fixed place of business through which the business is wholly or partly carried on'. When expatriate employment arrangements are set up care must sometimes be taken to ensure that a permanent establishment is not created. This may mean describing the employee's duties and restrictions on his ability to conclude commercial contracts in the employment documents. Employee activity will not necessarily be the only criterion. (See **4.39-4.48** and **13.12–13.15**.)

PERMANENT HEALTH INSURANCE (PHI)

A3.223 The employer may take out an insurance plan under the terms of which the employer will receive payments if the employee is unable to work after a qualifying period of absence. The employer then makes payments to the employee who remains in employment but does not work. The payments may be equivalent to, say, 75% of basic salary after 6 months' absence and might continue until retirement if the employee remains unfit to work. Whilst PHI may be a valuable benefit for employees, provision of PHI cover during an overseas assignment may create disproportionate complication and expense for the employer.

A3.224 PHI is sometimes known as 'long-term disability' cover, particularly in the US. PHI should not be confused with 'critical illness' cover, see above.

PERSONAL SERVICE COMPANY

A3.225 A colloquial term, normally used to describe a company that employs one employee who is also the sole director and shareholder.

PHANTOM SHARE PLAN

A3.226 Many multinational businesses offer employees share/share option/ stock plans that allow them to be awarded shares, or granted options to buy shares, usually in the parent company. In some countries participation in share-related plans is not permitted or is not tax effective. The employer may instead offer the employee an opportunity to participate in a bonus plan designed to mirror the share/share option arrangements that would otherwise be offered. Usually the plan provides for the employee to be awarded 'phantom' (ie notional or hypothetical) shares so that the eventual cash bonus payment can be linked to share price without share-related rights actually being awarded. (See **15.9–15.15** on share plans generally.)

POINTS-BASED SYSTEM

A3.227 The points-based system (also known as PBS) is the UK's points-based system for granting immigration permission (see **19.4–19.31**).

POLICY

A3.228 Policies are usually arrangements that employers apply to a number of employees to make administration more convenient. Normally they are not contractually binding (though they can be). They may be prepared for internal management guidance or for issue to employees, for example as part of a staff handbook or international assignment policy.

A3.229 If policies exist that may, or are intended to, relate to expatriate employment arrangements the status of the relevant policy should be made clear in the expatriate employment documents. It is usual for the employer to ensure that the normal home country staff handbook and/or policy documents do not apply during the assignment (see Chapter 9).

POSTED WORKERS DIRECTIVE

A3.230 Council Directive 96/71/EC, the EC Posted Workers Directive, broadly, requires member states of the EU to provide employment protection to employees 'posted' from an undertaking in one EU member state to work temporarily in another EU member state (see **10.50–10.55**).

POST TERMINATION RESTRICTIVE COVENANTS

A3.231 See 'Restrictive covenants' below.

POWER OF ATTORNEY ('POWERS')

A3.232 A power of attorney is legally binding authority given to somebody to act for someone else or do something for someone else.

A3.233 Powers of attorney may be provided in ordinary employment contracts (eg to facilitate intellectual property arrangements). In an expatriate context, 'power of attorney' or 'powers' may also be used to describe formal authority given to a company representative, for example to manage the payroll (see **13.26–13.29**).

PRIVILEGE

A3.234 In some countries certain communications are not subject to disclosure requirements, for example in the event of litigation or enquiry by tax authorities. Typically, advice given by a lawyer to his client will be 'privileged' whereas internal discussions, for example between an assignment manager and a line manager, or between home and host companies, are not privileged. The rules that determine whether privilege applies and, if it does, the scope of the protection offered varies between countries. Care should usually be taken to ensure that documents are produced in a way that minimises risk even if privilege does not apply. For example, drafts should be marked 'draft' or 'subject to discussion/consultation' as appropriate. (See also **15.123–15.128** on disclosure.)

PROPRIETARY INTERESTS AGREEMENT

A3.235 A US term used to describe an agreement with an employee confirming the employer's property rights, typically covering things like confidential information and intellectual property.

PROVIDENT FUND

A3.236 A term used in some countries to describe a pension arrangement.

REDUNDANCY

UK

A3.237 In the UK we have a definition of 'redundancy' that is used for the purposes of determining Statutory Redundancy Pay entitlement, and whether the reason for termination is 'redundancy' or not for the purposes of an 'unfair dismissal' complaint.

A3.238 The definition is contained in ERA 1996, s 139 as follows:

'For the purposes of this Act an employee who is dismissed shall be taken to be dismissed by reason of redundancy if the dismissal is wholly or mainly attributable to –

(a) the fact that his employer has ceased or intends to cease –
  (i) to carry on the business for the purposes of which the employee was employed by him, or
  (ii) to carry on that business in the place where the employee was so employed, or
(b) the fact that the requirements of that business –
  (i) for employees to carry out work of a particular kind, or
  (ii) for employees to carry out work of a particular kind in the place where the employee was employed by the employer,

have ceased or diminished or are expected to cease or diminish.'

A3.239 Essentially, redundancy arises where there is a requirement for fewer employees to do a particular kind of work or to do that kind of work in a particular place. In the UK whether or not an employee is redundant is factual and, usually, relatively easy to determine. An employee will not be 'redundant' if he is replaced by someone else because his work is unsatisfactory.

Elsewhere

A3.240 In other countries different concepts will apply, and it is common, even in the UK, for people to assume that 'redundancy' can cover dismissals in other circumstances. When using the word 'redundancy' in communications it is usually helpful to describe the relevant factual circumstances so the intended meaning is clear.

A3.241 Some advisers from other countries will refer to dismissal for 'economic reasons' which usually means roughly the same thing as 'redundancy'. Again, care should be taken to ensure that the intended meaning is understood.

REDUNDANCY PAY

A3.242 This term is used to describe a payment that is made to an employee because his employment terminates by reason of 'redundancy' (see 'redundancy' above). This should not be confused with a 'payment in lieu of notice' (see above) or a payment to someone who loses his job from a state insurance fund.

A3.243 Sometimes redundancy pay may be referred to as an 'indemnity' by European lawyers (see 'indemnity' above). This can be confusing for UK and US lawyers who will need to ask for a fuller explanation of what is intended.

A3.244 Sometimes the term 'redundancy pay' is used loosely to describe severance pay where the reason for dismissal is something other than redundancy.

RE-ENGAGEMENT

A3.245 This is a term usually used to describe the situation where an employee's employment is terminated and he is offered a different role with the same employer (compare 'reinstatement' below).

REFERENCE

A3.246 An employee who seeks new employment may seek a reference from a current or former employer to confirm details of his current or former employment. In some countries the way that references must, or can, be provided is prescribed by law.

REFERENCE SALARY

A3.247 See 'Notional salary'.

REINSTATEMENT

A3.248 This is a term usually used to describe the situation where an employee is dismissed and later offered the same job back again (compare 're-engagement' above). It is worth checking whether this is intended to mean dismissal, (ie a period when the employee is not employed and then recommencement of the same employment) or whether the intention is to describe a 'void' dismissal, for example, where a court or employment authority declares the original dismissal ineffective and the employee is treated as though there has been no break in his service.

RELOCATION

A3.249 This term is generally used to describe the employee's removal to the host country at the outset of his assignment. The term could also be used to describe removal to another country at the end of his assignment, though usually if the removal is back to the home country this would be referred to as 'repatriation'.

A3.250 Typically, the expatriate employment documents will include a promise that the employer will bear repatriation expenses on termination of the assignment, subject to conditions. Relocation expenses are not usually provided on the same basis as repatriation expenses (see **7.57–7.64** and 'relocation allowance' and 'repatriation' below).

RELOCATION ALLOWANCE

A3.251 Relocation expenses may, for example, include flights, shipping, temporary accommodation costs, furnishing costs, etc. Sometimes a relocation allowance is provided (see 'allowance' above and **7.57–7.64**) but reimbursement of expenses is more common.

REMITTANCE-BASED TAX TREATMENT

A3.252 If the arrangements are appropriate, then some remuneration earned outside a country may only be subject to tax on a 'remittance basis', ie the earnings may only be subject to tax if they are sent to the country, paid into an onshore bank account or spent in the country. (See **6.58–6.69** on dual employments (and warnings) and **19.39** on overseas workdays.)

REPATRIATION

A3.253 This term is generally used to describe the employee's return to his home country. This might, for example, be the employee's country of birth or nationality or the country from which he was originally assigned (usually these will be the same place). Typically, the expatriate employment documents will include a promise that the employer will bear repatriation expenses on termination of the assignment, subject to conditions. Repatriation support may also be a condition of immigration permission. Repatriation expenses may not be provided on the same basis as relocation expenses, and may be subject to additional conditions (see 'allowance', 'relocation' and 'relocation allowance' above and **7.57–7.64**).

REPATRIATION ALLOWANCE

A3.254 Repatriation expenses may, for example, include flights, shipping, temporary accommodation costs, furnishing costs, etc. Sometimes a repatriation allowance is provided (see 'allowance', 'relocation' and 'repatriation' above) but reimbursement of expenses is more common. This may have an impact on tax relief: this should be checked.

REPRESENTATIVE OFFICE

A3.255 Sometimes there will be no group company registered in a particular country and no 'branch', but a group company may nevertheless operate there. This may be referred to as a representative office. 'Representative office' may have a particular meaning in the home or host country, for example, under tax legislation.

RESIDENCE PERMIT

A3.256 This is the term usually used to describe permission granted by the host country immigration authority for the employee and/or family members to live in the country. The individual will probably require additional immigration permission to work. Permission to work and live in a particular country may be linked. For example, loss of a work permit may lead to loss of a residence permit or vice versa. The relevant permit(s) may be granted to the individuals personally or may be granted to the employer. There may be additional requirements, for example to register with the local police (see **3.3–3.26** in relation to immigration permission generally and **19.4–19.31** on the UK points-based system).

RESIDENT

A3.257 This is a term normally used to describe someone who lives in a particular country.

In the UK the term also has a particular meaning when used in a tax context (see 'tax resident').

RESIDENT LABOUR MARKET TEST

A3.258 A term used to describe UK labour market checks conducted for immigration purposes, eg advertising to see if there is an appropriate alternative local candidate before immigration permission is granted. (See **19.19.**)

RESIDUAL CONTRACT

A3.259 Where there is a host company employment arrangement the employee may retain some contractual relationship with his home company employer, for example to provide for some continuing benefit such as pension and return home at the end of the assignment. The document confirming the terms of that contract will not be an employment contract, as the host company will be the employer during the assignment. That contract is described as a 'residual' contract in this book but various different terms are used in different contexts to describe the same thing (see Chapter 6, **8.62–8.72**, checklist **A1.9** at Appendix 1 and framework document **A2.5** at Appendix 2).

RESTRICTIVE COVENANTS

A3.260 These are agreed restrictions on an employee's ability to engage in particular activities. For example, a promise to refrain from accepting employment with a competitor, from soliciting business from customers or persuading employees to leave a business.

A3.261 In the UK we often refer to these as 'post termination restrictive covenants' if they apply after the employment ends. Sometimes we refer to them as 'restrictions' or 'covenants'. In the US, and elsewhere, restrictions are often referred to as 'non-compete agreements'.

A3.262 This is an area where national practices are quite diverse. (See Chapter 11 on post termination restrictive covenants generally.)

ROME I

A3.263 Regulation 593/2008/EC of the European Parliament and of the Council of 17 June 2008 on the law applicable to contractual obligations ('Rome I') came into force, and replaced the Rome Convention (see 'Rome Convention' below), from 17 December 2009 (see **10.10** and **10.12** on Rome I and **10.3–10.29** on governing laws more generally).

ROME II

A3.264 Regulation 864/2007/EC of the European Parliament and of the Council of 11 July 2007 on the law applicable to non-contractual obligations ('Rome II') came into force on 11 January 2009. From 11 January Rome II has applied to every EU member state except Denmark (see **10.11**).

ROME CONVENTION

A3.265 The Rome Convention on the Law Applicable to Contractual Obligations 1980 is usually known as the 'Rome Convention'. The original Rome Convention has been amended by the Luxembourg Convention 1988, Brussels Protocol and Funchal Convention.

A3.266 The Rome Convention was used to determine which country's laws govern a document and applies to the tribunals and courts of EU member states (see 'European Union' above for a list of EU member states).

A3.267 The Rome Convention should not be confused with the Treaty of Rome (see the 'EU Treaty' above).

A3.268 A new EC Regulation ('Rome I' above) came into force in December 2009. (See **10.3–10.29** and 'governing law' above on governing laws more generally.)

ROTATOR

A3.269 An expatriate who works part of the year and whose job is covered by one or more other people for the rest of the year. Rotators may work in difficult locations eg on oil rigs or serving on military bases, and typically spend substantial periods of time at home on leave.

SALES TAX

A3.270 A tax on the supply of goods or services that may, for example, be applied to the supply of an expatriate from one company to another.

UK

A3.271 In the UK sales tax is known as 'value added tax' or 'VAT'.

SCHENGEN AREA

A3.272 See 'Schengen visa' below.

SCHENGEN VISA

A3.273 A 'Schengen visa' issued by a participating country allows free travel between countries within the 'Schengen area'. The area within which free travel is permitted includes EU member states (see above) and Liechtenstein, Norway,

Iceland and Switzerland, with the exceptions of Bulgaria, Croatia, Cyprus, the Republic of Ireland, Romania and the UK. Bulgaria and Romania are in the process of joining. (See **3.19–3.23.**)

SECONDMENT

A3.274 See 'assignment' above.

SENIORITY

A3.275 See 'continuous employment' above.

SERVICE AGREEMENT

A3.276 A UK term used to describe an employment contract for a senior executive or company director who is employed. (Compare 'contract for services' above.)

SERVICE COMPANY

A3.277 This is a term usually used in the expatriate context to describe a company that employs people and supplies those people to work for the business of another company. Typically, the supply of expatriates (and/or their services) will be the service company's only function (see 'employee leasing company' and 'GEC' above).

SETTLEMENT AGREEMENT

A3.278 See 'severance agreement' below.

SEVERANCE AGREEMENT

A3.279 An agreement between an employer and employee (and sometimes other parties too) to settle employment disputes that arise in connection with termination of employment. Whether a severance agreement will be effective, and the appropriate terms to be included, will vary considerably from country to country and with the circumstances. (See Chapter 16 on termination generally, checklist **A1.12** at Appendix 1 and framework document **A2.7** at Appendix 2.)

UK

A3.280 A 'settlement agreement' is, essentially, a severance agreement. However, in the UK 'settlement agreement' has a specific meaning prescribed by legislation. A severance agreement will not normally be effective to settle statutory employment claims in the UK (eg a complaint of 'unfair dismissal' or discrimination claim) unless it satisfies the criteria for a formal settlement agreement. For example, the agreement must be in writing and must state certain things. The employee must receive independent advice from a qualified person (eg a solicitor) regarding the terms and effects of the agreement before it is concluded.

Settlement agreements used to be referred to as 'compromise' agreements in the relevant UK legislation.

SEVERANCE PAYMENT

A3.281 See 'termination payment' below. The two phrases generally have the same meaning. See also the European expression 'indemnity'.

SOCIAL PARTNERS

A3.282 A European term often used to describe representatives of employees and management. 'Social partners' is broadly equivalent to the English phrase 'the two sides of industry', though the term is usually intended to express a more co-operative relationship.

SOCIAL PLAN

A3.283 This term is used in many European countries to describe a formal agreement that is reached between employer and employee representatives in relation to redundancies. The agreement is likely to specify the appropriate severance pay to be paid. A social plan may also cover a wide range of related matters such as selection criteria, individual consultation, timing, outplacement, rehiring, treatment of vulnerable employees etc. Participants in negotiations, procedural requirements and likely outcome of negotiations can vary considerably from country to country.

SOCIAL SECURITY REGULATION

A3.284 The EU countries, EEA countries & Switzerland are party to an agreement which prescribes where social security contributions should be paid.

SPLIT CONTRACT

A3.285 A split contract is a term that may be used to describe an employment contract where there are two distinct roles with the same employer. This term is also often used to describe a dual employment arrangement (see above), although this is not recommended. The essence of most dual employment arrangements is that the two employments must be separate, standalone arrangements. The term 'split contract' does not describe this accurately. Use of the term 'split contracts' can also lead to confusion between a 'dual employment' arrangement (see above) and a 'split payroll' arrangement (see below).

SPLIT PAYROLL

A3.286 This term is sometimes used to describe a situation where remuneration is paid through two separate payroll arrangements, usually in two different countries, by or on behalf of the same employer. This typically arises where there are discrete home country and host country duties for the same employer. It is worth checking that the arrangement is not intended to be a 'dual employment' arrangement (see above).

SPONSOR

A3.287 This is a term often used to describe an employer or other organisation that applies for work or residence permits, or other immigration permission, for an expatriate and/or his family. The sponsor is often required to comply with legal obligations in relation to the individuals sponsored and more general sponsor registration requirements may apply. For example, the sponsor may be required to inform the authorities if the role changes, remuneration is reduced, the employee is absent or the employment ends (see **3.3–3.26** on immigration generally and **19.4–19.31** on the UK points-based immigration system).

STATUTORY REDUNDANCY PAY (SRP)

A3.288 This is a UK term for 'redundancy pay' that must be paid in accordance with the Employment Rights Act 1996 (ERA 1996). SRP is determined in accordance with a formula based on age, length of service and a week's pay (see also 'redundancy' above).

SUBSIDIARY

A3.289 When talking about group companies we often refer to 'parent', 'sister' and 'subsidiary' companies. Sometimes, for example, for the purposes of confidentiality clauses or post termination restrictions, it is useful to have more precise definitions. The terms are usually defined by reference to legislation to reduce the risk of dispute over the meaning of the term. For example, if the agreement is governed by English law it may be appropriate to refer to a definition from companies or tax legislation (see 'affiliate', 'associated company' and 'group company' above).

SUBSISTENCE ALLOWANCE

A3.290   This is usually a regular allowance to cover the costs of, for example, hotel expenses, meals etc. A subsistence allowance is more likely to be offered where there is a shorter-term assignment and the employee is not living in permanent accommodation, but subsistence allowances can sometimes be provided throughout a longer-term assignment. Tax relief may be available in respect of all or part of the allowance (see 'allowance' above and 7.53). The allowance may be calculated as a daily rate in which case it is usually referred to as a 'per diem'.

SUPERANNUATION SCHEME

A3.291   This is a term used in some countries to describe a pension arrangement.

SUPERVISORY BOARD

A3.292   See 'Board'.

TAX CLEARANCE

A3.293   Sometimes it is possible for an employee or employer to apply to a tax authority for 'clearance' or 'approval' that a particular tax treatment is appropriate. The clearance given may or may not offer some protection against future claims from the tax authority.

TAX EQUALISATION

A3.294   This is an arrangement by which an employer, broadly, agrees to put the expatriate in the same position, from a tax and/or social security perspective, as the employee would have been in if he had received similar remuneration subject to home country tax. There are different ways of achieving this (see **7.80–7.98** and 'tax protection' below).

TAX ILLUSTRATION

A3.295 A calculation, typically prepared by an expatriate tax specialist, intended to show the employee how gross and net remuneration will be determined. For example, this may show the method by which tax equalisation is applied. Usually the calculation is made at a particular point in time.

TAX PROTECTION

A3.296 This is similar to tax equalisation, except that this term is used to describe the situation where the employer promises to ensure that the employee is no worse off, from a tax and/or social security perspective, than he would have been if he had received similar remuneration subject to home country tax. There are different ways of achieving this (see Chapter 7 and 'tax equalisation' above).

TAX RESIDENT

A3.297 An employee who is considered to be 'tax resident' in a particular country is likely to find his worldwide income subject to income tax in that country (see **5.4–5.19** on income tax and assignments generally). It is important to bear in mind that 'tax residence' in one country does not automatically mean exemption in another. It is possible for an employee to be subject to tax in more than one jurisdiction. See 'double tax'.

UK

A3.298 The UK tax residence text is based on number of days in the UK and ties, eg property and family ties.

(See also **19.33–19.56** on UK income tax and assignments to the UK generally, **20.6–20.13** on UK income tax and assignments from the UK generally.) Specialist expatriate tax advice should always be sought in relation to 'tax resident' status as the rules can be complex and the financial consequences can be significant.

TERMINATION BY MUTUAL AGREEMENT

A3.299 This phrase is used to describe the situation in which the employer and employee agree on the termination of the employee's employment. This can be contrasted with dismissal (where the employer terminates the employment unilaterally) or resignation (where the employee terminates the employment unilaterally). The distinction is important in some contexts. For example, if the termination is by mutual agreement in some countries there may be no requirement for approval of the termination by the employment authorities or some mandatory arrangements may not apply. Termination by mutual agreement may also affect the tax treatment of a termination payment if favourable tax treatment is only allowed on dismissal. (See Chapter 16 on termination of employment generally.)

TERMINATION DATE

A3.300   This term is usually used in employment documents to refer to the date on which an employment actually ends. Sometimes similar terms are used to describe related dates. For example, in the UK the termination date for the purposes of determining whether the employee qualifies for redundancy pay may be later if statutory minimum notice has not been worked. If the term is used without definition in employment documents care should be taken to make sure it has the intended meaning under the governing law.

TERMINATION PAYMENT

A3.301   This is a general term used in this book to include various types of payments that may be made to an employee in connection with termination of his employment. These might include, for example, payments in lieu of notice, redundancy pay, 'ex gratia' payments, payments under the terms of a social plan, etc made to the employee. It is important to be aware that in some countries termination payments are not made by the employer. The payment may be made by a third party, for example, an employment authority possibly funded by earlier contributions from the employer. (See Chapter 16 on termination of employment generally.)

TOP EXECUTIVE

A3.302   A colloquial term used in some jurisdictions to describe a director or other senior executive. (For example cadres in France or dirigenti in Italy.) In many jurisdictions top executives are subject to different employment, or other, rules from ordinary employees. For example, top executives may have less protection than junior employees on termination of employment. For this reason, it is often important to be clear about the status/seniority (in the UK sense) of individuals who will be assigned internationally.

TOTALIZATION AGREEMENT

A3.303   A US expression, usually referring to a bilateral agreement between the US and another country regarding social security contributions.

TRADE SECRETS DIRECTIVE

A3.304 'Trade secret' is, broadly, a term used to describe particularly valuable confidential information that gives a competitive advantage. Directive 2016/93 on the protection of undisclosed know-how and business information (trade secrets) against their unlawful acquisition, use and disclosure must be implemented by EU member states by 8 June 2018. There is a longer definition of trade secret set out in the Directive. See also Chapter 11 on confidentiality, competition and restrictive covenants.

TREATY ON THE FUNCTIONING OF THE EUROPEAN UNION (TFEU OR LISBON TREATY)

A3.305 See EU Treaty, above.

13TH MONTH PAYMENTS

A3.306 In some countries the employer must make the employee an additional payment once a year equal to a month's pay. Mandatory bonus payments are quite common. The method of calculation, timing of payment etc varies considerably between countries. In some countries the mandatory bonus payment can take the form of 'holiday pay'. The important thing for advisers is to ensure that the need to make additional payment is considered before remuneration is fixed and documented (see **8.26–8.28**).

TRANSFER PRICING

A3.307 Cross-border payments for goods and services, including the costs of supplying expatriates, may affect the corporation tax due in a particular country. The amounts paid between connected parties are often regulated by tax authorities to ensure that an appropriate amount of tax is paid in the relevant country. These regulations are usually referred to as 'transfer pricing' rules (see **13.16–13.18**).

TRAVEL ALLOWANCE

A3.308 Travel allowances or reimbursement of travel expenses may be offered in a variety of circumstances, for example, in relation to pre-assignment orientation trips, relocation, home leave or repatriation (see 'allowance' and 'expense' above).

'TUPE'

UK

A3.309 The Transfer of Undertakings (Protection of Employment) Regulations 2006 are often referred to as 'TUPE'. TUPE was intended to implement the Acquired Rights Directive (see above). TUPE goes beyond the minimum requirements of that Directive and can apply in situations where the Directive does not. The scope of TUPE is wide. Eg TUPE can potentially apply when the work of only one employee transfers from one company to another.

UK BORDER AGENCY

A3.310 Now 'UK Visas and Immigration'.

UK VISAS AND IMMIGRATION

A3.311 UK Visas and Immigration, part of Home Office, is responsible for issuing visas to people who wish to enter the UK. See **19.5** and https://www.gov.uk/government/organisations/uk-visas-and-immigration.

UNITED KINGDOM (UK)

A3.312 See 'Great Britain' above.

UTILITIES ALLOWANCE

A3.313 An allowance may be paid or expenses may be reimbursed in respect of 'utilities'. 'Utilities' does not have a consistent meaning. The preferred meaning should usually be clarified in the documents. 'Utilities' might include gas, electricity, telephone line rental, telephone bills, internet connection, service charges, water bills, waste disposal, local taxes, etc. (See 'allowance' above and **7.127**.)

VALUE ADDED TAX (VAT)

A3.314 See 'sales tax'.

WHITE COLLAR WORKER

A3.315 The term 'white collar worker' is often used to describe an office worker. Whilst the term is now rarely used in the UK it can be important in some other countries, for example Belgium, where the applicable collective agreement may depend on whether the employee is a 'blue collar' or 'white collar' worker. Care should be taken to ensure that the term is understood correctly in its context.

WITHHOLDING OBLIGATION

A3.316 This is the term to describe an employer's obligation to withhold income tax from an employee's pay and pay it over to the tax authorities (see also 'Pay-As-You-Earn' above).

WORKING TIME DIRECTIVE

A3.317 Council Directive 2003/88/EC, the Working Time Directive, requires that EU member states implement minimum standards, for example, in relation to maximum working time (the '48-hour week'), daily and weekly rest breaks, night work and holidays. There are currently proposals to amend the Working Time Directive.

WORKS COUNCIL

A3.318 Most European countries have collective employee information, consultation and/or co-determination arrangements. These may be referred to as works councils and the arrangements may, for example, vary from region to region or depend on the topic being discussed.

A3.319 If change is being introduced it is important to keep an overview of the collective requirements in relevant countries.

A3.320 Additional considerations will apply if the organisation has a multinational information and consultation arrangement in place (see 'European Works Council' above).

A3.321 Works councils do not often have a significant impact on the arrangements for individual expatriate assignments, but local works council arrangements should always be checked.

INDEX

References are to paragraph numbers.